Improving
Service Quality
in the Global
Economy

Improving
Service Quality
in the # Global
Economy

Achieving High Performance
in Public and Private Sectors

Second Edition

Michael E. Milakovich

Auerbach Publications
Taylor & Francis Group
Boca Raton   London   New York   Singapore

Published in 2006 by
Auerbach Publications
Taylor & Francis Group
6000 Broken Sound Parkway NW, Suite 300
Boca Raton, FL 33487-2742

International Standard Book Number-10: 0-8493-3819-0 (Hardcover)
International Standard Book Number-13: 978-0-8493-3819-9 (Hardcover)
Library of Congress Card Number 2005043912

Library of Congress Cataloging-in-Publication Data

Milakovich, Michael E.
    Improving service quality in the global economy : achieving high performance in public and private sectors / Michael E. Milakovich.—2nd ed.
        p. cm.
        Rev. ed. of: Improving service quality. 1995.
    Includes bibliographical references and index.
    ISBN 0-8493-3819-0 (alk. paper)
        1. Industrial management. 2. Service industries—Management. 3. Quality control. I. Title.

HD31.M435 2005
658.5'62—dc22   2005043912

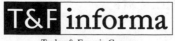

Taylor & Francis Group
is the Academic Division of T&F Informa plc.

Visit the Taylor & Francis Web site at
http://www.taylorandfrancis.com

and the Auerbach Publications Web site at
http://www.auerbach-publications.com

Contents

1 Introduction: The Need for Improved Global Service Quality 1

From the Industrial to the Knowledge Revolution 4

Quality Improvement (QI) Strategies 6

Quality Awards and Incentives for Change 8

The Internet and Beyond: www.customerservice.com 8

Demanding Total Quality Service (TQS) 11

Learning Customer-Driven TQS 17

Redefining TQS 20

Key Terms 23

Notes 23

2 Applying Total Quality Service Concepts to Public and Nonprofit Organizations 33

Origins and Evolution of TQS 36

Changing Perspectives on Quality and Control 39

Benchmarking for Service QI 43

TQS: A Working Definition 44

Developing a TQS Culture 45

CFM, Teamwork, and "Delayering" 45

Strengthen Customer–Supplier Relationships 48

Empower Employees to Meet Customer Quality Requirements 51

Understand Systemic Relationships 53

Carefully Monitor Results 56

Implement CQI 58

Reduce the Costs of Poor Quality 59

Summary and Conclusions 60

Key Terms 61

Notes 62

3 From Quality Control to Continuous Improvement 73
Evolution of Quality Control Concepts.. 74
Masters of Total QI.. 78
   W. Edwards Deming (1900 to 1993).................................... 79
   Joseph M. Juran (1904 –) 84
   Armand V. Feigenbaum (1920 –) 88
   Kaoru Ishikawa (1915 to 1989) 89
   Philip Crosby (1926 to 2001) 94
Selecting QI Strategies.. 96
Summary and Conclusions... 97
Key Terms 98
Notes 99

4 People Power: Total Quality Human Resources,
Participation, Training, and Empowerment.........................107
Total Quality Human Resource Management................................. 109
Total QI Guidelines 111
   Guideline No. 1... 112
      Implications of Guideline No. 1 113
   Guideline No. 2... 114
      Implications of Guideline No. 2 114
   Guideline No. 3... 115
      Implications of Guideline No. 3 116
   Guideline No. 4 and Guideline No. 5 116
      Implications of Guideline No. 4 and Guideline No. 5 117
   Guideline No. 6... 118
      Managing Fear in the Workplace.................................. 120
      Implications of Guideline No. 6: Creating a Stimulating
      Environment... 120
      Suggested Strategy.. 122
   Guideline No. 7... 122
      Implications of Guideline No. 7 123
   Guideline No. 8... 123
      Implications of Guideline No. 8 123
      Pinches, Detecting Devices, Measurement, and
      Information Lines 124
   Guideline No. 9... 125
      Implications of Guideline No. 9 126
   Guideline No. 10.. 126
      Implications of Guideline No. 10 127
Human Resources Topics Offered under a TQS Perspective 127
Summary... 129
Key Terms 130
Notes 130

5 Monitoring Process, Costs, Quality, and Productivity..........139
Measuring and Adding Value to Processes................................. 139

Understanding Process Variation and Control Techniques 142
Variation Due to Common and Special Causes 144
Statistical Process Control... 145
Six Sigma 146
Reducing the Costs of Poor Quality 147
Measuring Poor Quality: Getting Below the Surface................................. 149
Controlling Direct and Indirect Quality Costs.. 151
Defining Improvement Opportunities and Raising the Productivity
Ceiling... 154
Merging Costs, Quality, and Productivity Definitions............................... 155
Summary and Conclusions... 158
Key Terms 160
Notes 160

6 Rewarding Service Quality Improvement............................173
The Need to Improve Performance 175
International Charters, Quality Awards, and Standards............................. 177
Florida Power and Light Company and the Deming Prize 184
Encouraging Innovation and Rewarding Performance.............................. 188
State and Local Quality Awards.. 192
Conclusion: A 21st Century Trend or Passing Fad?.................................. 195
Key Terms 198
Notes 198

7 Managing Performance in the Public Sector........................207
Assessing Alternative Performance Management Strategies 208
Reinvention, Service Standards, and Results Orientation 210
Restoring Faith and Trust in Public Service 212
    Rebuilding Confidence and Trust.. 213
    Bureaucratic Empowerment and Citizen Relationship
    Management 215
    Accountability, Ideology, and Bureaucratic Mobilization 217
Alternatives to Public Management... 218
Balancing Public and Private Strategies.. 222
Restoring Faith and Trust by Improving Service Quality......................... 226
Key Terms 229
Notes 230

8 Preserving the Future: Improving Quality in Education 239
Defining Quality Education.. 240
Improving Quality Processes and Outcomes 243
    Teacher Education and Classroom Instruction 243
    Fiscal Policy and Resource Management.. 246
    Quality of Curriculum... 247
Measuring Quality of Results in Education 248
Rewarding Educational Quality Reform... 253
Summary and Conclusions... 255
Key Terms 256

9 **Implementing Continuous Quality Healthcare Improvement** **265**
   Increasing Costs and Shifting Priorities for Healthcare 266
   What Is Total Quality Healthcare Improvement? 270
   Implementing Total Quality Healthcare Improvement 273
   Changing Attitudes, Globalization, and Managed Healthcare
   Competition 275
   Strategies for Measuring Patient Satisfaction 278
   Implementing Organizationwide Healthcare Quality 284
   Conclusions and Action Steps 287
   Key Terms 288

10 **Leadership for Service Quality Improvement** **305**
   Implementing TQS for High Performance 307
   Barriers to Achieving TQS 313
   Action Strategies for Service Quality Improvement 316
   Leadership Challenges 319

Appendices

A **The Eternally Successful Organization Grid** **325**

B **Deming's 14 Points** **329**

C **Crosby's 14 Steps** **331**

D **2004 Criteria for Performance Excellence —
   Item Listing** **333**

E **Are We Making Progress?** **335**

F **State Quality Award Programs** **341**

G **Bibliography** **345**

H. **Glossary and Acronyms** **361**

Index **387**

Preface

Responding to customer demands for improved service quality is essential for entering and surviving highly competitive domestic and global service markets in the 21st century. Better design, execution, and daily management of customer-focused quality improvement (QI) strategies are vital for all types of organizations, especially those providing services or products to market leaders in the business, nonprofit, and public sectors (key terms are listed at the end of the chapter and defined in the glossary). Doing business in decentralized, individualized, and geographically distant markets requires mastery of technical skills, managing knowledge and information, motivating employees, and the control of complex processes. To remain competitive, market leaders must constantly meet (or exceed) higher external, customer-driven performance standards and internal quality requirements.

Sound theory and careful strategic analysis are always necessary when deciding — among many alternatives — which QI strategies to adopt. Matching appropriate theory with the specific service delivery environments is critical for success. Moreover, it is increasingly apparent that producers of goods or services who fail to adapt to the changing global environment are less likely to succeed in the 21st century (see Chapter 2 and Chapter 3 for details). Manufacturing-based quality improvement systems such as Total Quality Management (TQM) have been applied for decades to guide customer service and internal organizational change processes.[1] For manufacturing industries there is no option: either they have already deployed some variation of quality improvement or TQM, or they no longer exist.

In sharp contrast, service industries employ larger numbers of people (85 percent of all U.S. workers), impact a far broader range of agencies, companies, firms, institutions, and organizations, and are increasingly subject to the vagaries of global markets. If those working in manufacturing service support are included, the total number jumps even higher. The trend is unmistakable; nearly all the 135 million people in our workforce are employed in the public, private, and nonprofit service sector. In addition to offering a wider variety of essential market-based services, vital nonmarket services such as law enforcement, postal delivery, home-land security, and public utilities also realize the importance of adopting customer-focused quality theories.

One purpose of this revised edition is to guide workers, managers, and owners in developing knowledge management (KM) systems to select the essential elements and design systems best suited to meet their customers' needs (Furlong and Johnson, 2003; Liebowitz, 2003; Senge, 1990, 1994, 1996; Wimmer, 2002; 2004). Integrating customer-focused quality improvement (QI) and knowledge management (KM) systems is critical for service industries in rapidly changing global economic markets. The focus here is on changing managerial thinking to integrate QI and KM concepts and promote task-related leadership principles for decision makers to cope with the demands of the global economy. The sluggish world economy, increasing debt and deficits, and changing domestic and international priorities increase interest in quality improvement as a means to exceed customer expectations and improve productivity. Above all, leadership and vision are necessary to initiate and sustain these changes.

Emphasis here is placed on changing administrative management concepts to promote leadership principles and guide decision makers in complex service delivery environments. The concluding chapter summarizes lessons learned, barriers to implementation, and leadership skills needed to change internal organizational systems and sustain high performance and continuous process improvements.

The importance of applying knowledge and quality management practices in service industries is further underscored by the fact that this sector now generates over two thirds of the gross domestic product (GDP) in the United States and most other developed and developing economies. Included are such critical functions as public education, government, healthcare, construction, insurance, law enforcement, transportation, travel, and tourism, among many others. Step-by-step guidelines, recommendations, and action plans for implementing service quality improvements in many of these functions are provided in several chapters. But this book is not a how-to-do technical manual describing the details of E-commerce, quality auditing, inspection, planning, statistical process control, Six Sigma, or risk assessment. Others have already written such specialized studies, some of which contain self-assessments to determine whether an organization is ready to embark on the QI journey (Appendix E, 2004; Berry, 1991; Evans and Lindsay, 2005; Gilbert, 1992; Gitlow and Levine, 2005; Hunt, 1992; Omachonu, 2004; Schmidt and Finnigan, 1992).

In the competitive, mission-driven, and reinvented global service environment of the early 21st century, all organizations search for models to encourage innovation, improve productivity, measure performance, and raise service quality standards. The early chapters define the general concepts necessary to understand and achieve continuous quality improvement in services. The integrative concept of total quality service (TQS) is presented to capture critical components of many of the available strategies. These are described in subsequent chapters and include well-known, but difficult to achieve, goals such as changing internal management systems, "delayering" organizational structures, empowering employees, fostering teamwork, creating closer customer–supplier relationships, monitoring results, thinking systemically, and reducing poor-quality costs. Theory-based concepts and principles can and must be understood to initiate the organizational changes necessary to promote TQS. Chapter 3 presents a more detailed description of the various theorists and their theories to guide QI efforts.

The human resources training, motivational incentives, rewards, and process-monitoring techniques required to survive changing global service markets are discussed in Chapter 4 to Chapter 6. The importance of process monitoring, cost reduction, statistical process control, and merging definitions of cost, quality, and productivity is detailed in Chapter 5. The need to use quality awards as incentives to encourage employees to improve customer service is emphasized throughout the book. Awards can also advance knowledge about management and organizational learning theory, standardize processes, and assist managers in determining which strategies are best suited for their particular organizations. Chapter 6 describes in detail various quality award programs worldwide and analyzes the impact of awards on improving service quality in the United States. The foundation of knowledge and theory in the first six chapters prepares the reader for service quality case studies in the "Big 3" non-market-driven, regulated public and nonprofit services: government (Chapter 7), education (Chapter 8), and healthcare (Chapter 9).

Throughout the book, examples of successful QI efforts in both public and private service industries complement major points in each chapter. These cases are placed at the end of each chapter and include profiles of global service quality leaders such as Baptist Healthcare, Boeing Aerospace Support, Citigroup Card Services, Dell, Federal Express (FedEx), Marriott-Ritz-Carlton, United Service Automobile Association (USAA), and Xerox Business Services. But the primary focus here is on selecting the QI strategies for "regulated" public non-market-driven services: education, government, and healthcare.

The knowledge base in the field of customer service quality and productivity improvement is expanding so rapidly that no one book — no matter how current or comprehensive — can detail all applications in so many different types of services. Some may read this book to decide whether or not to invest in the training and organizational changes necessary to compete as a "world-class" global service provider; others may have already tried one of the many quality approaches and become disillusioned with the results. Still others realize that their choices are limited because EDI, TQM, SERVQUAL, CQI, TQS or "some other acronym" has already been designated "the way" by the direction of the market, your boss, his or her boss, your customers, the state or federal government, global markets, or your accrediting association. In many instances, your customers or clients are asking why your organization has not implemented a QI system already. They are insisting that you demonstrate statistically how your service quality is superior to others. Plainly, if your future depends on acquiring the knowledge and skills to compete in global service markets, then no further encouragement is needed to learn and apply these concepts.

Whatever the individual motivation may be to learn more about improving service quality, for most accountable managers and responsible employees, the challenge is to understand, design, implement, and monitor the most effective approaches to become high-performance service organizations. High-performance service quality delivery systems seek to go beyond these definitions, providing services or products that dazzle, electrify, or delight customers. The relative quality of competing providers, under these emotionally based definitions, can then be defined in terms of the customers' willingness to boast about the product or service. This extended network of satisfied customers then serves to market services among friends, relatives, and co-workers. Long-term success at achieving a level of service beyond current definitions of total quality depends on the ability to positively "surprise" the customer. In addition, high-performance firms develop the capacity to foresee or anticipate customer needs.

At this writing, more is known about high performance in the private sector than in the public sector. Public managers, however, are highly motivated and as concerned about improvement as their private sector counterparts; many are actively working to define and achieve high-performance status. Creating a high-performance workforce requires increasing training opportunities; developing new skills for employees; basing pay on skills, not position; teaching problem-solving tools; and encouraging more effective labor-management communication (Gibbons and Gogue, 2001; Hogan and Fernandez, 2002; Preuss, 2003). Obstacles to full participation remain, however, especially in regulated public service environments where heretofore there were fewer incentives to initiate customer-driven quality improvements.

Meeting the competitive challenges of domestic or global service markets requires workers, owners, managers, and suppliers to prepare themselves now with the communication tools, leadership skills, and managerial and technical training necessary to articulate a quality vision for the entire organization. That vision must be translated into understandable goals and objectives for each work unit. Individuals within each of those groups, in turn, must be trained to accept new responsibilities and apply new sets of skills. Guiding the QI effort requires formulating action strategies and implementing decisions using organizationwide quality control systems to monitor customer feedback and take corrective actions at the point of customer contact (Milakovich, 2003). Delays, inaction, and dubious appeals to supervisors only exacerbate existing customer frustrations and inhibit responsiveness. In market-driven business environments, responding to customers with higher-quality goods and services at lower prices is encouraged and expected. All market-driven for-profit organizations seek customer input to increase productivity while lowering costs and improving product or service quality. Ultimately, all types of service organizations — public, private, or nonprofit — are defined by their customer service quality.

To raise standards, internal management activities of all organizations must not only be focused, but carefully integrated to fulfill individual customer demands for consistent, higher-quality service, fairness, and more courteous treatment. Long-term commitment and support by senior managers, coupled with an understanding of the behavioral and statistical elements of QI systems, are necessary for competing in the ultracompetitive domestic and international service markets. There is an even more compelling reason to implement QI systems, especially in a recessionary economy.

The quality of American goods and services is a pressing national concern. Knowledge has evolved to the point where a quality consensus now exists among many world leaders in the public and private sectors. Effectively responding to challenges of global competition in manufacturing and service environments requires an understanding of the complexity of applying service quality concepts in all types of markets: mixed socialist, state–capitalist, and free-market economies. Ideology and culture play an important role in all societies, but knowledge management and quality improvement theories have proved to be viable anywhere in the world. As organizations based in the United States compete globally for a greater share of emerging markets, failure to deploy these strategies weakens the international competitiveness of the U.S. economy, increases budget debt and trade deficits, and contributes to the exportation or outsourcing of jobs to global competitors.

Recognizing the value and uniqueness of free-market competition, successful organizations accept the reality that there is no one way to best manage quality and improve productivity in diverse global markets. Relatively few businesses are still unaffected by international trade and government regulation. One of the virtues of competitive free markets is that they minimize short-term resource allocations and maximize resource efficiency. At the same time, however, senior business executives also tend to ignore the long-term interests of their companies by demanding higher salaries, outsourcing jobs, and undercutting the future of their own employees. This is reflected by actions that maximize quarterly profits over long-term investments and protection of employees: downsizing, excessive executive compensation, layoffs, leveraged buyouts, hostile take-overs, underfunding pension plans, and deliberate transfer of jobs over-seas. At some point, governments may take action to ensure the long-term competitive position of certain industries, especially those where American jobs are more likely to be affected by international competitive pressures.

This book is written for current and future managers of all types of organizations, private corporations, political institutions, public agencies, and nonprofit agencies who share a common need: to know how the global service quality revolution personally affects them and their daily work environments. If there is a bias in the presentation, it is an argument for the formation of multilevel "quality constituencies," organized interest groups demanding higher quality public and private services. They, in turn, can pressure owners to "stay the course" and improve domestic work processes, education, and healthcare to ensure jobs remain in the United States.

It is my sincere hope and expectation that the experiences, knowledge, and observations contained in these pages will assist leaders in providing better products, services, and support to world markets, thereby improving U.S. competitiveness abroad and job security at home. My goal is to help all those in competitive, as well as regulated markets, to better serve their customers and guide fellow citizens, employees, managers, owners and stockholders in the turbulent business, economic, political, and social climate ahead.

Key Terms

Global service markets
Quality improvement (QI)
Information
Total Quality Management (TQM)
Nonmarket services
Knowledge management (KM)
Gross domestic product (GDP)
Total quality service (TQS)
Management systems
High-performance service organizations
Work unit
Quality consensus
Outsourcing
Competitive position

Notes

1. Readers unfamiliar with the quality improvement theories and practices of quality theorists such as W. Edwards Deming, Joseph Juran, or Philip Crosby can find summaries in Chapter 2 and Chapter 3 of this book.

Acknowledgments

No book of this kind can be the sole effort of one individual. The concepts, ideas, insights, and strategies for improvement contained in the following pages evolved from the critical and supportive reviews of many readers. This collaborative effort would not have been possible without the thoughtful comments, reviews, and material contributed by Carlos Atienza, Jason Blunt, Cmdr. Chris Button, Royce Burnett, Federico Cuadra, June Teufel Dreyer, Lincoln Forbes, Jane Graham, Sara Grossman, Garrett Ho, Albert C. Hyde, Paul Koch, Bettina Larsen, Vincent Omachonu, John Rondinelli, David Sumanth, William Werther, Christian Wilson, and Kostas G. Zografos. I owe a special debt of gratitude to my faculty colleague, Jose Eulogio Romero-Simpson, who offered drafts of unpublished papers for Chapter 4.

The author also acknowledges the valuable support of a close circle of professional associates who reviewed earlier drafts. They include Professor George Beam, University of Illinois-Chicago; Gen. Robert L. Dilworth (ret.), Virginia Commonwealth University, Richmond, Virginia; Lincoln Forbes, Dade County Public Schools, Miami, Florida; Carol Greebler-Schepper, TQMPlus, Lucerne, California; Dr. Jack Miller, M.D., MBA; and Gordon Roston, Senior Advisor, Treasury Board of Canada Secretariat, Innovative and Quality Services, Ottawa, Canada. Their willingness to share experiences, frustrations, and insights about the challenges of daily leadership for service quality, greatly strengthened the book.

While the author accepts full responsibility for conclusions and interpretations, he gratefully acknowledges the support of all those who helped improve earlier drafts of the text. This includes Richard O'Hanley, Editor, Andrea Demby, and Claire Miller of Auerbach Publications for their encouragement and support for the project are recognized for their editorial, copyediting, and proofreading skills. Last but not least, I would like to offer a special thanks to the many colleagues, friends, and students with whom I have worked in executive briefings, graduate and undergraduate courses, public policy seminars, workshops and training sessions. Without your encouragement, this work would not exist.

Michael E. Milakovich
Coral Gables, Florida

About the Author

Michael E. Milakovich is a professor of political science and public administration at the University of Miami, Coral Gables, Florida. He teaches international comparative development, public and non-profit administration, and American government. He is co-author with George Gordon of *Public Administration in America* (Wadsworth/St. Martins Press, 2004) and author of *Improving Service Quality* (St. Lucie Press, 1995). He has published numerous articles in academic journals, served as a consultant to private companies as well as federal, state, and local agencies, and is a life member of the American Society for Public Administration.

Chapter 1

Introduction: The Need for Improved Global Service Quality

> The Twentieth Century will be remembered as the century of productivity, while the Twenty-First will come to be known as the century of quality.
>
> **— Joseph M. Juran,**
> **cited in *Quality Progress*,**
> **August 1994**

The United States became a global economic and political leader during the Industrial Revolution in the late 19th century. Our "Manifest Destiny" was predetermined 150 years ago by abundant natural resources, massive immigration of many willing (and unwilling) workers, unregulated laissez-faire capitalism, invention of the assembly line, and application of scientific management principles to industry.[1] In response to external pressures, ideological threats, and international crises, the United States gained economic strength and assumed global political leadership during the early 20th century. From the late 1940s until the mid-1970s, most Americans were generally satisfied (perhaps complacent?) with their status in the international economy and disinterested in making changes to then-dominant manufacturing and service systems. And why shouldn't they have been?

In the years following World War II, American industry mass-produced over half the world's manufactured goods, dominated its competitors, and was the economic superpower in nearly all world markets. Employment increased and the production of industrial goods such as aircraft, automobiles, and electronic appliances powered the domestic economy. Industry provided most U.S. jobs and generated two thirds of our gross domestic product (GDP). Continued dependence on foreign sources for energy resources, globalization of basic industries, and fierce international economic competition have changed that enviable position forever.

In the last 20 years, the United States lost nearly half of its manufacturing base; fewer than two of every ten Americans still work in a traditional factory job. New forms of high-tech global competition are rampant, and distribution systems have radically changed. Techno-service multinational corporations (MNCs) such as Dell, Hewlett-Packard, Intel, IBM, McDonalds, Microsoft, and Wal-Mart, now drive the U.S. GDP as well as large segments of the international economy.

Today, manufacturing is still a vital component of our economic strength, but the composition of our workforce, GDP, and growth sectors of our economy have shifted dramatically. So, too, have attitudes toward globalization, immigration, and emerging markets in developing nations that are now increasingly viewed as economic competitors. For example, China is now the world's second leading consumer of energy, competing with the United States, Japan, and other industrialized nations for petroleum products and other raw materials in several regions of the world (Figure 1.1). China's growing demand for energy, especially its dependence on coal, oil, and natural gas, poses economic, environmental, and political challenges for the United States.[2] If China continues to grow at its current rate, not only will it consume ever larger shares of scarce world resources, but overtake Japan as the second largest economy in the world by the early 2020s. The Chinese economy is developing under very different political and social conditions from past superpowers.

The United States dominated the old world economic order during the 20th century by promoting free-market capitalism, political freedom, and free trade among nations. With help from the United States, two of our former political enemies became robust economic competitors. During World War II, Germany and Japan were destroyed by Allied bombing and, after the conflict, their populations were forced to make dramatic alterations in their traditional political, economic, and social systems. Their economies and political systems were "democratized" and redesigned from the bottom-up on the U.S.-based capitalist-democratic post–World War II model. With help from Americans during the occupations, changes in political, managerial, and manufacturing quality control systems followed.

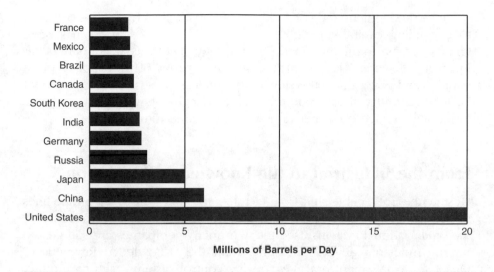

Figure 1.1   Global oil consumption.

The economic success of this long-term investment can be clearly seen by the peace, prosperity, and stability in Western Europe and Japan since the 1950s, especially when compared to the civil strife and political violence that has ravaged nondemocratic countries in Africa, Southeast Asia, and the Middle East where changes have yet to occur. When democratic and economic changes took place in Eastern Europe in the 1990s, several countries in this region joined their more affluent Western European neighbors and began to emerge as global competitors as well.

American industry received a wake-up call when former enemies, as well as newly emerging economies in Asia and Europe, began consuming more resources and producing better-quality, lower-cost products for sale in world markets. Increasing international competitiveness, currency devaluations, free-trade agreements, and consumer frustration with the quality of American goods and services combined to stimulate a long-overdue reexamination of quality control and productivity management systems. These competitive pressures subsequently forced U.S. service industries to reinvent management and control processes.

In summary, the U.S. economy has been impacted positively and negatively by five major trends shaping the global economy in the early 21st century: increased international competition, expanded technology, the emergence of MNCs, free-trade agreements, and social and political reforms in developing nations. The negative consequences of these trends include loss of jobs to less developed economies, unstable and changing global economic environments, shifting public attitudes, unfavorable trade balances, and violent antiglobalization demonstrations by groups opposed to expanding capitalist economic systems. The United States has been favored by its dominance of the technology sector, as headquarters for most of the world's largest MNCs, and as a result of the stability of its banking and governmental systems. Nonetheless, these megatrends cannot be ignored and will continue to impact all segments of global manufacturing and service economies for the foreseeable future.

From the Industrial to the Knowledge Revolution

Despite the irreversible shift from factories to offices, from telephone lines to the wireless Internet, and from the industrial to the information age, the organizational systems used today in many companies are still geared for the Industrial Revolution, rather than the "Knowledge Revolution." Obsolete management practices, quality control systems, staffing requirements, and productivity improvement methods based on pre-Internet, mass-production, manufacturing-era models impede full participation in the global economy. Many U.S. processes even lag behind those of other developing and industrialized competitors in the emerging markets, especially in service industries. Old habits change slowly.

Throughout most of the 20th century, the U.S. economy was dominated by large, highly centralized industrial giants capable of turning out millions of identical "widgets" in cookie-cutter fashion at maximum efficiency and lowest cost. Corporate behemoths such as Boeing, GM, Enron, Ford, IBM, and Dow Chemical dominated their respective markets. There was little need to change or innovate because virtually no competition for market share existed. For example, GM controlled half of the world's automobile production markets from the end of World War II until the late 1960s. Although GM sold nearly twice as many cars as a half-century ago, by 2003 its total market share had declined to just under 28 percent. During the same time period, Japanese auto makers increased their share of the U.S. market from near zero to over 40 percent for cars and light trucks (Figure 1.2).

With the expansion of communication and Internet technology, improved transportation, and more liberal free-trade agreements, more competitors are entering global markets. Industrial giants who modify their management structures and work cultures to accommodate 21st century customer demands are more likely to survive the rigors of competitive global capitalism. Those who refuse to change are being replaced by more efficient producers who offer lower-cost, higher-quality goods and services.

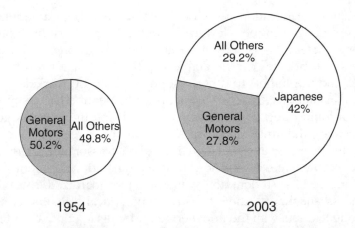

1954   2003

Figure 1.2   GM's shrinking share of North American auto sales.

Many of today's market leaders did not even exist 25 years ago. Global leaders such as Dell, Intel, Microsoft, Nokia, and Wal-Mart have changed internal management systems faster than their competitors and now lead their respective markets in market share, profits, sales, and return on investment (ROI). Only a small fraction of global corporations have sustained a leadership position as financial and market leaders during the past two decades.[3] Most have been replaced by faster, leaner, and more flexible producers who have benefited from internal management changes and less restrictive global markets. Manufacturers share an important advantage over services industries. They mass-produce a single product and benefit from sharing process improvements designed to increase internal efficiency and industrial output.

In contrast, there are many different types of service organizations, ranging in complexity from the corner retail store to multibillion dollar insurance firms. (In today's economy, the retail outlet may be the better managed and more efficiently run business.) Service industries such as banking, education, healthcare, government, and travel and tourism differ from manufacturing firms in several ways: (1) results are less tangible than those produced by manufacturers, (2) services are typically consumed at the time of purchase, and (3) customers must often wait years to evaluate their value. Although they vary considerably in size, ownership, locality, and type of service provided, all service firms share the common lack of tangible product output that distinguishes them from manufactured products. Their value, quality, and reliability are therefore more difficult to judge than a car, refrigerator, or computer. Despite these differences, the management and quality control systems used for the production of goods and the quality of services increasingly overlap.

For example, education in its broadest sense is both a service and a product. Students can be viewed as either "input" to or from other educational systems or as "raw materials" flowing through various stages or processes. Graduates can be defined as the "output" or results of these processes and the "input" to other systems such as job markets or higher-education institutions. Teachers can also be identified as "supervisors" who control and direct these processes and shape the knowledge, skills, and values of the final product. Administrators are "plant managers" responsible for achieving goals such as quality assurance (teacher competency), knowledge acquisition (curriculum), development (passing grades), and results (student achievement on standardized tests). In addition, schools encourage students to become critical thinkers, consumers, and lifelong learners with the knowledge and skills to critique and reinvent what is wrong with the information, goods, and services they receive. Obviously, there is a great deal more to high-quality education than merely processing students through a series of curricular challenges at increasingly higher levels. Quality is difficult to define because students receiving educational services from public or private schools, career-oriented institutions, colleges, or universities must often wait years before determining the ROI from the time spent, money invested, and degree earned from the institution they attended (detailed in Chapter 8).

Quality Improvement (QI) Strategies

To meet the demands of intensified international competition, many U.S. manufacturers initiated Total Quality Management (TQM), or derivatives variously known as *continuous quality improvement* (CQI), *business process reengineering* (BPR), or *total quality control* (TQC). These changes, previously defined and known collectively as *quality improvement* (QI) *strategies*, respond to customers by focusing on complex interrelationships between costs, competition, market share, productivity, and profit. For thousands of American firms, the application of QI resulted in impressive gains in productivity, increased market share, and improved global competitive position. For others, including many regulated domestic-service organizations less willing to accept change, the experience with off-the-shelf industry-based quality systems was disappointing. Progress was slower in regulated service monopolies such as public schools, telecommunications, and public utilities because they have fewer incentives to change and are often protected by quotas, tariffs, or government regulations isolating them from global competition. Given the bewildering "acronym-soup" of choices, and hoping to avoid the pitfalls of earlier postindustrial misapplications, selecting the most effective strategy for service industries can be a daunting task.

Various quality and productivity theories and methods have been unevenly applied in the past, as many organizations rediscovered just how difficult it is to consistently deliver results, especially in quasi-monopolistic, noncompetitive, and regulated nonmarket service environments. When thoughtfully applied and appropriately modified to meet all types of customer needs, various QI systems outlined in the following chapters can be used to respond to customer demands.

The 1990s witnessed a profound restructuring of many of our basic productive enterprises. In some instances, the principles underlying TQC and CQI (or other related acronyms) were misunderstood and misapplied. Many large multinational enterprises were literally reinvented from the inside-out using QI principles; others broke up into smaller, more manageable, decentralized units to establish closer working relationships with customers and suppliers. Given the sheer size and scope of the effort, mistakes, misplaced optimism, and poor execution were inevitable. Many QI programs failed to achieve the desired results or were poorly implemented, especially when imposed from "the top down" in a rote and mechanized "do it or else" fashion, reminiscent of early 20th century industrial bureaucracies (for example, see FPL Case Study 6.1 in Chapter 6).

Rather than empowering employees to serve customers well, many service firms used management systems that emphasized top-down command-and-control systems for processing all types of decisions. Consequently, there was often more talk about improving quality in all types of organizations than there are actual successes in implementing QI methods, service standards, and theories (Brown, Hitchcock, and Williard, 1994; Cole, 1993; Douglas and Judge, 2001; Hackman and Wegman, 1995; Koch and Fisher, 1998; Milakovich, 1998; Zbaracki, 1998). Although early efforts to apply quality theories in services met with initial successes, they were often followed by failures, frustration, and resistance; layoffs became necessary as the quality demanded by customers and management could not (or would not) be internalized and delivered by employees in both the private and public sectors (Dervitsiotis, 2004; Boyne and Walker, 2002). Nonetheless, TQM was "the thing to do" in corporate America during late 1980s and early 1990s.

Deploying these (then innovative) management strategies raised customer expectations about product quality and productivity levels to meet international competitors but did little to forestall the downsizing or outsourcing of American jobs in many U.S. industries. Indeed, hyping TQM in too many organizations created unrealistic expectations and controversial "quality bureaucracies" that hastened the demise of poorly designed programs. Predictably, a TQM-backlash, reflecting unrealistic expectations and failures to understand the complexities of global QI, dampened enthusiasm for further service applications during the late

1990s. In the early 21st century, increasing debt and deficits, changing domestic and international priorities, and worldwide recession have renewed interest in QI as a means to exceed customer expectations and improve productivity.

Quality Awards and Incentives for Change

In what is a longer-lasting legacy, a national "quality constituency" formed and successfully promoted a federal quality award, the Malcolm Baldrige National Quality Award (BNQA), in 1987. Using the BNQA as a model, numerous state and local awards, charters, and charter marks were subsequently created to recognize the quality achievements of public, private, and nonprofit organizations (detailed in Chapter 6). Initially, these awards promoted international competitiveness and the restoration of American industry, especially high-tech and telecommunications, and spawned the growth of numerous quality consulting firms with expertise in applying various QI theories in both manufacturing and services. In recent years, more educational institutions, hospitals, and public service organizations are being recognized for their QI achievements (For examples, see illustrative cases in Chapter 6 to Chapter 9).

The emergence of a global knowledge-based service economy presents both threats and opportunities for individuals and organizations prepared to respond positively to changes in domestic and international service markets. Past efforts to improve service quality often did not match the motivation of employees or the management capacity of many organizations to consistently meet customer expectations. Since the mid-1990s, the Internet-driven E-commerce revolution has presented new challenges as well as opportunities for service firms. The "dot.com" boom and bust of the late 1990s facilitated the spread of technology around the world, but did little to equip individuals and organizations with the motivation and training necessary to respond to customers in the new global economy. The challenge for service organizations is to understand the significance of the knowledge revolution and utilize new technology to establish closer customer–supplier relationships to increase loyalty and satisfaction.

The Internet and Beyond: www.customerservice.com

Bolstered by technology, free-trade agreements, and deregulated international economic markets, globalization of services is being stimulated by the transfer of information via telecommunications and the Internet. Global MNCs now outsource components, parts, people, and services to suppliers who offer higher quality, lower cost, reliability, and on-time delivery, often without regard to the impact on domestic economies. In-sourcing, outsourcing, and factoryless enterprises dominate the global economy and have prompted the expansion of quality management systems and measurement of customer satisfaction at each stage of manufacturing processes. The spread of information and technology is probably the least controversial component of globalization, in that both developing and developed countries benefit from increased global communications. Still, the economic and political consequences of global technology challenge corporate executives, union groups, and politicians alike.

What is new in the Internet-driven service quality revolution is that concepts and principles formerly used only in select multinational manufacturing firms are now being applied locally to access markets globally. Despite the expansion of capitalism worldwide and opening of global markets through free-trade agreements, many service firms are still affected by corporate and governmental decisions at the national, regional, and local levels. Therefore, it is equally important to apply QI initiatives in mixed regulated systems, as well as unfettered free markets. These concepts are being used to improve services in public, nonprofit, and other types of non-government organizations (NGOs). In addition, a shift in organizational culture is necessary, but not always sufficient, to apply these principles successfully in global service environments, especially within emerging markets in less developed countries (LDCs). Ironically, several developing economies, unfettered by large investments in older technology, have succeeded in applying knowledge management tools and technology at a faster rate than some more developed systems.

As more businesses and households plug into the Internet using electronic data interchange (EDI) for commercial activities, customer service, fund transfers, procurement of parts and service become ever more common in cyberspace. This worldwide communication system is drastically changing how companies obtain information about global markets, competitors, and future customers (Giovannetti et. al., 2003).

Older hierarchical, industrial-age, paper-based supply-purchasing and distribution systems, known as Theory X management systems, are rapidly disappearing along with many workers in nontechnology jobs who are finding their skills obsolete or outsourced. Traditional Theory X command-and-control vertical hierarchies (corporate or governmental) isolate managers, centralize authority, and distance those accountable from their customers (MacGregor, 1960). They are being flattened and expanded to include horizontal service networks consistent with the structure of the Internet and the World Wide Web. Customer-contact personnel at all levels must be "empowered" — trained to respond positively and effectively to customers in remote locations. Everyone must adopt a process approach to eliminate non-value-added (unnecessary) steps to meet customer-defined needs and requirements. Barriers to cooperation between departments within organizations isolate and limit communications. They must be eliminated, leadership roles redefined, and processes reengineered. Interlinked, flexible, horizontal service networks are replacing vertical hierarchies in businesses and governments throughout the world. A new global service management system, referred to as the *network model*, is rapidly replacing traditional industrial-era factories. In addition, a wider range of services are now being offered over the Internet. To see how one multinational firm is shifting its global operations to the networking model, see Case Study 1.1.

Global service quality organizations manage for results, place customers first, empower workers, and integrate computers, digital technology, knowledge management, technology transfer, and electronic commerce (E-commerce) to improve internal business-to-business (B2B) efficiency, enhance government-to-business (G2B) relationships, improve government-to-government (G2G) exchanges, and encourage citizen access to, information about, and participation in government-to-citizen (G2C) decision making. B2B systems are now replacing factory-based methods of production and distribution. G2C transactions include renewing drivers licenses, obtaining passport applications, renewing car registrations, registering to vote, finding government benefits, filing taxes online, government job postings, and obtaining case status with Social Security or other federal agencies. G2G contacts include grant applications, federal employee-background investigations, and collaboration and information sharing between local, state, and federal agencies. G2B transactions include wage reporting, business tax filing, purchasing supplies, business law and regulation posting, filing patents and trademarks, and posting contractor opportunities. Government purchasing agents must be particularly skilled in QI theory and practice. Both G2C and G2B transactions require greater citizen participation, defined by a readiness of both citizens and government to accept certain civic responsibilities and roles. In addition, over 20 U.S. states now process welfare applications and contract other services through outsourced employees in India and elsewhere.

At the U.S. Federal Government level, E-government initiatives strengthen G2C and G2G partnerships with so-called high-impact agencies to achieve measurable goals and standards for customer service. Among these agencies are the Internal Revenue Service (IRS), Environmental Protection Agency (EPA), Federal Aviation Administration (FAA), Food and Drug Administration (FDA), Occupational Health and Safety Administration (OSHA), and the Social Security Administration (SSA), which employ 1.1 million of the 1.8 million civilian employees and have the most direct contact with the public (G2C) and businesses (G2B). New technology is also being applied to communicate directly with citizens, to gather public comments, and to distribute reports from high-impact agencies on their progress toward reaching performance goals.[4]

Transfer of knowledge and exchange of information accelerates customer access to a broader range of choices and encourages cost competition among service providers previously isolated from global competition. Global trends further suggest that citizen expectations about the delivery of public services and their relationships with political regimes are changing even faster (Carr and Littman, 1990; Milakovich, 1995a; Kettl, 2002). In theory, greater citizen participation also brings better government, defined in cost–benefit terms as utilitarian decisions benefiting the largest numbers of citizens. Greater citizen participation occurs as a civic or partisan obligation, in response to threats against local economies or environments, and as a consequence of increased knowledge about the consequences of governmental actions. Citizen involvement stresses the individual and group benefits of participation, identifies appropriate groups receptive to citizen input, helps citizens find positive ways to respond to threatening situations, and creates opportunities for citizens to become better informed about issues and opportunities (Milakovich, 2002). Public employees and their professional associations are also promoting management practices aimed at reducing the need for outsourcing and responding to citizens as valued customers, within existing frameworks of bureaucratic–political relationships.

Demanding Total Quality Service (TQS)

All service organizations are concerned about costs, employee productivity, suppliers, and related customer service quality issues. Highly competitive service providers such as accounting firms, airlines, banks, import–export firms, insurance companies, telecommunications, as well as regulated service monopolies such as local governments, hospitals, schools, and public utilities, must demonstrate at least minimum QI understanding and application. In most cases, success is defined by the bottom-line ROI, better customer service, and improved results. In the private sector, strategies are guided by relatively visible measures of increased market share, profit margins, and earnings per share. In addition, more tax-supported, regulated, and nonprofit agencies now seek alternative measures to transform organizational cultures and improve customer service. In many instances, those measures must be developed in cooperation with a broad range of stakeholders, including appointed officials, regulators, taxpayers, elected officials, and consumers of public services.

During the last decade, more citizens became increasingly less tolerant of perceived inefficiency, mismanagement, and lack of responsiveness in the public sector. In response to such criticisms, many managers and politicians opted for third-party cooperative partnerships with select faith-based, private, or nonprofit alternatives, rather than either private or traditional public service providers (Auger, 1999; Eggers and O'Leary, 1995; Goldsmith, 1997; Hodge, 2000; Salamon, 1981; Savas, 2000; Schaeffer and Loveridge, 2002; Milakovich, 2004). Third-party government encourages the creation of public–private service delivery partnerships and describes the ideal mutual support relationship between nonprofit and government agencies. (In the United States, under IRS section 501[c] 3, donations to nonprofit agencies are tax deductible, board members serve without compensation, and rules governing boards are stricter than those applying to private sector corporate counterparts.) Prompted by reinvention reforms, corporate scandals, and reform measures, governments are deploying a much wider range of partnerships with NGOs as a means to change organizational structures, provide better customer service, reduce costs, and respond to all citizens.

As the missions of public, private, and nonprofit sectors overlap, the probability of divisive relationships between providers, competition for funds, and uncooperative interactions with customers increase. The shared goal of improving organizational performance and customer service is more challenging for public managers because (1) democratic governance encourages conflicting ideological (political) and group conflicts over the purposes of government, (2) pluralism encourages private-interest groups to compete for limited public resources, (3) regulatory agencies are constrained by political processes in setting and enforcing service standards, and (4) public agencies sometimes resist developing performance measures for fear that the results may be used against them. These, as well as other factors, create complex budgetary, legal, and regulatory issues that are inherently more contentious than those found in the private sector. Too often, unnecessary political wrangling focuses on who should deliver a service, rather than how it can best be delivered to citizens. Although both public- and private sector advocates agree on the need to base decisions on performance and results, the challenge for public administrators is to find ways to integrate the strongest features of various QI models.

There is now a general industrywide awareness of various QI strategies, and most service organizations realize the quality revolution's potential impact on their daily work environments (Berry and Parasuraman, 1992; Oliver, 1990). Several multinational world-class competitors recognize the competitive advantage of quality and productivity strategies to gain global market share as well as motivate their workforces. Significantly, those regulated and nonmarket services most in need of improved customer service quality are now facing the same global competitive challenges that manufacturers confronted in the 1980s.

Global competitiveness is impacting the daily operations of all types of service organizations in a variety of ways: definitions of service quality are merging, business environments are changing; information, capital, products, and services flow across international borders at speeds unheard of just a few months ago; and, unfortunately, jobs disappear as well. In the information technology (IT) sector alone, 500,000 jobs have already been "exported," and it is estimated that another 2.5 million Americans will lose their jobs through outsourcing in the next five years (2003 to 2008). Longer-term prospects are even dimmer. Forrester Research, a respected forecasting firm in Cambridge, Massachusetts, predicts that 3.3 million U.S. jobs, including about 200,000 service jobs per year, will be exported in the next decade. Although there is intense political debate about the economic impact of global outsourcing, this trend is likely to continue in the future. The United States alone spends nearly $500 billion and employs 4 million workers to outsource work formerly reserved for Americans. As more nations subscribe to open markets and liberal free-trade policies, competition increases and more governments "demonopolize" and deregulate many of their own service markets. Providers of critical public and nonprofit services, such as education, healthcare, telecommunications, transportation, law enforcement, and corrections, are increasingly aware of the implications of the new economic reality. Consumers and citizens have a broader range of choices for services they purchase and receive from private, public, or nonprofit markets, but many of those affected are suffering job losses as a result of being unprepared for changes in the competitive global economy.

Once isolated from the rigors of "do-or-die" competition in international markets by quotas, tariffs, subsidies, or favorable government regulations, regulated service monopolies also need to change. Without competition, inefficiencies in service delivery processes are protected, costs increase, and customer complaints are more likely to be ignored. Vital and necessary public sector infrastructure such as airports, schools, roads, security systems, and public utilities are potentially vulnerable to obsolescence. The August 2003 blackouts affecting 50 million residents of the northeastern United States illustrate the negative consequences of ignoring service distribution systems. Despite the relative security of their regulated local markets, many public agencies are increasingly aware that their jobs, as well as their organizations, could disappear overnight as rules change and world markets continue to merge. (In many localities, local cable TV providers compete with satellite networks.)

Rapid changes in political party leadership and voter loyalty following the 2000 presidential and 2002 Congressional elections, as well as state and local contests, reflect broad-based frustrations with government inefficiencies, overregulation, and unresponsive bureaucracies. Until recently, the phrase *public sector innovation* was regarded by many as little more than a bad joke or oxymoron. The chaos following the 2000 presidential elections and the 2002 primaries in Florida resulted in part from the continued use of obsolete (40-year old) technology and failure to invest in new voting machines. Congress passed legislation authorizing billions of dollars to update equipment, standardize procedures, and improve training to prevent such events from happening in future elections. But progress at the state and local level has been slow. There continue to be problems with electoral processes. Different states still use various voting methods, ranging from paper ballots to electronic voting machines, and civil rights and civil liberties groups have raised Constitutional concerns about procedures used to count and record votes.

The trend toward more responsive, customer-oriented, decentralized, and deregulated service units is accelerating worldwide as recommendations for change and success stories from a wide range of public agencies and private industries are publicized (Gore, 1993; Ingraham, Thompson, and Sanders, 1998; Spechler, 1991). According to advocates, the service quality revolution requires massive changes to be "catalyzed and guided" by government policy and action (Beam, 2001; Osborne and Gaebler, 1992; Osborne and Plastrik, 2000). Once considered bastions of regulation and resistance, governments are now deregulating outmoded laws, changing management systems, empowering employees to act in the citizen–taxpayer–customer's best interest, privatizing nonessential services, and streamlining procurement processes (Kelman, 1994). Public agencies are further responding to customer needs as partners and suppliers of essential services for millions of people who cannot or will not purchase them from private providers.

Consider the changes that have occurred in Asia since the 1980s, in Europe since the early 1990s, and in North America following the opening of free trade between Canada, Mexico, and the United States a decade ago. The passage of the North American Free Trade Agreement (NAFTA) in 1992 created tremendous opportunities for entrepreneurial ventures undreamed of just a few years earlier. The reduction or elimination of trade barriers have advantaged some and disadvantaged others in the United States, Canada, and Mexico (Hill, 2003; Hufbauer and Wong, 2003). Among the services that have benefited from the elimination of trade barriers are international banking and financial services, E-commerce, pharmaceuticals, textiles, and cross-border transportation. Those with the vision to see the potential of those changes are benefiting from the lifting of trade barriers in North America.

The European Union (EU) is another example of geographic neighbors coming together for the purposes of freer trade, a common market, and regional integration. Certain integration mechanisms remain largely unique to the EU experiment, including the adoption of the euro as a shared currency and a drafted constitution to govern its member countries. Many of the EU's critics worry that such advanced integration will ultimately weaken the individual countries by watering down their cultural beliefs and taking away their government's sovereignty. Although these are valid concerns, there are currently 25 European countries that earned membership. The payoff from EU membership can be boiled down to two words: trade liberalization. Under the influence of open international trade borders, increased competition from imports would serve to give consumers a lower-priced product with a higher level of quality. Also, the member countries enjoy international trade with fewer barriers and restrictions, thus leading to a larger consumer base for their goods in the European market. From a global perspective, and as a cohesive trading bloc of 480 million people, the EU will have significantly more negotiating power — especially with regard to the United States — than if separate nations negotiated trade policies as individual countries.

National security and foreign policy issues often supercede efforts to promote free trade, even among neighboring countries. Responding positively to the labor and transportation lobbies in the late 1990s, the Clinton administration baulked at NAFTA provisions that would have allowed Mexican trucks unrestricted access to U.S. highways. The Mexican government, in turn, insists on liberalization of immigration policies and amnesty for illegal emigrants. These, as well as other border issues, are transforming production lines, labor forces, and markets as no other change since the Industrial Revolution. At the same time, the consequences of neglecting global market shifts are becoming more severe for all types of service organizations. Future changes are likely to occur even faster, surprising some and shocking others.

If those providing services lack the management support, tools, and training needed to do the job, they are unlikely to be motivated to even meet — much less exceed — customer needs. Dissatisfied customers, if they have the choice, will turn to a competing provider. For those unwilling or unable to purchase services from a competitor, continued neglect of quality could lead to frustration and negatively impact a providers' bottom line. One of the strengths of free markets is that competition among service providers has been shown to reduce costs for consumers, as well as increase efficiency among providers. However, so-called "managed competition" in quasi-regulated services, such as education, government, and healthcare, does not necessarily guarantee increased productivity or better service to customers.

Those who depend on government agencies or nonprofit "third sector" voluntary faith-based or nonprofit associations (American Heart Association, Catholic Charities, Red Cross, YMCA, or the United Way, for example) often do not have a choice of competitive providers. (Nor can they switch providers if the service provided is less than acceptable.) For increasing numbers of recipients, the politically-regulated sector provides essential services, such as emergency disaster relief, job counseling, retirement assistance, unemployment insurance, education, healthcare, and public safety, typically without market competition. Continued neglect of service quality principles in the non-market-regulated service sector not only short-changes those who pay (directly and indirectly), but further alienates taxpayers and undermines confidence in government institutions. These so-called public service monopolies offer special challenges for learning and applying quality and productivity improvement principles and concepts. These themes are expanded in Chapter 7 to Chapter 9 dealing with vital government, education, and healthcare services.

Reduction of tariffs and quotas, free-trade agreements, and expanded use of IT enhance customers' ability to shop internationally to find best-value, highest-quality products and services, often at much lower prices than those offered by providers closer to home. This trend is irreversible: service organizations can no longer avoid domestic or global competition. Indeed, many U.S. and European service companies utilize E-commerce technology to reduce costs by employing workers in remote locations. Firms such as America Online (Time Warner), American Express, Dell, Delta Airlines, and Hewlett-Packard contract with Indian and Philippine companies to provide programming and customer services such as baggage handling, software development, and technical support. The results are not always conducive to customer satisfaction, especially in services that require close contact with customers and knowledge of local culture. See Case Study 1.2.

As more service firms enter the brave new E-world of global commerce, one result is certain: whether purchasing goods or services, all consumers want more value for their scarce resources. Plainly, any distinction (if one ever existed) between the quality and value received when purchasing a manufactured product or consuming a service has virtually disappeared.

To survive, all organizations must respond to customer complaints, as well as understand fundamental problems associated with changing global markets and economic cycles.

The spread of globalization in the early 21st century presents unique opportunities for refocusing public management systems. Juran's prophesy (epigraph in the preceding text) may become a reality sooner than many expected. As quality recognition becomes the main factor in judging an organization's performance, those that fail to accept the new demands of an increasingly competitive global economy will be less likely to survive (DeFeo and Janssen, 2001; Milakovich, 1995b).

Traditionally, organizations reacted to customer complaints by restructuring debt, seeking lower-cost labor markets, and laying off employees to reduce costs. In the short-run, this may once have protected corporate profits, but it causes severe disruptions for displaced workers and their families. As Henry Ford observed at beginning of the mass-production era nearly a century ago, this strategy is ultimately is self-defeating, as workers need jobs to buy products and services to fuel the economy. Firing workers or outsourcing jobs to foreign countries not only reduces the number of potential domestic consumers, but actually increases costs by shifting the burden of unemployment compensation and retraining costs from the private to public sector. To make matters worse, the federal government has curtailed retraining programs for those whose jobs have been eliminated. Downsizing, outsourcing, and proposals to reorient current unemployment compensation and job training programs have emerged as major national political issues and will remain so for the foreseeable future.

The global service quality movement recognizes that successfully responding to customer demands for improved service quality requires the elimination of the root causes of system flaws or defects that cause failures and dissatisfaction (among both customers and employees) so common in today's service encounters. QI principles offer an alternative to reducing the workforce, ignoring the complaints, or increasing costs. That strategy is to become more customer responsive, less bureaucratic, and more efficient. For this to occur, however, changes in government-support networks, organizational structures, and work environments are critical for motivating and empowering employees to assume new roles.

If initiated solely as a short-term response to financial crises or as a reaction to customer complaints, these, similar to earlier reforms, are destined to fail. Internal changes are necessary, but insufficient by themselves, to deliver customized, customer-designed services. They must be accompanied by a commitment from leaders, owners, and senior managers to initiate fundamental structural changes accompanied by rewards, resources, and training to sustain QI goals. As more and more service providers compete for greater shares of expanding domestic and international markets, customer-driven quality management is fast becoming the preferred method for improving organizational performance. In competitive global markets, this change is coming just in time for some but too late for others.

Learning Customer-Driven TQS

In the mid-1980s, Karl Albrecht and Ron Zemke sounded the alarm, identifying the "lack of a consistent model or framework for managing service" as the reason most often cited for customer dissatisfaction (Albrecht and Zemke, 1985). For most services, the means to consistently manage and monitor TQS to achieve customer success, empower employees, and improve productivity has still not been fully developed or consistently applied.

During the tech boom in the 1990s, some of the world's most profitable manufacturing industries, those producing computers, IT software, and telecommunications equipment, found it difficult to recruit qualified knowledge workers. These industries were among the chief lobbyists for deregulating immigration restrictions to import more qualified foreign workers to the United States. As a result, over half the Ph.D.'s in computer science and electrical engineering granted in the United States during the past two decades went to students from other countries — India, Taiwan, Korea, and China. (Ironically, many of our grandparents entered the country the same way during the 19th and early 20th centuries, albeit with work visas from the so-called old economy industrial giants such as Bethleham Steel, Ford, and GM, rather than as "guest workers" with work permits from Microsoft, Oracle, or Hewlett-Packard.) Today, although there are fewer Americans to fill the jobs, there are more employment options available to students interested in learning quality specialities.

In the past, with the exception of specialized fields such as industrial and electrical engineering, operations research, or production management, research, teaching, and textbook-writing focused on manufacturing quality assurance rather than services. There are now more books or courses dealing with the application of quality and productivity improvement principles to services. Moreover, more integrated service QI cases, examples, or self-study materials are now available for learning how to apply quality management concepts to specific services. There is still a gap between the statistically based quality and productivity improvement manufacturing models and the human-relations- and marketing-based labor-intensive customer relations approaches used in services. The result is a dearth of graduates as well as training materials available to current and future service industry leaders, especially for small (under 150) to medium-sized (under 1500) service firms.

Recognizing the recent growth of the service economy and understanding that recent graduates are most likely to find employment with small and medium-sized firms, several professional schools within leading research universities offer modules, courses, and degrees in quality management. Many institutions are redesigning curricula and developing new programs in total quality and productivity management concepts. In addition, several schools use quality methods to offer instruction to students (Brown and Murti, 2003; Sinn, 2002). Bowling Green University offers bachelor's, master's, and doctorate degrees in technology management with a quality systems specialization. Several business schools have degree programs and certificates in technology and operations management. Fordham University Graduate School of Business offers an MBA in management systems with a global business specialty, and the Monfort College of Business at the University of Northern Colorado received a Baldrige award for its undergraduate business education curriculum in 2004 (Case Study 6.2, Chapter 6). Engineering schools at the University of Arizona, University of Michigan, Oregon State University, and Pennsylvania State University have degree programs at all levels in TQM. Several schools have added or revised courses, developed specialized curricular material on quality management, and created programs or institutes to study quality: Columbia University; Rochester Institute of Technology; Samford University in Birmingham, Alabama; Sloan School of Business at the Massachusetts Institute of Technology; Texas Agricultural and Mechanical; University of Minnesota; University of Miami; University of Pennsylvania; University of Tennessee; and University of Wisconsin–Madison.[5]

Quality management curricula have been slow to reach mainstream academia because faculty members at most major research universities teach courses and conduct research in narrowly-defined specialty fields. Reward systems are individualistic and course textbooks are written in accordance with accrediting association guidelines within traditionally defined academic units, such as accounting, business law, computer information systems, economics, finance, management, marketing, or public administration, in which specialties prevail. There is little reward for interdisciplinary work and faculty who step outside the well-worn paths of their disciplines do so at considerable professional risk. The so-called practical disciplines such as business, education, engineering, and bio-chemistry have always been more connected to industries that support basic research and patent applications in their respective fields (Koch, 2003).

The absence of a quality focus in higher education may also explain why so many larger research universities are losing support, downsizing, and coping with increased stakeholder (i.e., faculty, parent, student, alumni, and, if state supported, taxpayer) dissatisfaction with the service provided (Seymour, 1992; Johnson, 2002) This neglect is especially harmful to recent graduates who have earned advanced degrees without acquiring a basic understanding of the importance of quality and productivity improvement for the future of the United States in a competitive global economy.

This neglect is more than ivory tower isolation, although some academicians will always disdain the practical applications of their theories. There are fewer incentives to approach topics such as quality and productivity management from an interdisciplinary or team perspective. Higher-education institutions, especially large research universities, survive on research grants, reputation and alumni support, rather than market-driven, competition-based teaching and research quality.[6] Consequently, few research universities encourage the interdisciplinary cooperation necessary to apply quality concepts to various business, educational, healthcare, governmental, or engineering services.[7] Occasionally, team-taught courses are offered, but academic reward systems, such as grading students in the classroom and individual performance rankings in business, reflect traditional specialties and discourage participation in cross-functional interdisciplinary projects.

Not surprisingly, specialization and fragmentation of curriculum restricts course offerings and results in a lack of self-study material for learning these concepts. Such neglect runs counter to industry trends, in which teamwork and horizontally integrated cross-functional management (CFM) and organizations are valued as a means to successfully implement TQM, CQI, or TQS. Unlike higher education, the application of these concepts often means the difference between extinction and long-term competitive survival for many service firms.

Successful organizations recognize the complexity and multidimensional nature of service quality, yet decide upon which aspects to compete and strategically focus their efforts on responding to those customer-defined areas. Why? Because it is less expensive to respond to customers' needs in the first place than to correct errors after they are made. The case study of FedEx (Case Study 1.3) illustrates how this successful global package delivery service firm uses CFM to balance internal and external definitions of quality while providing employees sufficient discretion to respond to individual customer needs.

Redefining TQS

The spectacular success of Japanese industry in producing higher-quality, lower-cost, and more reliable products using statistical process control methods forced U.S. manufacturing leaders to rethink their own perceptions about the relationship between cost, quality, productivity, and customer satisfaction. Efforts by U.S. manufacturers to catch up responded directly to Japanese and, to a lesser extent, European competition for greater shares of the international markets. Although competition from Europe and Japan prompted North American managers to improve the quality of manufactured goods, free-trade policies, technology, the threat of litigation, and increased consumer activism within the United States simultaneously focused attention on the need for TQS. Providers of poor-quality goods and services were more likely to be sued, making some of them defensive about initiating the system changes necessary to eliminate the causes of poor quality. Manufacturers' neglect prompted consumer anger over shoddy work and defective products, and resulted in the continuing liability insurance crisis. Perspectives are slowly changing as some service industry leaders are still skeptical about the costs and commitment required to learn, redesign, and apply TQS principles.

The complexities of QI have forced many firms to rethink their approaches to TQM. Quality is still and will probably always be perceived by some as a luxury, a subjective "warm and fuzzy" term, or loosely used to describe a goal or an objective (usually increased profits or sales) rather than a continuous activity — a final destination, reward, or prize, instead of a never-ending journey. The quest for workable systems to improve service quality at the point of customer contact has been described more realistically as "a pilgrimage rather than a panacea." Like so many other clichés, these have some basis in truth.

Selecting appropriate QI strategies requires a vision that is dynamic, flexible, and focused on exceeding valid internal and external customer needs (see Case Study 1.1). Current performance appraisal and internal reward systems must be reexamined in relation to achieving this transformation (Milakovich, 1991a; Bowman, 1994; Hellein and Bowman, 2002). As QI methods become better known, entire organizations are being evaluated (as high, medium, and low performers) in much the same manner as individual performance appraisals are conducted (American Quality Foundation and Ernst and Young, 1992; Bush, 2001).[8] Many organizations are mandating that their suppliers demonstrate a commitment to improved service quality by insisting on higher performance standards, enhanced responsiveness to customers, and demonstrable quality results. As the "quality circle" expands, more and more otherwise isolated, protected, and regulated public and private services are responding to customers by learning how to become more competitive.

TQS is a powerful, yet simple, method of process improvement for achieving customer satisfaction without the need for substantial additional resources (detailed in Chapter 2). Managers and workers are guided to anticipate future internal and external customer needs by systematically evaluating and validating customer requirements, streamlining internal processes, and merging customer satisfaction data with existing management control systems. TQS anticipates customer needs and encourages employee participation and ownership of work processes. TQS is an essential first step that allows an organization to define its own quality standards, compete on a higher level, exceed customer expectations, and increase market share. Although there is little agreement about the precise definitions of the term, there is value in accepting the diversity of definitions for TQS offered by others (Albrecht, 1992; Brown, 1992; Gilbert, 1992; Schneider and White, 2004; Sureshchandar, Ragendran, and Anantharaman, 2001).

Whereas industrial-era quality control methods often required statistical knowledge and applications, no previous exposure or extensive experience with advanced statistics is necessary to learn how to implement TQS. Concepts and principles are aimed at encouraging employee responsibility, reducing internal competition, promoting teamwork, improving decision-making processes, and lowering costs. When the organizational changes and simple statistical techniques outlined in the following chapters are combined, remarkable gains in market share, productivity, and competitive position can be achieved.

For the reasons outlined earlier, fewer service firms have consistently applied TQS systems capable of integrating, managing, monitoring, and improving all aspects of customer service satisfaction. Therefore, less is known about quality applications in such important competitive and noncompetitive, market and nonmarket services as construction, health-care, insurance, import–export, government, education, telecommunications, travel and tourism — all vital segments of the global economy that together comprise some of the nation's best opportunities for employment and economic growth.

In sum, it is apparent that quality and productivity management systems designed for large-scale, early-20th-century private manufacturing cannot simply be "installed" in complex service delivery environments. Nor can modern off-the-shelf, statistically based systems be applied, without substantial modification, to improve customer service quality. Concepts such as accreditation, competition, EDI, results-driven quality measures, and service standards are still well within the capacities of most organizations to acquire, learn, and consistently deliver.

Another important trend accompanying the need for better service quality is the disappearance of the distinction once made between public- and private sector quality standards. As both sectors strive to respond to customer-defined service quality standards, systems for defining customer needs and managing quality merge. In many ways, all organizations are becoming more public, especially complex regulated services such as communications, education, healthcare, transportation, and public utilities. The purpose of any organization is to deliver the highest-quality products, services, and product support to demanding and valued customers. Clearly, the public and private sectors have overlapping missions and purposes.

This book emphasizes the importance of integrating common elements such as customer responsiveness, empowerment, planning, process focus, marketing, system design, technology, and information management to achieve system improvement and customer satisfaction.

Key Terms

Scientific management
Global competition
Multinational corporation (MNC)
Knowledge Revolution (see also knowledge management)
Return on investment (ROI)
Continuous quality improvement (CQI)
Business process reengineering (BPR)
Total quality control (TQC)
Regulated service monopolies
Malcolm Baldrige National Quality Award (BNQA)
Service quality revolution
Less developed countries (LDCs)
Electronic data interchange (EDI)
Theory X
Vertical hierarchies
Horizontal service networks (See also network model)
Network model
Purchasing agents
Stakeholders
Third-party cooperative partnerships
Pluralism
North American Free Trade Agreement (NAFTA)
European Union (EU)
Teamwork
Cross-functional (horizontally integrated) management
1:10:100 Rule (FedEx)
Internal customer needs
External customer needs

Notes

1. Frederick W. Taylor, *The Principles of Scientific Management* (New York: Norton, 1967); first published in 1911. See also Robert Kanigel, *One Best Way: Frederick Winslow Taylor and the Enigma of Efficiency* (New York: Viking Press, 1997).
2. For details, see: "China's Energy Needs and Strategies," Hearing before the United States–China Economic and Security Review Commission," 108th Congress, Washington, D.C.: Government Printing Office, October 30, 2003; and "Hearing on China's Impact on the U.S. Manufacturing Base," Hearing before the United States–China Economic and Security Review Commission, 108th Congress, Washington, D.C.: Government Printing Office, January 30, 2004.

3. These changes can be seen in the several editions of Robert Levering and Milton Moskowitz's, *The 100 Best Companies to Work for in America*. (New York: Doubleday), published in 1984, 1993, and 2003. For other examples of changes in past two decades, see also Tom Peters and Robert Waterman, *In Search of Excellence: Lessons From America's Best Run Companies* (New York: Warner Books), originally published in 1982, revised edition 1988.

4. To establish stronger ties with other governmental reforms such as the Government Performance and Results Act (GPRA), high-impact agencies must publish their customer service standards, performance goals, specific measures, and results on the GPRA Web site (www.opm.gov/gpra/index. htm). Two other comprehensive Web sites for information on recent reforms are: www.firstgov.gov and www.planetgov.com

5. For a full listing of degree programs, see Corinne N. Johnson, College and university programs in quality, *Quality Progress*, Vol. 35, No. 10, October, 2002, pp. 33–43.

6. There is no "playing field" comparable to free markets between universities. In addition, there are few incentives to engage in genuine competition (except on the gridiron) between various institutions of higher learning. Thus, competitive "rankings" would accurately reflect the actual value of services received from investments in higher education only if Department Chairs and professors from individual academic specialties (Management, Marketing, Economics, or Political Science, for example) acted more like coaches and competed with others in teams made up of the best students in their departments.

7. Karen Bemowski, Restoring the pillars of higher education, *Quality Progress*, Vol. 24, No. 10, October 1991, pp. 36–42; Axland, Suzanne. A higher degree of quality, *Quality Progress*, October 1992, pp. 44–61.

8. For current performance management rankings of all federal executive branch agencies, see www.results.gov. The American Customer Satisfaction Index (ACSI) measures customer satisfaction in the private and public sectors. Customer satisfaction is now a key indicator in the federal agency performance and the ACSI results provide the baseline measurement for each agency. For comparative rankings, see www.bus.umich.edu/research/ nqrc/government.html.

▼

Case Study 1.1: Xerox Business Services (XBS)

Xerox Business Services, a 14,000-person division of Xerox Corporation, relies on a business philosophy that focuses on customers and continuous learning for all of its employees. On the strength of this approach, XBS — headquartered in Rochester, New York — has grown into a $2 billion business in less than five years. Revenues and profits have increased by more than 30 percent annually, and XBS's share of the U.S. document-outsourcing market has grown to 40 percent, nearly three times the share of its nearest competitor. The company has 4,300 customers and is adding several hundred new accounts each year. XBS management believes that every employee has the potential to affect the bottom line. Through compensation and recognition systems aligned with division objectives, all XBS employees have a direct stake in the success of the business. Employee satisfaction has increased as the business has grown — from a 63 percent favorable rating in 1993 to about 80 percent at the end of 1996 — significantly higher than the average for a peer group of companies.

The Global Business

With 80 percent of its employees located at customer facilities, XBS provides document-outsourcing and consulting services to businesses worldwide. Document-outsourcing services, such as on-site management of mailrooms and print shops, account for 80 percent of revenues. The remainder is derived from "document solutions" — customized services designed to meet customers' specialized requirements for creating, producing, distributing, and storing paper and digital documents. In 1996, XBS provided services at about 2,300 customer locations in the United States. It also serviced 2,000 accounts in 35 foreign countries. The U.S. operation also includes 14 document technology centers and 38 field operations offices. XBS is the second Xerox unit to win a Baldrige award. In 1989, Xerox Business Products and Systems won an award in the manufacturing category. Although paper-centered document services now account for the bulk of its revenues, XBS anticipates that advanced services focused on digital documents and advanced networking capabilities represent its greatest opportunities for growth.

Managing for Results

For virtually every business goal, customer requirement, and improvement target, there is an XBS process, measure, and expected result.

The division's Senior Leadership Team achieves this clarity of organizational focus through "managing for results" — an integrated planning and management process that cascades action plans into measurable objectives for each manager, supervisor, and frontline associate. The entire process, the company says, is designed to "align goals from the customer's line of sight to the empowered employee and throughout the entire organization."

Yielding five-year and three-year strategic plans and a one-year operating plan, the process attends to the past, present, and future. To encourage organizational learning, for example, the Senior Leadership Team diagnoses the past year's business results and reassesses business practices. The reviews generate the "vital few" — priorities for process and operational improvements. XBS also develops strategic initiatives based on its understanding of the division's strengths and weaknesses as well as its reading of opportunities and threats. This analysis draws on the division's extensive competitive intelligence, "voice of the customer," and "voice of the market" information systems (see Chapter 3). Other inputs include benchmarking (see Chapter 2), data analysis, and storyboarding scenarios, which help the division to home in on future customer requirements, anticipate potential risks and challenges, and quantify the resources and action plans necessary to accomplish strategic goals. Strategic planning generates a "strategy contract," priorities for investment, and business partnership plans. These are distilled into a human resources plan, an investment plan, and operational plans for each organizational unit, customer account, and employee.

Customers First

Customer satisfaction is the division's number one priority, and XBS has made knowing the current and future requirements of existing and prospective customers its business. It uses a three-pronged customer satisfaction measurement system to systematically track XBS and competitors' performance in this critical area and to furnish regular feedback to organizational units and account teams. An open, networked architecture provides XBS employees with rapid access to customer data. Four categories of customer requirements — service quality, sales support, performance of on-site XBS personnel, and billing and administrative support — are subdivided into detailed performance attributes that are measured in semiannual surveys and monthly reviews with customers. Through XBS's 10-Step Selling Process, on-site services are customized to meet the unique needs of each account. Dedicated account teams develop "standards of performance" according to customer service priorities. These standards, which XBS pledges to meet through its "total satisfaction guarantee," are formalized in operations handbooks developed specifically for each customer.

Empowered Employees

Empowered employees are at the heart of XBS's customer-focused culture. Jobs, work processes, and work environments are designed by individuals and workgroups to help ensure that they can satisfy the unique requirements of their customers. In monthly and quarterly reviews, the effectiveness of work processes is assessed against performance measures. The division invests more than $10 million annually for training, and it is continually searching for innovative learning approaches. Examples are minicamps — designed to help employees contemplate and prepare for future changes in the way they work and in how XBS addresses evolving customer requirements — and each employee's personal learning plan, which is regularly reviewed by assigned "coaches."

Within Xerox, XBS has been recognized for its efforts to create a culturally diverse workforce, a commitment shared by the parent corporation. In addition, XBS offers several innovative assistance options to employees and their families. For example, Life-Cycle Assistance gives employees a $10,000 account, which can be used to fund special needs, including adoption, elder care, and first home purchase.

Results

XBS's commitment to total quality — by the entire organization and by its individual employees — is generating multiple dividends. The company saw $1.5 billion in revenue in 1996. In addition to leading its competitors in overall customer satisfaction, the division tops the industry in 7 of the 10 high motivators of customer satisfaction. Performance in all four key categories of customer requirements continues to improve; average scores in 1996 ranged from 8 to 9 on a 10-point grading scale. In all five areas identified by employees as having the greatest impact on their motivation and satisfaction — trust, responsible freedom, teamwork, valuing people, and learning — XBS also is improving from year to year. In 1996, the division earned favorable ratings of 70 percent or better in each category.

Source: Baldrige National Quality Program, National Institute of Standards and Technology, U.S. Department of Commerce; Web site: www.baldrige.nist.gov.

▲

▼

Case Study 1.2: Complaints about Dell Outsourcing Tech Support

Dell is just one of dozens of companies that use offshore call centers to boost business performance by reducing the cost of customer support. The practice, along with outsourcing more technical jobs — such as software engineering — has come under fire from some U.S. workers' groups. In a move that could dampen the tech sectors' unbridled enthusiasm for low-cost outsourcing, Dell said it would stop routing some customer-support requests to call centers in India after customers complained about the quality of service.

Dell said it had received some complaints about the technical support through the overseas support center, with one executive saying that customers reacted unfavorably to the fact that Dell had changed how it handled those calls. Newspapers located near Dell's Austin, Texas, headquarters reported that customers were complaining not only about having their calls answered by technical support staff who spoke with accents but also about receiving scripted responses to their questions rather than one-on-one support.

Dell's own online user forum is rife with recent complaints about attempts to reach Dell for technical and nontechnical customer service. Tech-support calls from customers with certain types of computers will now be handled from existing call centers in Texas, Idaho, and Tennessee. The affected products are sold largely to business customers. Dell said its call centers in Bangalore, India, would remain fully staffed, with some customer calls still being handled overseas.

Analysts said that the Dell example might give some companies pause, especially given the extremely competitive nature of the personal computer market in which strong customer service can distinguish one company from another. "There's only so much price competition that can happen," said an industry analyst. In the case of computer sales, the customer is also looking for overall value, and if there is a sense that's being eroded by a lower level of service, that is a major concern.

Source: Abstracted from "Dell Recalls Tech Support from India After Complaints," by Keith Regan, *E-Commerce Times*, November 25, 2003. Web site: http://www.ecommercetimes.com/story/32248.html; accessed August 24, 2004.

▲

▼

Case Study 1.3: FedEx

At FedEx, dedication to customer satisfaction, on-time delivery, and continuous monitoring has produced measurable results. Many lessons can be learned by benchmarking this air carrier, a leader in the application of customer-driven service in the aviation industry. Twenty years ago, FedEx launched the air express industry. By constantly adhering to a management philosophy emphasizing people, service, and profit, the company achieved high levels of customer satisfaction and experienced rapid sales growth. Annual revenues topped $1 billion within just 10 years of the company's founding, an exceptional achievement for any new business. But past accomplishments do not ensure future success. That is why FedEx has set ever higher goals for quality performance and customer satisfaction, enhanced and expanded service, invested heavily in advanced technology, developed its human resources, and established its reputation as an excellent employer. Company leaders stress management by fact, analysis, and improvement.

FedEx began operations in 1973. At that time a fleet of just eight small aircraft was sufficient to handle demand. Just five years later, the company employed 10,000 people, who handled a daily volume of 35,000 shipments. Today, approximately 90,000 FedEx employees at more than 1,650 sites process 1.5 million shipments daily, all of which must be tracked in a central information system, sorted in a short time at facilities in Memphis, Indianapolis, Newark, Oakland, Los Angeles, Anchorage, and Brussels, Belgium, and delivered by a highly decentralized distribution network. The firm's air cargo fleet is now the world's largest. FedEx revenues totaled $7 billion in fiscal year 1990. Domestic overnight and second-day deliveries accounted for nearly three fourths of the total, with the remainder being international deliveries. The company's share of the domestic market in 1989 was 43 percent, compared with 26 percent for its nearest competitor.

FedEx's "People–Service–Profit" philosophy guides management policies and actions. The company has a well-developed and thoroughly deployed management evaluation system called *SFA* (survey/feedback/action), which involves a survey of employees, analysis of results by each workgroup's manager, and a discussion between the manager and the workgroup to develop written action plans for the manager to become more effective. The employee workgroups offer solutions and monitor progress. Data from the SFA process is aggregated at all levels of the organization for use in policymaking. Training of frontline personnel is a responsibility of managers, and "recurrency training" is a widely used instrument for service QI. Work teams regularly assess training needs, and a worldwide staff of training professionals devise programs to address those needs. To aid these efforts, FedEx has developed an interactive video system for employee instruction. An internal television network, accessible throughout the company, also serves as an important avenue for employee education.

Consistently included in listings of the best U.S. companies for the past 20 years, FedEx has a "no layoffs" philosophy, and its "guaranteed fair treatment" procedure for handling employee grievances is used as a model by firms in many industries. Employees can participate in a program to qualify frontline workers for management positions. In addition, FedEx has a well-developed recognition program for team and individual contributions to company performance. Over the last five years, at least 91 percent of employees responded that they were "proud to work for FedEx."

An internationally recognized quality leader and winner of the 1990 BNQA, FedEx is one of the nation's leading service quality package delivery firms. FedEx stresses the 1:10:100 rule in its employee training. If a mistake is caught at the source, it costs just $1.00 to correct; if the flaw is passed on to the next process, it costs $10.00, and if the mistake reaches the end user, it costs $100 to remedy. Every FedEx employee knows it is 100 times less costly to prevent mistakes from happening in the first place. Thus, rather than relying on inspection or customer complaints to detect errors, FedEx empowers each employee to deliver quality to customers by preventing errors. To achieve its goal of 100-percent customer satisfaction, FedEx initiated a comprehensive service quality indicator (SQI) system that describes how its performance is viewed by customers.

SQI replaced FedEx's old measure of quality performance — percentage of on-time deliveries — with a 12-component index that comprehensively describes how its performance is viewed by customers. Each item in the SQI is weighted to reflect how significantly it affects overall customer satisfaction. Through a process focusing on the 12 SQIs (noted in the following text), FedEx sets higher standards for service and customer satisfaction. Measuring themselves against a 100-percent service standard, managers and employees strive to improve all aspects of the way FedEx does business.

FedEx SQIs

Indicator	Weight
Abandoned calls	1
Complaints reopened	5
Damaged packages	10
International	1
Invoice adjustments requested	1
Lost packages	10
Missed pickups	10
Missing proofs of delivery	1
Overgoods (lost and found)	5
Right-day late deliveries	1
Traces	1
Wrong-day late deliveries	5

Performance data is gathered with the company's advanced computer and tracking systems, including the SuperTracker, a handheld computer used for scanning a shipment's bar code every time a package changes hands between pickup and delivery. Rapid analysis of data from the firm's far-flung operations yields daily SQI reports transmitted to workers at all FedEx sites. Management meets daily to discuss the previous day's performance and tracks weekly, monthly, and annual trends. Analyses of data contained in the company's more than 30 major databases assist quality actions teams (QATs) in locating the root cause of problems that surface in SQI reviews. Extensive customer and internal data are used by cross-functional teams involved in the company's new product introduction process.

To reach its aggressive quality goals, the company has set up one cross-functional team for each service component in the SQI. A senior executive heads each team and ensures the involvement of frontline employees, support personnel, and managers from all parts of the corporation when needed. Two of these companywide teams have a network of over 1000 employees working on improvements. The SQI measurements are directly linked to the corporate planning process, which begins with the chief executive officer (CEO) and chief operating officer (COO) and an executive planning committee. SQIs form the basis on which corporative executives are evaluated. Individual performance objectives are established and monitored. Executive bonuses rest upon the performance of the whole corporation in meeting performance improvement goals. And, in the annual employee survey, if employees do not rate management leadership at least as high as they rated them the year before, no executive receives a year-end bonus.

Employees are encouraged to be innovative and to make decisions that advance quality goals. FedEx provides employees with the information and technology they need to continuously improve their performance. An example is the Digitally Assisted Dispatch System (DADS), which communicates to some 30,000 couriers through screens in their vans. The system enables quick response to pickup and delivery dispatches and allows couriers to manage their time and routes with high efficiency.

Since 1987, overall customer satisfaction with FedEx's domestic service has averaged better than 95 percent, and its international service has rated a satisfaction score of about 94 percent. In an independently conducted survey of air express industry customers, 53 percent gave FedEx a perfect score, as compared with 39 percent for the next-best competitor. The company has received 195 awards over the last 13 years, and representatives of nearly 600 businesses and organizations have visited its facilities.

Source: Baldrige National Quality Program, National Institute of Standards and Technology, U.S. Department of Commerce; Web site: www.baldrige.nist.gov.

▲

Chapter 2

Applying Total Quality Service Concepts to Public and Nonprofit Organizations

I hear and I forget
I see and I remember
I do and I understand.

— **Confucius**

During the waning decades of the 20th century, U.S. manufacturers were slow to grasp the profound changes occurring in global competitive markets. Many learned harsh lessons on how not to compete in international manufacturing markets. As a result, several businesses experienced substantial losses and were forced to either respond to their customer's preferences (sometimes against their will) or withdraw from the markets altogether.

There are success stories as well, notably of U.S. automobile manufacturers, computer hardware and software makers, and telecommunication companies. Large manufacturers were first to recognize the need to improve customer service. These included many of our most financially successful and socially responsible manufacturing firms — quality leaders such as AT&T, Dell, Intel, Ford, 3M, Motorola, Microsoft, Johnson & Johnson, Texas Instruments, and Xerox, who define themselves as service organizations as well. Other smaller but equally successful manufacturing businesses, including Clarke American Checks, Dana Corporation, Operations Management International, Solectron, and STMicroelectronics, utilized quality management techniques to dominate sectors of domestic and global markets. (These are among the over 60 Malcolm Baldrige National Quality Awards (BNQA) winners, and their full profiles and contact information can be found at www.baldrige.nist.gov.) American service providers now face many of the same competitive challenges that manufacturers confronted in the last two decades.

The challenge for private, for-profit organizations is to respond to demands for better customer service at lower costs or withdraw from competitive markets. Likewise, neglect of quality standards in public, nonprofit organizations, and regulated markets breeds frustration, resentment, and resistance from customers.

The majority of non-market-driven services are provided by government agencies facing unique barriers to process improvements. These organizations vary in mission, purpose, and scope and include government corporations, publicly regulated utilities, local police departments, cable TV franchisees, many hospitals and healthcare providers, public schools, as well as federal agencies and 87,000 general purpose state and local governments. Reforms promoting customer-focused and nontraditional government service (networked internal processes responsive to citizen, customer, or user demands) have often conflicted with other public priorities and vested interests. Barriers to the implementation of networked, horizontally integrated, customer-responsive models include:

1. Adherence to hierarchical rule-driven management systems, instead of networked customer-focused work cultures
2. Inexperience with output or results measures for allocating resources
3. Lack of incentives to reward performance
4. Fear of the political consequences of not meeting customer standards
5. Failure of elected and appointed officials to cooperate
6. Divided accountability for achieving results, especially in regulatory compliance agencies (Milakovich, 1998)

Customers everywhere express concerns about the continued neglect of product and service quality, especially in non-market-driven services. Americans especially are frustrated with unacceptable delays, mistakes, rudeness, incompetence, defective materials, deliberate overcharging, and poor workmanship that characterize many service encounters today. One of the reasons that 1.6 million Californians signed a petition to recall Governor Gray Davis and subsequently elected Arnold Schwarzenegger in 2002 was the pervasive belief that "special interests" dominated Davis' administration and that state programs were wasteful and inefficient. Increasing numbers of citizens and customers are dissatisfied with local manufacturing and service firms and willing to shop internationally to find alternative providers. Demanding customers are not satisfied unless treated as members, guests, or associates who receive the service paid for and whose repeat business is valued. For most, the artificial distinction once made between the tangible quality of a finished product or a service consumed at the point of delivery is irrelevant. Informed consumers now demand higher quality and lower cost. Thus, continuously improving customer-driven service quality has become a top priority — if not an obsession — for all types of organizations.

Despite the high frustration levels between suppliers and customers and fierce competition among providers, many market and nonmarket driven service firms still have not responded to demands for better service. (Some would say they just "don't get it.") Either they have not yet heard the message from their customers, or they fail to invest in the resources necessary to redesign service quality monitoring systems to meet customer's needs. Some have tried but failed to consistently apply existing systems to monitor progress toward continuous quality improvement (CQI). Regardless, the results are equally damaging.

Those service firms that have heard the message and are responding with new strategies designed to eliminate barriers to CQI are more likely to prosper in the future. For them, total quality service (TQS) is as much a survival strategy as a means of satisfying customers or increasing market share.

Suppliers and providers must not only deliver initial product and service quality, but maintain a sustained commitment to excellence in follow-up services as well. Even when purchasing nondurable goods or professional services such as insurance, legal advice, higher education, or medical care, customers evaluate "total quality" as much by the before- and after-sale service as initial product quality. With the increasing availability and lower cost of technology, companies selling digital cameras, computers, cellular telephones, and software must offer service quality as good as or better than that provided with the initial sale of products. Many organizations do not meet this standard.

Improving the customer-defined quality position of any organization has emerged as a strategic opportunity for nearly all organizations, especially those competing for greater shares of expanding international markets. Not only do most people work in service industries, but over one third of all U.S. services are exported.[1] Compounding worker frustration, many jobs associated with global services are being outsourced to non-U.S. companies. For many American service industries, future expansion increasingly depends on access to global markets — and success in global markets means competition on the basis of cost, quality, and reliability.

There is a gap (some would say a chasm) between the theoretical understanding of quality improvement (QI) theories and their application in various service industries. Although strategies for improvement differ with the type of product or market, most service industries are now generally aware of the changes required to compete in a global economy. Even those services protected as monopolies or regulated by governments such as public utilities, cable TV providers, or government corporations are slowly accepting the need to change (See Chapter 7 to Chapter 9 for detailed examples).

In this chapter, we take a brief retrospective view of past attempts to raise quality and productivity levels by responding to customer needs and expectations. This is followed by discussions of the importance of benchmarking, changes in the definitions of quality, and the elements that constitute the TQS approach. The remainder of the chapter discusses the components of the TQS model.

Origins and Evolution of TQS

The evolution of the TQS movement is a mix of various American and Japanese philosophies and strategies linked to the global search for better quality and lower costs. Although greater numbers of Japanese firms first succeeded in applying the strategy later labeled Total Quality Management (TQM) in the United States, several Americans are recognized internationally as the intellectual founders of the concept. TQM comes in several different flavors, sizes, and variations, yet its essential ingredients reflect a continuous, cross-functional, interdisciplinary, and horizontally integrated management strategy applicable to all types of organizations. One of the lessons learned by large manufacturers during the 1990s is that it is vitally important to select a quality approach that best matches the working culture of the organization.

The importance of controlling the quality of industrial products accompanied the era of mass production manufacturing in the early 20th century. In the 1920s, Walter Shewhart first introduced statistical process control (SPC) charts to monitor quality in mass production manufacturing (Shewhart, 1931). At the Western Electric "Bell Labs" factory in Chicago during the 1930s, SPC techniques were expanded by Shewhart and his colleagues, including a young Ph.D. in statistics from Yale, W. Edwards Deming. SPC techniques provided an efficient method for controlling the quality of mass-produced goods (Deming, 1950). Several others contributed to the development and implementation of QI theories and methods.[2] They were expanded, perfected, and successfully applied to the mass production of weapons and war materials during World War II. Figure 2.1 describes the evolution of TQS concepts during the 20th century. In the boom years following the war, the lessons learned were largely forgotten. In the absence of competition, American industry leaders mistakenly believed that their products and management systems were superior.

Japanese manufacturing companies have used statistically based total quality control (TQC) since the early 1950s. These principles have evolved into a team-based management philosophy, referred to as TQC or companywide quality control (CWQC) (Ishikawa and Lu, 1985). Statistical quality control was strongly promoted by powerful political and economic forces, most notably the Japanese Union of Scientists and Engineers (JUSE). There was no organized lobbying for the quality effort in the United States until the promotion of the BNQA awards in the mid-1980s.

As a consequence, quality concepts were slow to reach American firms. The theories and techniques underlying TQM and CQI were ignored in favor of traditional, command-and-control, top-down, hierarchical, management by objectives (MBO), or results-oriented approaches. This approach directly challenged traditional hierarchies by emphasizing the need to change work environments to achieve customer-driven quality goals (Crosby, 1979; Deming, 1982, 1986, 1993; Ishikawa, 1985).

Deming, Juran, and Ishikawa are recognized as the intellectual "godfathers" of the Japanese economic miracle. Deming refined his teachings into "Deming's 14 Points" (Appendix B) intended to guide American quality and productivity improvement efforts. Juran's approach is less prescriptive, although he emphasizes the importance of cross-functional management (CFM) and breakthroughs (Figure 3.2) achieved through teamwork and process improvements. Both Juran and Deming agreed on the importance of teams and stress that at least 85 percent of an organization's quality problems are under management's control. Kaoru Ishikawa recognized the importance of self-managed work teams, statistical control, continual training, and worker participation. Each of these quality gurus, as well as others, contributed to our knowledge of how to balance the human relations approach with more quantitative SPC to enhance organizational behavior and management.

There is also a need to transform management attitudes, change organizational structures, and alter performance appraisal and reward systems to obtain employee "buy-in" for improved customer service. (Albrecht, 1992; Albrecht and Zemke, 1985; Berry, 1991; Clemmer, 1992;

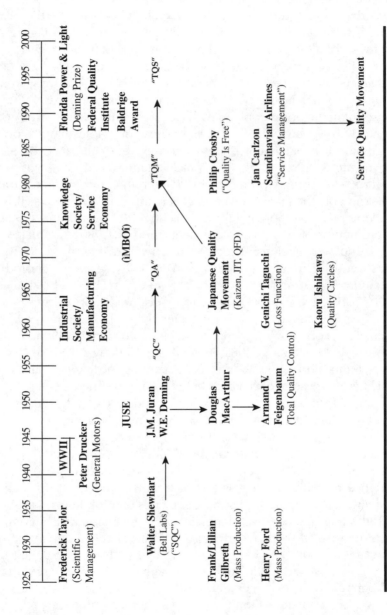

Figure 2.1 Evolution of TQS. (Adapted from Karl Albrecht/The TQS Group.)

Gilbert, 1992; Ouchi, 1984; Peters, 1987; Rosander, 1989; Zeithaml, Parasuraman, and Berry, 1990; Zemke and Schaaf, 1989). When accompanied by changes in the workplace, management systems designed to continuously monitor and improve processes have achieved remarkable gains in quality, productivity, and competitive position in two to three years (Deming, 1986; Scherkenbach, 1988, 1991; U.S. General Accounting Office, 1991). Concepts such as employee "empowerment" and "process ownership" describe the important organizational changes required to implement TQS (Block, 1991).

While there is an emerging consensus that broad-based participation is needed to implement service quality, several different theories exist (and sometimes compete) to explain how best to improve an organization's work environment. Some approaches are statistically based and aimed at better process control, improving measurement capability, and reducing variation. Others stress marketing and customer satisfaction, carefully assessing and measuring the gaps between customer expectations and perceptions, and motivating employees to provide better customer service (Berry and Parasuraman, 1997, 1992; Zeithaml, Parasuraman, and Berry, 1990). Others place greater value on the need to change top-management behavior to direct the change effort from the top down. The emphasis on process reengineering to redesign business systems extends these principles by identifying critical internal processes, focusing on customer requirements, and rethinking the mission of the organization (Hammer and Champy, 1993). As knowledge and appreciation of the power of various QI theories increases, these approaches are merging into a common set of principles (listed later in this chapter) reflecting successful applications in both manufacturing and service industries.

Largely as a result of the efforts of a coalition of business and public interests, TQM and CQI principles were rediscovered in the 1980s and applied primarily (but not exclusively) by large American multinational manufacturing firms. A detailed discussion of these quality principles (listed in Table 2.1 and Table 6.1) is presented in Chapter 3 and Chapter 6. Given the ideological resistance and general disinterest of many American businesses prior to the 1990s, it is not surprising that service organizations just began to experience the full impact of these changes in the early 21st century.

Changing Perspectives on Quality and Control

The adoption and implementation of modern quality theories has been accompanied by changes in the definitions of customer service, quality standards, and productivity (Table 2.1). Definitions based on the requirement

Table 2.1 Changing Organizational Values

Old	New
Hierarchical, Theory X, top-down organizational structure	Flatter, leaner, Theory Y or Theory Z, participatory organizational structure
Centralized command-and-control structure	Decentralized and empowered workforce
Productivity versus quality	Productivity gains are achieved through quality
Separate data systems	Integrated data systems
Blame workers for poor quality	Management is responsible
Quality achieved through inspection	Quality is built into systems and processes
Supplier relationships are short term and cost oriented	Supplier relationships are long term and quality oriented
People are viewed as variable costs and replaceable	People are viewed as assets for their contributions to the organization
Training is external to the mission of the organization	Training is integrated with quality and productivity goals
External definition of quality standards	Quality is measured by customer needs and process improvement
Quality is measured by degree of conformance to standards	Quality reflects continuous improvement and user satisfaction

of large-scale manufacturing industries are gradually being adapted to fit service delivery environments. Traditional manufacturing concepts include the *appropriateness of design* and *specifications* of a product's function and use, as well as the degree to which a finished product conforms to the design and performs according to customer specifications.

Quality of design reflects the designer's intention to include specific features (such as size, weight, or color) in a finished product. Design choices demanded by customers typically originate from marketing representatives who listen to and gather information from external customers. Because production resources are always limited, the end product or service usually reflects some compromise between the "voices of the customer" and the "voice of the process." Quality of conformance is to the degree to which goods and services are consistent with the intent of design. Factors that influence conformance include: the capability of equipment, the training and skills of employees, process monitoring to assess conformance, worker motivation, and management commitment. Lastly, quality of performance encompasses the reliability of the original product or service as well as the competence, integrity, and promptness of staff and support services. Different types of services can themselves be characterized by quality of design, conformance, or performance.

For some fortunate suppliers and a few well-to-do consumers, quality will always be defined in luxury terms as the best available — a Lexus automobile, Russian caviar, or a five-star hotel. One of the key lessons of the Japanese manufacturing "miracle" is that reliable high-quality goods can be produced at lower and lower costs. Thus, rather than being based solely on manufacturers' specifications, conformance to design, or luxury features, other dimensions of quality began to be considered by American producers in the 1980s.

Harvard Professor David A. Garvin (1984) proposed five distinct groupings of quality definitions: *transcendent* (quality is innate excellence), *product based* (quality as a measure of the quantity of some ingredient or attribute built into the product), *user based* (a reflection of the consumer's preference), *manufacturing based* (conformance to specifications), and *value based* (performance or conformance at an acceptable level of price or cost). Variations of these five definitions have since been used by academicians and practitioners in such varied services as clinical medicine, engineering, philosophy, economics, law, marketing, operations research, and construction management. These specialties define quality from the perspectives of their own professional standards and internal users. Different definitions have also emerged based on the unique research methods, procedures, information technology systems, and databases of each of these disciplines. Under all these concepts, customer preferences are typically interpreted by professionals.

Another reason why customer-based quality concepts have been slow to reach the American service culture is that each subspecialty has its own (sometime conflicting) definition based on design, conformance, or performance requirements. Without the motivation or technical capacity to measure improvements in service processes, definitions tend to shift as information, goods, or services flow through internal processes toward the point of final delivery. This problem of "entropy" — or the displacement of uniform standards as products flow through the production cycle — is recognized in all manufacturing and services systems.

Although the design, conformance, and performance approaches to defining quality have existed for some time, incorporating customer-driven or user-based perspectives on service quality is relatively new to the American service sector.[3] Garvin (1987) identified eight dimensions of quality as a framework for considering how customers define quality. This framework can be described as a multifaceted attempt to gauge quality on the basis of the following elements:

1. Performance
2. Features
3. Reliability
4. Conformance
5. Durability
6. Serviceability
7. Aesthetics
8. Perceived Quality

This multidimensional, customer-focused view of quality showed how quality theories can be used as competitive weapons in the struggle for international markets (Chapter 6). Understanding how these elements interact reinforces the importance of defining quality from the perspective of customer demands and needs. It enables all participants to strategically manage quality as an interdisciplinary and flexible resource for initially meeting, then exceeding, and subsequently anticipating customer expectations. Multidimensional definitions of service quality must be customer based, measured against the extent to which a service at least fulfills, if not surpasses, customer expectations. Recognizing multiple perspectives on quality within market and non-market-driven (competitive and non-competitive) service organizations, a working definition of quality used here is *customer* or *user determined*. Measures used to evaluate quality must be based on valid service quality characteristics[4] and reliable measures of customer satisfaction to anticipate, meet, and exceed customer expectations (for details, see Chapter 5).

To improve the delivery of services, it is also critical to develop "flexible use" criteria for determining and anticipating customer needs. Because services are less tangible than manufactured products, their production and consumption are often closely linked. For many other types of services, customers must wait months or even years to evaluate quality and reliability. Common examples are higher education, healthcare, or life insurance policies. Understanding how customers form expectations and perceptions is essential to service quality management. In addition to the criteria listed in the preceding text, services can be judged by the competence, courtesy, credibility, responsiveness, sense of security, and accessibility communicated by all employees providing the service. Several of the case studies of successful service providers presented in the inserts in this and other chapters underscore the importance of horizontal or *cross-functional integration* of organizational branches, departments, or divisions. (See concept (1), Section "TQS: A Working Definition" later in this chapter.) Thus, the subjective perceptions and expectations of customers must be considered when selecting a strategy for monitoring QI (Zeithaml, Parasuraman, and Berry, 1990). Strategies and monitoring processes are discussed in detail in Chapter 3 and Chapter 5.

At first glance, it would appear to be unrealistic to apply the same standard to public or nonprofit agencies, especially where services are not purchased on the open market or in situations in which regulatory, law enforcement, evaluative, or authority relationships exist. Customer-driven quality definitions, however, need not assume a competitive market and multiple providers of goods or services. Delivery of healthcare services, education, law enforcement, revenue collection, environmental protection, and building and zoning inspections are but a few examples of services where "delighting" the customers may seem to be an unattainable goal. On the contrary, it is precisely in nonvoluntary compliance agencies, such as state and local police departments, state bureaus, and federal agencies such as the Internal Revenue Service (IRS), in which extraordinary progress is being made in the application of service quality principles (Hellein and Bowman, 2002; Galloway, 1992; Kravchuk and Leighton, 1993; New York State Police, 1993; West, Berman, and Milakovich, 1994).

Benchmarking for Service QI

Benchmarking is a well-established methodology for improving governmental practices, transferring knowledge from one organization to another, identifying "best practices," comparing results, scientifically analyzing policy goals, highlighting achievements, and guiding results-oriented customer service efforts (Camp, 1989; Ammons, 2000; Coe, 1999; Keehley et al., 1997). Benchmarking examines internal organizational processes of recognized leaders in performing certain functions, studies those processes, and transplants them to other organizations. The speed of change accelerates by using tested practices, creating a sense of urgency when gaps are revealed and minimizing time spent reinventing processes. Agencies save time and money that they would otherwise spend on discovering more productive practices on their own. Benchmarking is an objective-setting strategy that must be developed, rather than a specific operationally quantifiable process that can be immediately installed. Through benchmarking, managers and agencies gain the "software" and general direction to follow, but not always the detailed processes used to achieve specific goals (see Case Study 2.1).

When appropriately researched, documented, and summarized, comparative methodologies offer managers detailed benchmarks for understanding customers' needs and training employees to meet them. In addition to ranking organizations, better understanding of organizational processes reinforces goals and standards, rewards success, and transfers best practices to guide in the transition to a customer-responsive, horizontally-integrated, networked, and results-driven government. Achieving exemplary (or even satisfactory) customer service outcomes is difficult because so many complex and varied participants and relationships take place in decision-making processes. In addition, government–customer transactions are often mandatory, involuntary, paid for indirectly, and not market based. In other instances, service relationships may be voluntary or fee-for-service based. Citizens and administrators benefit from empirically-based knowledge and theory gained from customer surveys that evaluate the level of service expected and delivered, especially by intelligence, law enforcement, and regulatory compliance agencies (Milakovich, 2003). For instance, benchmarking was recently used by local school districts to facilitate the exchange of school security standards developed by the U.S. Department of Education and the Secret Service (Vassekuil, Fein, Pollack et al., 2002; U.S. Secret Service, 2002).

Cities, counties, and states are benchmarking leaders of various processes, such as budgeting, E-government, procurement, personnel, systems integration, and customer relationship management. At the local level, public agencies learn from each other and from the private sector how to best respond to the needs of all their customers. Many nonprofits and local public agencies are joining the public sector's efforts as copartners in making management improvements based on experience, practice, and performance standards in other similar functions and jurisdictions. To demonstrate success over time, an organization must first measure results, show how management practices relate to the community and customers being served, and document a clear road map to show how processes evolved (Keehley et al., 1997; Coplin and Dwyer, 2000). Research findings generated by successful applications offer administrators a clearer understanding of their customers' needs and how they can empower employees to meet these requirements (Ammons, 2000; Ammons, Coe, and Lombardo, 2001; Coe, 1999).

TQS: A Working Definition

TQS is a continuous, cross-functional, interdisciplinary, and horizontally integrated approach applicable to all types of organizations. TQS is not an end in itself, but rather a carefully designed and executed strategy for improving processes, products, and services through continual improvements in quality, reliability, systems, and performance. Successfully applying TQS requires an unwavering commitment to rethinking existing production and delivery systems, not only from an internal systems perspective, but from the perspective of their many users. By definition and in practice, TQS must be multidisciplinary, customer driven, and organizationwide.

TQS is a powerful yet simple method of process improvement for achieving valid customer quality requirements and productivity goals without the long-term need for substantial additional resources. It streamlines internal processes and merges process measurement characteristics with customer satisfaction data. In the short term, additional resources may be required for retraining, but when organizational changes and simple statistical management techniques are combined, TQS reduces internal competition, fosters teamwork, improves decision-making processes, and lowers costs.

Developing a TQS Culture

The critical elements in developing a TQS culture are described in the following text and amplified in subsequent chapters. At a minimum, everyone must be trained to apply the following concepts:

1. Integrating crossfunctional management (CFM) through teamwork and flattening the hierarchy
2. Strengthening customer–supplier relationships
3. Increasing employee empowerment and participation
4. Understanding systemic interrelationships
5. Monitoring results and customer feedback
6. Implementing CQI or Kaizen
7. Reducing poor-quality cost practices

CFM, Teamwork, and "Delayering"

All organizations must make a visible companywide commitment to customer-driven QI. The importance of continually improving internal processes to better serve customers must be communicated to everyone. There is more, however, to implementing TQS, especially in nonmarket or regulated services: all internal management activities must be carefully integrated and aimed at anticipating customer demands for higher quality service and individualized treatment, often within preset budget limits or at costs suited to the prevailing market. Such system integration is difficult for all organizations but especially challenging for non-market-driven services. Unlike in the for-profit sector, budgets are less likely to increase as a result of greater demand for services. Quite the opposite would be the case, because operating revenues are typically set by charities, elected legislatures, regulatory agencies, or local government boards, not by the customers directly receiving the service. Without incentive systems to reward employees for better service, customers are often thought of and treated as recipients of services paid for by others.

Changes in the types of services delivered in government, education, and healthcare (detailed in Chapter 7 to Chapter 9) are rapidly changing this dependency relationship. In addition, public agencies receive a greater share of their operating revenues from direct charges, tolls, federal aid, or user fees. These include direct and indirect revenues for services such as airline landing, water and sewer districts, trash collection, highway access, special district assessments, and designated taxes. These types of assessments are the more rapidly growing sources of revenue for states and local governments. All public service organizations have entered an era of "no excuses" management in the market-driven, as well as non-competitive segments of the economy. Although the broad policies are set by others, operating parameters of regulated utilities, special districts, or general purpose governments are increasing responsiveness to customers. Operating revenues are much less elastic (expandable), so there are fewer incentives to reduce costs by improving internal processes and acting on customer preferences. Plainly, when services are paid for directly, customers of all types of public services demand and deserve the same level of quality provided by the private sector.

High-performance service firms know that individual customer needs differ and also that systems must be designed to accommodate those preferences. Whether or not the service is provided by the competitive or regulated sector of the economy, cross-functional teams, such as those employed at FedEx (Case 1.3) and Citigroup Card Services (Case Study 2.3), are the most effective means to achieve the vital goal of customizing service requirements for each valued customer (Katzenbach and Smith, 1992).

Service quality leaders are flattening hierarchies, training employees to respond to customers, and achieving improvements in response time and productivity. Organizations still operating under vertically controlled hierarchical and patriarchal systems are doomed. Organizational structures must be flattened and thinned; all employees, not just "customer service reps," must be trained to respond courteously, flexibly, and promptly to valid customer requirements. More than just "charm schools" for employees, the manner in which all employees are trained to respond to customers' needs often makes the difference between survival and extinction. (Training strategies are described in Chapter 4.) To better manage across an organization and respond to customers, barriers to internal communications between departments, divisions, and bureaus must be reduced or eliminated. Attention should be focused on creating better horizontal integration between groups or divisions, thus enhancing teamwork and reducing the distance between customer and supplier. Traditional top-down (vertically managed) or tall pyramid structures foster leadership styles that limit the ability of employees to act effectively to serve customers. Hierarchies further reinforce fear-based, top-down, and nonparticipatory (Theory X) management patterns. Further, they inhibit genuine empowerment of employees and increase the distance between senior management, employees, suppliers, and customers.

Leaders of all organizations are applying TQS principles to enhance their long-term strategic market position as well as improve internal management processes. The perceived benefits of an organizationwide cross-functional quality management strategy are:

1. Better communication between departments
2. Reduced rework
3. Greater productivity
4. Lower unit cost
5. Improved competitive position
6. Greater long-term job security for the entire workforce

Teams, committees, workgroups, community councils, or quality control circles can be used to create this seamless structure of cross-functional, horizontally integrated unity among the workforce. Achieving this goal has become easier with the publication of several excellent books on how to teach teamwork (Katzenbach and Smith, 1992; Scholtes, 1988; Shonk, 1992). With proper training and top-management support, service workforces can be empowered to respond to customer demands and needs.

The need to delayer or flatten hierarchical structures in service organizations was demonstrated by Columbia University Business Professor John Whitney, who analyzed insurance companies and food service providers and found in one case that there were 17 (!) layers of bureaucracy between the customer and top management (Whitney, 1989). In organizations such as these, even if senior management wanted to implement TQS, it would be highly unlikely that the multiple layers of middle managers would facilitate internal communication or respond effectively to customer needs. The need to reduce the distance between customers and senior management is increasingly apparent in all service delivery environments.

One of the basic values underlying most QI strategies is the need to transform existing vertical hierarchical structures. This involves everyone in process improvements and efforts to delayer and eliminate internal barriers between departments, sometimes referred to as "vertical chimneys" or "missile silos." These functional departments and the efforts expended to defend them violate TQS principles and limit communication and empowerment. Commitment to QI also means changing the relationships between departments, eliminating non-value-added costs, increasing teamwork among different branches, and reducing internal barriers by recognizing fellow employees as lifelong customers with valid needs.

CFM of internal processes is necessary and difficult to achieve within a vertical hierarchical structure. To implement TQS, managers require a broader horizontally structured system that emphasizes prevention and new service innovations and encourages all those involved in the redesign of service delivery processes to make suggestions for improvement. Frontline workers, supervisors, and middle managers often lack the sense of mission to respond to the many "moments of truth" that contribute positively to an organization's reputation and increase market share (Carlzon, 1987). To achieve closer customer–supplier relationships, many states and local governments (the most rigid of bureaucracies) are successfully applying total quality concepts, delayering hierarchical pyramids of unnecessary authority, training and empowering employees, and redesigning systems to better serve customers' needs (Kravchuk and Leighton, 1993; West, Berman, and Milakovich, 1994).

Strengthen Customer–Supplier Relationships

Whether to earn a profit for stockholders, carry out its role as a voluntary nonprofit association, or serve the broader public interest, the primary mission of any organization is to identify, nurture, and maintain the customer. The best way to keep current customers happy and increase the number of new ones is to offer quality services to greater numbers of people faster than the competition at lower costs. This has always been a wise strategy for competitive service because it costs five times more to acquire a new customer than it does to retain one.

In a quality-driven service culture, the concept of the customer or user as the final arbiter of quality standards must be extended to include internal customers (employees in departments, divisions, and bureaus) and external customers (buyers, vendors, and regulators) of a firm. Valid customer requirements thus become the essential "linchpin" that binds the provider or supplier of services with the internal and external customers in an extended process. Together, supplier and customer can streamline processes to eliminate non-value-added steps or activities. This results in substantial internal efficiencies and cost savings, which can be achieved without substantial additional resources but through better training and

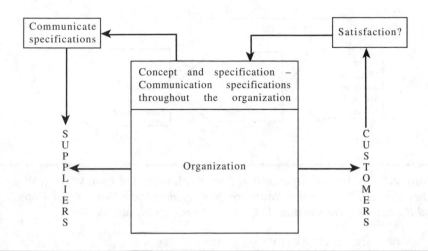

Figure 2.2 The extended process.

improved procedures. (See Chapter 4 for a discussion of training and Chapter 5 for procedures to add value to internal processes.)

The Japanese, who perfected these methods in manufacturing over 50 years ago, often say "the next process is your customer" to alert all employees to be more sensitive and responsive to customer–supplier relationships within the extended process (Ishikawa and Lu, 1985). Figure 2.2 shows the general model of process improvement. (Table 9.1 presents an extended definition of this relationship in a healthcare service environment.)

Getting all those involved in an organization to recognize the importance of listening to the customer is one of top management's initial and continuing challenges. Once customer–supplier relationships are established or "mapped" for all users, processes improve, costs decline (because fewer mistakes are made), there are fewer complaints, and market share increases. One excellent technique for mapping customer–supplier processes is flowcharting. A deployment flowchart is used to visually show how people and processes interact with one another. It is similar to those used in engineering and computer programming, except that internal customers are included as accountable for process outcomes (Tribus, 1989). Flowcharting in service organizations can be time consuming and is often politically sensitive, as members of a team or workgroup are aware that their work responsibilities (or lack thereof) may be graphically displayed. This technique can identify general problems, break them up into small units, clarify responsibilities, establish accountability for solutions, and initiate long-term process improvements.

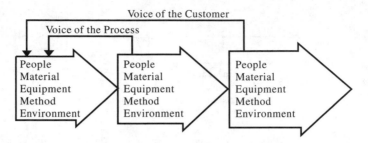

Figure 2.3   Sources of organizational feedback (Adapted from William W. Scherkenbach, *The Deming Route to Quality and Productivity: Road Maps and Roadblocks,* Washington, D.C.; CEEP Press, 1988, pp. 35–39).

Monitoring feedback to detect critical service quality and reliability problems before they become more serious (recall the 1:10:100 rule from Case Study 1.3 in Chapter 1) is challenging and very dependent upon employee participation. Often, the internal "voices of the process" such as personnel records, financial reports, and annual evaluations, tend to be biased indicators of performance. Moreover, they often conflict with external "voices of the customer" data (Scherkenbach, 1988; 1991). Therefore, it is critical that data reaching top management accurately reflect external, as well as internal customer feedback. All voices, especially those of dissatisfied customers, clients, or employees should be heard — loudly and clearly. As indicated in Figure 2.3, bringing the voice of the process in line with the voice of the customer strengthens customer–supplier relations, helps reduce process variation, and eliminates non-value-added expenses. Case Study 2.2 describes how Merrill Lynch Credit Corporation (MLCC) uses its voice-of-the-client process to target and deliver appropriate services. Achieving this in the absence of new resources is especially challenging for public and private service organizations. Significant differences exist among public sector agencies in the definitions of quality measures, citizens, customers, recipients of services, and taxpayers.

Quality characteristics must be carefully selected, applied, and validated to determine customer preferences for all types of service organizations (public, private, competitive, or market driven) as well as voluntary nonprofits. Here, process and performance techniques, such as customer surveys, focus groups, and internal monitoring systems, can be used to establish baseline data and validate customer quality characteristics (see the following text and Chapter 5). In addition, advanced systems and techniques are available to listen more carefully to the many voices of customers, measure results, and motivate employees. In addition to benchmarking, many service firms are applying advanced methods such as ISO

9000 certification (Chapter 5), gain sharing (Chapter 5), and quality function deployment (QFD). As covered in the previous section, benchmarking examines those firms that best perform a certain process or group of processes (for example, preparing a payroll), studying that process or group of processes, and then transplanting those methods into one's own organization. ISO 9000 is an international quality standard developed in Europe. Gain sharing is a variation of profit sharing in which all team members share equally in any gains or savings from successes. QFD is a comparison of the voice of the customer with the capability of the system to deliver specific characteristics. Customer preferences are identified, structured, and deployed throughout manufacturing and service delivery processes.[5]

Empower Employees to Meet Customer Quality Requirements

Empowering workgroups requires a fundamental change in the way an organization is managed. This begins with the breakdown of internal barriers to communication, as noted earlier. Training everyone to listen carefully and respond appropriately to the needs of all customers — internal, external, as well as individuals whose roles are changing — is a necessary requirement for TQS. Like early forms of worker self-management, empowerment is an area of intense controversy in some organizations.

Rather than a set of rigid rules, policies, positions, or practices, empowerment is a state of mind or attitude shared by all the members of an organization. Employees are empowered by the training, knowledge, and experience necessary to identify and respond to the needs of all customers. Empowerment is the delegation of authority and resources, within preset limits, to those serving customers. As process "owners," they are expected to make decisions and act on the customer's behalf in their work areas. It is the confidence, mutually reinforced by trust and experience among all members of a quality-focused service, that customer interests will be served. Concomitant with empowerment is the requirement to monitor results from the perspective of those being served. Empowered workers are integral to Xerox Business Services' customer-focused networked global work culture. Jobs, work processes, and environments are designed by workgroups to satisfy customer requirements. The effectiveness of empowered workers is assessed against results-driven performance measures (see Case Study 1.1, Chapter 1).

Within an empowered work environment, senior managers may have to give up some control, although line managers, supervisors, and workers will assume more responsibility for achieving customer satisfaction. The boundaries of individual decision making are not unlimited. They can be established by senior managers with the help of external customer-focused groups, internally focused teams, and process-redesign workgroups. This can, and does, include critical decisions regarding work redesign, as well as selection and retention of individuals as team members. Not all senior executives are equally enthusiastic about the potential (perceived) loss of power that might accompany genuine empowerment, but most realize that some modification of the traditional hierarchy is necessary to involve everyone in the process.

Similar to the concept of "bounded rationality" in organizational theory (Barnard, 1938; Thompson, 1967), empowerment is a participatory Theory Y management strategy that encourages employees to continuously analyze and redesign their jobs within preset limits. Douglas McGregor's Theory Y was in sharp contrast to what he called Theory X, which maintained that workers were lazy, wanted to avoid work, and needed to be forced to do it (McGregor, 1960). Theory X is the basis for most fear-based work environments. Because frontline employees best know what customers need, it is they who must be empowered to act. Management must recognize this critical linkage and listen to employees before making decisions that affect customers or workgroups. When accurate customer definitions of quality are added to an organization's repertoire of strategic planning skills, the determination of quality standards or outcomes becomes part of regular operations. Questions then asked are: Just who are the customers, what are their quality requirements, how are they defined, and how can they be met?

Described in the following text is a set of five simple questions that can be used within an integrated quality-managed organization to address the quality requirements at each customer–supplier linkage. Once these requirements are established for all customers, then top management can proceed with the reduction of poor-quality costs by integrating financial, customer service, and quality measurement systems.

1. What is your major product or service?
2. Who are your major users or customers?
3. What are the quality requirements demanded by your users or customers?
4. What is the most respected product or service offered by your competitors?
5. What kinds of comparative studies do you conduct to compare your service with your competitors' for the quality requirements of your customers?

(*Source:* Kano, N. and Gitlow, H. (1989), Lectures on TQC and the Deming Management Method, University of Miami Quality Program, Coral Gables, Florida [unpublished lecture notes].)

Strategies for developing an empowered and self-managed workforce include: human resources training, instilling teamwork, and understanding systems relationships. Serving customers directly and effectively requires training to perform each sub-task necessary to satisfy customers' needs. This requires an in-depth understanding of processes and systems, the capacity to exercise independent judgment, and familiarity with the mission of the organization. Toyota Motor Company has perfected this strategy to such an extent that any factory worker who observes a defect can stop a production line by pulling a rope called the andon cord. Can you imagine the chaos that would result if most American workers were given such empowerment? In exchange for the delegation of authority to control processes, everyone is expected to achieve results that meet or exceed and, ultimately, *anticipate* customer expectations.

Understand Systemic Relationships

Once the vision of the organization and mission of internal workgroups have been defined and communicated, applying TQS requires the understanding and application of problem-identification, problem-solving, and process improvement cycles. Peter Senge describes this aspect as *systems thinking*, the importance of understanding the behavior of nonlinear systems in a learning organization (Senge, 1990). Techniques can be taught as simple methods to identify problems and implement solutions (Chapter 5). The approach is an applied variation of the scientific method or problem-solving process (Figure 2.4) variously known as planning–activation–control–evaluation (PACE), focus–analyze–develop–execute (FADE) (Figure 2.5), or the Shewhart cycle or plan–do–study–act (PDSA) wheel (Figure 2.6).

The Shewhart cycle consists of four steps that form the basic systemic analytical approach to QI:

- ▪ Step 1: Plan — The initial step in an effort to accomplish a goal is to recognize an improvement opportunity. The problem or problems are defined and possible causes diagnosed. Planning recommends changes in areas that need improvement.
- ▪ Step 2: Do — Test the theory, recommend action, execute or implement the planned change, initially on a small scale. Establish measures and collect data.
- ▪ Step 3: Study — Observe the results, summarize data, identify root causes, analyze, evaluate, and compare the effects of the actual change with expected or planned outcomes.
- ▪ Step 4: Act — Take action on the results. Make changes in the plan where expectations are not met. Improve, test, and monitor the results. Hold the gain and repeat the process to achieve breakthroughs to higher performance levels.

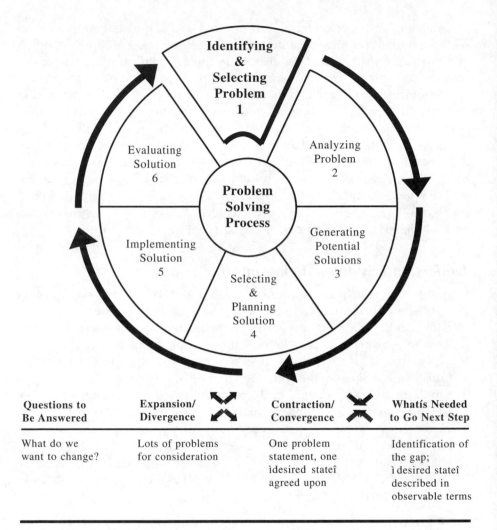

Questions to Be Answered	Expansion/ Divergence	Contraction/ Convergence	Whatís Needed to Go Next Step
What do we want to change?	Lots of problems for consideration	One problem statement, one ìdesired stateî agreed upon	Identification of the gap; ì desired stateî described in observable terms

Figure 2.4   Step 1: Identifying and selecting a problem.

The underlying purpose of these analytical cycles is to visualize and better understand the systemic causes of problems inherent in the critical systems of all types of organizations. As such, they are a process-oriented way of thinking about problems that emphasize the elimination of non-value-added costs and the achievement of higher levels of performance (see Figure 2.8). Systemic thinking involves viewing relationships in a nonlinear fashion, that is, without a beginning, middle, or end. Most problems can be solved by utilizing basic problem-identification and problem-solving techniques discussed by others (Cole, 2002; Evans and Lindsay, 2005; Omachanu, 2004). More complicated interactions within organizations may require the discipline of a FADE or PDSA cycle. Finding

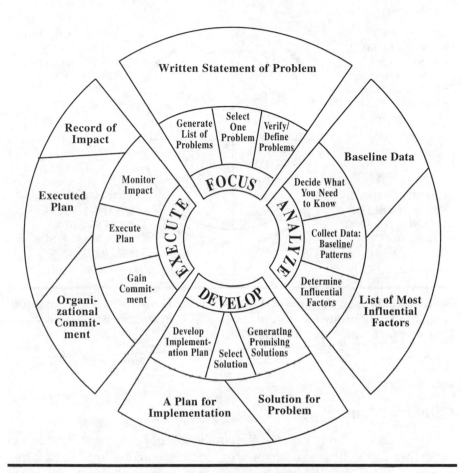

Figure 2.5 The focus–analyze–develop–analyze (FADE) process.

a permanent solution may require the combination of these techniques with a more comprehensive team approach to identify sources and eliminate the causes of variation (Chapter 5).

Successfully implementing TQS requires a process focus, systems thinking, teamwork, cross-functional management, and an understanding of how and why the output or results of one's work impacts the next process. That means coordination and communication across, as well as up and down, the organization. Combining CFM, teamwork, and systems thinking assists in the redesign of internal management systems to break down horizontal barriers between departments. Everyone's attention can then be focused on meeting valid customer service requirements. When this is achieved, managers become less preoccupied with control, inspection, and supervision and more concerned with improving systems and continuously meeting customer-defined quality requirements.

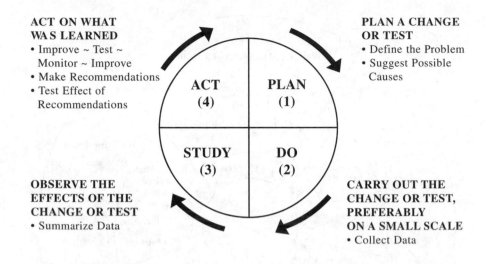

**ACT ON WHAT
WAS LEARNED**
- Improve ~ Test ~
  Monitor ~ Improve
- Make Recommendations
- Test Effect of
  Recommendations

**PLAN A CHANGE
OR TEST**
- Define the Problem
- Suggest Possible
  Causes

**ACT
(4)**   **PLAN
(1)**

**STUDY
(3)**   **DO
(2)**

**OBSERVE THE
EFFECTS OF THE
CHANGE OR TEST**
- Summarize Data

**CARRY OUT THE
CHANGE OR TEST,
PREFERABLY
ON A SMALL SCALE**
- Collect Data

Figure 2.6 The plan–do–study–act (PDSA) cycle. (From Michael E. Milakovich, Creating a Total Quality Healthcare Environment, *Healthcare Management Review*, Vol. 16, No. 2, p. 16, Spring 1991.)

Carefully Monitor Results

Customer satisfaction is a critical step in the journey to consistently deliver TQS. Measuring how customers respond is equally important. Only employees who have direct contact can "delight" customers. As described in Case Study 2.3, Baldrige award winner Citigroup (formerly AT&T Universal Card Services) has succeeded in achieving this goal by empowering line employees to act on behalf of customers' interests. Citigroup carefully measures customer satisfaction with elaborate surveys, including 8 primary, 18 secondary, and 125 key measurement indicators monitored and analyzed daily. These results are shared with customer-contact associates to provide error-free service (see Case Study 2.3). Various divisions of AT&T also won Baldrige awards in 1992 and 1994.

In one form or another, all organizations continuously receive feedback from customers, employees, and suppliers. Some listen more carefully than others to these voices. Feedback may be in the form of informal communications, complaints, surveys, responses in suggestion boxes, or more formal written comments. Most organizations do not deploy measurement systems as comprehensive as AT&T's (described previously), but many are now using customer surveys and other forms of direct customer-to-management evaluations to systematically collect data on both employee and customer satisfaction. It is especially important to listen and respond to internal as well as external customers and some companies have found it advantageous to set up formal channels for employees to express complaints.

These "safe harbors" for venting frustration (without fear of punishment or reprisal) are important for establishing genuine empowerment in the workforce. Such internal communication, especially if it is negative, may be as important as external feedback from customers. To be consistent in their service to all customers, employees must be capable of enjoying their work in a positive environment. Increased power or control over work responsibilities enhances feelings of empowerment and, in most instances, results in higher customer satisfaction. The opportunity to express frustrations freely and without fear is central to improving daily work.

Measuring the quality of service provided to customers involves more than assessing outputs, productivity ratios, or aggregate financial expenditures. Customer perceptions are equally important and often include the manner in which the service is delivered as well as its costs. See Figure 2.7 for a useful technique to analyze the differences between expectations and perceptions, known as *gap analysis* or the SERVQUAL model (Parasuraman et al., 1988; Zeithaml et al., 1990; Parasuraman et al., 1994; Wisniewski and Donnelly, 1996). Various gaps include discrepancies between top management and consumer expectations (Gap 1), internal barriers in meeting consumer expectations (Gap 2), employee delivery versus perceptions (Gap 3), and differences between expected and perceived services (Gap 4). The magnitude of the last gap (Gap 5) equals the sum of the first four. The use of SERVQUAL behavioral measures encourages consistency between employees' performance and customers' expectations of quality service.

With greater freedom to act as an empowered work team comes enhanced responsibility for better measurement of group results. Managers must focus on processes, rather than individual performance, narrow tasks, or reinforcing hierarchies. Performance measures reflect customer satisfaction rather than traditional profits or losses. Employees are rewarded for team performance, as well as individual performance. Specialists would be trained to measure results and communicate process improvement opportunities to all staff members. A few companies have gone as far as having subordinates rate their supervisors on team skills. Current efforts to improve government performance focus on monitoring results as well as processes (DiIulio, Garvey, and Kettl, 1993; Kettl, 2002). Whatever the monitoring system selected, empowerment, performance measures, and better understanding of systems relationships are required.

ServQual Model

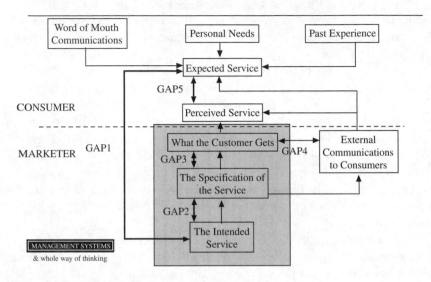

Gap 1   What managers and customers see as important

Gap 2   What managers see as important and the specifications

Gap 3   The specification and the delivery

Gap 4   The delivery and the claim/promise

Gap 5   Expectations and perceptions

Figure 2.7   ServQual model. (From http://www.mngt.waikato.ac.nz/depts/ mnss/courses/emba/sqm/sld002.htm) Originally developed by L. Berry and A. Parsuraman (1991).

Implement CQI

Underlying all QI theories is the concept of CQI, known to the Japanese as *Kaizen*. The term was coined by Masaaki Imai and is used to describe organized attempts to achieve constant improvement through efforts of the entire workforce. According to Imai (1986), a *Kaizen* strategy:

> maintains and improves the working standards through small, gradual improvements. A successful Kaizen strategy clearly delineates responsibility for maintaining standards to the worker with the management role being the improvement of standards … In process-oriented management, a manager must support and stimulate efforts to improve the way employees do their jobs.

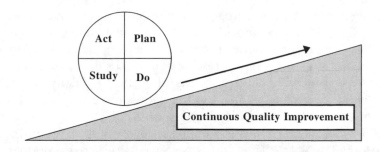

Figure 2.8   The Shewhart cycle and Kaizen breakthroughs to higher levels.

Rather than a firm list of policies or procedures, CQI is an attitude of mutual support between management and labor, instilled in the workforce, which encourages gradual improvements in work processes and rewards employees for their efforts to reduce process variation. The goal is to achieve breakthroughs to higher levels of work performance and productivity (Imai, 1986; Juran, 1988). Simply put, CQI recognizes that there are always processes that can be improved and provides statistical–analytical tools to achieve the improvements.

The diffusion of quality consciousness and a commitment to CQI are clearly linked to increasing competitiveness in world markets. Japan's success in applying CQI principles to continuously raise product quality at lower costs further strengthens the concept's appeal as a tool for international economic competition. Figure 2.8 shows how the concept of CQI can be combined with systems thinking (the PDSA cycle) to reduce variation and raise the level of quality within an organization.

CQI can also be used to reduce the costs of poor quality by eliminating non-value-added costs. Statistical tools and techniques are available to manage systems, flatten existing hierarchies, eliminate the need for performance appraisals, empower employees, and minimize external control systems. All participants can analyze problems and base decisions on facts, data, and information. As a result, processes become more "visible," non-value-added costs of poor quality are discovered and eliminated, and empowered teams can be held accountable for results.

Reduce the Costs of Poor Quality

The general condition of the economy, as well as the specific condition of one's business, influences the need to uncover and eliminate poor-quality costs. In an expanding market, there are fewer incentives to measure the costs of poor quality and to take actions to reduce rework, defective systems, and returns. Thus, hidden losses attributable to poor underlying quality processes are routinely covered by expanding revenues. The prevailing attitude becomes: when you are making money, who cares how — just make more! In the short run, it may appear to be a less costly alternative to bury causes of poor-quality processes in obscure accounting systems or to ignore quality problems altogether by denying that they exist. Without systematic attention to the causes of poor quality, however, cost reductions will be superficial and short-lived.

Philip Crosby highlighted the importance of understanding the costs of poor quality with "The Eternally Successful Organizational Grid" (Appendix A). Using a healthcare analogy, Crosby classified organizations (or work units within them) as being at one of five stages of quality management, from comatose to wellness (Crosby, 1979, p. 31). Dimensions of performance, such as quality, growth, customer orientation, change (flexibility), and employee morale, were evaluated against the "health" of an organization. The progressive, healing, or wellness organizations understand and minimize both the visible and hidden costs of poor-quality practices.[6]

The journey toward a healthier organization begins when everyone is capable of managing across functions, expresses pride in working for their employer, has accurate feedback from customers, is willing to objectively examine customer–supplier relationships, and understands systems relationships. When these elements are applied by a "critical mass" of individuals working together toward a common set of goals, then organizations can themselves learn and change to reflect the "new" values outlined in Table 2.1.

Summary and Conclusions

The modern quality revolution began in Japan during the early 1950s. Its concepts and theories were exported along with Toyotas, Hondas, digital cameras, DVDs, and VCRs to the United States and the rest of the world. It has forever changed how corporations, hospitals, governments, schools, colleges, and small businesses are managed. Customers are demanding more and better service satisfaction and are willing to shop worldwide to obtain it. The sheer size of the U.S. service sector (two thirds of our economy), competing demands for scarce public resources, and the poor reputation of many products require national leaders to seriously consider the consequences of not improving service quality. This is especially true in vital nonmarket areas such as education, healthcare, public assistance, and law enforcement. The globalization of service industries has created viable markets for quality services in a wide range of public, private, and nonprofit services.

Educational institutions, for example, are redesigning teacher training, curricula, and testing to reflect quality and productivity principles and prepare students for productive careers in the new competitive global market economy (Lewis and Smith, 1994; Seymour, 1992). The connection between improving teacher training, curriculum, classroom education, and competition in world markets has become the focus of many conferences at the elementary, secondary, and higher education levels, and several school districts have been recognized as quality leaders (Chapter 8). Corporate leaders recognize the need for educational quality, and greater numbers of school districts are applying quality theories to improve educational services at all levels (Arcaro, 1995; Kember, 2002; Murgatroyd and Morgan, 1993).

Without an organizational environment conducive to empowerment, motivation, and training, the changes required to achieve this transformation can be very threatening to the workforce, especially middle managers already experiencing on-the-job pressures for increased productivity. Resistance or even paralysis can result. Such reforms must be supported by resources and, above all, commitment to active leadership and training for advanced knowledge of the importance of quality as a means to respond to customers and expand future markets.

The following chapter offers a more detailed description of the theoretical basis for major quality strategies. No one approach is favored. In practice, most organizations adopt a hybrid approach, borrowing elements from each of the major quality theorists. It is important to understand how each of the components interacts to strengthen each other. These interrelationships are shown in the figures and tables discussed in this chapter. When the basic principles described here are understood and incorporated as part of the TQS effort, then the journey to apply them can begin.

Key Terms

Non-market-driven services
Walter Shewhart
Statistical process control (SPC)
Japanese Union of Scientists and Engineers (JUSE)
Management by objectives (MBO)
Human relations
Marketing
Customer satisfaction
Quality of design
Quality of conformance

Quality of performance
Multidimensional quality
Quality characteristics
Benchmarking
Total quality service (TQS)
Flattening the hierarchy
Customer–supplier relationships
Empowerment
Results and customer feedback
Systemic interrelationships
Kaizen or continuous quality improvement (CQI)
Hierarchical structures
Stockholders
Deployment flowchart
Gain sharing
Quality function deployment (QFD)
Andon cord
Theory Y
Systemic causes of problems
SERVQUAL
Poor-quality costs

Notes

1. *Source:* From *The Economist*, February 20, 1993.
2. The theoretical work of several world leaders in the field of QI paved the way for service professionals to apply these principles to their organizations. In the early 1950s, Armand V. Feigenbaum (1983) coined the term TQC, and both W. Edwards Deming (1982, 1986, 1993) and Joseph M. Juran (1964, 1980, 1988), among others, were invited by Gen. Douglas MacArthur to teach SPC techniques to the Japanese during the occupation. Deming and Juran both met and influenced Kaoru Ishikawa (1985), who became Japan's foremost expert in CWQC. Phillip Crosby (1979, 1984, 1992) alerted the public to the importance of quality at a time when few skeptical American managers listened. (The details of their contributions are described more fully in Chapter 3.)
3. University of Miami statistician Howard S. Gitlow defines quality as "a predictable degree of uniformity and dependability, at low costs and suited to the market," Gitlow, Howard S. et al., *Quality Management,* 3rd ed., (Homewood, IL: Dow Jones-Irwin, 2005, p. 18).
4. How to develop these characteristics is a critical element in the application of TQS to services. The methodology is described further in Chapter 5.

5. Advanced quality approaches are just now being applied to services. They include benchmarking (Camp, 1989), gain sharing (Gartman and Fargher, 1988; Masternak, 1993), QFD (King, 1987; Hauser and Clausing, 1988; Griffin and Hauser, 1993), and SPC (Bothe, 2003; Wheeler and Chambers, 1992).
6. See Figure 5.2 in Chapter 5 for a description of the "Cost of Poor Quality Iceberg," showing how neglect of hidden costs of poor quality further impact service delivery systems.

▼

Case Study 2.1: Pal's Sudden Service

A privately owned, quick-service restaurant chain, Pal's Sudden Service serves primarily drive-through customers at 17 locations, all within 60 mi of Kingsport, Tennessee, where its first restaurant opened in 1956. Carefully following its formula for standardizing high levels of product and service quality, Pal's has since grown to become a major regional competitor. Pal's is the first business in the restaurant industry to receive a Malcolm Baldrige National Quality Award.

Today, Pal's employs about 465 people, 95 percent of whom are in direct production and service roles. It competes directly with national fast-food chains, earning a steadily increasing — and now second-best in its region — market share of almost 19 percent, doubling since 1994. In 2001, sales totaled about $17 million. The company aims to distinguish itself from fast-food competitors by offering competitively priced food of consistently high quality, delivered rapidly, cheerfully, and without error. The majority of customers live or work within 3 mi of Pal's locations, and nearly two thirds are women.

Highlights

- Customer scores for quality in 2001 averaged 95.8 percent, as compared with 84.1 percent for the best competitor.
- Pal's order handout speed has improved by over 30 percent since 1995, decreasing from 31 to 20 s, compared to its competitors' performance, which increased from 73 to 76 s over the same period of time.
- Even in the current economic situation, with substantially decreased sales and profits throughout the hospitality industry, Pal's sales continue to increase.

Business Excellence Process

For everything organizational and operational, Pal's has a process. And almost everything — from new product introductions to hiring decisions to the design of support processes and work systems — is done with a thorough understanding of its likely impact on customer satisfaction. The company's Business Excellence Process is the key integrating element, a management approach to ensuring that customer requirements are met in every transaction, today and in the future. Carried out under the leadership of Pal's two top executives and its 17 store owner-operators, the Business Excellence Process spans all facets of the operation — from strategic planning (done annually with two-year horizons) to online quality control. Every component process, including those for continual improvement and product introduction, is interactively linked, producing data that directly or indirectly informs the others

Benchmarking underpins the entire Business Excellence Process. Managers are continually on the lookout for benchmarking candidates, and each one compiles a running list of potential subjects. For the Leadership Team, benchmarking yields meaningful competitive comparisons, new best practices for achieving higher performance goals, or new organizational directions. For the entire organization, benchmarking results are a constant reminder that performance can always be improved. Pal's is exhaustive in its pursuit of useful data, the basis for sound planning and decision making. In particular, customer, employee, and supplier feedback is central to all processes, and it is gathered in numerous formal and informal ways. For example, Pal's owner-operators must devote part of every workday to "marketing by wandering around." A portion of this period is spent engaging employees and customers to hear their views on how a location is performing and to solicit ideas for improvement. Owner-operators also go door-to-door within a 3-mile radius of their restaurants, seeking direct input on customer requirements and satisfaction levels. Answers to predesigned questions are recorded, compiled, and later analyzed at the store and corporate levels.

Owner-operators also maintain a communications log to record what they have learned about sales, expenses, customers, staff, products, services, equipment, and suppliers, and they list ideas for improvement. Weekly logs are sent to Pal's senior executives, who comb the entries for issues and opportunities to be addressed at formal monthly management reviews of organizational and business results. Data is gathered systematically at all levels — process, shift, individual store, and entire business. The company's enterprise resource planning system, SysDine, is a key tool, generating store-level and companywide data on sales, customer count, product mix, ideal food and material cost, and turnover rates. This information supports daily operational decisions. It is also used to update Pal's Balanced Scorecard of Core Performance Measures, which links directly to its key business drivers: quality, service, cleanliness, value, people, and speed. Managers regularly review the value of the data collected, and the company employs an outside statistician to evaluate the type of information tracked, how it is used, and how it is collected.

Employees with "Positive Energy"

Pal's aims to provide the "quickest, friendliest, most accurate service available." Achieving this objective is a real challenge in an industry with annual employee turnover rates of more than 200 percent. The company's success in reducing turnover among frontline production and service personnel, most of whom are between the ages of 16 and 32, has translated into a competitive advantage. Since 1995, the turnover rate at Pal's has decreased from nearly 200 percent to 127 percent in 2000, and it continues to fall. In comparison, the best competitor's turnover rate in 2000 topped 300 percent. Moreover, since 1998, sales per labor hour at Pal's improved by about $6.

Developed with the aid of benchmarking studies, the company's training processes support improvement in operational and business performance. Owner-operators and assistant managers have primary responsibility for staff training. They use a four-step model: show, do it, evaluate, and perform again. Employees must demonstrate 100-percent competence before they are certified to work at a specific workstation. Initial training for all employees includes intensive instruction on effective listening skills. In addition, in-store training on processes, health and safety, and organizational culture is required for new staff at all facilities via computer-based training, flash cards, and one-on-one coaching. Cross-training is required of all store-level staff to ensure their complete understanding of all production and service procedures as well as quality standards.

Customer-Focused Improvement

In customer satisfaction, including food quality, service, and order accuracy, Pal's is outperforming its primary competitor. For example, customer scores for quality in 2001 averaged 95.8 percent, as compared with 84.1 percent for its best competitor. Pal's order handout speed has improved more than 30 percent since 1995, decreasing from 31 to 20, almost four times faster than its top competitor. Errors in orders are rare, averaging less than one for every 2,000 transactions. The company aims to reduce its error rate to one in every 5000 transactions. In addition, Pal's has consistently received the highest health inspection scores in its market and in the entire state of Tennessee.

Source: Malcolm Baldrige National Quality Award recipients, Small Business category, National Institute of Standards and Technology; U.S. Department of Commerce, Web site: www.baldrige.nist.gov.

▲

▼

Case Study 2.2: MLCC

When MLCC first began operations in 1981, its singular focus was providing financing to customers by offering a new, highly innovative credit product — home equity credit lines. Today, powered by intimate knowledge of its customers' needs and a systematic, data-driven approach to performance excellence, MLCC offers a diverse line of credit products and services. MLCC strives to enable its clients to manage their liabilities to optimize their entire financial portfolio. Building client net worth and total balance sheet management over the client's financial life cycle is the dominating business strategy to ensure that MLCC not only survives the accelerating consolidation in the financial services industry but also significantly increases its market share. At the heart of MLCC's aggressive strategy is the conviction that quality service is not a goal; it is an imperative in achieving growth objectives.

The Business

A wholly owned subsidiary of Merrill Lynch & Company, MLCC offers real-estate- and securities-based consumer credit products — including home financing, personal credit, investment financing, and commercial real-estate financing — to primarily affluent individuals. About 90 percent of its approximately 830 employees, known as partners, are located in MLCC's Jacksonville, Florida, headquarters. The company's field representatives, the Mortgage & Credit Specialists, are MLCC's primary sales force. These partners market all MLCC products through the nationwide network of over 14,000 Merrill Lynch Financial Consultants. MLCC originated over $4 billion in loans for 1997 and has a servicing portfolio of nearly $10 billion. MLCC also has been a leading force in creating new vehicles for managing liabilities. For instance, by enabling investors to pledge stocks and bonds as collateral against home financing, personal loans, and investment financing, MLCC offers its clients a way to borrow without liquidating those assets. The investment portfolio remains intact and continues working for the client. With a host of competitors — including major banks and investment firms — MLCC distinguishes itself with a comprehensive line of innovative products. MLCC's senior managers set the direction and tone while seeking future opportunities for the company through a systematic business planning process (BPP), quarterly meetings with all partners, monthly management reviews to evaluate overall performance, regular training, and continuous interaction with partners at all levels. Leaders are expected to serve as role models in every respect, with a premium placed on involvement with community and industry organizations.

"Data-Rich" Systems

Data-rich aptly describes MLCC's management-by-fact approach. Relying heavily on a continuous flow of information, the company's BPP encompasses both long- and short-term plans. Its longer-term, strategic-planning component is a continuous process; the business development department constantly adapts this plan to business factors and information about trends in the mortgage, credit, and financial services industries. Company strengths and weaknesses, as well as opportunities and threats, are identified. Monthly and quarterly information about MLCC's performance in eight core processes and ten support processes needed to generate and complete a transaction are factored into this plan — as are customer characteristics and market data. Every July, as part of the BPP, senior managers translate the strategic imperatives into the company's Critical Few Objectives (CFOs), key performance measures for those CFOs, and specific short-term targets. (For example, a CFO to improve process productivity with the aim of increasing shareholder value is measured by the number of days taken to approve applications against specific, ambitious, and measurable goals.) In turn, these CFOs provide the basis for determining partner performance management plans. By involving all partners in obtaining information for the business planning process, and in regular refinements and progress reviews, MLCC ensures that its plans are fact-based and linked to individual goals and objectives.

Voice of the Client

MLCC segments its market into several categories of current and potential customers, stratified by their asset levels and age. Working with its parent company, MLCC uses in-depth research to target and deliver appropriate products and services. Its "voice of the client" process spells out customer satisfaction "drivers" for each client segment and for each of its credit categories. These priority requirements provide the basis for aligning the company's processes and workgroups and for identifying indicators and key performance measures for each of its eight core processes. In turn, each of those indicators are tracked and used to identify and put in place improvements in areas having the greatest impact on customer needs and satisfaction. Information about the customer is truly paramount for MLCC. To ensure that its market research is always current, MLCC continuously evaluates and improves its data on what its clients need and what they might want in the future. The client data comes from an array of sources, ranging from surveys of clients and financial consultants in the field to written or telephone feedback, internal audits, syndicated research, and benchmarking studies. Satisfaction levels of competitors' clients also are used in analyzing client needs. Customer complaints are analyzed in depth, reviewed monthly, and reported back to MLCC regions to identify any sudden changes and to share lessons learned. Negative trends and recurring problems trigger process improvement teams to develop countermeasures and to prevent recurrences. Clients receive acknowledgment of any complaint within two business days, and resolution is arrived at in no more than five business days.

Empowered Partners

MLCC considers partner empowerment critical to its success. Partners are encouraged to take initiative and responsibility, especially in being flexible, responding rapidly to customer needs, and in individual development. An example: MLCC partners received an average of 74 hr of training in 1996, nearly twice that of benchmarked companies. The company strives to be the employer of choice in a tight labor market. Alternative work arrangements are provided in an approach that is clearly working: partner satisfaction with the company's recognition programs improved from 42 percent in 1994 to 70 percent in 1996. And in an industry that typically has not put technology at the forefront, MLCC is placing far greater emphasis on technology approaches to enable partners to meet the ever-increasing expectations of clients and the company's financial consultants.

Results

MLCC has impressive results to show that its focus on quality management and performance excellence is a wise investment. Net income rose 100 percent from 1994 to 1996 and exceeds the industry's average. Return on equity increased approximately 74 percent, and its return on assets improved approximately 36 percent in the same period. Key indicators for loan delinquency rates and write-offs compare favorably with the rest of the industry and are clearly improving — as are the firm's total loan originations, market share in originations, wholesale volume as a percentage of first mortgages, and size of servicing portfolio.

Source: Malcolm Baldrige National Quality Award winners, National Institute of Standards and Technology; U.S. Department of Commerce, Web site: www.baldrige.nist.gov.

Case Study 2.3: Citigroup (Formerly AT&T) Card Services

Customer focused; that is what AT&T Universal Card Services (UCS) believes it must continue to be if it is to maintain the rapid ascent that, in 30 months, made its Universal Card the second largest in the credit card industry. Indeed, the young business was designed around the use of the quality principles to "delight" the customer. A comprehensive data and tracking system helps the AT&T subsidiary chart a well-marked course for continuous improvement in its customer relationships, internal operations, supplier partnerships, and business performance. For example, determinants of customer satisfaction — the starting point for all quality planning — are studied in layers of detail. UCS's eight broad categories of "satisfiers," including price and customer service, are used to define the company's quality focus. In turn, these prioritized determinants of how customers perceive the value of credit card services are underpinned by 125 satisfiers, each one also weighted to reflect its relative importance.

One practical result of this increasing specificity is an exhaustive set of concrete performance measures linking internal operations to customer satisfaction. Another is a clear picture of what UCS must do to better its services, performance, and market share. Management knows what improvements are likely to yield the greatest gains in quality. Each part of the business, from UCS as a whole to individual work units, has a list of ten most-wanted QIs. UCS reports that it leads the credit card industry in such areas as speed and accuracy of application processing and customer satisfaction. UCS also cites its industry leadership position in all eight primary customer satisfiers.

UCS — a Snapshot

Since AT&T established UCS in March 1990, the AT&T Universal Card — a combination general-purpose credit and long-distance calling card — has attracted 16 million cardholders. UCS now employs 2,500 people, or 10 times more that its initial payroll. Nearly 90 percent work at UCS's main facility and headquarters in Jacksonville, Florida. The collections operation in Houston and the payment processing center in Columbus, Georgia, employ the remainder. Two thirds of all employees are in customer-contact positions. AT&T views its Universal Card as a strategic tool for protecting and bolstering its long-distance customer base. In 1991, UCS's first full year, AT&T documented a 40-percent annual increase in calling-card revenues from UCS customers. UCS competes against some 6000 national, regional, and local issuers of general-purpose credit cards.

Delight Customers

UCS began with a straightforward strategy: Offer a credit card with a comprehensive set of competitive services. Then, through a carefully conceived and executed strategic plan, continuously improve internal performance and pursue enhancements in product and service offerings. The twofold aim was delighting the customer and differentiating the Universal Card from competitors' products. Fundamental to the strategy was the need to listen to customers — resulting, for example, in eight customer-related databases and eleven monthly surveys that track overall satisfaction and the quality of specific services. Also fundamental was an organizational structure that would respond quickly to changing customer requirements and competitive conditions by efficiently carrying out QI initiatives.

Although a top-management business team develops UCS's annual and long-term strategic plans, mechanisms that go beyond evaluating relevant trend data provide other avenues for getting customer and employee inputs in setting quality and business goals. For example, during 1992, all employees met with a senior executive to exchange ideas in gatherings of no more than ten people. Employee suggestions were also fed into the planning process. In 1992, UCS personnel sub-mitted more than 6200 suggestions, compared with 1727 in 1990. Nearly half of all suggestions made last year were accepted and acted on by management. All business team members are required to devote some of their time to meeting with customers. Several also serve on the Customer Listening Post Team, which evaluates the effectiveness of UCS procedures for gathering, responding to, and evaluating cus-tomer comments and survey results. The business team translates goals into key initiatives. At the top of the list are the business team's "ten most wanted" QIs. All key initiatives are assigned to teams com-posed of representatives from various UCS units.

In support of each initiative, these cross-functional teams develop specific programs as well as the associated performance measures that link programs to UCS's strategic goals. Another tier of cross-functional teams, which include supplier representatives, implements the pro-grams. If the goal of the program is to develop a new service, customer focus groups also participate in the process. If the goal is to improve an existing process or service, a companywide quality assurance group helps the team establish measures for assessing how changes affect levels of customer satisfaction.

Employees — the Key

UCS exhibits a strong culture of concern for its people. Associates are made to feel that they are the key to delighting the customer. This is made real by empowering line employees. Intending to move beyond project-focused quality teams, the company has begun a pilot program to introduce self-directed work teams responsible for all day-to-day activities and decisions. Customer-contact employees already have considerable authority to act on their own. For example, they can grant credit-line increases and adjust customers' bills without management approval. Training opportunities are numerous, ranging from tradi-tional classroom sessions to computer-based instruction. In 1991, hourly employees underwent, on average, 84 hours of training, not including the eight-week orientation for new customer-service employees. Monthly surveys track employee satisfaction. UCS has developed a list of employee satisfiers that guide improvements in training, recogni-tion programs, and other human resource activities. Widespread use of advanced information technology supports important components of QI efforts. A strategic systems plan, now in its final phase, will provide the company with world-class online processing and analysis capabilities. In 1991, UCS spent $20 million on computer workstations, providing customer-support personnel with easy access to detailed card-member information. In many key areas of performance and customer satisfaction — for example, speed in processing telephone applications (three days versus ten days for the nearest competitor) — UCS ranks as best in its class. In setting ever-higher standards for itself, the company is nurturing customer loyalty. The company reports that over 98 percent of customers rate overall service as better than the competition.

Source: Malcolm Baldrige National Quality Award winners, National Institute of Standards and Technology; U.S. Department of Commerce, Web site: www.baldrige.nist.gov.

▲

Chapter 3

From Quality Control to Continuous Improvement

In complex and diverse service delivery environments, internal management issues, such as cultural change, diversity, customer relations, human resources, training, and process redesign, often frustrate the most disciplined attempts to achieve permanent quality improvements (QIs). Suppliers of goods and services to all types of markets — foreign or domestic, public or private, regulated or free — attempt to anticipate customer and employee needs, monitor progress, and demonstrate results to current and potential customers. Changes in the way services are delivered at the point of customer contact are critical for establishing quality control and sustaining continuous improvement. It is especially important for employees to recognize how their behavior represents the customer's perception of the entire organization.

Most service organizations say they realize the importance of meeting or exceeding valid customer needs, but lack consistent strategies or theories to guide internal organizational change processes necessary to reach this goal. Employees not only ask what is required, but also seek guidance for improvement and opportunities to actively participate. They, too, want to assist in the achievement of the total quality service (TQS) transformation. Most books on the subject are written by consultants and are little more than rehashes of a 1-min method for quality salvation: just buy this book, and your business will be saved from global extinction! Obviously, if it were that easy, more customers would express delight, rather than disgust, with the services they receive.

Experienced managers know just how difficult it is to convince others to accept any type of change. Defining and maintaining a long-term commitment to delivering high-performance services is even more demanding. Those firms that have mastered the means to achieve success reap rewards, such as employee job security, increased market share, and higher profitability. For others contemplating the adoption of TQS, reflecting on the various theories of recognized experts (given in the following text) may provide inspiration and direction. Despite the occasional (and inevitable) misuse of the term "quality" to sell books and create unrealistic expectations, several prominent world-class quality masters have positively influenced the direction of modern (post-1950) efforts. Their theories and strategies provide the basis for a more informed choice of available alternatives. First, this chapter presents a brief look at the evolution of thinking about quality control to provide a framework for the discussion of how modern service QI concepts developed.

Evolution of Quality Control Concepts

Societal concern with the productivity of workers and quality of products and services can be traced back to ancient civilizations. Documents such as the Code of Hammurabi (2150 BC) show that society was willing to impose severe penalties to deter those who practiced unsafe production and service techniques. Under the code, if an unsafe dwelling was built and it collapsed, killing the occupants, then the builder would forfeit his life.[1] The principle of retribution (an eye for an eye) has been codified and substantially modified by modern liability insurance requirements. However, holding those who produce poor-quality goods or services causing injuries accountable for errors in the production or delivery process remains a powerful deterrent force to ensure the quality of residential and commercial construction. Likewise, manufacturers of goods posing inherent dangers to consumers face lawsuits if their cars, drugs, toys, or other products cause injury or death to consumers.

Apprenticeships, guilds, and trade associations developed in the Middle Ages as early efforts to ensure the quality of goods. The definition of quality standards was personal and individual — a contract between the artisan who produced the goods and the consumer who purchased them. During the Industrial Revolution in the late 19th century, quality control became bureaucratized as government agencies began setting standards and inspecting the quality of mass-produced goods. Inspection of agricultural products and services, such as meat and poultry processing, followed in the early 20th century.

The need to improve productivity and ensure consumer safety has been recognized in the United States since the founding of the Republic. Political economist Adam Smith advocated the division and specialization of labor in his classic treatise *The Wealth of Nations*, first published in 1776. Eli Whitney made a significant contribution to U.S. productivity in the late 1700s with the interchangeability of musket parts, built in the same factory that first used Smith's concepts of specialization of labor.[2] These concepts influenced 19th-century production, allowing factories to inventory parts and maintain supplies for future use, rather than having to produce customized parts for each product. There was no widespread need to ensure the quality of finished products because each piece was custom-built, and its quality was guaranteed by the producer.

Modern concepts of quality, productivity, and quality control evolved rapidly as major quality and productivity management theorists advanced the knowledge base of the field (see Figure 2.1). Quality control concepts were significantly influenced by the aforementioned inspection and product liability principles as well as: (1) assembly line and mass production techniques, (2) division of labor and interchangeability of parts, (3) changes in management–labor relations, (4) behavioral expectations within organizations, (5) changes in prevailing social values, economies, and political conditions in different cultures, and (6) knowledge revolution and the emergence of global markets.

Frederick Winslow Taylor's *Principles of Scientific Management* was published in 1911, about the same time Henry Ford applied these concepts to the automobile assembly line. Under the scientific management approach, complex tasks were broken down into simple operations that could be performed by semiskilled laborers. Thus, highly technical products could be mass-produced at lower costs while inspections maintained quality standards. Management did the thinking while labor did the work. Scientific management rested on four underlying values reinforced by rigid hierarchy: (1) efficiency in production, obtaining the maximum possible from a given investment of resources, (2) rationality in work procedures, the arrangement of work in the most direct relationship to objectives sought, (3) maintaining the highest levels of productivity possible, and (4) profit, which Taylor conceived (and Henry Ford enjoyed) as the ultimate objective of everyone within the organization (Milakovich and Gordon, 2004). Quality control was further depersonalized as a necessary part of the end-product inspection process.

Organizational management concepts were based on military and religious principles dating from ancient civilizations. Max Weber's seminal work, *The Theory of Social and Economic Organization*, was written in 1922 but was not translated and published in English until 1947. The central themes of the Weberian (Theory X) model are discipline and control of behavior within organizations. Preoccupation with control lies at the heart of virtually every element of this formalized, closed system of organization. Rules, procedures, personnel files, and exercise of authority through a hierarchy reinforce the need for organizations to be effectively managed, i.e., for managers to tightly control employee behavior. Control over all organizational activities has to be exercised "from the top down" to reinforce hierarchy and maintain command and control. Many organizations still use Theory X principles such as span of control, hierarchy, professionalism, and specialization of functions to maintain control and establish accountability. These closed systems were not designed to respond to customers' needs, but rather to defeat outsiders, enemies, or nonbelievers. The use of strict internal command-and-control structures requires absolute discipline; independent judgment or empowerment in response to customer needs is explicitly forbidden.

New approaches in psychology and sociology focused on those who made up the workforce of an organization. The human relations approach constituted a major change in the evolution of organization theory and signaled the advent of the participatory Theory Y tradition (Chapter 2). Those who embraced this approach did so because they were increasingly dissatisfied with one or more dimensions of scientific management. This triggered an intense controversy over the nature of organizations and the aspects of organization that were most appropriate as building blocks for successful management. In a sense, that controversy, begun in the late 1920s and early 1930s, continues to the present day (Milakovich and Gordon, 2004).

Matrix organization was introduced in the late 1950s. Under a matrix structure, employees report to multiple superiors in separate control structures. For example, a construction engineer in the South American division of a large multinational firm would be simultaneously accountable to the head of the geographic division, the construction division, and the engineering division. All of these theories of organization implied a closed, formal structure dominated by a hierarchical superior–inferior relationship between management and the workforce. These models actively discouraged participation and responsiveness to customers; worse, they failed to encourage workers to positively interact with other employees and managers. Pleasing your superiors, by any means, to advance your own position in the hierarchy became the road to success.

Participatory or Theory Z management systems developed in response to the low productivity rates generated by the inspection-based hierarchical systems. Japan's postwar success with less control-dominated quality circles, team problem solving, and worker participation accelerated the movement toward the participatory organizational model (Ouchi, 1981). Since the 1960s, many American firms applied the human relations approach to organizational behavior (MacGregor, 1960). By the late 1970s, as international competitors challenged U.S. manufacturers, concern with inspection-based quality assurance (QA) and production control reemerged.

Historically, QA was based on the need to carefully inspect end products to ensure that they met predetermined standards and specifications. Ensuring that defective products did not reach the market protected manufacturers against liability (recall the FedEx 1:10:100 rule in Chapter 1). Since the early 1950s, W. Edwards Deming and others criticized inspection-based quality control systems as costly and ineffective (Deming, 1982). Inspection can identify defective products only after they have been manufactured. Then, the only action that can be taken is either to repair the defective products or to discard the entire product. In either case, inspection-based quality control wastes resources and decreases productivity.

In service industries, in which production and consumption are generally simultaneous, end-process inspection is even more wasteful and ineffective. Without a system to monitor performance at each point of customer contact, analysis of errors leading to complications or dissatisfaction with the service encounter can be very costly, as well as ineffectual. In many instances, the documentation required to audit or reconstruct errors in service delivery processes exceeds the cost of the service. (Consider medical malpractice suits or any errors that result in litigation, for example.) How can you ensure the quality of the advice given by physicians to their patients? Or that provided by attorneys to their clients? The reason most often cited by plaintiffs for the actions against physicians or hospitals is not lack of technical competence, but the attitude or treatment of a service provider, most of whom are licensed and therefore assumed to be competent to practice. It is very difficult to verify if individuals working in a service organization are serving their own best interests or those of their customers.

Nonetheless, inspection will always be one of the central concepts of quality control. It is increasingly obvious, however, that continuous quality improvements (CQIs), especially in complex service delivery environments requiring intense human contact, cannot be achieved by inspection alone. The shortcomings of inspection-based QA led to the development of concepts that emphasize the continual improvement of internal systems and processes to prevent the need for inspection.

As mentioned in the previous chapter, CQI is achieved by training everyone, particularly customer-contact workers, and building quality features into each step of the service delivery processes. Therefore, this approach requires widespread employee participation. Whereas QA is based exclusively in the inspection division, process-control-oriented CQI requires involvement of several divisions of an organization — for example, admissions, purchasing, customer service, marketing, as well as the cooperation of all suppliers. The Japanese refer to this type of comprehensive system as *total quality control* (TQC) or *companywide quality control* (CWQC). Companywide participation is required because each division — as an internal customer — must participate in quality control activities. Moreover, CWQC includes employee-friendly aspects such as employee assistance plans (EAPs), flextime, organizational restructuring, interorganizational agreements (in both private and public sectors), and retraining employees for new responsibilities. In contrast to the Weberian "tall" hierarchical (Theory X) or more contemporary matrix approaches, CWQC emphasizes "flat" organizations, independent judgment, peer review, worker participation, and multilevel managerial leadership (Theory Y and Theory Z). The entire system is redefined to support those who assume the responsibility for quality at each step in the process.[3]

In sum, QA is inspection based and aimed at minimizing defects in a product or service received by an end user before it is delivered. Quality control uses sampling techniques to achieve the same ends after the product or service is produced. Both TQC and CWQC seek to minimize defects during production processes to achieve CQI. TQC, or CWQC, is widely practiced in Japan. Understanding the theoretical basis for CQI as distinct from QA and control is important in making the transition from traditional to more advanced QI practices.

Masters of Total QI

Commitment to QI is rooted in the teaching, research, and consulting of five pioneering leaders of the quality movement: W. Edwards Deming, Joseph M. Juran, Armand V. Feigenbaum, Kaoru Ishikawa, and Philip B. Crosby. Their philosophies are not limited to the statistical management of quality alone. Rather, all are leaders and teachers who encourage companywide integration of purpose (vision), recognize the importance of process variation on job performance, and possess a genuine respect for people. All recommend a systems approach to improving quality, from the design, procurement of supplies, production, and delivery stages to service after the sale and consumer education. The remainder of this chapter provides an overview of the theories of these American and Japanese experts who advocate both statistical and behavioral (nonquantitative) approaches to motivate employees and respond to customers.

W. Edwards Deming (1900 to 1993)

An American raised at the turn of the century in northwestern Wyoming, W. Edwards Deming was a national hero to the Japanese for over 40 years. He gained widespread recognition in the United States in June 1980 when NBC first broadcast the documentary "If Japan Can ... Why Can't We?." The Deming philosophy stresses that production processes and equipment must be designed to meet customer quality objectives. His basic message was that blaming employees for poor-quality products or services does no good, unless all system-caused sources of variation leading to poor productivity are eliminated. According to Deming, it is the management system (94 percent of the time), and not the worker, that causes productivity problems, defective products, and poor-quality service. Most workers are judged by performance figures that contain both common and special variations (detailed in Chapter 5), over which they have no direct control. It is the top management's responsibility to provide employees with the proper training and tools to meet or exceed customer requirements. Top management is responsible for working on and continuously improving the system, whereas workers work in the system. Deming further advocated the use of the scientific method, what he referred to as plan–do–study–act (PDSA) cycle, a systems approach, CFM, and the use of self-managed work teams (Chapter 2). Not surprisingly, his theoretical formulations were considered unnecessary or too radical and thus largely ignored by American business leaders until the 1980s. Often with blunt and caustic language, Deming chided North American managers to:

1. Stop punishing workers for defects and continually improve internal processes.
2. Identify and meet the valid requirements of internal and external customers.
3. Minimize the influence of external processes unrelated to the extended process (Figure 2.2) upon which the quality of the product or service is based.

Resistance to Deming's management philosophy (prior to the 1980s) provides a plausible explanation for the weak status of U.S. exports and the poor quality of services at home. Reasons for this ignorance differ, but include such explanations as:

1. Most U.S. corporate leaders were trained in accounting and finance, disciplines not generally recognized for valuing human assets, flexibility, and innovative thinking.

2. From the post-World War II era until the late 1970s, the United States had little if any competition from the recovering European and Asian economies, so there was little incentive to change management systems.
3. Consequently, there was no need to systematically address customer-driven quality requirements as all products manufactured by U.S. firms were assumed to be of high quality.

The continuing dramatic loss of U.S. share of global markets for goods and services in the early 21st century shows just how accurate Deming's predictions were. One disturbing reason for the attitude change is the increasing loss of market share of basic U.S. industries, including automobile manufacturing, once dominated by U.S. producers (see Figure 1.2, Chapter 1). Similar losses in market share have occurred in consumer electronics, computer chips, steel production, and a wide range of manufactured goods once dominated by U.S. producers. Under current economic forecasts, it will be very challenging for U.S. manufacturers to regain their dominance in many global markets. One of Deming's major contributions was to implore American managers to rethink the relationship between costs, productivity, and quality.

The emphasis on quality as an integrative management function is based on Deming's *Chain Reaction of Quality Improvement*, a theoretical relationship first proposed in the late 1940s. Before Deming's theories were accepted in the United States, a common belief was that quality and productivity were inversely related. That is, if one is increased, the other must be decreased. The chain reaction of QI shows how improved quality reduces waste and rework, and increases efficiency with better use of people, time, materials, and equipment. Commitment reduces losses due to poor quality, pleases customers, increases productivity, expands market share, and secures jobs. Another result is increased sales through word-of-mouth advertising (Figure 3.1). Once a theory, the chain reaction of quality has

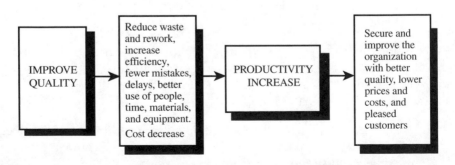

Figure 3.1 The chain reaction of QI.

become a reality in thousands of service organizations throughout the world (Groocock, 1986).

In his book *Out of the Crisis* (1986), Dr. Deming identified several deadly diseases and obstacles to transformation of American management and prescribed a 14-point remedy to correct them (Appendix B). Removing the causes of these diseases can have profoundly positive effects because of the still-lingering "past sins" and current practices that diminish the quality of services, lower productivity, and distract employees from serving customers. The deadly diseases are:

1. *Lack of Constancy of Purpose* — Results from a failure to plan for services that will be needed in the future, provide leadership for change, and guarantee productive and rewarding employment opportunities. This includes loss of U.S. jobs to global competitors. One reason American firms lack direction is that management treats employees as replaceable assets, not unlike physical plant or equipment. Underinvestment in training further undermines employee motivation and reinforces poor service.

2. *Short-term thinking* — Decisions are made on a short-term, often crisis-to-crisis basis, reflecting annual budget cycles and pressures for immediate profits. Predictably, continual improvement of processes, training of employees, and upgrading of services are ignored. Unless companies are on the verge of bankruptcy, senior managers have no incentive to guide the transformation to a quality-oriented work environment. Because they enjoy greater job security, it is in their best interests to support TQS as a means of enhancing job satisfaction and security.

3. *Individual performance appraisal* — As commonly used, evaluations are a means to control and discipline the workforce, rather than improve performance. They rob management and labor of motivation, foster mediocrity, instill fear, prevent teamwork, and remove the intrinsic joy of work. Annual performance reviews and other internally competitive punishment–reward systems that lack methods for accomplishing objectives distract everyone from their primary mission of service to the customer. Often, those who conduct the performance reviews lack the incentive to change because they were promoted to their current positions under the same system.

4. *Mobility of senior management* — Although less significant in recent years as the world economy stalled, failure to make the grade in annual (short-term) performance ratings encourages senior managers to move to competitors. The emphasis in graduate business education on rapid upward mobility by showing quick results

encourages many younger managers to job-hop without becoming familiar with the critical functions of their current positions.[4] In the public sector, regular turnover of elected officials every 2 to 4 years limits service quality and productivity efforts.

5. *Managing by numbers alone* — This practice is endemic to all types of service organizations, especially governments. Like the tip of an iceberg, they give only a superficial picture of the organization. Rather than relying on visible numbers (weekly worksheets, bank statements, hospital patient censuses, and audits), managers must carefully study underlying processes to uncover the hidden causes of losses from poor-quality cost practices (see Figure 5.2). Substantial empirical research supports this assertion, and Deming's points 10 and 11 call for the elimination of numerical goals and quotas (Appendix B).

6 & 7. *Excessive medical and liability costs, swelled by lawyers who work on contingency fees*[5] — Losses from unnecessary procedures, waste, and inefficiency in the health service delivery area alone equal nearly $1 out of every $4 invested in healthcare. With the national healthcare bill now exceeding $1700 billion (17 percent of the GNP), losses from poor-quality practices exceed $400 billion. For most businesses, employee benefit costs alone exceed 50 percent of total net revenues. Worse yet, costs for employee health insurance have been rising at an astronomical 25 to 30 percent per year, therefore doubling every 30 months. This has forced many businesses to either curtail benefits or charge employees and their families higher rates for insurance.

Compounding the last two deadly diseases is the legal profession's well-known greed, resistance by educators to outside evaluation of performance, and the medical profession's callous disregard of the patient's view of quality. Organizational cultures of professional service firms are often driven by the paternalistic notion that "management knows best." The paternalistic and self-serving attitude among many lawyers, teachers, and physicians that only they can define the parameters of quality limits the application of customer-driven service quality monitoring systems. Healthcare service delivery is a complex mix of public and private sector resources, roles, and responsibilities. Efforts made by the public sector to reallocate resources are often resisted by special interests that control these resources. Still, the federal government subsidizes over half of the total cost in Medicare, Medicaid, Veterans' Hospitals, and other tax-supported healthcare programs. The Clinton administration attempted to reform this vital area in the early 1990s by implementing health security for all Americans. These efforts encountered the strongest resistance from many of those who expressed reservations about changes, but also benefited from the status quo (see Chapter 9 for details).

Hopes for applying market-based formula solutions to achieve sudden results, using technology to solve problems, and inadequate testing of prototypes are all common barriers to acceptance of Deming methods. Application is further limited by false starts, poor-quality practices ("It's OK if it's within specifications"), management blaming unions or employees ("Our trouble lies entirely in the workforce"), professional excuses ("Our problems are different"), and negative attitudes ("We installed quality control").

Leadership for change, knowledge of quality, and enhanced technology are critical responses to competition in world markets. Without greater knowledge of how to strategically manage quality, productivity suffers, costs rise, employee morale plunges, and market position declines. For those who listen, Deming offers an alternative.

In contrast to other QI strategies, the Deming method is a statistically based system that identifies *process variation* as a major problem. Various analytical tools such as run charts, histograms, cause–effect diagrams, and statistical control charts are used to identify the causes of and reduce common and special variations (detailed in Chapter 5 and defined in Glossary). In what has become a classic statement of goals for an aspiring quality organization, Deming has summarized his recommendations for change into 14 principles intended to be a philosophy for transforming American managerial thinking. Service organizations can remedy the ills they face by implementing both statistical process control (SPC) as well as behavioral management techniques to improve quality. Both aspects are equally important, because it is the synergistic implementation of all the 14 points that improves quality in a never-ending fashion.[6] In other words, knowing what to do is as important as knowing how to do it. Deming also believed that enlisting a critical mass of committed workers within the organization was key to successful implementation.

Deming's statistical methods show how variations are endemic to all systems and processes. In the "funnel experiment," he demonstrates how tampering with a process by compensating for each observation results in greater variation than if no midprocess adjustments are made.[7] This experiment demonstrates the danger of overcontrol and shows that only the most carefully reasoned changes in a stable system can improve quality. Repeatedly tampering with the system only makes things worse. To further illustrate the random nature of process variation, Deming also devised the "red bead experiment," which is still used in Deming seminars. Each of six workers (seminar participants selected at random) stirs a mixture of 3200 white beads and 800 red beads, and then removes 50 beads. Red beads simulate defects, so the object is to produce as many white beads as possible. The results in a typical experiment are:

	White	Red
Marsha	35	15
Bill	41	9
Barney	40	10
Michelle	46	4
David	43	7
George	41	9
Total	246	54

Under traditional hierarchical management theory, if the number of white beads represented daily or monthly performance, Michelle with 46 would be recognized as the "Employee of the Month." Marsha, on the other hand, with only 35 would probably be demoted or fired. In fact, a simple statistical analysis of variation shows it was just luck that Michelle drew the high score.[8] Next month it could just as easily be David, George, or Barney. With flaws remaining in the process, Michelle did nothing special to be emulated. The red bead experiment demonstrates statistically that about 85 percent of problems traditionally blamed on individual workers are the fault of the system in which they operate.[9] Deming's message is simple and clear: people should not be punished or rewarded for performance over which they have no control. All systemic causes of variation must be eliminated before individuals are blamed for poor performance.

In a TQS organization, teams of workers are fully trained as participants aspiring to become owners of work processes. As owners, they are empowered to anticipate and prevent errors from happening in the first place. (Recall the example of the andon cord in Chapter 2.) Incentives and reward systems may be adjusted to enhance the ability of a work team to eliminate causes of system problems (see Case Study 3.1).

Joseph M. Juran (1904–)

Statistical quality control (SQC) expert, popular author, lecturer, and consultant Joseph M. Juran is the century-old leader of the quality movement. As editor-in-chief of the established quality control guide for industrial engineers,[10] Juran stresses that productivity gains will only be achieved through emphasis on quality. His pragmatic and mechanistic approach emphasizes rationality, analysis, diagnosis, and management processes to achieve what he calls quality breakthroughs to higher levels of performance (represented in Figure 2.7, Chapter 2).

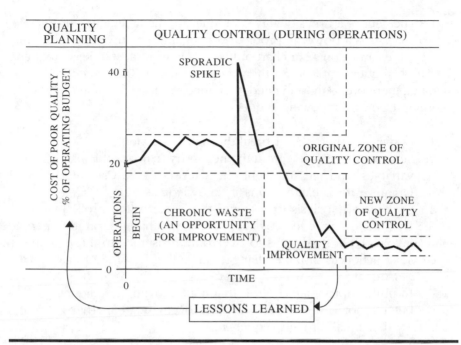

Figure 3.2 The Juran Trilogy.

Unlike Deming, Juran offers few recommendations for changing organizational structures to accomplish quality goals. He is far less prescriptive than Deming in his recommendations for managerial change and defines quality simply as customer-based fitness for use (Juran, 1964). Juran advocates translating criteria into language that is easily understood by the technicians who are responsible for detecting problems, monitoring, and improving a process. In the classic definition (first mentioned in Chapter 2), he further divides quality into three components: design, conformance, and performance. The theoretical basis of Juran's quality control system is known as the *Juran Trilogy*: planning, control, and breakthrough (Figure 3.2), which together form a cycle, interlocked with a second cycle: the old standard, breakthrough, and the new standard. The Juran Trilogy is repeated in a never-ending cycle of continuous improvement (Juran, 1980). Proper quality planning yields processes that reduce poor-quality costs by meeting quality control goals. This, in turn, leads to a new zone of quality control. Unlike Deming, Juran encourages organizations to manage by objectives and work toward defined goals. On this last point, as well as on the need for performance appraisal, he and Deming strongly disagreed.

Juran believes that management can and must seek continual improvements in quality. He shares Deming's faith in the Pareto principle that at least 85 percent of a firm's quality problems are management controllable. Pareto analysis is a powerful problem-solving and priority-setting tool that arranges the causes on a bar chart or histogram from most to least frequent. The most frequent causes can then be given the greatest attention. Management, therefore, is most in need of change resulting from breakthroughs emerging from the following sequence:

1. Convince others that a breakthrough is needed.
2. Separate the vital few from the necessary many problems, activities, variables, and measurement characteristics (see Case Study 3.1).[11]
3. Organize for breakthroughs in knowledge.
4. Conduct an analysis to discover the cause of the problem.
5. Determine the effect of the proposed changes on the people involved, and find ways to overcome resistance to these changes.
6. Take action to institute changes, including training of all involved personnel.
7. Institute appropriate controls that hold new improved quality levels but do not restrict continued improvement — perhaps through another breakthrough sequence.

In services, breakthroughs involve evaluation of actual performance, comparing both with a standard, and adjusting to the difference. (For an example of how different firms diagnose results to generate data on the vital few priorities for process improvements, see Case Study 3.1 as well as Case Study 1.1 in Chapter 1.)

Planning deficiencies contribute to chronic waste that stricter control processes would reduce. Similar to the Japanese *Kaizen* (CQI) approach, Juranian quality control goes beyond previous limits by breaking through to higher levels of performance. The basic sequence involves breakthroughs in attitude, knowledge, culture, and results:

■ *Breakthrough in attitude:* Rather than reacting to a crisis, Juran believes quality attitude changes must be based on "fire prevention, not firefighting." Attitudes should reflect a willingness to innovate, to enlist change agents within the organization, and encourage leadership and creative solutions to problems.
■ *Breakthrough in knowledge — diagnosis:* This step includes problem identification and problem solution techniques (Figure 2.4 to Figure 2.6) as well as flattening the hierarchy. Nonhierarchical participation is essential to diagnosing the cause of system problems. Plainly, those closest to the customers are best able to diagnose and respond to customer needs.

- *Breakthrough in cultural patterns:* This breakthrough has seven steps: (1) planning, including participation by advocates, those affected, and third parties (for balance and objectivity), (2) eliminating technical and cultural baggage not needed for change, (3) working with recognized leadership of corporate culture, (4) treating everyone with dignity, (5) reducing the impact of changes by weaving them into an existing pattern of behavior or acceptable other changes, (6) using empathy by putting yourself in the other's place, and (7) making use of a wide variety of methods to deal with resistance to change.
- *Breakthrough in results:* This breakthrough has six steps: (1) set up a steering group to organize the drive, (2) convince people of the importance of safety, cost, and quality, (3) show everyone how to contribute to safety, cost, and quality, (4) solicit ideas from everyone, (5) establish goals for improvement and a scoreboard to follow progress, and (6) incorporate new techniques into the standard operating procedures (SOPs).

During each of the "standard" periods, a manager should encourage activities aimed at eliminating the root causes of special variation, when any observation falls above a preset upper control limit (UCL) or below the lower control limit (LCL) of a process control chart (see note to the red bead experiment in the preceding text). When special variation is eliminated, a process is said to be in statistical control. The next step is identifying the root causes of special variation. To prevent a recurrence of the problem, statistical tools, especially Pareto analysis, are required.

Detecting a problem is the first step toward greater process control and reduction of variation. Some mechanism is needed to scan performance and to convert the data monitored into communicable language. This is the *sensor,* a sensing device that is highly specialized to recognize certain stimuli and to convert the data into information (useful knowledge). In service organizations in which contact with customers is often direct, human beings act as sensors. The sensor should use a system of measurement to compare actual performance with the standards. The comparison becomes the basis for decision making. The feedback loop is an excellent technique for improving participation and establishing team standards. Organizational feedback consists of components such as a sensing device that detects what is occurring, a control center that compares results using data from a sensing device to recalculate the nominal value of a quality characteristic, and a motor device that takes action to adjust a process as necessary and to bring results in line with standards. A monitor determines whether or not a stable process exists and a steering arm directs the discovery, dissemination, and subsequent use of new knowledge. Feedback is provided by a diagnostic arm responsible for the design of experiments and the collection, analysis, and interpretation of data (Juran, 1988, pp. 85–100). In services, these tasks are typically performed by line-level customer service employees having direct contact with customers and supervisors who monitor customer–employee interactions.

Juran and his associates also advocate SPC, SQC, and management by self-control (MSC), in which employees and managers establish and monitor performance objectives. SPC uses statistically valid methods for the collection of statistics and provides feedback. SQC is the use of scientific quality management (QM) to perform quality control instead of QA. Scientific QM is the philosophy that everything about any task necessary to meet valid customer requirements can be measured. This is not the same as Frederick Winslow Taylor's scientific management, the idea that there is one best way to do any task (Taylor, 1911). MSC, which was the original idea behind Peter Drucker's management by objectives (MBO), occurs when managers negotiate quantitative objectives and performance measurement criteria with superiors, then receive autonomy to execute (Sedell, 1991).

Although less prescriptive than other quality gurus in specifying ultimate goals, Joseph Juran offers very specific suggestions for managers to create a stimulating environment:

1. Never ask an employee to do something without explaining what and why first.
2. Never tell an employee to do something without first asking how he or she thinks it should be done.
3. Either tell the employee what result you want and leave the method to him or her, or explain what you want to be done and assume responsibility for the result (Juran, 1988, pp. 272–273).

Armand V. Feigenbaum (1920–)

In 1951, decades ahead of its application in either manufacturing or services, A.V. Feigenbaum defined TQC as the "composite product and service characteristics of marketing, engineering, manufacture, and maintenance through which the product and service in use will meet the expectations of the customer" (Feigenbaum, 1991, p. 7). Feigenbaum is a mathematician best known for originating the concept of TQC, which he explains as follows:

The underlying principle of the total quality view, and its basic difference from all other concepts, is that to provide genuine effectiveness, control must start with identification of customer quality requirements and end only when the product has been placed in the hands of a customer who remains satisfied. Total quality control guides the coordinated actions of people and information to achieve this goal (Feigenbaum, 1991, p. 11).

As a harbinger of today's intensive customer-friendly services, Feigenbaum recognized that significant gains would be made only when quality control systems were applied to white-collar services. In contrast to Juran and Deming, Feigenbaum initially placed the responsibility for quality control with the makers of the part or the providers of the service, rather than top management of the organization. In recent years, he, similar to Deming and Juran, has become increasingly critical of top management's reluctance to initiate QI systems.

Feigenbaum was an early proponent of the idea that doing it right the first time is cheaper in the long run than inspecting for defects. His rationale for such breadth of scope is his view that quality is influenced at all stages of what he calls the "industrial cycle." The cycle's stages are marketing, engineering (design), purchasing, manufacturing engineering, manufacturing supervision, shop operations, inspection and testing, shipping, installation, and service. Similar to Deming and Juran, Feigenbaum also recommends the use of statistical methods such as histograms, control charts, sampling tables, linear and multiple regression analysis (including t-tests and F-tests), cumulative curve probability graphs, Taguchi experiments, and design of experiments to better control processes (see Glossary). He further suggests that a feedback cycle should be applied to each of the eight steps of the industrial cycle mentioned earlier.[12]

The hidden plant and undercapacity scheduling are two other important concepts developed by Feigenbaum that apply equally well to services. The hidden plant is the proportion of plant capacity that exists to rework unsatisfactory parts. Undercapacity scheduling refers to providing enough time to do the job right instead of maximizing output without concern for the quality of the output. He clarified quality costs, and, with his example of the hidden plant, estimated that the proportion of total capacity that exists to rework unsatisfactory parts (the hidden plant) ranges from 15 to 50 percent. If anything, this estimate is likely to be higher for most service organizations.

Kaoru Ishikawa (1915 to 1989)

Kaoru Ishikawa was a highly respected Japanese authority who acknowledged the influence of Deming, Feigenbaum, and Juran on his thinking.

Ishikawa made several original contributions toward understanding processes and implementing change. He proposed quality control circles (QCCs) in both concept and practice to encourage participation and attention to detail by all workers ranked at and below the level of foreman. QCCs are groups of seven to ten workers from the same division of a company who volunteer to meet for an hour or so once or twice a month. After work (usually they are paid overtime), they discuss ways to improve the quality of their products, the production process in their part of the plant, and the working environment. Their long-term objective is to build a sense of responsibility for improving quality, but the immediate goal is to exchange ideas in a place uninhibited by barriers of age, sex, or company rank. QCCs are lead by a facilitator who meets to identify problems, potential problems, and solutions. QCCs address problems using an eight-step process:

1. Determine the problem
2. Select the subject for discussion
3. Fix a time limit
4. Study the present situation (using the basic tools)
5. Analyze the factors
6. Work out a policy (brainstorming, scenario writing, etc.)
7. Implement a policy
8. Confirm the result

The idea behind QCC is that there is no person in an organization who knows a production or service task better than the individual worker who actually performs that task. (A similar approach, aimed at shifting the burden of quality from the inspector to the worker, is the *Saratov* system used in the former Soviet Union. Others are the Polish *Debra Robota* [good work] and the German *Ohne Fehler* [without defects] systems.) All these systems are variations on the theme of worker self-management, a suspect ideology during much of the Cold War and, therefore, resisted in the United States.

The formation of a quality circle starts by providing training in SQC and opportunities for participation of the workforce. The quality circle meets on company time at scheduled intervals to discuss possible projects that could lead to improvements in quality. Once these projects are selected, the circle as a group sets priorities and implements solutions through the use of the "quality story" technique. (See Chapter 6 for a description of the quality story technique applied by an American public utility.) Although QCCs developed a bad reputation within some U.S. firms, it was not the concept but its execution as a fad during the 1970s that was faulty (Bowman, 1989). Indeed, they may take generations to bear fruit, and cannot be expected to succeed if they are ordered from the top down. One of the most important features of QCCs in Japan is that they did not originate with senior management. Rather, they sprang up from a voluntary, grassroots, bottom-up movement of workers and middle managers from across the nation. In the first decade of their use in Japan, over five million QCCs were formed. The average savings per group was thousands of dollars, so the effect of quality circles has been widely felt in Japan. QCCs, however, hold little promise of short-term gains.

Japan's experience has revealed several preconditions for successful QCCs. Some may be indigenous, others cultural. First, the workforce must be intelligent and reasonably well-educated. Members of the circle must be able to use statistical and industrial engineering analysis methods. They must know what it takes to make things work on a nuts-and-bolts level and they must be able to brainstorm together. Japanese companies that have been most successful with these circles and other participatory methods for improving productivity are also well known for their careful recruiting and internal training programs.

To be successful, management must be willing to trust workers with cost data and important information, and empower them with the authority to implement their ideas. In Japanese companies with successful QCC programs, managers work their way up through the ranks. They believe in their workforce, and it is no surprise to them that groups of workers, if given information and authority to experiment by trial and error, will reduce downtime and waste, and rework processes that circles are most effective in addressing. In addition, workers must be willing to cooperate with each other. Unlike the suggestion box and other worker-incentive programs that reward individuals, QCC programs reward groups. A genuine team spirit is therefore necessary. Workers must be willing to express themselves and find fulfillment by reaching an agreement. Moreover, if authority in production decisions is to be decentralized down to the level of these circles, then the circles have to be able to cooperate with each other. Unless there is a spirit of cooperation within the workforce (the attitude that talking a problem through with peers is more rewarding than taking it up with management), a company is better off using individual carrots instead of the circles. Otherwise, it may find night shifts undoing the improvements of day shifts.

QCCs do not run themselves. They must be directed and revitalized. Most important is the specific set of goals they are given and a strong manager who coordinates QCC changes with corporate objectives. In companies that use both the suggestion box and QCCs, management can gather ideas directly from workers, which may require significant capital expenditures, and at the same time use the suggestion box to encourage QCC efforts. Managements spend more time today on sustaining existing circles than starting new ones, understanding that their effects are incremental and cumulative. In 1951 Toyota got 700 proposals from its new workers participation program. By the early 1990s, it received 500,000 per year, which saves a reported $500 million. But there are limits to what the circles can do. QCCs, composed of workers from a single division, cannot come up with innovations such as the elimination of inventory and the Just-in-Time (JIT) or *Kanban* system originally developed at Toyota. Nor can they replace strategic thinking. In many industries, a single-minded focus on productivity improvements and quality control activities may be less important than focused R & D and targeted marketing. Innovation is a key aspect of CQI and innovation. QCCs work best when they are part of what the Japanese call TQC, which embraces concerns about the entire spectrum of a business, from production to distribution to after-sales service. QCCs are one of a number of productivity improvement techniques that work best when put together. As the Japanese say, it is like collecting dust to make a mountain … somebody has to envision the mountain and know which way the wind is blowing.[13]

The quantum leaps in cost reduction that the Japanese have achieved in industries as diverse as automobile production and consumer electronics do not result from QCCs alone. They come from major strategic decisions about new technologies and plants and entirely new ways of producing and delivering a product or service. Paying attention to details is vital for participatory management to succeed, but thinking big is equally important for encouraging continuous innovation. In the late 1990s, Toyota made a single change in its vehicle production line that eventually resulted in cost savings of $2.6 billion by 2003. This change was to substitute a single brace to hold automobile frames together rather than the 50 different braces previously used on the assembly line for each model. This system helped reduce the costs of refitting production lines by 75 percent and, over time, lead to huge savings that could then be passed on to dealers and customers. Toyota's global competitiveness and market share increased, and customer service and satisfaction improved with increases in vehicle-quality ratings.

Kaoru Ishikawa, Maasaki Imai, Shigeo Shingo, and Genichi Taguchi are well-known advocates of the Japanese school of CWQC. When it comes to cost–benefit analysis (both in terms of an organization and society as a whole) applied to productivity, procurement, and materials-testing issues, the work by Genichi Taguchi is recognized worldwide. Taguchi defines quality as a value-added process of maximizing the net benefit to society in cost–benefit terms (Taguchi and Clausing, 1990). The basics of Taguchi methodology are taught to every industrial engineer in the free world, and they are spreading to newly democratized Russia and Eastern Europe. Advanced Taguchi methods have been used in both the private and public sectors in Europe and Japan by engineers and statisticians trained in TQC or CWQC. Similar in methodology to the Deming method, CWQC seeks to set the nominal, eliminate special variation, and reduce common variation. Once a process is under statistical control, it is possible to reduce variation even further by locating and eliminating causes of common variation. CWQC also advocates the use of PDSA and that of the basic, intermediate, and advanced tools.

Following Ishikawa's death in 1989, Noriaki Kano of Tokyo University has been increasingly recognized as a leader of this school (Lillrank and Kano, 1989; Kano, 1993). Genichi Taguchi (1986) defines quality in terms of maximizing the net benefit to society in cost–benefit analysis terms. CWQC uses SPC, SQC, and the total care concept (TCC) for both QA and quality control. Under the Japanese TCC, employees are divided by seniority into permanent status and those on probation. Permanent employees receive full company benefits and services, including the use of in-house travel services, assistance in locating child and elderly-care facilities, help in placing children in schools, and in locating housing. Job enhancements such as dual-career couple recruiting and EAPs are also used as incentives under TCC. The spouse of dual-career couples is assisted in finding employment either within or outside an organization, and both jobs are offered as a package deal. Under most EAPs, employee files are inaccessible to supervisors. Employees with substance abuse problems (such as alcohol, drugs, etc.) receive appropriate counseling and treatment (Sedell, 1991). Maasaki Imai (1986) advocates teaching all workers an attitude of *Kaizen* to achieve CQI at the level of the individual employee. The late Dr. Shigeo Shingo (1986; 1989) served as president of Japan's Institute of Management Improvement and created many of the internationally known features of Toyota's *Kanban* or JIT production system. Shingo is also credited with developing the concept of *Poka-Yoke*, which allows manufacturing companies to fail-safe their processes from human error (Shingo, 1986). These systems are now being applied to services such as education and national security and integrated with new technology. Many schools are adopting JIT learning systems to provide students with up-to-date knowledge and scientific studies.

Although crediting Feigenbaum for his development of the TQC concept, Ishikawa favors an extension beyond the quality profession. Feigenbaum includes all company divisions in his call for TQC, whereas Ishikawa argues that there is not enough reliance on contributions to quality from nonspecialists. In 1968, Ishikawa began using the term "Companywide Quality Control" to differentiate the Japanese approach to TQC from the more specialized and hierarchical view attributed to Feigenbaum. The exchange of views has caused both to evolve, and today the terms TQC and CWQC are used almost interchangeably.

Feigenbaum, Ishikawa, and Deming favor a total, companywide involvement in commitment to quality.

In his revealing book *What is Total Quality Control? The Japanese Way* (1985), Ishikawa reflected philosophically on why the Japanese were more successful than Western industry in applying QI concepts. In the West, he suggests, quality control was delegated to a few staff specialists or consultants, and then only when a crisis forced Western leaders to consider their options. (This opinion is not shared by Americans who recognize the value of CQI and accept the costs of training the entire workforce in teamwork and basic statistical methods necessary to apply concepts to complex service organizations.) In most U.S. organizations, crisis resolution "firefighting" is the basis for promoting and rewarding managers. By contrast, in Japan the commitment to quality has been total and, until recently, lasted throughout the company's life. Fire prevention is encouraged and rewarded as well.

Philip Crosby (1926 to 2001)

The least statistically driven of the quality masters, Philip Crosby was corporate vice president of ITT for 14 years. He became a consultant, lecturer, and author of several popular books, including *Quality is Free* (1979). The concept of this book, which explains his overall approach, is that:

> Quality is free. It is not a gift, but it is free. What costs money are the unquality things — all the actions that involve not doing jobs right the first time. Quality is not only free, it is an honest-to-everything profit maker. Every penny you don't spend on doing things wrong, over, or instead becomes half a penny right on the bottom line (Crosby, 1979, p. 2).

Crosby's philosophy is based on four primary ideas he calls "absolutes." These rules include:

1. The definition of quality is conformance to requirements. The output must conform to design, and the design and price must conform to customer requirements.
2. The system of quality is prevention. Do it right the first time. Fire prevention, instead of firefighting, is advocated.
3. The performance standard is zero defects. Eliminate the practice of issuing waivers and variances. Do not use sampling tables or acceptable quality level (AQL).
4. The measurement of quality is the price of nonconformance, or the cost of poor quality, which Crosby estimates as "20 percent or

more of sales in manufacturing companies and 35 percent of operating costs in service companies" (Crosby, 1984, pp. 85–86).

His approach to quality, which he simply calls QM, is guided by 14 steps (Appendix C), and stresses individual and organizational changes rather than SQC. His method involves three primary management tasks: (1) Establish the requirements that employees are to meet, (2) supply the wherewithal that the employees need to meet those requirements, and (3) spend time encouraging and helping the employees to meet those requirements.

Crosby's approach represents a very different concept of QM. Similar to Deming, he emphasizes that organizations must be committed to building quality into the culture of the company, rather than relying on inspection to minimize defects. In contrast to numbers- and variation-based approaches of Deming, Juran, and Ishikawa, Crosby's method is based on individual attitude, awareness, and a more behavioral–managerial orientation. Crosby stresses that quality means conformance to requirements and proposes zero defects as a goal. He criticizes one often-used figure, the AQL, which originated in manufacturing and is widely used in services. He says that an AQL is not really a standard or target, but a commitment to produce a certain amount of imperfect material — before delivery or production is even started. It is simply acceptance of the status quo and inconsistent with the commitment to continuous improvement. Taking the consumer's view, Crosby makes his point quite clearly:

> Consider the AQL you would establish on the product you buy. Would you accept an automobile that you knew in advance was 15 percent defective? 5 percent? 1 percent? One half of 1 percent? How about the nurses that care for newborn babies? Would an AQL of 3 percent on mishandling newborns be too rigid? (1979, p. 146)

Too many service organizations continue to accept a certain percentage of errors or defects. Usually, the acceptable range is from 1 to 5 percent, depending on the type of business. Even 99.9 is not good enough, especially if you are among the unlucky one-tenth of one percent whom the error affects 100 percent! When it comes to critical processes, less than 100 percent is simply not good enough. If other vital services accepted the 99.9 percent AQL standard:

- 25,000 checks will be deducted from the wrong bank account in the next 60 minutes.
- 20,000 pieces of mail would be lost or delivered to the wrong address, every hour.

- There would be two unsafe aircraft landings at major airports, every day.
- 30,000 prescriptions for drugs would be incorrectly filled each year.
- Surgeons would perform 500 defective medical procedures each week.
- 1,000,000 documents will be lost by the IRS this year.

The quest for zero defects is endless, especially in critical services such as healthcare, government, and education, in which the continued use of AQLs results in low performance standards.

Selecting QI Strategies

U.S. business executives (in both large and small firms) now view quality or Total Quality Management (TQM) or QI as important strategies to respond to customers. Definitions of these terms vary considerably, however, depending on their application. These terms are sometimes misused as a hollow advertising slogan to demonstrate commitment to end users or as a consultant's siren for generating higher profits.

Without a management system capable of monitoring quality control efforts, such a commitment represents little more than scam marketing. When asked to show results with comparative statistics (facts and data comparing performance with competitors), many pseudoquality efforts disintegrate. In time, companies practicing cosmetic quality soon fall behind the competition. Submission of QM systems to rigorous neutral evaluations, such as that required for the Malcolm Baldrige National Quality Award (BNQA), provides an objective basis for comparison between quality providers. (See Chapter 6 and Appendix D for a description of the criteria used by BNQA examiners.)

Advocates of various approaches can point to success stories, primarily, but not exclusively, in manufacturing. Although service managers have used various productivity improvement methods such as profit sharing, work redesign, and suggestion boxes, the most revealing research on the application of these techniques is still based on manufacturing systems.[14] Although less frequent, service quality success stories are increasing as breakthroughs occur in various sectors formerly isolated from competitive quality considerations.

One insurance and financial services company that has been nationally recognized for its customer quality systems and use of benchmarking to identify improvement opportunities is United Services Automobile Association (USAA). USAA is the fifth-largest auto and homeowners insurer in the United States (see Case Study 3.2). The company is member-owned and was created in 1922 by a group of army officers who could not get private insurance on their automobiles. Its mutual insurance division serves military officers and their dependents and has grown to over five million members. USAA Federal Savings Bank has become the second largest MasterCard provider in the United States (Gass, 1992; Spechler, 1988).

More than ever, service firms must demonstrate customer service with statistically valid data, not necessarily based on one of the recognized quality awards, but at least from an independent and reliable source: for instance, J.D. Power for automobile service, A.M. Best for insurance, and *Conde' Nast Traveler* for hotels, travel, and tourism. Having a comparative basis for judging quality is especially important for services, because there are fewer examples to benchmark for successful applications. In addition, variations in internal processes tend to be greater. The lack of a tangible product (such as a car, radio, or TV) and consumption of the service at the time of delivery further complicates efforts to compare and evaluate performance over time. Nonetheless, methodologies are available, and service firms are increasingly willing to submit to the same rigorous examination standards as manufacturers.

Thousands of companies use various principles espoused by quality masters such as Philip Crosby, W. Edwards Deming, Maasaki Imai, Joseph M. Juran, Kaoru Ishikawa, and Shigeo Shingo. These quality leaders have drawn from different theories to produce in-house strategies (as noted in the following text). Many have been recognized as recipients of Japan's prestigious Deming Prize, the BNQA, or the Shingo Prize for Excellence in American Manufacturing. The origin and purpose of these prizes is described in greater detail in Chapter 6.

Summary and Conclusions

Following their exportation to the United States in the early 1980s, QM principles spread rapidly, if unevenly, in American firms. Different theories competed for the attention of service organizations seeking to improve quality. Rarely consistent in their definitions, some are strongly associated with a single theorist, whereas others are based on hybrid theories, reflecting several approaches.

From the early 1950s to the late 1970s, the quality ideal was nurtured by visionaries in the field of QM. Although the specifics of their philosophies differ, pioneers such as W. Edwards Deming, Joseph Juran, A.V. Feigenbaum, Kaoru Ishikawa, Philip Crosby, and their students have positively impacted businesses and consumers alike. They preached the quality gospel at a time when few American leaders listened. Ironically, although most of the early work in SQC was done by Americans, U.S.

industry leaders were unwilling to initiate the management changes required to implement customer-driven QI until Japanese and European competitors gained market share. For many markets, this change was too little and too late to save American jobs.

The Japanese shrewdly avoided the criticism that buying foreign products is "un-American" by constructing manufacturing plants in and hiring workers from the United States. The cars and auto parts produced at these "trans-plants" meet the same quality standards as those produced in Japan. This is further evidence that QI concepts and techniques, when properly applied, will succeed with any well-trained, motivated, and empowered workforce. The Japanese deserve credit for the application, implementation, and subsequent refinement of QM techniques. Without their competitive challenge to American industry, it is unlikely that the current push toward TQS would have occurred until even later (if at all).

Each quality master has contributed important insights, ideas, and terminology to the discipline of service QI. Those organizations that understand the strengths and weaknesses of various QI strategies are better able to customize their TQS applications. Approaches that merely admonish the workforce to adopt the 8 or 10 or 14 guidelines for quality, without changing the underlying organizational culture in which they must be implemented, tend to be frustrating, short-lived, and unsuccessful. In practice, most organizations shop for an approach that best suits their needs, or mix and match elements from various schools, often creating new, hybrid schools in the process. In the end, it is less what is said than what is done to achieve internal process changes that will allow trained and committed employees to act in the interest of customers. Having outlined the basics, we now turn to the organizational changes and training needed for service organizations to reach high-performance status.

Key Terms

Code of Hammurabi
Frederick Winslow Taylor
Henry Ford
Scientific management
Max Weber
Human relations
Matrix organization
Theory Z
Quality assurance

W. Edwards Deming
Chain reaction of quality improvement
Deadly diseases and obstacles to transformation
Process variation
Critical mass
Funnel experiment
Overcontrol
Red bead experiment
Joseph M. Juran
Fitness for use
Monitoring
Juran Trilogy
Pareto principle
Breakthroughs
Histogram
Vital few
Causes of special variation
Sensing device
Armand V. Feigenbaum
Hidden plant
Kaoru Ishikawa
Quality control circles (QCCs)
Facilitator
Kanban
Total care concept (TCC)
Poka-Yoke
Philip B. Crosby
Acceptable quality level (AQL)

Notes

1. Zografos, Kostas G., Integrating total control and QA concepts in construction project planning, unpublished research paper, University of Miami Department of Civil Engineering, June 1990.
2. The first documented use of the term "productivity" was by Samuel T. Coolridge in the early 1800s. Toward the end of the 19th century, modern industrial systems emerged. J.B. Clarke first used the concept of productivity to refer to a ratio of outputs to inputs in 1899.
3. Toyota has a system in which 98 percent of its employees submit suggestions with a 95 percent acceptance rate; the ratio of suggestions to total employees was 360 to 1 in 1990. Globe Metallurgical, a 1988 Malcolm Baldrige National Quality Award (BNQA) winner, and Saturn Automotive have employed similar systems with positive results. Such a cooperative

work optimization procedure allowed the 1988 BNQA winner Motorola and its suppliers to reduce the time it took to fill a phoned-in order for cellular telephones from an average of 40 days to an average of 2 h. Although the results from service applications may be less spectacular than these, significant successes can be achieved with greater employee participation.

4. This contrasts sharply with the traditional Japanese practice of lifelong employment and loyalty to one's primary employer. The protracted economic recession in Japan has required employers to modify this promise in recent years.

5. The United States is the only advanced industrialized nation that does not offer universal healthcare to all its citizens. The lack of a healthy workforce is associated with the lack of competitiveness in global markets. This, combined with low achievement scores in math and science, disadvantages many of our industries. This problem is now becoming more severe for U.S. service quality and productivity as more jobs are being outsourced to foreign companies.

6. Gitlow, Howard S., Gitlow, Shelly, Oppenheim, Alan, and Oppenheim, Rosa, *Tools and Methods for the Improvement of Quality*, Homewood, Illinois: Irwin, 1989, p. 15.

7. This can be accomplished by first making a target by marking an X on a convenient surface. Then place a funnel in a holder such that the end points towards the X. Drop a marble through the funnel, and place a dot where it rests. Repeat as many times as desired. There are many possible combinations for adjusting the funnel between drops, but it can be shown mathematically that the best results will be obtained by not adjusting the funnel at all.

8. Consider the following statistical analysis of this hypothetical group of workers. The average number of red beads (defects) per worker is 54/6 = 9. The overall percentage of red beads to total beads extracted is 54/300 = 18 percent. The UCL is: (average number of defects) + 3_ (average number of defects) × (1 percentage of defects), or 9 + 3_9 × (1 − .18) = 9 + 3_7.38 _ 17.15. The LCL is 9 − 3_9 × (1 − .18) = 9 3_7.38 _ 0.85. Thus, someone would be doing exceptionally well if he or she drew 50 white beads. Someone would be doing exceptionally poorly if he or she drew less than 33 (50 − 17) white beads. The range 33 to 49 white beads represents common variation. Calculations drawn from unpublished research paper by Ken Sedell, Department of Political Science, University of Miami Public Administration program, revised, Summer 1990.

9. For details of the Red Bead Experiment, see Deming (1986), *Out of the Crisis*, pp. 110–112, 346–350, and 459–464.

10. *Juran's Quality Control Handbook* with Frank M. Guyna, Associate Editor, 8th edition, New York: McGraw-Hill, 1999.

11. Several of the BNQA profiles presented in this book reinforce the importance of separating the "vital few" from the "necessary many" in private services. This concept is difficult to convert to public and nonprofit services because all citizens expect equal treatment.

12. The feedback cycle is a never-ending cycle with the following steps: (1) planning what should be done, (2) measuring whether it is being done, and (3) analyzing how to improve the plan.
13. Portions of this section abstracted from Kenichi Ohmae, Quality Control Circles: They Work and Don't Work, *Wall Street Journal*, March 29, 1982.
14. There is evidence that the quality gap between American and Japanese products still exists but may be closing. Ford Motor Company and Cadillac Division of General Motors have been recognized for their quality successes. Other widely cited examples of successful quality companies in the United States are AT&T, Corning Glass, Federal Express, Milliken, 3M, Ritz-Carlton, and Xerox.

▼

Case Study 3.1: BI, Minnesota

BI's business is helping other companies to achieve their own goals by enhancing the performance of the people who hold the keys to success. That usually means customers, employees, distributors, or consumers. As one of the three major players offering full-service business improvement and incentive programs across the country, BI employs more than 1,400 associates. Most are located at its headquarters in Minneapolis, Minnesota. Others are in Eden Valley, Minnesota; Sioux Falls, South Dakota; and in 21 U.S. sales offices. During the 1950s, BI became an early innovator in the incentive programs that companies began to offer to employees and consumers. BI is more sophisticated today with a diverse mix of offerings, and its products and services are used by some of the largest firms in America. BI works behind the scenes to help customers succeed by integrating communications, training, measurement, and rewards to improve performance. Almost every BI account requires a customized product or service.

Highlights

- Over the past two years, 546 QI teams demonstrated improvements and disbanded.
- For the past three years, BI's customer satisfaction ratings have outperformed its two key competitors.
- Associate retention is 83 percent, whereas unemployment in twin cities is just 2.9 percent.
- BI associates designed and teach a School-to-Work curriculum in local schools.

Try, Try, and Improve Again

BI first began using the Baldrige approach to quality and performance improvement in 1990. In fact, the company applied for the Baldrige award for ten consecutive years. Like many others, they did it to improve and learn, not to win the award. Along the way, they won the Baldrige-based Minnesota Quality Award in 1994. The company adopted a formal QM approach even earlier — the same approach it offered its customers. Improvement efforts are driven by the goal of customer delight and grouped under a process management system known as the BI Way, which includes training, problem-solving techniques, process improvement, incentives, and a focus on results. Every BI associate takes part in the improvement process, but the company's leaders drive the process and give it priority and energy. BI is organized around teams. Teams made up of the owners, office of the president, and other senior leaders comprise the business team, productivity team, and strategic planning team. They offer senior leaders the opportunity to stay in touch with key stakeholders and to communicate company strategies, expectations, values, and direction. The business team, for example, consists of the owners, office of the president, and 18 additional vice presidents representing all aspects of the business.

BI has identified five corporate objectives that are front-and-center at every decision made by the company: revenue, productivity, customer satisfaction, associate satisfaction, and added value. Every action at BI must support at least one of these objectives, and all plans, improvement teams, and measures that track progress and quantify the company's success are tied to these objectives.

Linked directly to its corporate objectives, BI's Vital Few indicators are sales and margin, sales per associate, transactional customer satisfaction indices, and associate retention. These indicators provide a snapshot of the health of the organization — a snapshot that is reviewed during biweekly business team meetings. BI's performance ratings in these categories, coupled with a few strategic measures and operational measures decided on throughout the company, are compiled into a leadership scorecard that is tied to the company's strategic business and quality plan.

Teaming, process improvement, and continuous improvement are staples of business strategies at BI. In fiscal year 1998 to 1999, 84 percent of associates participated in quality or process improvement teams and completed courses enabling associates to work more effectively on teams. Every associate has the power to launch an improvement team. The number of QI teams that have demonstrated improvements and disbanded has more than doubled over the past two years — from 201 to 546, showing pervasive involvement in BI's team-based, empowered work system.

Customer Satisfaction is King

BI's Customer Delight Process provides the process road map for discovering, defining, designing, and delivering products, making certain that BI knows what the customers' needs and wants are. Then, BI uses three key measures to evaluate customer satisfaction. Top on the list is the transactional customer satisfaction index, or TCSI. The TCSI is a quick way for account managers and company leaders to judge customer satisfaction. If an account receives an overall satisfaction rating of 7 out of 10 or lower, a business team member is assigned as champion to investigate and present an action plan to the business team. If a score of 10 is earned, the account team earns special recognition. To keep on top of customer satisfaction, the full business team reviews aggregate TCSI numbers at biweekly meetings.

The relational customer satisfaction index, or RCSI, offers another window on how customers respond to BI's products and services. Customers are asked annually to rate specific attributes of BI and to identify areas for improvement, the likelihood of repeat business, and overall satisfaction. BI also funds an annual competitive study conducted by an independent research firm. Consisting of surveys sent to BI customers and those doing business with its two largest competitors, the yearly study offers insights into strengths and opportunities for improvement.

Rewards Work Both Ways

Constructing business improvement programs to motivate its customers' employees, distributors, and consumers is BI's primary business — and what is good for the customer is good for BI. Associates work on a profit-sharing plan based on BI's financial performance — a plan that has paid benefits in 17 of the past 18 years. Associates are also eligible for performance bonuses, which in 1998 were given to more than 78 percent of those eligible. New hires not yet eligible for performance bonuses are not forgotten: they earn BI award credits redeemable for merchandise or restaurant and movie certificates. They are not alone. All associates can earn rewards by participating in the BI Way improvement system. Rewards vary from $20 in award credits to credits equal to 20 percent of cost savings achieved. BI teams can apply for an annual quality award based on the Baldrige criteria, with internal and external examiners reviewing applications.

Generous rewards are one way in which BI demonstrates the importance of its associates. The fact that employee retention is one of its four Vital Few measures is another. So is the BI Culture Scan — an annual survey of its associates — which shows that associate satisfaction has increased since 1995. Approximately 97 percent of BI's associates received training in 1998. That figure is notably higher than benchmarks and the national average cited by the American Society for Training and Development.

Results

If the four Vital Few indicators are the measures that really count for BI, then the results it has been producing have made BI's owners and profit-sharing associates very happy. Company revenue has grown by a cumulative 47 percent over the past five years. That success reflects BI's customer focus, improvement efforts, and the company's decision to target strategic, large accounts rather than overall market share. Productivity of its associates, another vital indicator, has been topping the 5 percent annual improvement goal.

BI has consistently outperformed its two key competitors for the last three years on customer-focused results. Last year, an independent study concluded that BI's TCSI results were 8.5 on a 10-point scale for overall satisfaction compared with competitor ratings of 7.9 and 7.6; 8.1 for on-time performance compared to 7.9 and 7.7 for competitors; and 8.1 for accurate performance versus 7.8 and 7.7 for competitors. A full 70 percent of BI's top customers have been with BI for more than five years.

Now at 83 percent, associate retention, another Vital Few indicator, has been particularly strong — especially when considering the Twin Cities' unemployment rate has averaged just 2.9 percent during the 1998 to 1999 fiscal year, creating a tight labor market.

Source: Baldrige National Quality Program, National Institute of Standards and Technology, U.S. Department of Commerce; Web site: www.baldrige.nist.gov.

▲

▼

Case Study 3.2: USAA

USAA is a mutual insurance company that services more than five million customers, primarily current and former military personnel and their families. Its products and services include property and casualty insurance (only for military personnel), banking, life insurance, brokerage, and investment management. USAA also provides financial services with its MasterCard, auto, home loan, and retirement-planning divisions. The company employs 21,000 people and also has a large mail-order catalog business, and offers long-distance telephone services, travel planning and group discounts, and Internet access to its members.

BI is a private-member-owned Fortune 500 (number 185) company, with sales of $10.6 billion and annual sales growth of nearly 15 percent in 2003. USAA is the highest-ranking financial services company for customer advocacy, according to an independent survey by Forrester Research. The company scored highest on simplicity (making it easy for customers to do business); transparency (being up front about rates and fees); benevolence (taking the customers' side when problems arise); and trustworthiness (doing what is right for the customer). USAA relies extensively on technology to direct market its services, reaching clients via telephone and the Internet.

What respondents said about USAA:

- 67 percent would consider USAA for their next insurance purchase. Only one other firm received a higher rating than 50 percent.
- 43 percent would consider USAA for their next banking purchase. This is 10 times higher that the average score for industry peers.
- 42 percent would consider USAA for their next brokerage purchase. This is eight times higher than the average score for industry peers in the Forrester survey.

▲

Chapter 4

People Power: Total Quality Human Resources, Participation, Training, and Empowerment[1]

> In a time of drastic change, it is the Learners who inherit the future. The Learned find themselves equipped to live in a world that no longer exists.
>
> **— Eric Hoffer**

High-performance service firms anticipate customers' needs, meeting the demand for high quality goods and services from suppliers, and continuously respond to changing domestic and global environments. As a result, leading firms in various service sectors are reaping benefits such as increased market share, cost savings, greater customer loyalty and satisfaction, and reductions in complaint rates. Some of these firms (and sectors) include Citigroup (financial services), Disney (entertainment), FedEx (package delivery), Knight-Ridder (publishing, information systems), L. L. Bean (mail order), Metlife, New York Life, Paul Revere,[2] and USAA (diversified financial and mutual insurance), Hyatt, Loews, and

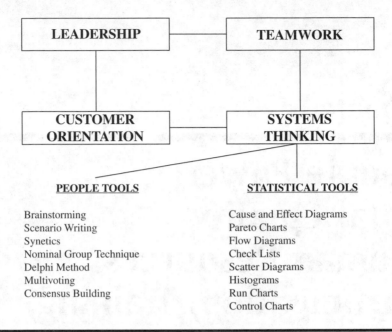

Figure 4.1   An interactive model for total quality service.

Ritz-Carlton, which is an independent division of Marriott (hotels) (Spechler, 1991; Tisch, 2004).

Within any organization, the interaction of employees with equipment, surroundings, policies, procedures, and technology influences the level of service quality delivered to customers. To allow for systemwide improvement, training in total quality service (TQS) must be participatory and process oriented, as opposed to the more traditional control-based and results-oriented approaches such as management by objectives (MBO), planning–programming–budgeting system (PPBS) and, when outputs fall short of goals, "management by exception." Training for this new way of looking at (see Chapter 2, Table 2.1) the interaction of customers, employees, managers, and suppliers is critical to the success of organizational change strategies.

This chapter explores the implications of TQS for human resource management, organizational behavior, and training to encourage participation and overcome resistance within internal work cultures. The purpose of this training is described in the form of an "interactive" model linking leadership, teamwork, customer orientation, and the statistical management capability of the organization (shown on Figure 4.1). This conceptual model represents an alternative to traditional results-oriented, fear-based, number- and control-driven systems that emphasize reinforcement of authority, centralization, hierarchy, performance appraisal, ranking employees, and MBO.

Total Quality Human Resource Management

Some still mistakenly assume that service quality improvement (QI) cannot be accurately measured, because it is composed primarily of human resources (people), and human behavior (they say) is inherently too difficult to change. In the past, that may have been an excuse (or perhaps even the truth) in some organizations or businesses. Service processes are often more complex, less tangible, and more difficult to measure than manufacturing processes and systems. The need for QI in services increasingly depends on *participation, personal involvement, and training.*

The TQS guidelines and their implications for organizational development and training are discussed in the following text. Each one, or a combination, could be incorporated into any training exercise for service organizations interested in the critical human and behavioral change aspects of TQS (the seven elements of TQS are described in Chapter 2). Organizations frequently rotate their employees through training seminars to learn the latest techniques for customer service QI. Many also maintain schools or training centers to orient new and experienced employees to corporate policies, standard operating procedures (SOPs), and changes in work culture. Behavioral change is explicitly or implicitly a goal of TQS, so modifications of attitudes, behaviors, perceptions, and authority systems are part of any training exercise.

TQS is a comprehensive approach that includes a wide range of subsystems referred to as hardware (physical assets), software (procedures and processes), and humanware (people) within the organization (Kano and Gitlow, 1989). The level of service experienced by a customer results not only from the human interactions between customer and provider but from a combination of all the three, each providing legitimate areas for measurement and improvement. TQS reflects customer satisfaction with:

1. *Physical surroundings* (furnishings, structures, and equipment) are tangible factors that can be measured just as any manufactured product would be measured. For example, a broken bed in a hotel room, the cleanliness of a rental car, a bus or an aircraft in need of maintenance, or a faulty transformer all impact service quality. The mere fact that such repairs need to be made can create a negative customer–provider relationship. When a customer reports the need for maintenance improvements, the system must respond. The time it takes from reporting the need to making the repair is as valid and reliable an indicator as is the customer's satisfaction with the person sent to make the repair.

2. *System processes* (procedures, policies, and "software") are less visible, but no less important as valid sources of satisfaction or dissatisfaction with services. For example, the speed with which

the maintenance technician responded to the call for service? The functioning of the software for a computer information system, check-in and check-out policies at different hotels, police procedures for responding to citizen complaints, and airline reservation systems are all examples of various measurable system processes. These elements are more difficult to measure, but may be the most important in terms of overall customer satisfaction.

3. *Human resources* (people, personnel, and training) are perhaps the most variable, but nonetheless important, component. The actual service provided by an employee, such as in repairing a car, bus, or aircraft, filling out a claim form, booking a reservation, or in correctly reading a utility meter often determines customer satisfaction. Training for performing the tasks required in a manner that exceeds customer expectations is essential. Without adequate systems, tools, or the knowledge to perform the task, even with the best of intentions, the most motivated employee will fall short of customer (and probably employer) expectations.

Although all of these elements are important to control, when measured against valid customer needs, the success of nearly all service organizations begins and ends with its people. Regardless of how well quality and productivity improvement systems are designed, it is the responsiveness of an organization's human resources in applying the technology, distributing resources, interpreting rules, serving customers and producing value-added processes that ultimately determines the level of performance. Continuously improving quality systems without the active participation and full cooperation of all those affected virtually guarantees failure. This is why the "top-down do-it-or-else" approach may succeed initially, but in the long run fails to change underlying organizational behavior.

As previously discussed, TQS can be understood in terms of its priorities, nature, and orientation. Perhaps the most striking feature of TQS is that it makes the needs of the customers and the quality of work life for employees its priorities (Romero-Simpson, 1990). Leadership, planning, and policies must reach beyond the traditional short-term "immediate profit-making" approach geared solely toward a limited number of interested parties (usually boards of directors and stockholders), and aim instead at changing the organizational subculture to reward customer-directed service QI. Service firms must pay particularly close attention to employee satisfaction especially in customer driven "high-touch" services such as banking and financial management. For examples, see the description of the New Mexico State Quality Award and of the Malcolm Baldrige National Quality Award (BNQA) winner Los Alamos National Bank in Case Study 4.1.

The human resources training necessary to understand and apply TQS principles requires active participation in cross-functional teams or task-forces that aim at overcoming traditional barriers to participation and cooperation (Milakovich, 1991a). The purpose of such teams is to identify and solve problems that cut across different staff areas by forming work-groups with representatives from each responsible work unit. Groups are led by a facilitator, or lead team member, trained in organizational behavior, statistics, and group dynamics, who chairs the team meetings and interacts with other lead team members.[3] Plainly, employee participation, cooperation, and cross-functional teams are as important to management today as MBO, quality control circles (QCC), and performance appraisals were to administration in the 1980s.

In sum, achieving TQS involves training and development in human and technical subsystems dynamically interrelated through a closely knit organizational "value structure" that is oriented toward constantly improving customer service processes and systems. This holistic approach significantly departs from the more specialized compartmentalized management systems used by most organizations. Thus, TQS requires a different style of training based on total QI guidelines.

Total QI Guidelines

The following guidelines were chosen on the basis of the values and principles discussed in previous chapters. They include:

1. Unwavering commitment to the customer
2. Recognition by the management of the importance of quality and a willingness to accept the responsibility for system improvement
3. Accepting the crucial role of education and self-improvement in accomplishing the change
4. Teaching the spirit of *Kaizen* or constant improvement through the efforts of the entire workforce
5. Adopting a process orientation (as opposed to a results orientation)
6. Developing and emphasizing the importance of a stimulating environment, free from fear
7. Implementing a team-based approach to cross-functional management and facilitating breakdown of internal barriers to cooperation
8. Using communication channels such as the Internet and the World Wide Web rather than relying on regulation or inspection to overcome obstacles, improve the system, and achieve high standards in quality

9. Thinking systemically and using appropriate statistical tools to measure and control variation

10. Personal commitment to the diffusion of TQS based on a conviction regarding its value in each employee (Romero-Simpson, 1990)

It is clearly beyond the scope of this book to describe in full the quality training required to implement TQS within a particular service organization. The preceding ten principles of TQS form the basis for the teaching philosophy in any training course on human resource development. In this chapter, they are posed as questions to be answered by the members of any organization seeking commitment (Point 10) to implement TQS.

In most training activities (short courses or workshops), students, instructors, the classroom, and the available resources comprise a "learning systems environment" consisting of several interconnected processes. The main purpose is to constantly improve learning processes through the joint efforts of the participants and the instructor. The ultimate goal is to empower each employee with the confidence and knowledge to meet or exceed customer requirements. In the learning environments, all participants are expected to make maximum use of self-improvement opportunities as well as contribute to the development of better versions of similar training courses in the future.

Guideline No. 1

Is the organization committed to its customers?

As noted earlier, the term *quality* has many different definitions, dimensions, and interpretations (Garvin, 1984; 1987). Throughout this chapter, the term is used to define the pervasive concern with developing the human resources of an organization or work unit. This concept reflects the continuous commitment to improving the environment in which work takes place, sometimes known as Quality in Daily Work (QIDW). This is one component of a TQS strategy, aimed at increasing the productivity of a service workforce by improving the quality of working conditions.

TQS practitioners must perceive the customer as the center of their activities, with other employees, policies, and systems responsive to customer needs. This is a fundamental premise. One of the best known quality practitioners, Peter Scholtes (1988), who also once served as a city manager, writes of this assumption — "an organization's goal is to meet and exceed customer needs by giving lasting value to the customer. The return will follow as customers boast of the company's quality and service." In essence, the goal is to create satisfied employees and customers who then become an extension of the marketing and advertising efforts of the organization.

Implications of Guideline No. 1

Everyone the organization has contact with is viewed as a current or potential customer whose needs must be anticipated and met or exceeded. Those undergoing training play the role of "internal customers" who are eventually responsible for process improvement and "external" customer satisfaction. This approach reflects the "extended process" of suppliers and customers (Chapter 2, Figure 2.2) and illustrates how the "voices" of all the processes link together as part of an integrated service delivery system (Figure 2.3). Communicating how the seemingly isolated decisions of individual internal customers (employees) add or detract value as "moments of truth" when serving external customers is another key to successful TQS transformation (Carlzon, 1987; Liswood, 1990).

This lesson is important not only for training, but for customer retention as well. Not only does it cost five times more to acquire a new customer than to satisfy a current one, but complaints from customers reflect only a fraction (less than 10 percent) of the estimated number of dissatisfied customers. This means that for every one vocally dissatisfied customer, there are at least ten others who, for various reasons, do not register complaints about the offending service. Reasons for not complaining or mishandling a complaint differ. Many who do not bother to complain just disappear. Others complain to their friends, neighbors, and business associates, who hear and often repeat the negative comments. Similar to "buzz" or "word-of-mouth" advertising for motion pictures, this informal marketing network can result in significant loss of business, especially for a small or medium-sized service firm. For nonprofit and public agencies, negative interactions often generate "mountains of paperwork" in the form of complaints, appeals, investigations, grievance procedures, and unnecessarily duplicative efforts.

The reverse is also true. Satisfied customers will generate new customers by making positive comments about the service received. Accurate data is difficult to obtain, but a single satisfied customer can influence the buying decisions of many others to "shop" at the same business.

Customer responsiveness training should be designed to satisfy the learning needs of all participants, and hopefully will extend beyond obtaining a certification, clearing a departmental evaluation, or securing a higher rank. If employee learning needs are understood and met, then the workers will change their behavior in relation to those they must satisfy. They will internalize the principles, behave in a manner consistent with them, and recommend them to others (fellow employees and prospective customers). Thus, instructors are encouraged to perfect their learning systems (workshops or courses) as examples of fulfilling the present and future needs of other internal and external customers.

Guideline No. 2

Is management committed in word and in deed to quality and are they willing to accept responsibility for system well-being and improvement?

As more service industries develop their high-performance skills, leadership efforts consume a greater share of senior management's time and effort, perhaps as much as one quarter in initial phases. Awareness, knowledge, and understanding of basic TQS principles and concepts is no longer optional — it is required of most senior executives. The ultimate payoffs from commitment to service QI can be substantial. Without top-level involvement, valuable training and implementation resources are wasted.

At the Ritz-Carlton Hotel Company (an independently operated division of Marriott Hotels), for example, winner of the 1992 and 1999 Malcolm Baldrige National Quality Award, employee commitment to total customer satisfaction not only requires executive support but adherence to customer service standards, detailed planning, and quality data. Once these gold standards were achieved, the hotel chain received widespread recognition as a quality provider in an extremely competitive industry. (See Case Study 4.2).

To initiate, learn, and sustain a quality transformation, visible commitment from top management is absolutely crucial. This principle is perhaps the most important one for "change agents" to keep in mind when pursuing organizational transformation (Bennis and Nanus, 1986). Once there is commitment from top management, maintaining credibility with employees is the biggest single challenge: they can never underestimate how often their commitment needs to be demonstrated and reinforced. If employees detect inconsistencies or perceive mixed messages regarding the company's commitment to quality, or if the management fails to meet established requirements, then its credibility suffers.

Implications of Guideline No. 2

In any learning environment where new skills and work habits are being taught, the instructor represents the management. Thus, consistency and commitment in this role are crucial as well. Instructors must be well versed in company quality policy and should be able to communicate clearly and effectively. Similar to any good teacher, the course instructor should lead by example, "walk the talk," and become a role model to his or her students. It is extremely important that the instructor's behavior be consistent with the principles taught in class. The instructor should be constantly operating under a TQS framework throughout the duration of the training. In several companies, senior executives have themselves taken the lead and taught others. This becomes a vehicle for understanding TQS as well as a tangible example of companywide commitment.

Guideline No. 3

Is education and self-improvement recognized as the means to accomplish change?

Education is defined by *Webster's New World Dictionary* as: the process of training and developing the knowledge, skill, mind, and character, especially by formal schooling; teaching or training. *Self-improvement* is defined as improvement of one's status, mind, abilities, etc., by one's own efforts. Finally, *change* denotes making or becoming distinctly different and implies either a radical transmutation of character or replacement with something else.

Education for self-improvement requires the acquisition of both specific technical knowledge, as well as learning new attitudes, behaviors, and skills to build mind and character. This cannot be a passive experience: a display of personal effort is required. Some have likened this to a religious experience or metamorphosis. Education helps smooth the transformation process, and training is seen as a means to fit people to jobs and to responsibilities for which they are best suited. In addition, a personal commitment is required from those undergoing training to advance these principles.

Employee training is the essence of effective QI. Questions every manager in the United States should ask himself or herself are:

- "Was I ever trained for my job?"
- "Who trained me?"
- "When was I last trained for my current position?"
- "Were my subordinates or staff every trained for their jobs?"
- "Who trained them?"
- "Do I really know what the jobs of my subordinates entail and is it accurately reflected in their job descriptions?"
- "Do I even know where their job descriptions are?"
- "When did I last revise my job description?"
- "Does my boss know what I do?"
- "Do I agree with my job description and job classification?"

Efforts to increase participation, such as the formation of labor–management committees, labor–management task forces, and QCCs are all part of, and originated from, the quality movement. Without TQS to support team efforts, the tendency is for group efforts to become diffuse and unfocused. At the same time, too much control can stifle creative solutions to problems presented to "empowered" teams of employees. Reflecting a longer-term view of the importance of human resources in increasing productivity, a Japanese factory will have negligible output the first six to twelve months after becoming operational, as defined by U.S. standards. That additional time is spent training workers in all aspects of companywide quality control (CWQC). Every employee is trained to do her or his job, learn who his or her customers, subordinates, superiors, and suppliers are, and learn also about fellow employees' jobs (Imai, 1986). This approach has also been successfully used by both European and Japanese manufacturers operating factories in the United States.

Implications of Guideline No. 3

There is an established technique known as *experiential learning* that is particularly well suited for TQS training. Experiential learning is defined as the process whereby knowledge is created through the transformation of experience (Kolb et al., 1984), and it is appropriate for QI training because (1) it is geared toward continuous change, (2) requires the learner to take an active rather than passive role in his or her learning, and (3) goes beyond the immediate classroom environment, and yet can be enhanced in the classroom. Several critical elements of the learning process can be enhanced by the experiential perspective.

The first aspect is emphasis on the process of adaptation and learning as opposed to the content or outcome of the learning process. Knowledge is viewed as a transformational process that is continuously created and re-created, not as an independent entity to be acquired or transmitted. The second aspect is that learning transforms experience in both its objective and subjective forms. Finally, to understand learning, the nature of knowledge itself must be understood. Rather than being passive receivers of knowledge, everyone assumes an active role in transforming the educational process itself. This is often difficult to expect from American workers trained from elementary school to be passive recipients of knowledge in a nonparticipatory learning environment.

Guideline No. 4 and Guideline No. 5

Does the organization practice *Kaizen* and continuous process-oriented learning?

Although each concept has its own separate definition and identity, *Kaizen* and process improvement go hand in hand. Together, they help focus the entire organization toward customer-driven QI. *Kaizen* is a process rather than a results-oriented concept, with a "people," as opposed to budgetary or financial, orientation. Teaching everyone to be alert for process improvement opportunities requires changing organizational, as well as the individual, behavior. To reiterate, familiarity with problem identification and process control tools is also necessary. The extent to which these tools and techniques are data- or statistics-driven depends on the nature of the service offered and the complexity of the processes being improved.

Organizational behavior has been defined as "the study of the behavior, attitudes, and performance of workers in an organizational setting; how the organization and subgroup impact the worker's perceptions, feelings, and actions; the environment's effect on the organization and its human resources and goals; and the effect of the workers on the organization and its effectiveness" (Cohen, Funk, Gadon, Willits, and Josefowitz, 1992; Szilagyi and Wallace, 1990). Thus, changing organizational behavior(s) must be viewed within a broader context of factors dynamically interacting with each other.

The basic unit of analysis is the individual worker, dealing with his or her own expectations and those of the organization. Perhaps the most complex unit is the organization's dynamic interaction with its environment. The field also contains units of intermediate complexity such as interpersonal communication, formal and informal groups, teamwork, organizational change, and work redesign. In quality-managed environments, all these elements must be integrated within a systems perspective (Chapter 2, Figure 2.6) with leadership focusing on strategy, planning, redesign, and implementation.

This *opens systems model* of organizational behavior and change represents a dynamic rather than static vision of the organization's interaction with its environment (Thompson, 1967). Throughout the process of developing new and better quality-related solutions to team-defined problems, creative efforts should be focused not only on producing new knowledge, but on combining traditional knowledge with new knowledge in small steps to gradually improve processes.

Implications of Guideline No. 4 and Guideline No. 5

During training, instructors must constantly improve the learning systems (training sessions and workshops) under their responsibility, just as operations managers are responsible for constantly improving the systems under their control. Also, the learner is responsible for maintaining standards and taking the initiative to suggest positive changes to improve the system. This forms the basis for team-based problem identification and reduces the need for external control and evaluation.

An important objective of any training exercise is to encourage participants to "learn how to learn" within realistic, work-related situations. The focus of a TQS-oriented course should be on constantly perfecting processes leading to system learning. This may be accomplished through the joint efforts of different student teams and the instructor (i.e., simulating the entire workforce). Everyone must convey an attitude of respect toward each other as fellow customers and suppliers. The instructor must deliver each topic enthusiastically and maintain a strong belief in QI along with the learning process. If such an attitude prevails, the spirit of *Kaizen* will be translated into observable behavioral changes. Once this spirit is conveyed, it should be nurtured so that it transcends the training sessions and permeates the organization.

Guideline 6

Is the work environment stimulating and free of fear?

After having been exposed to the basics of TQS, it is difficult to believe that anyone, regardless of his or her position, would question the benefits of a nonstressful, stimulating, and secure work environment. It is not uncommon, however, to experience high stress levels and nonstimulating environments in many different organizational settings. This reality, combined with personal and family pressures, results in increased absenteeism, family breakup, drug and alcohol dependencies, disability claims, and excessive healthcare expenses. Training efforts must not only promote the spirit of continuous improvement, but address and eliminate the underlying causes of stressful work environments (Ryan and Oestreich, 1991).

Among the most important research conducted in organizational behavior is that of Abraham Maslow, who wrote of "self-actualizing" workers achieving the highest degree of fulfillment on the job through maximum use of their creative capacities and individual independence (Maslow, 1954). Maslow viewed workers as having a "hierarchy of needs," and suggested that each level had to be satisfied before they could go on to the next one.

The first level was physiological needs — food, shelter, and the basic means of survival. Next was a minimum job security — a reasonable assurance (but not necessarily a guarantee) of continued employment. Following these essentials came social needs — group acceptance on and off the job and interpersonal relationships that are positive and supportive. Ego satisfaction and independence needs represent the fourth step in Maslow's hierarchy, and are derived from accomplishments in one's work and public recognition of them. Finally, Maslow's highest level was self-actualization — feelings of personal fulfillment resulting from independent, creative, and responsible job performance.

As the worker satisfied the needs of one level, he or she was seen as being further motivated to work toward satisfying the needs of the next higher level. Thus, Maslow emphasized interactions among the essential needs of the employee on and off the job: the work being done, the attitude of both management and employee toward work performance, and the relationship among employees in the work situation. The hierarchy of needs, like other theoretical formulations in the application of approaches referred to as *organizational humanism*, assumed that worker satisfaction could be affected by many factors in the organization, both close to the work situation itself and more distant from it; it did not assume that all workers would be motivated by the same set of needs.

Another influential organizational theorist, Frederick Herzberg, proposed the *Dual Factor Theory*, two independent sets of factors that account for worker dissatisfaction and satisfaction (Herzberg, 1966). The first set of "external" factors are the basics: minimum conditions that include adequate hygienic facilities in the workplace, proper illumination, ventilation, and space. The second set of "internal" (or motivational) factors are more important to individuals. If external factors are properly managed, there should be no cause for dissatisfaction among the workers. However, external factors are related to basic needs such as fringe benefits, salary, security, group identity, and social needs. Internal or motivating factors are related to the higher-level self-actualization needs that contribute to worker satisfaction. One such factor is the comfort experienced by a worker when there is compatibility between skills, preferences, and the specific nature of work. Recognition for achievement, responsibility, and pride stemming from a service rendered are more significant motivating factors for most workers.

Because they are the more satisfying aspects of one's job, these intangibles, according to Herzberg, are far better motivators than the more tangible rewards such as pay for performance, bonuses, or additional fringe benefits. Rewards actually "punish" workers by destroying the intrinsic value of the work itself. Growth and individual development are derived from the job itself, and most people not only work to live, but live to work. External factors should be carefully controlled to prevent dissatisfaction at work and internal factors should be properly managed to promote job satisfaction. High-performance service organizations even go one step further.

Because training should be aimed at improving workers' identification with the primary mission of the organization, any kind of system improvement related to either external or internal factors should trigger positive feelings in the entire workforce. These feelings would originate from the commitment to an organization that has a value-related mission and thus takes on some of the characteristics of a political cause or social movement.

Thus, internal work-related stress is minimized when management and employees communicate openly, humor rather than fear is encouraged, jobs are well defined, compensation is adequate for the tasks expected, and workers can relax or exercise during the day.

Managing Fear in the Workplace

To some extent, all employees are apprehensive about some elements of the workplace. Even trying to do one's best creates some degree of anxiety. This is a natural, physiologically based concern about the quality of one's work. Protracted anxiety, defensiveness, and the negative fear caused by overcontrol and unnecessary command structures is (or should be) of more concern to quality managers. To reduce the consequences of this latter type of fear, management must establish "long-term goals that are consistent with the new philosophy" (Gitlow and Gitlow, 1987). Reflecting Deming's management method, workers are not blamed for faults inherent in the system. Rather, their opinions and suggestions are sought by management to improve the system. Only when employees sense that management can be trusted do they become less defensive and more honest and open in discussing the barriers that hinder job performance. Only after the elements of fear are removed, and the workers treated with dignity and respect, can they be properly trained. They are then more likely to treat customers with the same degree of respect and courtesy.

Implications of Guideline No. 6: Creating a Stimulating Environment

The following factors contribute to a more stimulating learning environment and to effective training:

1. A clear specification of objectives offered at the beginning, giving all participants an opportunity to ask questions and resolve any doubts they may have and to contribute their suggestions. It is important that the nature of the training is understood and procedures consistently followed. It is also important that all participants are involved during the entire instructional process; this can be accomplished by requesting and offering immediate feedback throughout the course.
2. Training should be designed so that everyone can realize the advantage of immediate feedback as measured by the level of mastery of the subject matter. Because of their previous experience as students, some may place a greater emphasis on grades. It is

important that participants shift that emphasis to the sense of pride and accomplishment in "learning how to learn." This is accomplished to a great extent via personal application assignments (PAAs). These are written goal statements designed to reflect learning from a specific exercise, knowledge of the readings, application to real situations, and self-knowledge. They become the basis for workshop participants to express problems in such a way that they can be addressed by other team members (Romero-Simpson, 1990).

3. An atmosphere of openness to questions and suggestions from the participants and enthusiasm toward learning should be strongly encouraged from the beginning of the course. This should enhance commitment to achieve course goals, to its objectives, and to the procedures being followed.

4. Learning should stem from experiences (structured situations and simulations) to which individuals can relate. Workgroups should be encouraged to develop problem-solving and process-improvement exercises from their own unit's daily work experiences. (If the training is held "on campus" in the work facility, the opposite problem may occur; too many daily work problems could interfere with the workshop.)

5. Participants should be given an opportunity to discuss the experiences related to a specific topic as team members and in the light of different theoretical models, Deming, Juran, and Crosby, described in Chapter 3.

6. Everyone should be given an opportunity to state the practical implications and limitations of the subject matter in the light of his or her present and future supervisory or managerial experience.

Although some anxiety can enhance learning, dysfunctional levels of fear can inhibit constructive learning. Fear in a learning environment, as in the workplace, can actually hinder a person's capacity to realize that there is a need for improvement, to discern its real nature, and to generate possible solutions. Past educational experience may precondition some when entering an on-the-job learning environment. Many have the fear of being punished for "getting a low grade" or of being criticized by the instructor if they make the "wrong" statement. In a competitive environment, some may be afraid of their own associates. They may also be afraid of themselves and how they perform under pressure. This reflects upon the interactions they might engage in within an organization, as they do not know what their strengths and weaknesses are.

Many have also been taught by past educational experiences to be passive recipients of the instructor's knowledge. Few attended classes with the conviction that they would actually learn useful concepts. Thus, they merely took notes and prepared for quizzes and competitive examinations. In any TQS course or training activity, a special effort is made to link the material to be learned to the actual needs and expectations of the learners, taking into account their specific problem-solving styles. Interactive learning and team-based evaluations result. Grading or ranking of participants, if done at all, should reflect quality management principles and interactive learning environments.

Suggested Strategy

Training should be as relevant and interesting as possible in light of the objectives to be accomplished. Although not all employees are self-starters, special efforts should be made to encourage intrinsic motivation and thorough enjoyment of the process as well as the results of learning. To accomplish this, the following is suggested: (1) the terminology should be geared to the learner's level of experience, (2) the concepts should be explored within situations familiar to the learners, (3) participants should take active responsibility for their own learning and problem solving (PAAs are useful for this purpose), and (4) the classroom should become a stimulating environment in which transactions among students and between students and the instructor are the rule, not the exception (Romero-Simpson, 1990). In an organization committed to TQS, this could involve "creative backtalk" or feedback between workers and managers at all levels. Indeed, the freedom to express concerns about necessary process improvements cannot take place in a work environment where there is fear of reprisals for comments that could perhaps be considered at first to be negative. (Recall the earlier discussion of "safe channels" for complaints to relieve workers' frustrations with workplace conditions.)

Guideline No. 7

Is teamwork used to determine how to meet or exceed customer expectations?

Breakthroughs to higher levels of organizational performance are most likely to be achieved by team effort. Some of the other benefits that can be attributed to a team approach are: better meeting of social needs, fulfillment of ego needs, and self-fulfillment. Self-motivated and properly trained teams eventually increase organizational responsiveness to all customers, internal or external.

Peter Scholtes (1988) expresses the rationale for teamwork as follows: Where once there may have been barriers, rivalries, and distrust, the quality company fosters teamwork and partnerships with the workforce and their representatives. This partnership is not a pretense, a new look at an old battle. It is a common struggle for the customers, not separate struggles for power ... The notion of a common struggle for quality also applies to relationships with suppliers, regulating agencies, and local communities (Scholtes, 1988, pp.1–13).

Implications of Guideline No. 7

Workshop participants should be organized in teams according to their specific learning needs and problem-solving styles. This should be done very early in the training session. Every topic is approached within a team and among teams. The careful matching of teams by problem-solving style may reduce variations attributable to differences in style and minimize the homogeneous outcomes that are prone to emerge from each team. This is a useful strategy to reduce the common causes of variation that are attributed to individual differences in work styles and to the varying ability to work with others.

Guideline No. 8

Are communication channels other than inspection used to overcome obstacles, improve the system, and achieve quality?

TQS involves the entire workforce in never-ending process improvement. It inherently requires leadership, mutual trust, and open communication. Quite the contrary, according to W. Edwards Deming, mass inspection is an attitude born out of mistrust, misunderstanding, and failure to monitor and improve the process. Mass inspection must be modified because it fosters fear and distrust. What is the alternative, then, to achieve goals and maintain standards? As mentioned earlier, using teams as human sensors to develop "feedback loops" within the work unit is one feasible alternative.

Implications of Guideline No. 8

The traditional grading system in schools is comparable to organizational inspection policies (checking whether or not the student has in fact memorized the material) as well as to performance appraisals. Gitlow et al., 1989, use Deming's classic funnel experiment (see Chapter 3) to illustrate the absurdity of such procedures to improve organizational quality. They show how performance appraisals are a form of overcontrol based on common or random system variation. Performance appraisals can artificially increase the system's variation in a significant way. Alternatives to traditional performance appraisal are now available to organizations concerned about the destructive competition fostered by individual performance reviews. Under a quality evaluation system, the entire organization is considered a system of interlocking processes. The institution, rather than the individual employee, becomes the object of performance improvement (Bowman, 1994).

Another point is that inspection and performance appraisal, similar to grading, does not reflect learning, if learning is equated with problem solving. Typically, those being tested are reinforced for recalling the "right" response (fill-in-the-blank) or for recognizing the correct response among several multiple-choice answers. Concept memorization and concept recognition, however, are just two of many components that are present in the learning process. This definition of learning is beginning to change as high school graduates are now being tested on writing and reasoning skills (detailed in Chapter 8).

Inspection devices such as quizzes, exams, and ranking workshop participants should be minimized in the light of the above arguments, among others. It is important, however, to realize that many of those in training will have been conditioned by the present educational system, which relies heavily on individual grading procedures. Many participants may find it difficult to understand learning without quizzes, exams, and grades. Thus, a complete removal of quizzes and grades could generate a great deal of confusion and possibly lead to dysfunctional effects. Quizzes may be used during the early stages to benchmark technical information acquisition and gauge retention of the critical skills needed to solve problems. However, they should account for only a small proportion of the final evaluation (less than 25 percent). There should be a gradual transition from quizzes, to problem-solving exercises, to the use of PAAs. Also, the emphasis of the evaluation should shift from individual performance to team performance assessed via a feedback loop similar to that described earlier.

Pinches, Detecting Devices, Measurement, and Information Lines

Using Juran's terminology, each service worker becomes a "detecting device" aware of possible "pinches," or situations the Japanese call *warusa-kagen* (things that are not yet problems, but are still not quite right). Left untended, they may develop into serious problems. *Warusa-kagen* are often the starting point of improvement activities identified by team members. Communication or feedback between management and the employees must encourage immediate action to deal with any problems that may emerge. (Recall Ritz-Carlton's efforts to "move heaven and earth" for customers.) In the instructional setting, all participants should be encouraged to bring forward their concerns and questions to clarify any issue related to the content of readings, classroom procedures, and expectations before the learning experience begins. Thus, each team plays the role of a measuring and analysis station by processing information and critically evaluating it.

Establishing a nonthreatening atmosphere in the workshop allows participants to bring their concerns, doubts, and frustrations out into the open. Such pinches should be dealt with as soon as possible by the instructor and fellow students as a team. Team-focused activities become useful as "control centers" by comparing and contrasting actual behavior with ideal or stipulated behavior.

Finally, the PAA is a highly useful tool and quite compatible with TQS process orientation. PAAs become the information lines between the participants (workers) and the instructor (management). The assigned PAA evaluation should reflect the balance between the different stages of the learning process (feeling, observing, thinking, and acting). PAAs are ideal for such purposes. They also promote participation and may include criteria such as discipline, time management, skill development, participation, involvement, and communication (Imai, 1986). Its final stage, active experimentation, is particularly useful as a "motor device." In this stage, students describe the specific steps they intend to take as a result of his or her experience pertaining to the specific topic of concern. The PAAs then become "learning contracts" upon which future progress can be measured and evaluated.

Guideline No. 9

Is systems thinking used to measure and eliminate variation?

In a quality-managed service organization, management's key mission is to lead in the direction of never-ending and continuous improvement, followed by continual reduction of variation in an organization's processes. By closely monitoring a process using statistical methods, management can determine if its various subsystems exhibit common or special variations. Failing to deal with the system in statistical terms can actually increase process variation and reduce management's ability to strategically control, lead, and direct. Thus, even if a team is process oriented, lack of leadership to direct change processes could result in failure.

Management without TQS makes it more difficult to establish policies, set goals, or improve performance. Failure to differentiate common from special causes of variation means that rewards and punishments are assigned arbitrarily (the "Red Bead" experiment). Even though performance is system focused rather than worker related, decisions that are arbitrarily made reinforce and penalize individual behavior. This inevitably leads to low morale and resentment among the workforce. The lack of a connection between effort, performance, and rewards can be extremely detrimental, particularly for those workers who are penalized. In the light of the learning and imitation theory, workers are expected to engage in behaviors that are conducive to future rewards. When rewards and punishments are awarded without an understanding of variation and its impact on the workforce, results can be quite dysfunctional for the entire organization.

Implications of Guideline No. 9

There are two different implications for Guideline No. 9. Both relate to participation: one touches upon the manager or instructor's role and the other upon the participant or worker's role as a future manager. The instructor who plays the role of management in the classroom should be technically competent to differentiate common from special causes of variation. This will prevent him or her from rewarding or punishing in an arbitrary way, and from making other mistakes. Equally important, participants must learn to "think statistically" if they want to become efficient managers. They must learn to "map" processes, identify critical problems, and to constantly reduce variation in the specific process under their control. Learning to "think systemically" as well as statistically can present an obstacle to new learning.

Past instructional experience may have conditioned the students or workers to view statistics as a highly abstract and unrelated discipline. They may fail to see the connection between statistics and job performance. This is partially attributable to the fact that instructors do not always clearly establish such connections in the classroom. Instructors, regardless of their topic, should teach their subject matter using the most appropriate statistical tools to illustrate their points with task-related examples.

Guideline No. 10

Is everyone in the organization personally committed to the achievement of TQS, based on personal conviction of its value? (If not, begin again at step No. 1!)

The word *committed* implies active involvement in process improvements, doing more than just planning and directing. Not only is commitment a willingness to learn, but a pledge or promise to do something with the acquired knowledge. Although it carries certain emotional overtones, the word *conviction* implies a strong belief and is more reflective in nature. It is possible for a strong conviction to evolve into a commitment, eventually triggering a specific behavior. Those who really believe in TQS seldom remain passive. They are eager to share its advantages with others. Thus, the diffusion of TQS becomes a natural next step for them.

Implications of Guideline No. 10

TQS principles will not be fully understood by participants if they are merely asked to study them. Rather, they should be encouraged to "walk the talk" as active participants and role models familiar with the organization's QI strategy. They should consciously transmit it, talk about it, discuss it, and take advantage of any opportunity to analyze situations within this framework. The instructor (representing management) should "take on leadership for change" and encourage workers as students to do the same thing. This is perhaps the most difficult element of TQS, as the slightest deviation from top management's commitment and conviction will be viewed by workers as a signal that they should withhold active participation.

Human Resources Topics Offered under a TQS Perspective

Listed below are some examples of the topics typically included in quality-oriented training (such topics are relevant to the need to institute change and are consistent with the ten TQS guidelines mentioned earlier):

1. *Worker–organization bonding:* There should be organizational socialization through the gradual interchange of expectations, norms, and values, among others. Workshop participants will be exposed to the organization's quality philosophy and introduced to the need to be responsive to reducing the costs of poor quality.
2. *Leadership and communication:* Leadership is exercised at all levels as a common effort to reduce special and common causes of variation via interpersonal skills, statistical thinking, and learning to apply appropriate statistical tools. Leadership principles can be taught as any other cognitive skill. One technique to instill multi-level leadership skills is the use of audiovisual equipment. Videotaping leadership exercises allows individuals or team members to view and critique their own performance. It also rewards participants for

teamwork and mutual support. The exercise offers an excellent opportunity for a team of supervisors and workers to exhibit leadership and learn from each other. The videotape, which is an objective measure, offers the opportunity to discuss what happened and decide what needs to be changed to improve the system. (Chapter 10 expands on the details of the leadership skills required to achieve high-performance status.)

3. *Teamwork:* While working toward the improvement of work processes, members learn to assess their own strengths and weaknesses and those of their fellow team members. The literature on quality learning recognizes the importance of individual differences when referring to employee work skills. The concept of problem-solving style is extremely useful and could be included in the TQS approach. It recognizes differences among human learners in the way they adapt to the environment and act upon it. This concept is particularly important when analyzed within a problem-solving team perspective. Each team can be assembled in terms of problem-solving styles, each participant's style being determined by the Learning Style Inventory (Kolb et al., 1984).

4. *The organization as an open system:* Co-workers and team members learn how to deal effectively with other workers and organizational units, divisions, and departments. This emphasizes the value of exceeding the needs of external customers as an organization's ultimate goal. Techniques for opening channels of communications to obtain feedback and thus improve existing processes and systems are taught.

The purpose of training for high performance is to deal with the different areas of human behavior within organizations from a quality perspective. Effective organizational socialization implies giving up old values and assuming new ones (Table 2.1). This socialization issue becomes particularly crucial when someone joins a "quality" organization. The new worker goes through the typical anxieties and apprehensions related to facing the unknown. Moreover, the worker is joining an organization with a different way of perceiving, thinking, and acting. Because socialization is the first unit taught, it offers an ideal opportunity to expose recruits to a different philosophy. Such a philosophy also calls for a different instructional strategy and for different roles for both managers and workers.

The learning strategy applied throughout a training session is horizontally interactive and process oriented with the following required from the learners: (1) study of the specific topic as well as problem-solving exercises to be covered in class, (2) participation as a member of a team, based on problem-solving styles (a special effort must be made to achieve a balance in styles), (3) participation in a topic-related experience that could be a case study or a simulation, (4) participation in team discussion and interaction, (5) presentation of team reports by representatives who share the team's decisions in public, (6) involvement in discussions leading to specific conclusions pertaining to the subject matter, and (7) presentation, at a later date, of PAAs containing the above points (Kolb, Rubin, and McIntyre, 1984).

The course must convey TQS concepts, particularly during the unit on "worker–organization bonding," designed to expose learners to quality, processes, and systems thinking. The process-oriented nature of the course focuses on learning how to learn, combined with the instructor's specific instructional philosophy, and thus eases the inclusion of quality-oriented concepts in other technical and nontechnical courses. The "worker–organization bonding" and "leadership" units are very useful in acquainting learners with the most relevant concepts and tools of QI. It is important to stress that the feedback given by the customers (employees) is the result of their efforts to evaluate the course both from an individual and from a team perspective.

Going one step further, principles of TQS (i.e., teamwork, closer customer–supplier relationships, empowerment, systems thinking, continuous quality improvement or CQI, and cost reduction) should be presented as a way of thinking, regardless of the field of training. Under this perspective, the instructor's role is geared to pulling together the efforts of different teams. Team members take active responsibility for their own experiential and conceptual learning and for that of their fellow members.' They all work together toward a common goal: an improved system.

Summary

To summarize, several interrelated elements must be included for successful organizational change training. In addition to worker–organization bonding, other general topics should include customer orientation, leadership, teamwork, and thinking systemically. As a teaching philosophy, TQS is attractive because it recognizes the importance of treating individuals fairly, yet incorporates a "hard-data" approach to better results management. Human resource training must be integrated with job performance expectations and emphasize the soft and hard thinking and systems interface unique to a TQS culture.

As noted below, the interaction of each of these elements is critical to the development of a high-performance workforce. Once these conceptual principles are learned, training in specific job-related statistical skills and tools can proceed. The relationship between human resource and statistical training is diagrammed in the interactive model described in Figure 4.1.

Key Terms

Management by objectives (MBO)
Planning–programming–budgeting system (PPBS)
Management by exception
Performance appraisal
Hardware subsystem
Software subsystem
Humanware subsystem
Cross-functional teams
Commitment to the customer
System improvement
Education and self-improvement
Constant improvement or *Kaizen*
Process orientation
Environment, free from fear
Team-based approach
Communication
Think systemically
Personal commitment
Quality in daily work (QIDW)
Formal groups
Informal groups
Self-actualization
Dual factor theory
Intrinsic
Extrinsic
Personal application assignments (PAAs)
Feedback
Performance appraisal

Notes

1. Portions of this chapter are adopted with permission from the creative work of Jose Eulogio Romero-Simpson, Department of Management, University of Miami. "Management: Introducing Quality Concepts in Advanced Organizational Behavior," unpublished paper, June 1990.

2. For a revealing and well-written account of the QI effort at Paul Revere, see: Patrick L. Townsend with Joan E. Gebhardt, *Commit to Quality* (New York: John Wiley and Sons, 1990).
3. The theoretical basis of this cooperative team-based approach is derived from three sources: Deming's Points 5 and 9, which call for management to continually work to improve systems by optimizing the efforts of teams, groups, and staff areas toward the aims and purposes of the organization; Ishikawa's observation of the need to establish a structure for cross-functional management to achieve companywide quality control; and Juran's emphasis on fitness-for-use criteria used to identify and achieve customer-defined expectations.

----------▼----------

Case Study 4.1: Los Alamos National Bank

Established in 1963, Los Alamos National Bank (LANB) is the largest independent bank in New Mexico. LANB is owned and operated by Trinity Capital Corp., a one-bank holding company. With assets of $700 million, LANB has 184 employees and branches in Los Alamos, White Rock, and Santa Fe. It offers Internet-accessible banking services, which, as of 2000, were offered by only 5 percent of community banks.

LANB provides a full range of financial services to consumer, commercial, and government markets in northern New Mexico. LANB was created originally to address the banking needs of its unique namesake community, created to house what is now known as the Los Alamos National Laboratory, site of the Manhattan Project during World War II. The bank has become an integral component of the community. Nearly 80 percent of Los Alamos' 18,000 residents use LANB's financial services. Two thirds of the residents consider LANB to be their primary bank, and 30 percent of all customers use five or more services, as compared with the national average of 6 percent for all banks. The business takes great pride in its designation as a community bank. Nearly every dollar deposited with LANB is loaned to borrowers in the local community. Community commitment was greatly in evidence during the spring of 2000, when fire ravaged over 48,000 acres and destroyed 280 homes in the region. The bank offered zero-interest loans to anyone affected by the fire, suspended loan payments on burned homes, doubled the limit on withdrawals from automated teller machines, and took other extraordinary measures to help the community overcome the crisis.

High on Service, Low on Cost

In an era of banking mergers and acquisitions, LANB capitalizes on the advantages earned by successful homegrown businesses. As a locally owned and operated financial institution, it strives to be more customer driven than its competitors. It is organized to identify customer needs more readily and more accurately and, then, to respond more quickly and more satisfactorily. Success translates into more loyal customers who are more willing to use LANB products and services and to refer new business.

In its chosen markets, LANB has positioned itself to be a low-cost, full-service provider. For example, service charges generate less than an eighth of annual income, as compared to about a third for regional and national banks. Yet, LANB offers rates of interest on deposits that match or exceed those offered by competitors, and the rates it charges for loans typically are among the lowest — if not the lowest — in the market. Consequently, LANB's net interest margin (NIM), which is the spread between the interest rate paid on deposits and the rate charged for loans, is significantly narrower than that of most other banks. This, in turn, leaves LANB with smaller margins for errors in operational performance or business judgment.

By holding down administrative costs, the bank's highly efficient workforce more than counterbalances this potential vulnerability. On average, one LANB employee services more than $6 million in assets, which is more than twice the banking industry average. As a result, overhead expenses average 50 percent of income, a rate that ranks among the best in the industry. Effective management of its NIM and overhead expenses has enabled LANB to deliver solid returns to shareholders, while foregoing ATM fees and holding other service fees to a minimum.

Emphasis on Empowerment, Innovation, and Flexibility

Senior leaders set the bank's long-term strategic direction and annual corporate objectives, following detailed analyses of leading and lagging indicators of trends in the economy, markets, customer behavior, technology, employee skills, supplier capabilities, and other key factors. At the departmental level, planning becomes an organizationwide activity, involving all personnel. Corporate objectives are accomplished through action plans that often transcend several departments. These action plans, totaling about 90 in the year 2000, are converted into individual work goals for all employees, about a third of whom participate on long- or short-term teams.

This last step in plan development and deployment — implementation at the level of the individual worker — has been refined considerably since the mid-1990s. That is when employee survey results revealed that workers did not understand their role in the strategic direction of the bank. Under the leadership of LANB's Quality Council, which has members from every area and level of the company, the performance appraisal system was redesigned to magnify the direct link between job performance and corporate performance.

The form used for this system lists corporate goals, departmental objectives, and the annual and long-term goals of the employee, which he or she writes in consultation with a supervisor. Employees also complete a personal self-assessment of their strengths and of opportunities to improve their customer-service skills and technical competence. Once they complete the annual appraisal process, employees have a complete snapshot of what they must do to perform at a high level and to earn the attendant incentives and rewards, which includes profit sharing and employee stock ownership. Such incentive payouts average over 21 percent of an employee's annual salary.

Employee empowerment is vital to accomplishing LANB's goals for performance improvement and double-digit growth in annual income. Management consciously acts to distribute leadership responsibilities throughout the organization. In fact, over 90 percent of LANB's employees received leadership training in 1999, as compared to 8 percent of bank employees nationally. Employees are expected to create value for customers, and they are given the authority and resources to act proactively and decisively. For example, all workers have the authority to resolve complaints on the spot. Also, high lending limits and flexible underwriting standards enable loan officers to respond innovatively to loan applicants with special circumstances. Yet, LANB's charge-offs for loan losses (measured as a percentage of average assets) have been declining since 1997, to about one third the average percentage for local competitors and less than half the percentage for a national bank that LANB benchmarks.

Leveraging Technology

After a skilled, customer-focused workforce, LANB ranks technology as vital to executing its strategy of providing low-cost service, achieving high levels of customer satisfaction and loyalty, and, in the process, sustaining above-average profitability. It credits its client/server information network and relational database system with enabling the speed, dexterity, and analytical insight needed to manage risks and to respond rapidly to changing customer requirements and emerging market opportunities. LANB also uses a comprehensive simulation model to help it forecast the consequences of different business strategies.

LANB was quick to embrace the Internet and to provide online banking services, which have been received enthusiastically by customers. Introduced in March 1999, the service was being used by more than 6000 LANB customers as of the end of 2000. While on the lookout for new technology that will help it distinguish itself from the competition, LANB often offers to "test-drive" its suppliers' new hardware and software offerings while they are being developed. These collaborations help LANB evaluate how well new technology can be adapted to help it meet anticipated customer needs and future business goals.

Highlights

- In its most recent survey, 80 percent of LANB customers said they were "very satisfied" with the service they received — considerably better than the levels achieved by its primary competitors and the national average of 55 percent for all banks.
- Returns on key financial indicators exceed that of local competitors and the national average. For example, the bank's net income has increased by more than 60 percent over the last five years, and earnings per share increased from $1.20 to nearly $2.00.
- For the past three years, employee satisfaction levels have been well above those of other banks its size in five of eight key indicators of employee satisfaction.
- In 1999, LANB received New Mexico's highest quality award, the Zia. In 1996, *Inc.* magazine named LANB one of the 26 "Banks We Love," for its service to small businesses, and in 1995, *Money* magazine named LANB the best bank in New Mexico.

Source: Baldrige National Quality Program, National Institute of Standards and Technology, U.S. Department of Commerce; Web site: www.baldrige.nist.gov.

▲

▼

Case Study 4.2: The Ritz-Carlton
Hotel Company, Service Category

The only two-time recipient of the Malcolm Baldrige National Quality Award in the service category, the Ritz-Carlton Hotel Company manages 36 luxury hotels in North America, Europe, Asia, Australia, the Middle East, Africa, and the Caribbean. All have received four- or five-star ratings from the Mobil Travel Guide and diamond ratings from the American Automobile Association. The Ritz-Carlton competes against nearly 10 hotel groups in the "luxury" and "upscale, deluxe" categories in the industry. Sales totaled almost $1.5 billion in 1998, with services provided to meeting and event planners accounting for 40 percent of the total. Independent business and leisure travelers constitute the next largest customer segment. More than 85 percent of the company's 17,000 employees — known as "The Ladies and Gentlemen of The Ritz-Carlton" — are frontline workers in hotels. Through extensive training programs and by offering opportunities for professional development, the company encourages personnel to advance in the organization. An independently operated division of Marriott International, Inc., since 1997, the 16-year-old company is headquartered in Atlanta.

Highlights

- In an independent survey, 99 percent of guests said they were satisfied with their overall experience; more than 80 percent were "extremely satisfied."
- Any employee can spend up to $2,000 to immediately correct a problem or handle a complaint. First-year managers and employees receive 250 to 310 hours of training.
- Pretax return on investment and earnings (before income taxes, depreciation, and amortization) nearly doubled since 1995.
- From a field of 3528 nominees, it was selected "Overall Best Practices Champion" — in a 1998 study by the Cornell School of Hotel Administration and McGill University.

"To be the Premier Provider ..."

Winning the 1992 Baldrige award was both an acknowledgment that the Ritz-Carlton was an exemplary performer in the pursuit of excellence and an impetus for further improvement. Company management raised the threshold throughout the organization. Goals for customer satisfaction were raised to the "top of the box." Earning ratings of "very or extremely satisfied" became a top priority as well as a key element of the Ritz-Carlton strategy to achieve 100-percent customer loyalty. In its operations, the company set a target of "defect-free" experiences for guests, implementing a measurement system to chart progress toward elimination of all customer problems, no matter how minor. Management took action to realize other major opportunities for improvement. It revamped its strategic planning process to make it more systematic, and it refined its Total Quality Management (TQM) system, with the aim of achieving fuller and deeper integration into the organization. One result of this reassessment is the *Greenbook*. Now in its second edition, the *Greenbook* is the Ritz-Carlton handbook of quality processes and tools, a nearly constant reference that is distributed to all employees. Efforts to reduce employee turnover and to address employee morale issues — challenges faced by the entire hotel industry — also were undertaken. For example, hiring and selection processes were refined and streamlined, and a new initiative — "Pride and Joy" — gave employees a larger role in the design of their jobs. Turnover rates have declined nine years in a row and levels of employee satisfaction are trending upward.

Pyramid Concept

To help set a clear direction for continuous improvement and to align actions at all business and operational levels, the Ritz-Carlton has developed its pyramid concept. Positioned at the top is the company's mission: To be the premier worldwide provider of luxury travel and hospitality products and services. Succeeding levels consist of the Ritz-Carlton ten-year mission (product and profit dominance), five-year mission (broken down into fourteen "vital few objectives"), tactics for improving key processes, and strategies and action plans for sharpening customer and market focus. These tiers are underlaid by the company's TQM system and methods.

Finally, the Ritz-Carlton values and philosophy make up the base of the pyramid, serving as the foundation for all continuous improvement efforts. The company goes to great lengths to instill and reinforce the philosophy and values in all employees. Everyone receives a wallet-sized copy of the "Gold Standards," which consist of the company's motto, credo, employee promise, the Three Steps of Service, and the Ritz-Carlton Basics — essentially a listing of performance expectations and the protocol for interacting with customers and responding to their needs. These are reinforced in training (which totals 250 hours for first-year frontline employees), in the daily 5- to 10-minute briefing at the start of every shift, and through the company's reward and recognition system.

A new pyramid is developed every year during strategic planning. To set the stage, an extensive macro-environment analysis is performed and the results are distributed to senior leaders well before the first strategic planning session. The analysis considers factors ranging from the world economic outlook and global supply of hotel rooms to the actions of key competitors and from indicators of customer and employee satisfaction to supplier relations. A key output of the planning process that follows are the "vital few objectives" for the next three years. These are organized into categories corresponding to strategic goals, such as 100-percent customer retention, or to an organizational unit, such as new product development. Appropriate performance measures are identified for all objectives, and senior managers are assigned responsibility for ensuring the quality and reliability of data used for tracking them.

Understanding Customers in Detail

At every level, the Ritz-Carlton is detail oriented. Steps for all quality-improvement and problem-solving procedures are documented, methods of data collection and analysis are reviewed by third-party experts, and standards are established for all processes. Key processes also are dissected to identify points at which errors may occur. For example, to meet its goal of total elimination of problems, the Ritz-Carlton has determined that there are 970 potential instances for a problem to arise during interactions with overnight guests and 1,071 such instances during interactions with meeting event planners.

To cultivate customer loyalty, the Ritz-Carlton has instituted an approach of "customer customization," which relies on extensive data gathering and capitalizes on the capabilities of advanced information technology. Information gathered during various types of customer contacts, such as responses to service requests by overnight guests or post-event reviews conducted with meeting planners, are systematically entered into a database, which holds almost a million files. Accessible to all Ritz-Carlton hotels worldwide, the database enables hotel staff to anticipate the needs of returning guests and to initiate steps that will help to ensure a high-quality experience.

This attention to detail and the company's commitment to continuous improvement is delivering benefits. For example, in 1998, more than 80 percent of meeting planners reported that they were extremely satisfied with their overall experience — up from fewer than 70 percent a year earlier — and 99 percent said they were satisfied. Among overnight guests questioned in an independent survey, nearly 75 percent reported extreme satisfaction with their overall experience at the Ritz-Carlton, as compared with fewer than 70 percent for the nearest competitor's guests.

Financial performance also is trending upward. Total fees; earnings before income taxes, depreciation and amortization; and pretax return on investment have nearly doubled since 1995, with return on investment increasing from 5.3 percent in 1995 to 9.8 percent in 1998. Revenue per available room (the industry's measure of market share) continues to grow, exceeding the industry average by more than 300 percent.

Source: Baldrige National Quality Program, National Institute of Standards and Technology, U.S. Department of Commerce; Web site: www.baldrige.nist.gov.

▬▬▬▬▬▬▬▬▬▬▬▬▬▬▲▬▬▬▬▬▬▬▬▬▬▬▬▬▬

Chapter 5

Monitoring Process, Costs, Quality, and Productivity

Assuming new organizational relationships between management and labor, individuals and teams, and suppliers and customers while consistently delivering services at performance levels above customers' expectations and organizational quality requirements is challenging — even for the most experienced and best-trained managers under the most favorable market conditions. Long-term success requires the assumption of new (and often unfamiliar) roles, creating opportunities for genuine employee empowerment, as well as measurement and control of critical processes. Increasingly, these relationships need to be maintained across thousands of miles in different cultures and with workers speaking different languages.

Measuring and Adding Value to Processes

Evidence of improved service quality must be demonstrated with objective measures that are comparable, fact based, and consistent with the methods used by other providers. This, in turn, requires the design (or redesign) of internal management systems capable of setting quality standards, defining customer requirements, monitoring them accurately, and providing continuous statistical feedback and control to eliminate the underlying causes and costs of poor quality. The losses associated with not knowing how many resources are wasted as a result of poor-quality practices vary among different types of service providers. Some losses are inevitable, but most are system caused. They occur because of differences in the complexity of services provided, the sophistication of the technology used, and the reliability of performance-monitoring systems. Nonetheless, it is nearly impossible to add value to processes without controlling the costs of poor quality. Value-added processes are changes that increase the value of a product or service to customers without additional production costs.

As previously mentioned, the addition of value-added processes or the elimination of non-value-added (poor-quality) costs are heavily influenced by the training of human sensors who act as system monitors. To detect problems and prevent them from worsening, human sensors perform the vital early warning function. Not unlike highly sensitive instruments, the measurement characteristics they monitor must be precise, valid, and reliable — easily understood by those who must perform critical tasks within tolerable limits of bias, error, and precision. As shown in Case Study 5.1, the bank teller's refusal to validate a shabby customer's parking ticket shows how poorly trained monitors can impose extreme costs on service organizations. In this case, the bank lost $2,000,000 as a result of one employee's failure to validate a customer's parking ticket.

The customer's goal can be something as simple as getting a parking ticket stamped or as complex as having an automobile repaired. The degree of complexity in no way diminishes the importance of monitoring results. On the contrary, everyone's attention should be focused on the process improvement necessary to satisfy customer needs. Monitoring progress requires a team focus — as opposed to an individual focus — and ends with the application of appropriate statistical tools and techniques to reduce variation and eliminate non-value-added costs. The objective of statistical analysis is to make decisions about a process under conditions of uncertainty and imperfect information. Statistical analysis plays an important role, especially for airports, banks, financial institutions, hospitals, schools, and governments, where intensive customer contacts and large paper flows are involved. This, in turn, leads to lower costs, increased quality, and productivity gains. Case Study 5.2 describes how BNQA winner Dana Commercial Credit Corporation adds value to customer services by carefully monitoring systems with the use of customer expectation scorecards.

The service quality revolution is accelerating process improvement within all types of organizations. Understanding of processes as a means of transforming knowledge and responding to customers faster than the competition is at the heart of total quality service (TQS). Reducing even a small portion of the generally accepted 20 to 30 percent non-value-added waste and unnecessary expenses present in most organizations can generate enormous and immediate benefits. Prevention and control of variation is stressed because operational systems in all types of service industries are highly complex and variable. Although statistical process control (SPC) techniques can be applied to reduce variation and improve service quality, special care must be taken to first identify and then monitor valid customer measures. Although process improvement is a transformational activity involving teams, workgroups, and systems focusing on customers, what is evaluated under a TQS model are the *quality characteristics* of the unique process. Valid customer requirements are often referred to as quality characteristics of the product or service being measured. Quality characteristics are attributes of a process or service deemed important enough to warrant some control. By analyzing and understanding the distributions of these factors, entire processes can be studied and better understood.[1]

Valid customer characteristics are operational definitions or operational measures of what is needed to fulfill customer requirements. These measures are usually well known by the recipients — end users or external customers (who receive the finished goods or services). Opinions of the end users, or those who receive a service produced by work units, are critical in evaluating the performance of each unit. For example, operational measures could include the number of units sold per month, budgetary figures, or complaint rates per number of customers. In addition to the traditional measurement elements (specification, test, and criterion) definitions must also be SMART: (specific, measurable, accountable, realistic, and team based). All services need to improve to stay in business, but it is the rate of process improvement that increasingly separates high performers from adequate providers. Not only must the criteria for operational measures capture essential elements of customer-defined quality, but they must also be accurate, on time, reliable, and meet the technical standards for survey methodology. For an example of one research firm's methodology for measuring results, see Case Study 5.3.

In the global economy, the speed at which organizations eliminate non-value-added costs and improve processes increasingly determines the winners and the losers. When responding to valid customer demands, firms must develop accurate internal and external measures of performance. Often overlooked in a service environment are the needs of internal customers who receive a (partially finished) product or service (e.g., forms, data, or orders) produced by another work unit within the organization. The rate of process improvement can also be accelerated by organizing quality control circles, workgroups, or self-managed work teams and training them in the use of problem analysis tools. These groups may be formed as needed to resolve specific problems. A quality improvement (QI) "swat team" is a project team of line employees and technical support staff formed to study and solve a specific problem and then disband. These activities only work when there is already a companywide commitment to quality, when the circle includes a customer (i.e., a recipient of the output from the last process), and when the group is assigned problems rather than left free to select its own topics for study.

In a TQS environment, everyone either already owns or is working toward becoming an owner of a process or set of processes. Generally, the greater the number of processes under one's supervision, the higher the level of responsibility and compensation. The challenge of leadership for TQS (Chapter 10) is to direct these activities without interfering with the teams' enthusiasm to define problems and resolve them at the point of origin.

In theory, empowered frontline employees earn the authority to make decisions within prescribed limits at the point of customer contact by focusing on customer service, performance, productivity, and results. This encourages more accountability to customers (i.e., citizens, users, or recipients) as well as supervisors in the organizational hierarchy. Such a transformation in thinking can be very difficult for some managers in certain types of public service organizations, especially regulatory officials (e.g., in law enforcement, tax collection, and building and zoning code enforcement) who are committed to a top–down hierarchy and believe that they are exempt from such empowerment because of the evaluative judgments they exercise over their "customers."[2] Empowerment does present unique challenges for "unreinvented" public agencies, especially among intelligence, law enforcement, and regulatory compliance officials who are typically in conflict with many of their "customers" and may require close supervision of frontline employees to avoid corruption, liability problems, and potential conflicts of interest (Brehm and Gates, 1997; Pegnato, 1997). Far more empirical and theoretical work needs to be done in this area to guide elected and appointed public officials in establishing process control techniques to empower internal customers in their service quality and performance management efforts (Milakovich, 2003; Sureshchandar et al., 2001).

Understanding Process Variation and Control Techniques

What is a process? Simply put, a process is a transformation of inputs (such as materials, manpower, and equipment) into outputs that meet or exceed customer quality requirements. Process-oriented managers are constantly seeking better ways to control and improve the quality of goods and services provided to customers. They are continually seeking methods and tools to stabilize processes that, in time, improve a system composed of many interconnected processes. In this way, organizations, similar to individuals, learn to adapt to their environments and change as necessary to learn, grow, and survive (Senge, 1990). All modern QI theories stress a process or systems focus to manage knowledge. Operational processes are complex because they are composed of interrelated elements that interact in a nonlinear fashion to determine the performance of organizational subunits and systems.

SPC techniques have been used in manufacturing for decades. The classic study of modern methods of quality and reliability was published by Walter Shewhart (1931) and identified the seven common elements that constitute a process: (1) Materials (raw materials or components), (2) manpower or personnel (the human factor), (3) methods (product and process design), (4) machines (tools and equipment necessary for processing), (5) measurement (techniques and tools used to gather data on process performance), (6) maintenance (providing care for process variables), and (7) management (policy, work rules, and environment). Understanding how these elements interact is the key to improving processes. All organizational processes may be viewed as unique sets or groupings of elements from the seven M's. Financial management processes, for example, are a series of repetitive operations that are performed under conditions presumed to be identical for each operation. Ordering laboratory tests in a hospital, processing requests for parking vouchers, underwriting an insurance policy, or grading student papers are unique because they impact just one individual. Yet, all still involve processes that do not change wherever the provider is located. Figure 5.1 illustrates a basic transformation process.

Although all processes transform inputs (the seven M's) into outputs (results), applications within different services vary greatly. Processes exist in administrative systems, sales, employee training, and personnel and buyer–seller relations. Processes vary in the volume of transactions and the speed at which information (throughput) is available to the next customer. Validating parking tickets or check cashing, for example, involves millions of separate processes each hour where the potential for error is extreme. Diagnosis of a medical problem, giving legal advice, or grading student papers, by contrast, are labor intensive and customized activities. The relatively distinct process of filling out an insurance claim for a disaster victim is less prone to error, however, but no less complicated. Thus, although inputs, speed of processing, and volume differ, the common elements of each process for several types of transactions can

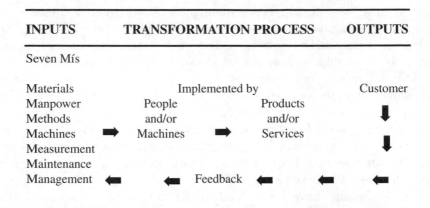

Figure 5.1 Transformation process: from inputs to outputs.

be identical for various service providers. This provides the theoretical basis for benchmarking of processes (Chapter 2) among different service delivery organizations.

All quality characteristics used to monitor processes exhibit a certain amount of variation. For example, in getting to work on time, various predictable and unpredictable factors such as your alarm clock, car's battery, traffic, road conditions, and the weather influence when (or if) you leave and whether you arrive on time. Therefore, efforts to improve processes must aim first at reduction of controllable variation within preset or known limits (e.g., if your car is slow to start, have the battery checked; if it is raining, leave home a few minutes early). These are relatively predictable causes of variation. Two types of variation occur in all processes: *common* (random, but predictable) and *special* (less predictable) variation. It is vital to distinguish between the two, because the appropriate action in response to each type of variation is quite different.

Variation Due to Common and Special Causes

This category of variation is inherent in any process and is caused by minute changes in one of the seven M's: raw materials, worker behavior, calibration of machines, design products, and so on. Common variation results from the inability of any process to repeat itself with the same precision on each successive output unit. Common variation exists even when processes are "in statistical control" because small fluctuations in a process are difficult to detect and remove. Common variation arises from so many sources that even if some of the sources were found and eliminated, the overall impact would be negligible. Common variation may be due to a specific component of a machine, defective material, or a definable local condition. It has been estimated that about 85 percent of all internal fluctuations stem from common variation, whereas the remaining 15 percent are caused by special variation. When operating with all common causes of variation within upper and lower specification levels, processes are said to be in a "state of statistical control" or merely "in control."

Special (random) variation results from some specific fault or malfunction that occurs outside the upper or lower limits of a process. Random causes may affect systems and processes at any time. For example, even if you leave early to get to work on time, the weather or an accident on the highway may still cause you to be late for work. The discovery and removal of special causes is the responsibility of those closest to the source, usually line workers. They should be concerned whether special causes develop gradually over time, or whether the changes are abrupt and infrequent. Various techniques such as run charts and control charts (described below) are useful for this purpose.

Process improvement is primarily concerned with managing special variation. A broad set of problem-solving and decision-making tools is used to identify process improvement opportunities. When common variation is distinguished from special causes of process variation, then management can stop blaming employees and focus on the elimination of quality problems through organizational change and the application of SPC methods.

Statistical Process Control

Walter Shewhart's SPC model helps managers control the quality of output in any process and respond appropriately to different types of variation. As mentioned earlier, an important component of the SPC model is a monitor, who determines whether or not a process is stable or out of control. The monitor distinguishes between the many small, random fluctuations that perturb the process (but do not affect output) and the relatively large or unexpected causes of variation that could affect system operations. Something can and must be done about special causes because they are unwanted and identifiable. The SPC model establishes a procedure for monitoring processes and removing common or assignable causes of variation, such as tellers deciding whether or not to validate parking slips based on how a customer is dressed.

At the same time, it could be equally harmful to confuse the two types of variation. The monitor, who may be a receptionist, police officer, salesperson or a bank teller uses SPC methodology to observe that something seems to be changing, a process that is no longer following an established (stable) pattern. When properly trained, the monitor can recognize which type of variation exists. Once identified, common causes can be reduced and special causes can be removed or anticipated.

It is vital that customer-contact personnel distinguish between the two types (or causes) of process variation and recognize the difference. Management must guide workers in eliminating both causes of variation. In the example given at the beginning of this chapter, the errant bank teller and the manager should have known that all requests for parking validation should be honored (a common variation), regardless of the demeanor of the customer. Instead, the teller and the manager treated the customer differently, as a special case needing differential treatment. If they had acted properly, the bank would be financially healthier today.

Process-monitoring techniques include flowcharts, cause–effect diagrams, run charts, check sheets, Pareto analysis, and histograms and scatter diagrams. The process flowchart identifies how a service is delivered so that each step may be analyzed as a possible cause of error. The cause–effect or fishbone chart displays a main quality characteristic as the spine bone on a drawing resembling a fish's skeleton. The chart focuses attention on the sources of defects, which may then be plotted on run charts or check sheets to isolate unusual or out-of-control factors. The scatter diagram correlates changes in process inputs and shows whether a relationship exists between two or more process characteristics. Using team problem identification and resolution techniques, these seven basic tools provide the process monitoring necessary to instill an attitude of TQS in each owner. Less attention is paid to statistics in this section because the subject is highly technical and requires specialized training.

Six Sigma

For the last decade, several U.S. corporations have refocused their internal quality management efforts to reduce defects and increase customer satisfaction. *Six Sigma* is a nearly zero-defect rate first championed by another BNQA winner, Motorola, which set a process failure rate of 3.4 defects per million as a corporate slogan and quality goal. Six Sigma is more than a numerical objective — it is a process-outcome goal that has been adopted by several leading manufacturers, including General Electric (GE), Raytheon, Citibank, and Kodak, among others. The basis concept is to create a cadre of internal consultants ("black belts") to redesign work processes (Blakeslee, 1999; Fontenot et al., 1994; Gitlow and Levine, 2005). Caterpillar Financial Services (see Case Study 5.4) also adopted Six Sigma and its efforts have led to significant productivity improvements.

Reducing the Costs of Poor Quality

Anyone familiar with the day-to-day operations of any type of business or public agency knows the value of service quality, but many still think of the concept in abstract, subjective, and vague terms. Some still believe that quality, similar to beauty or affection, is "in the eyes of the beholder" and cannot be precisely quantified. Especially in the minds of budget or financial officers, costs, revenue and "hard" productivity measures, rather than quality indicators, tend to be more immediate "drivers" for many organizations. So long as quality is defined in "softer," less quantitative terms, integrated process-focused TQS systems are less likely to be regarded on equal terms with financial measures.

For most firms struggling to stay ahead in a competitive market, subjective measures have nothing to do with the harsh realities of the bottom line, traditionally defined as profits or losses. Costs may be more tangible, but not necessarily more accurate, indicators of an organization's fixed expenses, growth potential, or total productivity. Most concerned managers also acknowledge that the value of any business is more than that represented on a financial statement or an organizational chart: human resources interact with complex processes, subject to cost restraints, to form interdependent networks of people, materials, methods, and equipment to support common purposes and mission. Thus, many of the most costly determinants of low productivity are hidden below the surface (Figure 5.2) and inaccessible to most financial management systems.

Most managers admit, at least privately, that they lack a thorough understanding of the losses incurred as a result of poor-quality practices. The "hard numbers" approach prevails because the total costs of inputs labor average workload per capita, and value of outputs can be more accurately estimated for each work unit. Implementing TQS can substantially reduce the costs of poor quality by eliminating non-value-added expenses. Thus, making the transition to a quality-managed, cost-effective, and continuously improving service culture requires an understanding of the complex interaction between costs, quality, and productivity.

Cost of poor quality analysis is a financial accounting methodology for estimating how much an organization spends, as a proportion of either total sales or gross income, in direct and indirect losses incurred for non-value-added activities. These activities include: excess paperwork and documentation, correction of defective outputs, inspection, and risk management. Direct and indirect losses may be due to liability costs for defective products or services, lawsuits, litigation insurance and retainers, customer allowances, warranty and guarantee costs, low employee productivity, absenteeism, stress-related health insurance costs, and lost sales or discounting to clear excess inventories. Non-value-added costs are all

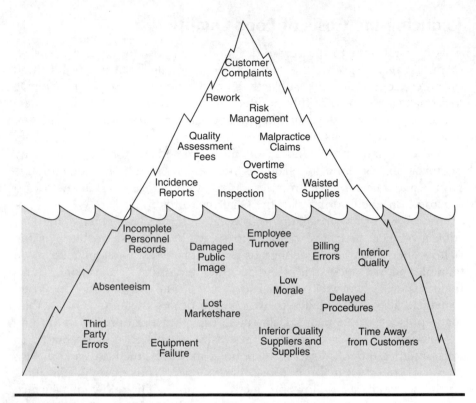

Figure 5.2 Visible and hidden poor-quality costs.

expenses for processes that can be eliminated without loss of value in delivering the final product or service to the customer.

The costs generally associated with poor-quality practices have been used in the past to establish manufacturing guarantees and warranty charges. Rather than adding value or continuously improving processes, a service contract or warranty is a potential future expense that "covers" the customer (and producer) against excess costs of repairs. Because customers pay for service calls and most warranties are time-dated or "capped," the potential future risks to manufacturers are limited. Although useful in marketing, they provide less incentive for providers to continuously improve process quality, and make the guarantee unnecessary in the first place.

As with their counterparts in manufacturing, managers of service firms recognize that errors made continuously throughout the assembly process require substantial and costly rework to correct. In healthcare, for example, the cost of administrative errors, increasing malpractice insurance premiums, and duplicate inspections are all expensive consequences of poor process control, which may require costly and unnecessary rework. For special causes of variation that can result in a malpractice suit against a hospital, the costs of legal fees and documentation alone could far exceed the insurance reserves set aside for such a contingency. Rather than issuing a warranty, it would be far less expensive to prevent the occurrence from happening in the first place. It is very difficult, however, to train service workers to think in such "preventive" terms.

As mentioned earlier, when business is good, there are fewer incentives to measure the costs of poor quality and to take action to eliminate the need for rework. Thus, expanding revenues usually covers the hidden losses attributable to poor underlying process quality — when you are making money, who cares how, just make more! Thus, it may appear to be the less costly option, in the short term, to bury the causes of poor-quality processes in obscure accounting systems or to ignore quality problems altogether by denying that they exist.

Quality costs are influenced not only by the training and motivation of employees but by the perception of service quality by customers and the sensitivity of management systems used to monitor progress. In addressing these behavioral quality measurement issues, the essential differences between manufacturing and service quality control are almost negligible, because most manufacturing companies also compete for business by defining after-sales service as one of their primary products.

Measuring Poor Quality: Getting Below the Surface

To use quality as a strategic management tool, managers must first acknowledge the existence of visible (above the surface) and hidden (submerged) problems contributing to poor quality (Figure 5.2). Next, measurement systems must be designed to accurately translate these costs, establish measurement characteristics for each quality function, and designate and carefully train "sensors" to monitor progress. This recognition phase precedes the design and implementation phases and must involve the entire organization in the critical task of identifying which of the system characteristics that are not presently being monitored must be measured. Critical, but less quantifiable factors such as relationships between headquarters, suppliers, and ancillary service staff often erode beneath the surface as well. Managers must strive to go below the "tip of the iceberg" to accurately diagnose the impact of hidden costs on the financial health of the organization.

To more accurately assess the impact of ignoring poor-quality costs, Philip Crosby developed the "Eternally Successful Organization Grid" (Appendix A), which illustrates the impact of poor-quality costs at various stages within different types of organizations. His concept is based on variations in the level of understanding most managers have about the costs of poor quality. Organizations are classified as being at different stages of the quality spectrum ranging from total uncertainty to absolute certainty. Most services are at the first stages of the quality grid (uncertainty), where there is little comprehension of quality as a management tool, the costs of poor quality are hidden, quality measures do not exist, and problems are resolved as they occur or their existence is denied in the first place. The ultimate objective of initiating a TQS planning and management control system is to reduce poor-quality costs, perhaps not to zero, but at least below the 5 percent level.

To some extent, these problems are common to all organizations that focus only on profits and losses as measures of well-being. Nearly all professional organizations, for instance, initially deny the existence of quality problems or define quality narrowly in technical terms as conformance to accepted professional standards. For purposes of understanding the relationship between costs, quality, and productivity, the costs of quality can be conceptually divided into two areas: (1) the price of nonconformance and (2) the price of conformance.

The price of nonconformance includes all the expenses accrued because of doing things wrong, often repeatedly, for long periods of time. Healthcare service examples run the full gamut of routine activities from corrections of incomplete purchase orders to scheduling and laboratory errors to the need to keypunch orders for the second or third time, to the more time-consuming and damaging liability costs and subsequent litigation incurred as a result of administering the wrong medication to a patient.[3] Joseph M. Juran (1988) offers a chilling example of the possible consequences of not having a quality-monitoring system to discover such problems in a hospital:

> For years the hospital industry had only the vaguest idea of the extent of errors in the process of giving medication to patients. All hospitals posted rules requiring nurses to report medication errors promptly ... however, in many hospitals the nurses had learned that when they made such reports they were often subjected to unwarranted blame. Hence they stopped making such reports. In due course a classic study made by a qualified outsider showed that: (1) about 7 percent of the medications involved errors, some quite serious, and (2) the bulk of the errors were management-controllable, not worker-controllable. (Joseph M. Juran, 1988, p. 95).

The price of conformance is what it would cost to do things right in the first place; examples of this include most professional quality assurance functions, education and training, all prevention efforts, and actions taken to improve supervisory skills. In an organization with a reasonably high degree of certainty about its quality costs, these expenses represent between 10 to 15 percent of total expenses. Previously discussed tools and techniques such as Pareto analysis, control charts, quality control circles, brainstorming in team sessions, and surveys of internal and external customers are useful in identifying and reducing these non-value-added costs. It is important to employ these techniques and collect appropriate data so that the organization will have baseline information for determining where the most effective and least costly opportunities for preventive action exist.

Controlling Direct and Indirect Quality Costs

To measure the total losses due to poor quality, organizations must further analyze the costs that go into the efforts to repair defective work. In general terms, these quality losses can be broken down into direct and indirect costs. Direct quality costs can be broken down further into: (1) controllable quality costs, which include prevention and appraisal costs, and (2) resultant costs, which include internal and external error costs (Harrington, 1987). Controllable (or assignable) quality costs are those over which management has direct control to ensure that only prescribed services are delivered to customers and that it is done in an acceptable manner. They can be either prevention costs necessary to help an employee do the job correctly every time, or appraisal costs expended to determine if a standardized activity was done properly every time. Typical prevention costs are those incurred for developing and implementing a data collection and reporting system, quality-related training, specialty training, vendor surveys, packaging inspections at the shipping-receiving docks, and for preparation and documentation for outside inspections.

Probably the most effective way any organization can spend its limited resources is to invest in preventive actions. Unfortunately, most facilities neglect these investments because: (1) they are time consuming and (2) the expense, as opposed to equipment or personnel costs, is often considered by budget and financial officers to be too difficult to tie to a tangible return on investment (ROI). Consistent with the example cited earlier regarding a malpractice lawsuit, the rewards of prevention could far exceed the cost of paying for errors. With effort, quality characteristics can be developed to complement financial and personnel measures. The underlying problem is generally not lack of technical competence, but too much concern about visible numbers and not enough attention to customer service quality.

Appraisal costs are an example of rework expended to determine if an activity was done right every time. These include outside audits, financial reports, approval signatures on various interdepartmental documents, outside endorsements (such as those from underwriters' laboratories), maintenance and calibration of laboratory instruments, inspection of equipment, payload audits, and proofreading letters and memos. One reason appraisal costs are necessary is that management is often not 100-percent confident that the money and time already expended in prevention costs has eliminated the possibility of error. Similar to inspections, appraisal costs tend to be wasteful and are an example of too little too late. Often, they reflect a poor understanding of basic system processes, yet are necessary as an inspection measure to prevent further waste of resources. They do little to identify and eliminate the causes of errors or to prevent them from recurring.

The resultant costs of poor quality make up a second broad category of direct costs and include all of the expenses that result from errors and all of the money spent because activities were not done right every time. These costs are called resultant because they are directly related to management decisions made in the controllable poor-quality category. They may be divided further into subcategories of internal and external error costs. Internal error costs are those that occur before a product or service is accepted by a customer. They occur because everyone did not do the job right every time. Internal error costs are preventable, under control of management, and include examples such as:

1. A customer's refusal to submit a completed application because it was neither explained properly nor done according to an acceptable schedule
2. Costs of accounts receivable due to the billing system not producing bills on time
3. Mistakes on documents or computer reruns
4. Returning to a construction work site for a second or third time because the previous work was not performed to the customer's satisfaction

External error costs are from outside sources due to poor-quality work done by insufficiently trained service personnel. The most familiar example is a malpractice suit; others are the loss of package delivery contracts and revenues due to poor financial analysis of proposals, late delivery of supplies, and poor record keeping. With the proper development of measurement characteristics, all the above costs could be incorporated into an integrated TQS monitoring system.

More difficult to measure, but equally important to monitor, are those indirect "below the surface" costs not directly measurable on a profit–loss ledger, yet attributable to lack of quality control. Most of the indirect costs of poor quality are related to customer dissatisfaction with employee behavior and the resultant erosion of market share because of dissatisfied customers who complain to their friends and relatives. Not having systems to monitor even relatively minor inconveniences at a critical time in a customer service encounter can create major problems. Law enforcement and other public service agencies must pay special attention to these indirect costs due to the extraordinary legal, financial, and social costs incurred when something goes wrong on the street.

Customers' evaluation of a service will reflect a combination of their expectations and their perception of the quality of service given by a provider. Regardless of the quality assurance systems in place, if service levels do not meet customer expectations, any facility can incur indirect hidden costs by losing customers to other providers. Dissatisfied ex-customers telling others about their negative experiences could create a negative "ripple effect" that is very difficult to counteract. Recall that reliable estimates of this negative ripple effect suggest that as many as ten potential customers, immediate family members or friends, can be influenced by a single negative evaluation. Worse still, as many as nine out of ten dissatisfied customers fail to complain to the offending provider, so there is no "voice of the customer" to alert management that a problem exists. This can devastate the reputations of small- or medium-sized facilities and dramatically reduce repeat visits. Because these word-of-mouth evaluations affect attitudes and the perceptions of total quality of the facility as a whole, loss of a good reputation affects all other goods and services as well.

Rather than waiting for and responding to complaints, customer dissatisfaction can be prevented by using process flow checklists or carefully designed surveys administered at appropriate intervals following delivery of service. Service providers find TQS attractive because it helps them to better understand the full range of customer needs. This can avoid the tendency to design customer service systems around the small portion of customers who do complain. At Toyota Motors, for instance, each time a customer brings a car in for service, a representative from the dealer will call the customer within 48 hr for an evaluation. Toyota personnel provide training in the latest theory and customer service techniques for customer service workers twice a month. Customers not only receive a phone call but are also mailed a detailed survey questionnaire to assess their satisfaction with the services received. This survey is mailed to the service center, not the dealer. Individual dealers and service advisors are evaluated by this independent monitoring. Toyota service representatives commit themselves verbally and in writing to fixing the problem, and if service was unsatisfactory, the customer is told to bring the car back for a loaner car or same-day service to complete the work. The standard is to complete the service on the same day.[4]

In summary, an accurate picture of the full benefits of total QI is the price of nonconformity, or the costs of continuing to do things wrong. As outlined above, these costs can be divided into various categories of prevention, appraisal, and failure to comply with standards, and may have either direct or indirect consequences on customer service evaluations. Measurement characteristics can be established to monitor the overall costs of quality and determine the current status of specific services or procedural compliance. These measures can be used initially to guide management to target areas for quality and productivity improvement. Refined systems may be used later for independent monitoring and improved implementation, and as visible proof and recognition of productivity improvement (Milakovich, 1991b).

Defining Improvement Opportunities and Raising the Productivity Ceiling

Productivity is a commonly used term that means many different things to different people. What does it mean to be productive? Simply put, productivity is a ratio measure of how much an organization makes, divided by how much it costs to make the goods or services it provides. The less it costs to produce the goods or service, the higher the productivity; the more it costs or the less efficiently it makes a product, the lower the productivity. Productivity can be raised by either lowering costs or increasing efficiency, or some combination of both approaches.

D. Scott Sink, Director of the Virginia Productivity Center, offers a seven-part productivity index that measures items such as the cost of quality, innovation, inventory, time to process a travel claim, and leadership (Sink, 1991). David Sumanth (1984) advocates the use of a total productivity model (TPM), which includes tangible output, human input, material input, and capital and energy costs, to measure productivity. In this chapter, productivity will be defined as the complex interaction among these and other factors, including:

- Efficiency (the ratio of outputs to inputs)
- Effectiveness (the effects of a job, task, or project on bottom-line profits, the local economy, society, or the environment)
- Cost containment or reduction in expenses

- Employee benefits, goodwill, and morale
- Growth of a work unit's power base or budget
- Ability to coordinate between work units
- Stability or equilibrium (minimization of worker and managerial absenteeism, stress, conflict, and turnover)

The objective of any productivity improvement strategy is to balance the resources available with the level of service needed to satisfy the valid requirements of all internal and external customers. Listening to both types of customers is equally important to improve productivity. The only difference between internal and external customers is that the former receive a product or service produced by another work unit within the same organization, whereas the latter receive a product or service produced by another organization. All organizations strive to meet the valid quality requirements of both types of customers, albeit differently. Recall that valid customer requirements are operational measures that reflect both the "voices of the process" (i.e., profit–loss statements, financial costs, overtime, health benefits, and fixed expenses) as well as the "voices of the customers" (i.e., sales, output, contracts, grievances, survey results, and customer needs or complaints). High-performance services strive to raise productivity levels to meet higher customer satisfaction standards with the same or fewer resources.

In any organization, there is a theoretical limit above which productivity cannot rise using established and well-defined systems, even under perfect conditions. In QI terms, such a system is predictable or "in control." Traditional productivity improvement tools alone cannot raise productivity above the productivity ceiling. However, when SPC and TQS tools and techniques are combined, the ceiling can be raised. TQS sets a higher ceiling where only 75 to 85 percent of the old level of inputs are necessary to produce 85 percent of the old level of workload, resulting in the following improvements: (1) a work unit can either reduce inputs or utilize excess inputs to expand operations or diversify, (2) the quality of daily work life is improved through a reduced workload, and (3) more of the workload is shifted from invisible to visible output done right the first time, so the output substantially increases.[5]

Merging Costs, Quality, and Productivity Definitions

Improving service processes requires successive cycles of identification, analysis, measurement, and performance evaluation and controlling for consistency (see Chapter 2, Figure 2.4). Ideally, these cycles should never end, although the amount of measurement may decrease over time as procedures for measuring consistency are standardized and the whole system improves. This results in less labor content, fewer defectives, better communication, and more efficient processing. Process measures and customer satisfaction indicators must be reliable and valid. The objective is to eliminate the non-value-added elements from a process. When a process is fully improved, only the essential or value-added elements remain.

Productivity improvement is a systematic strategy for increasing a work unit's ratio of inputs to outputs using some combination of the following: cost–benefit analysis, needs assessment, work redesign, process improvement, incentive systems, job enrichment, labor–management committees (less commonly called labor–management task forces), flextime, or quality control circles. The basic tools of statistical process and quality control, numerical goals set by those who have to meet them, new technology, organizational restructuring, interorganizational agreements (in both the private and public sectors) to pool resources, resource reallocation, employee retraining, and modification of perceptions, attitudes, and authority systems can also be used (Sedell, 1991). Some of these methods have been described or are self-explanatory; others are defined in the glossary.

When facing budgetary reductions, privatization, or increasing market competition, many service managers discover that the means listed in the previous paragraph are necessary but insufficient to achieve desired quality or productivity goals. When traditional tools prove insufficient, managers increasingly turn to extended versions of the tools. For example, quality control circles can be combined with CQI to demonstrate that everyone is responsible, including vendors, end users, and internal customers. Labor–management committees and task forces lend themselves to *gain sharing* (Chapter 2), or shared incentives for improvement. Groups of employees are eligible for bonuses or commissions determined by a sliding scale based on the amount of money saved or generated through cost-cutting or productivity-improving suggestions. When applied in one federal government agency, self-managed task forces were allowed to keep 50 percent of any savings generated from cost savings. It is important to creatively combine these tools to fit organizational cultures and meet local service delivery requirements.

Service managers increasingly recognize that quality of life issues, the interrelationship between employees and their families, and nonmonetary rewards affect recruiting, retention, morale, and productivity. Benefits such as flextime, parental leave, employee assistance plans (EAPs), and provision of care for elderly parents and children are becoming as important as statistical measurement of output to raise productivity. Many benefits costing very little on a per-employee basis, such as nonmonetary awards presented by a supervisor in front of an employee's peers, can raise productivity on a limited budget. Increasingly, managements in both the private and public service sectors have found it profitable to tailor benefit packages to the needs of their employees and thus to invest in long-term family care and other nonmonetary benefits as a means to improve work performance.

Productivity improvement systems that encompass these features are consistent with elements of both Total Quality Management (TQM)- and TQS-defined strategies that (1) attempt to prevent defects instead of catching them after they have been made, (2) employ true participatory management practices, (3) are oriented toward identifying and satisfying both internal and external customers, (4) drive out fear, and (5) establish pride of workmanship (Milakovich, 1990a). The first two components of this definition are considered to be state of the art in productivity improvement.

The other three components, however, have also increased productivity by eliminating non-value-added costs. For example, in terms of satisfying internal customers, if a form can be rearranged so that all of the data that unit X requires remains on the form, but unit Y's time to fill out the form is reduced, and there is no impact on the time that it takes unit X to process the form, then why not rearrange the form? If unit X requires information from unit Y about project 1, and the information is on two forms, why not merge the two forms into one? Does a certain project required by standard operating procedure still have a purpose or has its purpose been superseded by changing times? To add value to processes, a TQS manager asks: (1) Is there something he or she can do to reduce the receiver's time and cost that would cost the organization less if it were done upstream? and (2) Is there something that can be done to reduce the supplier's time and cost that would cost the organization less if it were done downstream? (Sedell, 1991).

Driving out fear is compatible with removing dissatisfiers (hygienic factors) such as those mentioned in the earlier discussion of Frederick Herzberg's dual factor theory. Removal of dissatisfiers does not in itself provide productivity incentives to the employees (Herzberg, 1966). However, the removal of dissatisfiers is as necessary as the provision of incentives to motivate employees; this second point is often either forgotten or overlooked by management. Applications in both the private and public sector in the United States, Canada, Japan, and Mexico have shown that there are alternatives to punishment-based Theory X management that not only increase productivity, but actually improve managerial control by preventing the time-consuming special causes that prompt angry phone calls from superiors or important customers.

The fifth component is to "establish pride of workmanship." William L. Ginnodo, Director of the American Productivity and Quality Center in Houston, Texas, offers a ten-point plan to establish pride of workmanship (Ginnodo, 1989). These points include:

1. Developing a mission statement and then strictly following the intent of the statement
2. Emphasizing continuous improvement
3. Employee involvement
4. Eliminating anything that keeps people from performing at their best
5. Measuring and sharing the results of comparisons between work units within the organization as well as the results of interorganizational comparisons
6. Gain-sharing, incentives, and recognition systems where rewards are presented to an employee by his or her supervisor in front of other employees (even if it is a symbolic reward such as an extra vacation day)
7. Identifying the issues to be addressed
8. Championing causes about which subordinates and staff will be enthusiastic
9. Starting small
10. Each manager should aim at getting employees (both under him or her and in other work units) to identify barriers to pride in workmanship and, where it would improve the manager's own work unit's productivity, help them to eliminate those barriers

To improve productivity and simultaneously reduce costs, needs assessment and process reengineering are done at the design and implementation stages, periodically, or both. The identification of fraud, waste, and abuse is done on an irregular basis. State-of-the-art productivity improvement efforts are ongoing processes conducted by every employee using participatory management, needs assessment, work redesign, and the identification of poor-quality costs. New technologies, organizational restructuring, and resource reallocation, where appropriate, are usually by-products of adopting QI even if they are not part of the original initiative.

Summary and Conclusions

Productivity improvement is generally defined as the systematic study of a work unit's output using some combination of TQC, SPC, and TQM concepts and tools. Understanding the costs of poor-quality practices is essential to integrating quality and productivity improvements as well as in raising the organization's productivity ceiling. Organizations are typically run on "hard" numbers such as costs and expenses, probably because there is less understanding of the actual losses from continued poor-quality practices.

There are almost as many definitions for productivity as there are those who seek to improve it. As a ratio of inputs to outputs, productivity is the complex interaction of efficiency, effectiveness, cost containment or reduction, employee goodwill and morale, growth of a work unit's power base and budget, ability to coordinate, and stability or equilibrium. SPC and TQS can work together to improve productivity.

Without using SPC and TQS, there is an upper limit or ceiling on how much one can raise productivity using traditional productivity tools. Thus, components of SPC and TQS become logical and applicable extensions of traditional productivity improvement tools. Combining SPC and TQS with traditional tools leads to a higher productivity ceiling, but other tools may also be used to raise productivity beyond that ceiling. There are many examples in the private, public, and nonprofit sectors that show how to raise productivity, increase outputs, and either reduce inputs or utilize excess capacity to expand operations or diversify.

TQS can serve as a bridge between traditional methods and two international QI strategies: total productivity improvement and CWQC (the mainstream management philosophy in the Japanese private and public sectors). Merging definitions of quality and productivity concepts make TQS, together with SPC, effective tools for organizational cost control and productivity improvement.

The U.S. service industry has displayed a growing interest in the improvement of quality and productivity, but the ascendancy to "world class" performance can only be achieved when all involved achieve congruence in several main factors: uniform definitions of productivity and quality, consistent systems of measurement (to enable the necessary process of continuous improvement), a "professionalization" of training and staff, and shifting the focus from mass inspections to a culture of "building it right the first time." Efforts to date represent a jigsaw puzzle with many pieces missing. Industrial engineers and other quality-management professionals should heed the call to use their expertise as change agents to supply the missing pieces, and pave the way to global competitiveness. Above all, top management of all involved organizations — owners, designers, instructors, and managers — must be committed to the concepts of productivity/quality improvement and must provide necessary funding and staff support to ensure success.

Key Terms

Underlying causes and costs of poor quality
Human sensors
Value-added processes
Non-value-added (poor-quality) costs
Variation
Quality characteristics
Operational definitions
Work unit
Common and special variation
Flowcharts
Cause–effect or fishbone chart
Run charts and check sheets
Scatter diagram
Basic tools
Six Sigma
Cost of poor quality
Conformance
Price of nonconformance
Price of conformance
Controllable quality costs
Resultant costs
Indirect quality costs
Productivity
Productivity ceiling

Notes

1. Analysts often use two numbers — the *mean* and the *standard deviation* — to represent the performance of an entire process. This is a simple, cost-effective way to understand, and improve processes. Once the mean or average process characteristic is determined, then the standard deviation (upper and lower limits) around the mean can be calculated.
2. Many federal (national) government functions (and agencies responsible for them), such as customs inspection (Immigration and Naturalization Service, INS), emergency management (FEMA), environmental protection (EPA), federal tax collection (IRS), procurement (General Services Administration), and social security administration (SSA) have shown dramatic improvements in customer service during the past decade. The U.S. Customs Service has been identified as a model federal reinvention effort for reducing the time required to process inbound airline passengers. The SSA has been recognized for improving the responsiveness of its 800-number

information system. Others, such as air traffic control and aviation security (FAA), INS, the National Park Service under the Interior Department, and environmental cleanup "Superfund" management have been less successful.

3. For details of methodologies for analyzing poor-quality costs in healthcare, see the section on adaption of QI principles to medical service and hospital settings in W. Edwards Deming's *Out of the Crisis*, pp. 199–206. For an elaboration of the concept of how to define the needs of "extended customers," see Joseph M. Juran's *Juran on Planning for Quality*, pp. 17–59. These are particularly useful for managers as step-by-step guides for designing total quality measurement systems.

4. Conversations with Customer Service Representative, Kendall Toyota, Miami, Florida, February 24, 2004.

5. Ken Sedell, in an unpublished paper gives an example: If 60 percent of the portion of the workload that previously produced invisible output now produces visible output with a pre-TQM cost of poor quality of 30 percent, then only 85 percent of the old input level would be needed to produce an output of 100.3 percent of the pre-TQM output level, even without any changes in productivity. The output:input ratio would increase by 18 percent with a 0.3 percent increase in output and a 15% reduction in input.

▼

Case Study 5.1:
Shabby Customer Teaches Bank a Lesson

A bank learned an expensive lesson by refusing to validate a 50-cent parking slip for a destitute-looking man, who retaliated by withdrawing his million-dollar account.

"If you have $1 in a bank or $1 million, I think they owe you the courtesy of stamping your parking ticket," John Barrier told the Spokane Spokesman-Review this week.

The 59-year old man said he was wearing his usual clothes — wrinkled old jeans, a cap with old grease stains, and shabby sneakers — when he pulled his pickup truck into the Old National Bank parking lot.

He paid a quick visit to his broker, cashed a check at the bank, and headed back to his truck.

The lot attendant said that there was a 50-cent parking fee but that Barrier could take his slip inside to get it validated.

No problem, Barrier thought, because he had done business at ONB — now U.S. Bank of Washington — for more than 30 years. But a teller took one look at his grubby clothes and refused to stamp the parking bill.

The millionaire asked the teller to call a bank manager, who also refused.

"He looked me up and down and stood back and gave me one of those kinds of looks," Barrier said, turning up his nose to imitate the manager.

"I said, 'Fine. You don't need me, and I don't need you.'"

Barrier withdrew all his money and took it down the street to Seafirst Bank.

"The first check he brought me was for $1 million," said Dennis Veter, the vice president of Seafirst's main Seattle branch. "You'd never know by looking at him, but you and I should be so lucky."

The incident has allowed Barrier's new bank, Seafirst, to puff out with pride. Not only did Barrier defect — his son and daughter now bank there.

Source: Report from Washington; AP, Spokane, Washington

▲

▼

Case Study 5.2:
Dana Commercial Credit Corporation

Dana Commercial Credit Corporation (DCC) provides leasing and financing services to a broad range of commercial customers. The Dana Corporation subsidiary has developed a collection of quality-linked scoring processes that assess how the company is progressing in its pursuit of continuous improvement goals set for all key areas of the business.

Since 1992, when DCC embarked on an effort to improve teamwork and organizational communications, the company has scored gains in the quality of its performance, customer satisfaction, and the percentage of repeat business. For example, DCC's largest product group, the Capital Markets Group (CMG), has closed all of its multimillion-dollar transactions on time for the past five years. Dealer Products Group–U.S. (DPG), the next largest group, has reduced the time it takes to approve a transaction from about 7 hours in 1992 to 1 hour or less in 1996.

Since 1994, CMG's customer satisfaction scores have exceeded four on a five-point scale and, in 1995, topped the industry average by almost two points. DPG has scored between eight and nine on a ten-point scale, or nearly three points higher than the average for its industry. DCC competes on the basis of value-added lease products and services, not just financing. Since 1991, the dollar volume of DCC leases has more than tripled, to more than $1 billion.

About DCC

Since 1980, when it was started with a $2.5 million investment by its corporate parent, DCC has grown to become the 11th largest among 2,000 U.S. leasing companies, with 1995 revenues of nearly $200 million and total assets of $1.5 billion. Headquartered in Toledo, Ohio, DCC consists of seven major product groups, each aligned with a different market segment. These include leveraged leases for power generation facilities and real estate properties with values up to $150 million, and leases to help commercial equipment resellers, manufacturers, and distributors sell equipment ranging in price from $4,000 to $3 million. Unique transactions are DCC's speciality, such as arranging the short-term lease of microcomputers for the television network covering the 1994 Winter Olympic games, providing full-service leasing of on-site photo processing equipment to retail outlets, and helping put a major gas processing facility in the North Sea online. DCC lease contracts ultimately are prepared for businesses and organizations that lease equipment, facilities, or buildings. However, the company views financial intermediaries, such as investment bankers, and equipment manufacturers and distributors, as its primary customers, because they are the major source of leasing recommendations and referrals. Most of DCC's 547 people are located in Toledo and Maumee (Ohio), Troy (Michigan), Toronto, London, Paris, and Zurich. The company's continuous improvement process is led by the Division Operating Committee, which is chaired by DCC Chairman and Chief Executive Officer Edward Shultz, and includes heads of the seven product groups and major support units.

Adding Value for Customers

DCC aims to be the preferred financial services provider in its selected markets. To achieve this objective, DCC is increasing customer satisfaction through the commitment, skills, and innovativeness of its people and through its QI system. The system provides the strategy, direction, incentives, tools, and resources necessary for continuous improvement, but, by design, it is customized so that each group concentrates on the particular requirements and expectations of customers in its market niche.

DCC's strategic plan integrates customer, operational, people, supplier, and quality plans into seven guiding plans, one for each product group. Product group improvement goals are translated into actions that address the company's key business drivers: customer satisfaction, knowledgeable people, quality processes, and profit for the shareholder. In all groups, action plans are linked directly to anticipated improvements in meeting four key customer requirements, which are determined by the division operating committee but adapted to each market. Customer-related performance metrics are established for each process and each improvement project.

Measurements are tracked closely. Each month, scorecards are compiled to inform all DCC people of progress toward reaching goals for customer satisfaction, human resources, and key processes. A monthly competitor scorecard also is prepared to compare DCC performance on key customer satisfaction measures. In 1995, DCC piloted a customer expectation scorecard, compiled largely from information gathered by cross- functional transaction teams that work closely with customers in the design of leasing arrangements and new products. Now deployed companywide, this scorecard helps alert DCC to changing customer requirements and indicates how well the company is responding. DCC's SWOT analyses compare company performance to benchmark measures. Performance in the key process areas is flagged as a "strength" or "weakness" compared to the benchmark, and as an "opportunity" or as a "threat" to the business.

Knowledgeable People

DCC's mission statement and the Dana Style of Management assert that people are our most important asset. To promote organizational flexibility and responsiveness to customers, DCC limits the number of management layers within its groups to five or fewer, and its "just do it" policy empowers DCC's people to act on their ideas for improvement without prior approval.

Major emphasis is placed on retaining people and cultivating company loyalty, accomplished through a "promote from within" policy, mentoring programs, educational opportunities, and an extensive reward and recognition system. Currently, all executive positions and 95 percent of supervisory and management slots are filled by people who advanced through the company.

The company uses education and training to differentiate itself from its competitors. In 1992 it created the Education Group to develop and teach courses in interpersonal communication, quality, and marketing, as well as in technical areas needed to structure customized leases. In all, more than 40 courses are offered. Each DCC person received an average of 48 hours of formal education and training in 1995, better than chief competitors and almost three times the leasing-industry average. The company also provides 100-percent reimbursement for successfully completed college courses. Training and education needs and effectiveness are reviewed monthly. Careful attention is paid to further enhancing the skills of people, including senior managers, who have direct contact with customers.

Results

DCC is continually alert for opportunities to improve its leasing products and service delivery. Averaging about 10 per person in 1995, employee ideas have been an especially productive means for improving DCC's performance and for diversifying and adding value to its product offerings. About 78 percent of all ideas were implemented. The company's progress in improving performance and increasing customer satisfaction is mirrored by its gains in financial performance. Rates of return on equity and assets have increased more than 45 percent since 1991. DCC also credits its continuous improvement efforts with helping to lower borrowing costs, the company's largest expense. DCC now accounts for at least 10 percent of the Dana Corporation's overall profitability, and it was the first division to achieve the gold level of performance in the annual competition for Dana's Quality Leadership Award, which is modeled after the Baldrige award. As it does with its customers and suppliers, DCC works in partnership with the communities where its offices are located. For example, it has provided computers to local schools and charities. In Toledo, when negotiating tax incentives for relocating its new headquarters building, DCC committed the equivalent of 45 percent of the resultant tax savings to the Toledo School Board. As a result, the public school system will receive 1.5 times more money from DCC than from a normal tax distribution. The city has adopted this approach for future tax incentive offerings.

Source: Baldrige National Quality Program; National Institute of Standards and Technology; U.S. Department of Commerce; Web site: www.baldrige.nist.gov.

▲

▼

Case Study 5.3:
Custom Research, Inc.

Custom Research, Inc. (CRI), a national marketing research firm, leverages an intensive focus on customer satisfaction, a team-oriented workforce, and information technology advances to pursue old-fashioned ends: individualized service and satisfied customers. Since 1988, when CRI adopted its highly focused customer-as-partner approach, client satisfaction has risen from already high levels, and gains in productivity, sales volume, and profits have outpaced industry averages.

CRI's steering committee is responsible for crafting CRI's goals and strategies, and views customer loyalty as the firm's most valuable business asset. With all CRI employees as members of customer-focused teams, a flat organizational structure helps make executives immediately accessible to employees, customers, and suppliers. Well-developed systems are in place for understanding customer expectations, soliciting customer feedback, and monitoring each facet of company, team, and individual performance. Together, these systems help set the course for CRI efforts to meet or exceed customer expectations that can serve as a model for other professional services firms.

A Quick Look

Founded in 1974 and based in Minneapolis, privately owned CRI conducts survey marketing research for a wide range of firms. The bulk of its projects assist clients with new product development in consumer, medical, and service businesses. Revenues of more than $21 million in 1996 place CRI among the 40 largest firms in the highly fragmented $4 billion marketing research industry that is characterized by low entry costs and tough competition. The firm credits its reputation for quality for making it one of only a handful of companies that has remained independent while growing over the past two decades.

Besides its Minneapolis headquarters, the firm has electronically linked offices in San Francisco and Ridgewood, New Jersey, as well as telephone-interviewing centers in St. Paul, Minnesota, and Madison, Wisconsin. It employs approximately 100 full-time staff members, most of whom are cross-trained to create the flexibility needed to accommodate the demands and schedules of research projects. Contractors assist CRI in doing the interviewing. Choosing, in 1988, to concentrate its business on high-volume, repeat customers, CRI has reduced the number of clients it serves. In 1995, CRI's clients numbered 67, down from 138 clients in 1988; the number of large clients during this period increased from 25 to 34. This emphasis on large accounts has paid off with a doubling in revenues, achieved without increasing staff size.

"Surprising and Delighting" Customers

In recent years, CRI senior management aimed for a new level of consistency and competence in delivering quality services by organizing, systematizing, and measuring quality. CRI's steering committee distilled requirements for each research project to four essentials: accurate, on time, on budget, and meeting or exceeding client expectations. Before the first survey data is collected, criteria defining these requirements are determined in consultation with clients when CRI executives and project team leaders interview them, and they do that extensively.

The company was reorganized to make maximum use of customer-focused teams and to merge support departments to reduce cycle time, a growing client priority. All CRI teams have the same goal of surprising and delighting their clients. Quality at CRI is client driven, the center of the star, and is integrated into the company's business system as represented by the five key business drivers that are the points of the star: people, processes, requirements, relationships, and results. With extensive employee involvement, the steering committee annually sets corporate goals for the company, which then tie to the goals for each work unit. Quarterly, account teams review with the steering committee the business plans and results for each client.

Meeting customer-specified requirements depends on efficient execution of well-documented, measurable processes. Most professional services firms believe their services cannot be standardized. At CRI, although each project is custom-designed, the process for handling it flows through essentially the same steps across all projects. CRI has developed and heavily uses a project implementation manual for interviewing. Internal "project quality recap" reports completed for every study track errors in any step of the project flow. CRI measures the accuracy of results and the quality of personal and telephone interviewing. For example, over the last several years ratings for interviewers show sustained average quality scores of approximately 95 points out of 100, up from 83 points in 1990.

Customers have ample opportunity to advise and critique CRI. At the end of each project, clients are surveyed to solicit an overall satisfaction rating based on the customers' expectations. Each month the results of the client feedback are summarized and distributed to all employees. Internally, end-of-project evaluations also are conducted for CRI support teams and key suppliers. Personnel interviewing contractors, for example, are evaluated on performance and contribute ideas for improving the quality of their service.

People Make the Difference

CRI uses a "high-tech, high-touch" approach to satisfying customers. On the high-touch side, CRI uses its flat organizational structure and relatively small size to ensure that information flows freely within the company. Just as importantly, they view continuous improvement as part of their jobs. Staff members are surveyed annually, giving CRI senior managers specific feedback, including data on their own performance as viewed by CRI-ers.

A variety of recognition programs, bonuses based on achievement of corporate, team, and individual goals, and a peer-review system for evaluating personal performance serve to reinforce worker commitment to continuous improvement.

CRI has a companywide education plan, used to align individual training with business and quality goals. Each employee has a development plan, which sets annual and long-term goals for improvement and helps to identify training needs. In 1996, the average CRI employee received over 134 hours of training. All new employees receive companywide and job-specific training that addresses quality and service issues. CRI bases companywide training requirements on client feedback, performance reviews, CRI's education plan, CRI development plans, on-the-job reviews, interviewer monitoring, and employee surveys.

A Technology-Driven Approach

The "high-tech" component to CRI's business is reflected by its alertness to technological opportunities to improve its performance or to devise new services that respond to customer needs. Managing work through technology-driven processes is one of CRI's key business drivers. CRI led, for example, in the use of computers to assist in telephone interviewing, data collection, and analysis. Software enables CRI to use technology to integrate all stages of a project: produce a questionnaire for computer-assisted interviewing, control the sampling and autodialing for interviewing, edit and then tabulate the answers from the questionnaires, display them in tabular format, and generate report-ready tables for the final report and presentation. The use of computers has reduced cycle time for just one of these steps — tabulating data — from two weeks to a single day.

CRI views its major software supplier as a key partner. The long-standing relationship extends to annual planning sessions during which CRI shares its goals and the two firms determine how the software maker can contribute to meeting the goals.

These and other quality-promoting actions including an unconditional satisfaction guarantee aim to build client confidence and loyalty, which, in turn, generate a variety of business benefits. Since 1988, feedback from clients on each of its projects shows steadily improved overall project performance. CRI is now meeting or exceeding clients' expectations on 97 percent of its projects. Seventy percent of its clients say that the company exceeds their expectations. CRI is rated by 92 percent of its clients as "better than competition" on the key dimension of "overall level of service."

Source: Baldrige National Quality Program; National Institute of Standards and Technology; U.S. Department of Commerce; Web site: www.baldrige.nist.gov.

▲

▼

Case Study 5.4:
Caterpillar Financial Services Corporation

With total U.S. assets exceeding $14 billion and managing more than 100,000 contracts monthly, Caterpillar Financial Services Corporation U.S. (CFSC) is the second largest captive equipment lender in the United States. With a U.S. workforce of nearly 750 employees, CFSC has more than $1 billion in revenues as the financial services business unit within Caterpillar, Inc., a manufacturer of construction and mining equipment, gas and diesel engines, and industrial turbines. Based in Nashville, Tennessee, CFSC was incorporated in 1981 to finance Caterpillar's lift trucks. By 1985, the company was providing financing for the complete line of Caterpillar products as well as financing services to users and dealers of Caterpillar equipment and the Caterpillar business units. From 1998 to mid-2003, CFSC has increased assets by 34 percent and products by 54 percent although industry performance has declined by 21 percent and 35 percent respectively. CFSC has maintained strong ratings from the top three credit rating agencies.

Highlights

- CFSC's total contribution to Caterpillar's total earnings has increased from 5.6 percent in 1998 to more than 25 percent in the first nine months of 2003.
- Customer satisfaction levels exceed industry and American Customer Satisfaction Index (ACSI) world-class benchmarks.
- CFSC's Six Sigma improvement efforts have led to significant after-tax savings since the company embraced the methodology in 2001.
- In 2002, 80 percent of employees said they would recommend CFSC as a good place to work. The national norm is 55 percent.

Never-Ending Journey to Excellence

As a service organization based within a large manufacturer, CFSC measures its success by the success of Caterpillar, Inc., and its customers. That is why CFSC decided early on that excellence was going to define the company's culture and be its guiding principle. Today, CFSC's business model integrates excellence into its vision, mission, six critical success factors, and shared values. Tellingly, customer satisfaction and employee satisfaction are the first and second of CFSC's critical success factors. The others are growth, leadership, reliable returns, and world-class core processes. Leaders, managers, and employees work together to develop key business strategies and annual plans linked to these six factors and performance in these areas is continuously monitored. True to its mission of "helping Caterpillar and our customers succeed through financial service excellence," CFSC maintains a constant focus on process improvement.

Tools such as Six Sigma, a highly disciplined, data-based methodology, help CFSC prioritize and manage projects, design products, and improve processes. Ninety-seven percent of employees are trained in Six Sigma procedures for designing new processes, called DMEDI (Define, Measure, Explore, Develop, Implement), and for improving existing ones, called DMAIC (Define, Measure, Analyze, Improve, Control). Specially trained employees called "Black Belts," experts in the Six Sigma process and team facilitation; "Green Belts," subject matter experts; and "Yellow Belts," trained in the basics of Six Sigma, constitute teams of employees that implement these procedures. Since 1993, CFSC also has been using the Baldrige performance excellence criteria as the overall framework to assess the organization and guide improvement efforts. Other improvement and analysis tools include a four-year strategic plan, a one-year tactical plan, and a balanced scorecard of measures to assess organizational performance. CFSC's Six Sigma improvement efforts have led to significant after-tax savings since the company embraced the methodology in 2001. From 1997 through mid-2003, productivity improved by more than 10 percent and the current level of performance is nearly 35 percent better than the average of the industry's top 100.

Investing in Technology

Handling over 100,000 contracts monthly and working with customers and equipment dealers who demand accurate, timely, complete, and responsive service have led CFSC to invest in leading-edge information management systems and hardware. The company was one of the first in its field to launch three Web-based services available 24/7: Financ*Express*SM helps to streamline financing by automating quotes, credit approval, and document preparation; Account*Express*SM gives customers and dealers online access to accounts; and Customer*Express*SM provides employees and dealers one convenient portal to customer information. All employees have access to these services through either a networked desktop or laptop personal computer. Although access to data is necessarily liberal, it also is tightly controlled. Full-time security coordinators carefully manage the processes for granting access and quickly remove rights no longer required. Other systems and programs are in place to ensure information integrity, accuracy, and reliability and to protect confidentiality. Investments in technology along with a continuing focus on excellence and process improvements are helping CFSC achieve its corporate vision: "to be a significant reason why customers select Caterpillar worldwide." Seventy-nine percent of customers considering the purchase of Caterpillar equipment say that CFSC products and services favorably influenced their decision. Research also verified that CFSC exceeded customers' expectations twice as often as competitors. Only one to two percent of customers were dissatisfied with the service or options they received from CFSC. Satisfaction of end users, one of three key customer groups, has increased from 89 percent to 93 percent over the past five years in the equipment division. User satisfaction with loan origination in the marine division, which was already high at 91 percent, increased to 97 percent from 1999 to 2002. In the power division, satisfaction rose from 90 percent in 2002 to 93 percent in 2003. These levels of performance exceed industry and ACSI world-class benchmarks.

Environment of Growth and Achievement

Employee satisfaction is second only to customer satisfaction as a critical success factor, even ahead of growth and reliable returns. This is evident in the company's commitment to professional development — more than $2 million was spent on training in 2003. Investment in employee recognition programs, such as Eye-on-Quality Awards and Cat Bucks — which allow employees to instantly recognize other employees — has increased by nearly four times, from $84,000 in 1999 to $263,000 in late 2003. CFSC also recognizes employees with incentive pay, which is paid quarterly and directly aligned with company goals. Improvements in employee satisfaction are helping CFSC meet its strategic goal of attracting and retaining skilled employees. The overall Employee Satisfaction Index has risen from 67 percent in 1995 to 89 percent in 2003. Employee satisfaction with the job exceeds the financial services norm and is consistent with the score achieved by best-practice organizations. Employee retention has improved four points to 94 percent since 2000, with the current level of performance significantly better than the top quartile comparison. In 2002, 80 percent of CFSC employees recommended the company as a good place to work, up from 67 percent in 2000.

CFSC is committed not only to employees' satisfaction, but also to their well-being. An on-site, fully staffed fitness center is used by 60 percent of CFSC employees. Ninety-three percent of employees participate in the Caterpillar Healthy Balance program, which earned a national C. Everett Koop Award for Wellness Promotion in 1999 and the Wellness Councils of America "Well Workplace Award" in 2002.

Caring for Others

As part of its shared value of "caring for others," CFSC provides assistance to both local and international organizations, including The United Way, the Red Cross, and the Salvation Army. Giving to the United Way exceeds $300,000 annually, earning the company that organization's highest honor, the Iris Circle Award. Four times a year, Cat Financial hosts blood drives, which enable the Red Cross to assist more than 4,000 patients. More than 150 gifts for children and the elderly were provided through the Angel Tree program. CFSC also fosters professional development of local youth through support to Wharton Elementary School, the program "Exchange City" that teaches about business and free enterprise, and the "School to Work" program for high school students.

Source: Baldrige National Quality Program; National Institute of Standards and Technology; U.S. Department of Commerce; Web site: www.baldrige.nist.gov.

▲

Chapter 6

Rewarding Service Quality Improvement

All types of organizations are integrating advanced training, information technologies, and new equipment to meet administrative, institutional, and customer service challenges. As a result, reforms are accelerating in many organizations and at all levels of business, industry, and government.

It is especially difficult for public service organizations to integrate the human, material, and technical resources necessary to improve customer relationships and cross-functional (departmental) communication across jurisdictional (geographic) boundaries. In contrast to past customer service QI efforts, many new initiatives require extensive intragovernmental, as well as intergovernmental, coordination and cooperation among federal, state, and local agencies. Selecting the wrong type of incentives or rewards, or partnering with the wrong type of organization, can negatively impact progress. In addition, applying for an inappropriate award program can also limit quality progress (for example, see Case Study 6.1). State and local government agencies are also hampered in their TQS efforts because they depend on declining general revenue sources and competitive federal assistance programs. Public service organizations must demonstrate enhanced capacities for inter- and intragovernmental coordination, organizational learning, knowledge management, and QI to achieve integrated horizontally linked networked system reforms. More important, they must understand and apply these practices to compare results, exchange information, integrate human assets with technologies, and standardize performance measures. All public and private service organizations seek a common framework to determine if goals are being achieved within the revenue parameters set by private markets or public budgets.

Continuing security threats, reorganizations to improve intelligence capabilities and protect homeland security, and heightened tensions in the Middle East, as well as other regions of the world, expose weaknesses in critical public service delivery and regulatory systems. Numerous public agencies, including units of the armed services, intelligence and security agencies, the Environmental Protection Agency (EPA), the federal and state departments of health and human services, and several state military reserve units, are expanding their missions with limited training and resources. The Transportation Security Administration (TSA), a division of the newly created Department of Homeland Security (DHS), faces unprecedented challenges in meeting Congressionally imposed deadlines and requirements for improving and maintaining aviation security. Private corporations are increasingly partnering with public agencies to achieve mutual goals.

Regardless of the type of reform, employees require some form of recognition to encourage innovation, improve performance, and sustain management changes. The central questions guiding this chapter are:

1. How do quality awards contribute to overall improvement of customer service and productivity?
2. What organizational values do quality awards reward and recognize?
3. How is success measured, and what lessons can be publicized and transferred?
4. What can we learn from failures to maintain service QIs after they have been successfully implemented?
5. Does applying for an award provide the comparative standards, objective assessment, and outside perspective needed to evaluate the performance of internal systems and results?
6. Are private or state-sponsored awards being used to recognize, reward, and disseminate successful organizational change strategies?

These are long-term questions that can only be answered with integrated knowledge management systems capable of linking diverse databases across many microgovernmental functions (Agor, 1997; Senge, 1994, 1996; Wimmer, 2002). This chapter also presents the findings of a survey of all state quality award offices examining the importance of standardizing processes for all organizations.[1] In addition, the chapter categorizes BNQA winners according to their tax-status, state sponsorship, and extent of corporate support (Table 6.1); discusses how awards can serve as models for improved performance; describes different types of recognition programs; highlights problems that service organizations can encounter by

Table 6.1   Distribution of Baldrige Awards by Type of Program and State
(Number of Baldrige Awards Received by the State as of 2002: N = 62)

Nonprofit Awards	State-Sponsored Awards	Corporate Sponsor Awards
Alabama	Florida (2)	Colorado (2)
Arizona	Georgia (2)	Connecticut
Arkansas	Idaho	New Hampshire
California (6)	Kentucky	Ohio (3)
Delaware	Maine	South Dakota
Hawaii	Maryland	Tennessee (4)
Illinois (2)	Massachusetts (1)	
Indiana	Michigan (1)	
Iowa	Minnesota (5)	
Kansas	Mississippi	
Louisiana	Missouri (3)	
New Jersey (4)	Nebraska	
New Mexico (1)	Oklahoma (1)	
New York (6)	South Carolina (2)	
North Carolina	Virginia	
Oregon	Wyoming	
Pennsylvania (3)		**BQNA in States That Do Not Offer Quality Awards**
Rhode Island		
Texas (11)		Alaska (1)
Utah		Montana
Vermont		Nevada
Washington		North Dakota
Wisconsin (1)		West Virginia

applying for awards outside their own countries; and discusses various U.S. and state quality award programs (listed in Appendix F) and how they influence local quality initiatives.

The Need to Improve Performance

Failure to continuously improve internal processes, human resources, and management systems is a pervasive problem for many different types of organizations. Service firms find it especially difficult, even under the most favorable circumstances, to improve performance with limited resources. Computers, software, and other technological devices change so rapidly that equipment, systems, and training protocols become obsolete after only a few months of use. Even if systems and skills are continuously updated, many employees are demoralized, and organizations understaffed following years of downsizing, union busting, endless reinvention, and threats to privatize. Others suffer from inadequate supervision, lack of public support, outdated organizational structures, and poorly trained personnel to maintain and operate equipment (Brehm and Gates, 1997; Rosen, 1998). These examples may only reveal the tip of the poor-quality iceberg (see Chapter 5). In addition to state and local electoral systems, other vital and necessary public sector infrastructure potentially vulnerable to human and material obsolescence include airports, schools, roads, seaports, security systems, and public utilities.[2]

Governments face multiple pressures that may inhibit the adoption of new equipment, systems, training, and technologies. If effectively implemented, these changes would result in better performance and increased public trust. Organizational changes are difficult to initiate and sustain, however, because state and local governments are constitutionally separate from the national government, isolated from the policymaking authority of the chief executive, notoriously resistant to change, and vulnerable to outside pressures. Improving performance is more challenging because:

1. Compared with the market-based and profit-driven private sector, governments experience uneven capacity (and willingness) to measure performance.
2. Political interests multiply preexisting problems of defining citizen and customer needs.
3. Private interest groups compete with each other and with government agencies for limited public resources.
4. Public agencies often find service standards difficult to set and enforce.
5. Outcomes, performance, and results are less tangible and more difficult to measure (deLancer Julnes and Holzer, 2001; Donaldson, 1999; Haque, 2001; Milakovich, 1998, 2003; Sanderson, 2001).

In addition to these factors, a dearth of relevant examples of successful models in specific functions contributes to a pervasive need for hands-on, practical models to guide organizational changes in many public and nonprofit agencies.

In the current political environment, barriers to change, including weak negative stereotypes and fading institutional memories from past reforms, are less likely to prevent adoption of the latest technologies because of heightened domestic and international security threats, greater acceptance of the need for more regulation — especially in homeland security, public safety, and transportation — and increased public trust since the 9/11 terrorist attacks. These forces present unique opportunities for public administrators to reform organizational processes.

The standardization of various performance measurement methodologies is no longer an optional exercise for most public agencies. Public administrators and elected officials at all levels of government now share a common mission: to provide the highest-quality services with the most efficient management systems to all users at the least cost. Organizations often lack a common methodology to achieve these goals. Awards, benchmarks, or quality audits will not eliminate all the ambiguity in debates over the use of public or private sector models to resolve complex issues, define customer needs, motivate employees, or articulate organizational missions. Ideological and political preferences will continue to impact electoral results and public-sector decision making. Standardized performance measurement methods do, however, provide rich comparative databases to assist managers in defining their main purposes, comparing performance, setting service standards, and reaching out to citizens, the primary recipients of improved services.

International Charters, Quality Awards, and Standards

The global trend toward decentralized, flexible, and results-driven government is accelerating worldwide as more attention is being paid to successful models for managing change. Many other governments take actions to implement customer-oriented and performance-based changes, and lessons from these countries may be applicable in the United States as well (Sanderson, 2001; Heinrich et al., 2000). Widely used in Asia, Australia, Canada, and Europe, various methodologies such as citizens' charters, charter marks, and accrediting standards help to spread success stories from an expanding number of governments (Chuan, 2000; Debia, 2001; Puay et al., 1998; Tummala and Tang, 1996). Globalization of the reinvention effort, with heavy emphasis on electronic government (E-gov) technology, encourages citizen access to information, knowledge management processes, and participation in public decision making (Fountain, 2001; Gronland, 2002; Heeks, 1999; Ho, 2002; Moon, 2002; West, 2001; Wimmer, 2002, 2004).

International comparisons may be applicable as well, as many governments also utilize customer satisfaction, performance management, and information technology to form customer-oriented public–private partnerships. Examples of recent reform efforts include the expanded use of citizens' charters that guarantee specific levels of service, charter marks that recognize agencies for exemplary service, secret shopper programs that use public employees to evaluate levels of service in other agencies, and the publication of complaint procedures for others to follow when agencies fail to meet the service standards (Davison and Grieves, 1996; Van Thiel and Leeuw, 2002).

Citizens' charters are similar to a "bill of rights" (for airline passengers, consumers, healthcare patients, taxpayers, travelers, etc.). They originated in Europe and have grown in popularity during the past two decades in nearly 20 countries, including Australia, Belgium, Canada, Denmark, Finland, France, India, Ireland, Italy, Norway, Portugal, Spain, Singapore, Sweden, as well as governments in the United Kingdom (Schiavo, 2000). At the organizational (micro) level, several steps are being taken to maximize a charter's effectiveness. Charters are bolstered by well-developed systems and procedures, and providers must make sure that all employees understand the terms and standards stated in a charter. Each employee receives a copy of the document, is trained to respond to customer concerns, and is charged with upholding service standards. Everyone knows how to give feedback, report on standards violations, and offer suggestions for improvement. To make such reports, users know who to contact and how to contact them via phone or e-mail. Providers assure citizens that they value feedback and that top management will not ignore such information. Staff members are trained to competently and respectfully handle complaints at the point they occur and report them to supervisory management. Although relatively new to the United States, where charters are yet to be widely implemented, shared elements and goals, such as best-practice techniques, customer bills of rights, and improved accountability, could make this strategy an important new trend in American public administration.

Charter marks reward excellence in public service, reinforce standards, and raise the level of public service provided. Because charter marks are identified as the highest honor in the field, organizations conduct internal audits to determine if they should apply. Different regulations, guidelines, and characteristics in various services make this decision very difficult. They also improve public service via feedback to and from applicants. In the United Kingdom, there are over 200 national charters and an estimated 10,000 local charters, all designed to boost service quality for citizens. The U.K. national charter program began in 1991 and was renamed "Service First — The New Charter Programme" by the Labour Administration in 1998. Nine principles parallel the U.S. reinvention movement and underlie the initiative:

1. Set published standards of service.
2. Be open, and provide full information about costs and performance.
3. Consult and involve present and potential users.
4. Encourage access and promotion of choice.
5. Treat everyone fairly, respect their privacy and dignity, be helpful and friendly, and pay particular attention to those with special needs.

6. Put things right when they go wrong.
7. Use resources effectively to provide the best value for taxpayers and users.
8. Innovate and improve services and facilities.
9. Work with other providers.

Citizens' charters and charter marks continue to face challenges, such as spanning all public service sectors and being recognized by citizens as service guarantees and badges of excellence. As a result of these reforms, customer service standards are being applied successfully in two dozen countries, as well as in a few state and local governments in the United States. In the United Kingdom, the number of applicants and winners continues to increase almost every year since the creation of the award. Governments use citizen's charters to guarantee specific levels of service and charter marks to recognize agencies for exemplary service. Other agencies conduct focus groups, implement secret shopper programs, use public employees to evaluate levels of service, and utilize E-government technology to publish complaint procedures on Web sites for citizens when agencies fail to meet the service standards.

The leading international awards and standards for quality include the Deming Prize in Japan, the ISO 9000/14000 series, European Quality Awards, and the Malcolm Baldrige National Quality Award (BNQA) in the United States.[3] These prizes, awards, and audit accreditation programs influenced the creation of numerous state-sponsored U.S. "mini-Baldrige" programs that recognize success at the state and local level as well. Nearly all states and many communities now share similar missions using the BNQA criteria to advance service quality initiatives. In the United States alone, over 1,750 private, nonprofit, public service organizations have received recognition with state and local awards for service quality and productivity improvements in the past decade. In addition to awards, benchmarking and E-gov initiatives are being used to enhance citizen participation (Chapter 2). Applying for an award or an audit certificate provides incentives for employees to improve their processes and services, and recognition by outside examiners offers objective evidence of performance gaps. Awards can also serve as a cost-effective way to disseminate knowledge about the best practices for managing personnel and technology. This eliminates much of the risk from a "trial and error" approach to different improvement strategies and allows less experienced organizations to participate. Organizations that already received awards can use benchmarking for self-promotion and to implement newer, more innovative ideas. Most important, providing incentives such as awards, charter marks, and audit standards to achieve organizational goals encourages public agencies to overcome barriers to innovation.[4]

The Deming Prize is the oldest of the major awards (established in 1950), and many Japanese consider it to be as prestigious as the Academy Awards or the Nobel Prize for quality recognition.[5] Criteria for the Deming Prize include clarity of policies; appropriateness of organizational structure; information collection and communication; standardization of systems, performance, and technologies; human resources development; quality assurance and process control; maintenance of quality control systems; improvement methods; customer and employee satisfaction; and future plans for improving problems. Although less well-known in Europe and North America, the Deming Prize significantly influences development of quality control and management practices in Asia. Continuing the global trend in recognizing quality management, in recent years companies from India and Thailand have received nearly all the Deming prizes: 6 out of 6 in 2004, 6 of 7 in 2003, 2 of 2 in 2002, and 3 of 4 in 2001. The prize recognizes individuals and applicant companies and divisions of companies, including increasing numbers of non-Japanese companies and service organizations, for their theories and new approaches to total quality control. Organizations that compete for the prize demonstrate effective internal quality management systems, establish structures for implementation, and deploy total quality control methods. Furthermore, applicants must understand current markets, establish their own themes and objectives, and transform themselves companywide. Examiners evaluate whether or not the themes established by the applicants meet the needs of business environments, whether or not activities are appropriate for their circumstances, and whether or not their strategies will likely achieve future objectives.[6]

ISO 9000/14000 Series, the fastest-growing quality assurance system in the world, applies to most types of organizations. Although neither a quality award nor a charter *per se*, the International Organization for Standards audit certification series — commonly known as the ISO 9000 through 14000 (for environmental standards) — uses many of the same objective criteria and review by outside examiners required by the BNQA, Deming, and European awards. (ISO is not an acronym, but the shortened Greek word for *equal*.) To date, only a few governments are ISO certified, and there is a need for more research on its effectiveness in improving the management capacity of public service organizations (Chu and Wang, 2001; Lowery, 1998). Nonetheless, the ISO series maintains a commitment to customer service QI and shares many of the same criteria as the Baldrige, Deming, and European quality awards (Nakhai and Neves, 1994; Tummala and Tang, 1996). Together, these methodologies form a standard multinational definition of criteria used to evaluate quality processes in any type of organization (see Table 6.2). ISO 9000 audit certification standards create a greater awareness of the need to implement QI strategies and

Table 6.2   Global Criteria for European and American Quality Awards

1. **Leadership:** How senior executives guide the organization, and how the organization addresses its responsibilities to the public and practices good citizenship.
2. **Strategic planning:** How the organization sets strategic directions, and how it determines key action plans.
3. **Human resource management:** How the organization enables its workforce to develop its full potential, and how the workforce is aligned with the organization's objectives.
4. **Information analysis and technology:** The management, effective use, and analysis of data and information to support key organization processes and the organization's performance management system.
5. **Quality systems and processes:** How key production/delivery and support processes are designed, managed, and improved.
6. **Customer/market focus:** How the organization determines requirements and expectations of customers and markets.
7. **Customer/user satisfaction:** Documents how the organization meets customers' requirements.
8. **Corporate governance and social responsibility:** Responds to post-Enron concerns about corporate corruption and social responsibility.
9. **Supplier/partner relationships:** Just-In-time delivery and supply chain management.
10. **Results:** The organization's performance and improvement in its key business areas: customer satisfaction, financial and marketplace performance, human resources, supplier and partner performance, and operational performance. For private businesses, this category also examines how the organization performs relative to competition.

Source: Adapted from Criteria for European Quality Awards and the Baldrige National Quality Program. Web site: http://www.quality.nist.gov/BusinessCriteria. htm.

serve as a model for many international quality and excellence awards (Puay et al., 1998). Public and private organizations need to understand audit-based accreditation systems as a means to improve their performance and service quality initiatives.

The European Quality Award, created in 1990 by the European Foundation for Quality Management (EFQM), went into effect in October 1991 at the EFQM's annual forum. The European Quality Award spawned many national and regional quality awards throughout Europe and influenced development of the ISO 9000 standards. The newest categories for the award were added in 1994: the Public Sector Award and the Small and Medium Size Enterprises Award. Each applicant is reviewed by a team of award assessors, which determines a total score for the application. Based on the final report of the team of assessors, the jury selects the most outstanding organizations for the award.

Public Law 100-107 created the Malcolm Baldrige National Quality Award (BNQA) on August 20, 1987, in honor of a former Secretary of Commerce in the Reagan administration who died in a rodeo accident. The awards, established because the United States (manufacturers in particular) had fallen behind Japanese and European competitors in producing quality goods for sale or trade in international markets, recognize U.S. organizations for their achievements in business performance and raise public awareness about the importance of quality. Organizations and companies that demonstrate productivity, results, and the highest levels of customer service are eligible to apply for the award, but the number of awards is strictly limited. The Baldrige criteria also parallel and reinforce recent U.S. federal performance management legislation, such as the Government Results and Performance Act (GPRA), that encourages results-driven budgeting in all federal agencies (detailed in Chapter 7; see also GPRA, 2000).

The framework and evaluation criteria for the BNQA are the product of input from over 200 quality experts and include most of the philosophies and strategies embraced by theorists in the United States, Europe, and Asia (Appendix D). Thousands of organizations also use the BNQA criteria for self-assessment and training and as a tool to develop performance and business processes (Brown, 2004). Over 2 million copies of the criteria have been distributed since the first edition in 1988, and heavy reproduction and electronic access multiply that number many times. Nonmanufacturing organizations have also benefited from using the *Baldrige Criteria for Performance Excellence* (included in Table 6.2) as the foundation and self-assessment for their quality strategies (see Appendix E). Winning an award is very challenging, but whether or not an organization wins, the application process provides a comparative framework for self-assessments to see how to improve and what changes are needed.

When President Reagan signed the Malcolm Baldrige National Quality Improvement Act nearly 20 years ago, many supporters viewed it as "a declaration of war" against poor quality by the United States government. The annual quality award also sought standardization of performance measures by "mandate[ing] the development of a common framework upon which judgments of quality processes and outcomes could be based" (Winn and Cameron, 1998). The BNQA originally aimed at improving manufacturing quality and productivity by stimulating greater competition (and profits) through the use of quality initiatives. Public recognition of improvements and achievements provide examples for others to benchmark. Winners must publicly share information about quality strategies at a national conference to guide other organizations and to encourage them to become part of the QI effort.[7] This requirement is important because learning from the experience of other agencies can stimulate government organizations to become part of the quality process and find effective ways to improve their performance. Although federal agencies are ineligible and there is no specific category for government agencies, the BNQA accepts applications (since 1995) from educational and healthcare organizations. Every year, the BNQA gives a maximum of two awards in each of five categories (manufacturing, healthcare, education, service, and small business), in contrast to other awards with an unlimited number of winners. Like the BNQA, many state and local organizations also encourage recipients to share their success formulas.[8]

As a public–private partnership to reward exemplary and innovative management processes, the BNQA recognizes successful innovation strategies. Its criteria acknowledge the importance of results and require an organization to prove that its program has positively affected the quality of its outputs. Since its inception, 62 organizations (37 large and small private manufacturing firms and 25 public and private educational, healthcare, and service organizations) received Baldrige awards. In 2001, for the first time in the history of the awards, three of the five award winners came from the education category, two large and one small. All were public agencies: the Chugach School District in Anchorage, Alaska; the Pearl River School District in Pearl River, New York; and University of Wisconsin–Stout in Menomonie, Wisconsin.[9] In 2002, SSM Health Care of St. Louis, Missouri, became the first such organization to be recognized with a Baldrige award. In 2003, two hospitals, a financial services organization, and a school district were chosen. In 2004, two of four winners were service organizations, including the first college of business profiled in Case 6.2 at the end of this chapter (for list of additional recipients, see www.baldridge.nist.gov). Competition for these awards is formidable. Since 1999, over 50 healthcare organizations submitted applications for the BNQA, including 17 in 2002, with only 4 winners. Many of the other applicants in various categories have received high scores on evaluation criteria (Appendix D) and could serve as benchmarks for others to follow.

Since 2001, the focus of the awards has changed with the mission of the BNQA. Although the awards still emphasize private sector international competitiveness in manufacturing, they now acknowledge the equally important need to raise the quality of domestic public services, especially in education and healthcare. The new Baldrige mission is reinforced by the numerous other national, subnational, and regional awards programs that also use the BNQA criteria to encourage innovation, measure performance, and reward achievement.

Florida Power and Light Company and the Deming Prize

Few large service organizations even attempted large-scale service QIs until the 1980s. Florida Power and Light Company (FPL) of Juno Beach, Florida, began its ambitious quality improvement program (QIP) in 1981 and was recognized internationally a decade later for its companywide QI efforts as the first American service firm to successfully compete for the prestigious Deming Prize in Japan (Milakovich and Dan, 1990). Following a change in top management in 1989, FPL then largely dismantled its effort due to financial exigencies unrelated to the success of QIP.

This section describes how the QIP was designed, implemented, incorporated into company policy, and subsequently dismantled. First, it is important to provide a brief corporate history and recognize the business environment in which FPL operated in the early 1980s. Worldwide shortages of fossil fuel, anti-nuclear-power activists' campaigns, and cogeneration of electric power all threatened to reduce the long-term market share. Publicly regulated utilities such as FPL were in the midst of a hostile business environment while inflation was skyrocketing and fuel and oil prices showed no signs of decreasing. The inflation-adjusted price of crude oil reached $80 a barrel during the Iran hostage crisis of 1980. In addition, there was a great need for heavy capital expenditures, and several aspects of operations had grown cumbersome and overly bureaucratic. In the words of one senior manager, organizational growth at FPL had "created a rigid bureaucracy capable of acting in a set fashion ... but unable to react to new and changing circumstances." It became evident that a new management strategy was needed to deal with a series of major crises and successfully guide FPL into the future.

To achieve its new mission "to become the best-managed electric utility in the United States and an excellent company overall," FPL created a three-phase QIP. In July of 1981, FPL management announced (optimistically) that QIP would be used to conduct business for the rest of this century and the next as well. The program promised to attain QI, assist every worker to receive personal satisfaction for a job well done, and an opportunity to help achieve a common goal. Doing things right had always been a goal, but with the new strategy came the ideal of doing "the right things right," and doing so the first time. The goal was quality in everything, but the true test would be customer satisfaction.

Drawing from the theories of quality experts such as W. Edwards Deming and Joseph M. Juran as well as Japan's 1984 Deming-Prize-winning Kansai Electric, FPL settled on a mixed strategy, introducing the first phase of its QIP program in 1982. In the process, quality was redefined as conformance to the valid requirements of the customer. Customers were redefined as well, and in a way that clearly reflects Juran's "fitness for use" concept (Chapter 3). FPL defined a customer as not only the ultimate ratepayer but the person in the next department who receives a product or service in the next step of a manufacturing, assembly, or service delivery process. Closer internal relationships were an explicit goal of the program as well.

Four principles underlie FPL's QIP:

1. *Customer Satisfaction* — Quality is defined as satisfying the customer, which consists of meeting their needs and reasonable expectations.
2. *Plan–Do–Study–Act Cycle* — A four-phase methodology (Chapter 2, Figure 2.6) for problem solving was embedded everywhere in FPL's QIP processes.
3. *Management by Fact* — This has two meanings, not only for managers, but for all employees. First, objective data must be collected, and second, the company must be managed according to that data.
4. *Respect for People* — This principle asserts that all employees have a capacity for self-motivation and creative thought. Each employee needs to listen to and support this capacity in every other employee.

As it was impossible to instantly instill these principles in the 15,000-employee workforce, FPL implemented QIP in three phases. Quality improvement teams (QITs) started in 1982 and soon there were over 1,000 employees trained in team dynamics and over 100 teams in operation companywide. In 1984, policy deployment (PD) was implemented to allow management to prioritize and review problem solving companywide. Third, quality in daily work (QIDW) was introduced in 1986, and all employees began applying the quality techniques to their individual tasks. It took FPL almost five years to fully introduce this program.

At its peak in 1989, FPL had approximately 1,700 teams composed of 12,000 employees, representing an impressive 75-percent participation rate. At the same time, hundreds of employees were engaged in projects specifically designed to achieve the objectives delineated through the PD phase. Furthermore, regardless of their involvement in the prior two phases, every FPL employee was introduced to the QIDW concept. A quality council, composed of FPL's top officers assisted by a quality development team, guided the overall direction as well as the top-level QIP development and maintenance (Berry, 1991). FPL also charged the QI department with pushing, supporting, facilitating, and tracking quality progress for the entire organization.

The purpose of QITs and stories was to develop the skills, abilities, and attitudes of the team members as well as to improve the quality of FPL's services. The team approach proved to be very successful. Groups of workers become adept at addressing problems at their source and resolving them in accordance with companywide policy and customer needs. Four different types of QITs were in operation at FPL:

1. *Functional teams:* Usually formed from formal groups or natural work units, such as payroll, and all volunteers from that unit.
2. *Cross-functional teams:* Deal with problems that cut across organizational barriers, such as accounts payable.
3. *Task team:* Members are appointed from one or more organizational units to work on a specific problem, such as a cost allocation issue. When that problem is solved, the team is disbanded, and its members return to their original work units.
4. *Lead teams:* Headed by a manager, serving as steering committees, and guiding the activities of other teams in their area. They are responsible for the selection of the frequency and duration of team meetings.

As described in Chapter 3, *facilitators* are team leaders specially trained in statistics and human resources and appointed to help coach teams. They communicate and coordinate the efforts between cross-functional, task, and lead teams, and functional units. FPL also created an information clearinghouse known as Information Central (IC) to track team progress. IC kept files on team membership and documented their quality improvement (QI) stories. These stories were an important element in the QIP and became the standard way of displaying a QIT's efforts. Each story had seven steps in which each team was encouraged to do its work: (1) reason for improvement, (2) current situation, (3) analysis, (4) countermeasures, (5) results, (6) standardization, and (7) future plans.[10] This centralized approach to QI later stigmatized the QIP as overly bureaucratized and prone to creating separate "quality bureaucracies." Ideally, the entire organization should have implemented the QIP, but resistance to the extra overtime required to learn the QIP methodology became apparent after a few years.

Just as a body at rest tends to stay at rest, a company tends to change its policies very little unless stimulated by an outside force such as quality award examiners. Hence, policy deployment was the essential action phase of the QIP. Its objective was to achieve breakthroughs by concentrating company efforts and resources on a few priority issues. There were many reasons for the implementation of policy deployment, such as the improvements it could generate in response to customer needs. According to a senior vice president in charge of the QIP, PD enhanced FPL's ability to focus on the most critical corporate improvement issues. It improved the linkage between the annual improvement plans and the long-term corporate vision. Finally, it increased participation in and commitment to annual and long-term plans (Woodall, 1988). PD promised greater management efficiency due to the prioritization of corporate goals, and this contributed to FPL's overall process to achieve corporate improvement. Quality goals and quality-oriented activities at all levels support the corporation's vision. By concentrating its resources on a few priority issues, FPL targeted breakthrough objectives in performance. Significantly, PD was not put into effect without input from all segments of the company. It is a process that involves everyone in management. The process is systematic and thorough, involving planning, teamwork, and feedback. In addition to stimulating quality, PD improved communication between corporate departments and had stimulated companywide participation in the QIP.

QIDW was the application of the PDSA cycle to each individual's job. The main purpose of QIDW was to meet the needs and expectations of customers. Unlike the first two phases of the QIP, QIDW is a never-ending process of QI at FPL. This phase is considered the most difficult to implement because it involves the modification of the behavior of every single employee. To do so, a ten-step process that supposedly helped the implementation of QIDW was provided to every employee. This approach was later abandoned as overly detailed and unnecessarily complicated.

Following other industries that used QI techniques, FPL began to enlist vendors in their quality effort. The importance of vendors in the process is quite clear, considering that 60 percent of FPL's revenues are spent on the procurement of materials and services from vendors. This was a logical step to ensure that suppliers worked toward the same quality goals. In an effort to do this, FPL changed its procurement policy to emphasize development and maintenance of a long-term business relationship with vendors who, by virtue of their management philosophy and practice, ensure that a quality product or service is provided. FPL expected that its new procurement policy would establish long-term ties with high-quality vendors, therefore improving quality in another way. The communication lines established through these relationships were extremely valuable in the area of specification setting by FPL as vendors were allowed to contribute to the process, and better service resulted.

As mentioned previously, it can be difficult to measure quality in the service sector, so assessing the success of FPL's QIP was quite challenging. Many would look at the bottom-line ledger figures as a guide to whether the program was successful or not; however, looking at such figures alone will not necessarily reveal the true successes. Nonetheless, QI has shown up in the financial records in the form of increased revenues for FPL Group, Inc., as well as Qualtech, Inc., a software and consulting subsidiary of FPL. Among the other measurable results, there was a decrease in the number of customer complaints to the Florida Public Service Commission. During the five years from 1984 to 1989, this number dropped by an impressive 37 percent. Also, the average length of customer service interruptions has been cut to approximately 48 min, which is down from 100 min in 1981. And in the important category of safety, lost time due to injuries has decreased by 38 percent (Milakovich and Dan, 1990c). These were impressive numbers, especially compared to other utilities.

Those results confirm that the QIP was well on its way to becoming an international success story. According to a survey of *Wall Street Journal* subscribers, FPL Group, Inc., is the nation's "best-managed public utility." More important, the recognition FPL sought arrived when they were presented with the Edison Electric Institute Award for QI in a utility. In November 1989, FPL received the prestigious Deming Prize for QI: the first non-Japanese company ever to win the award. With so much support and recognition, why was the program dismantled? Case Study 6.1 addresses that issue and the controversies surrounding FPL's decision to apply for a "foreign" quality award.[11]

Encouraging Innovation and Rewarding Performance

In this era of increased internal and external challenges, managers must adopt the best theories and implement the most effective methods for managing resources and training employees. If resources become inadequate or unavailable to fully equip and staff public agencies (as frequently occurs), administrators must innovate and seek models for improvement elsewhere. Private firms that have not adjusted have already been downsized, outsourced, or eliminated. Public agencies that fail to compete in this new arena may also face reinvention, reduction, or elimination. Governmental hiring practices, internal management processes, procurement decisions, performance standards, and technologies are no longer immune from the need to innovate. Like manufacturing firms, service organizations must continuously improve people, processes, and performance.

Public organizations that cannot manage the required workloads become more vulnerable to the public sector equivalent of "hostile takeovers," i.e., contracting out or privatization (Goldsmith, 1997; Savas, 2000). The Bush administration, ideologically committed to a strategy of competition, outsourcing, E-government, and privatization, as well as partnerships with faith-based and nongovernmental organizations, now enjoys considerable public support for contracting out with private, nonprofit, and nongovernmental organizations. Although there is often more conflict than consensus about the long-term efficacy of such policies, recent Supreme Court decisions and public opinion thus far support this approach.

Operational design, planning, and policy decisions, based on collection, analysis, and interpretation of objective information is challenging for most organizations. Achieving goals in high-performance, results-driven organizations further requires annual strategic planning and performance reviews (Koehler and Pankowski, 1996; Milakovich, 1995b; Thompson and Strickland, 2002). Performance management strategies reinforce core values (i.e., collaboration, cost reduction, participation, process improvement, results-measurement, satisfying external customers, teamwork, etc.). External assessments can help identify neglected customers, underperforming processes, or unfulfilled purposes. Awards motivate and reward employees, serve as self-assessment tools for updating or refining performance initiatives, and provide incentives for changing employee behavior. Rewards can be *internal* to the agency in the form of appeals to patriotism, better working conditions, peer recognition, or *external* with bonuses, European charter marks, pay incentives, cash prizes, or recognition by competitive quality award programs.

In contrast to the beginning of the government reinvention era in 1993, hundreds of quality award programs, created worldwide in the past two decades, now exist. Their recipients, a largely untapped, but increasingly rich, reservoir of detailed information, demonstrate how various organizations successfully change internal processes to measure and meet performance goals. The full global impact of these many awards is too extensive to describe here, but the evolution of several national quality awards has been described elsewhere (Chuan, 2000; Debia, 2001; Flynn and Saladin, 2001; Nakhai and Neves, 1994). In the United States alone, 54 state, regional, and local quality awards, patterned after the BNQA, exist in 45 states (Green and Brill, 2002; Malcolm Baldrige, 2002). Most of these programs, in existence for over a decade, depend heavily on volunteer support, are incorporated as independent nonprofit corporations under IRS regulations section 501(c) 3, and receive only limited state funding (Survey, 2002). In addition, several nonprofit, publically sponsored, privately funded recognition and reward programs also publicize quality and performance management efforts and acknowledge individual employees for exemplary public service (Harvard University, 2002; Public Employees, 2002; President's Quality Award, 2001). See Table 6.3 for details.

The Ford Foundation Innovations in American Government program recognizes outstanding examples of creative problem solving in the public sector. Competition is intense because every program that receives an award is also given some monetary reward. The Exemplary State and

Table 6.3 Comparisons of U.S. Quality Award Programs

	Ford Foundation Innovations in American Government Program	Exemplary State and Local Awards (EXSL)	National Public Service Award (NPSA)	Public Service Excellence Awards (PSEA)	President's Quality Awards
Purpose	Recognizes outstanding examples of creative problem solving in the public sector. The purpose of these awards is to draw attention to exemplary achievements in government problem solving and to amplify the voices of public innovators in communicating their practices	Recognizes public initiatives that improve the quality of government services and operations, as well as innovations and programs that have produced measurable increases in quality and productivity, significant cost savings, and improvements in efficiency and effectiveness of government services	To honor individuals who make outstanding contributions to public service	To educate American citizens about the contributions made by public employees to the quality of their lives; to encourage *esprit de corps* among government employees; and to promote public service careers	Recognizes federal agencies that demonstrate high levels of service quality and results
Public/ Private	Private: The Council of Excellence in Government serves as the administrator of Ford Foundation awards and as a resource to all winners and finalists in their efforts to replicate and publicize their innovations. Among its resource services, the council helps identify existing forums and helps create new platforms for communication to support applicants, finalists, and winners in their replication, dissemination, and communication activities	Public: Administered by The National Center for Public Productivity at Rutgers University in Newark, New Jersey	Private: Sponsored by the American Society for Public Administration (ASPA) and the National Academy of Public Administration (NAPA)	Public: Sponsored by the Public Employees Roundtable, U.S. Office of Personnel Management, Federal Executive Boards/ Federal Executive Associations, International City/County Management Associations, National Governors Associations, National League of Counties, National League of Cities, and U.S. Conference of Mayors.	Public

Cash Award?	$18 million given since inception	No	No	No	No
Date of Inception	1986	1989	1983	1985	1988
Eligibility Requirements	All units of government are eligible, as long as they receive at least half of their funding from one or more governmental agencies, have operated their program for more than one year prior to the start of the awards cycle, are presently operating their program, and the submission is made by the overseeing government entity	Public agencies and community organizations receiving at least 50 percent of their funds from a public source, and in existence for at least one year, are eligible for nomination	Nominations may come from any level of public service and public service nonprofit organizations. Legislators and legislative staff are eligible, so long as they have public management experience	Programs with two or more employees administered by any U.S. federal, state, or local government agency may compete for all awards except for the Community Service Award, which must be performed on an unofficial, off-time basis	Federal executive agencies with at least 100 employees offering services to external customers, an administrative support agency for a cabinet department, or an executive branch agency are eligible
Number of Awards Given Annually	Twenty finalists are chosen annually. Ten winners receive $100,000 in grants. The other ten receive $20,000 in prizes	As many as 25 finalists are chosen annually to receive awards at the Public Sector Productivity Improvement Conference	As many as five winners may be awarded a Steuben crystal eagle at the annual award ceremony	One award is given in each of seven or eight categories annually	Approximately three awards are presented annually (48 awards since inception); however, judges are not required to award any participants if they feel that a standard of excellence has not been achieved
Web sites	www.innovations.harvard.edu	www.newark.rutgers.edu/~ncpp/exsl/exsl.html	www.aspanet.org	www.theroundtable.org/	www.opm.gov/quality

Local (EXSL) awards showcase innovations and programs that have produced measurable increases in quality and productivity, cost savings, and improvements in the efficiency and effectiveness of government services. Recent award winners include projects such as Affordable Housing, University of North Carolina Performance Measurement Project, Teen Pregnancy Prevention, and Medical Care for Children in communities such as Los Angeles County; Auburn, Alabama; Tucson, Arizona; Colorado Springs, Colorado; and the State of Washington (Holzer and Callahan, 1998). The National Public Service Awards (NPSA) recognize individuals who exhibit the highest standards of excellence, dedication, and accomplishment over a sustained period of time and are creative and highly skilled career managers at all levels of public service, including local, state, and federal governments, and international and public service nonprofit organizations (NPSA, 2002). Public Service Excellence Awards (PSEA) support governments in a three-part mission: to educate American citizens about the contributions made by public employees to the quality of their lives; to encourage *esprit de corps* among government employees; and to promote public service careers. Awards are made to all levels of government along with an award given for community service (Public Employees Roundtable, 2002). The President's Quality Awards recognize applicants that demonstrate more mature development of performance excellence and document world-class results (Lumney, 2000). Agencies must define their mission, products, services, size, major markets, organizational structure, and the type of equipment and technology used. Applicants are evaluated on whether the organization's methods are appropriate for its requirements; the effectiveness of its methods; whether learning cycles and a pattern of improvement are implemented; whether the data collected is objective and reliable; whether transactions with customers support functions and processes; and on performance levels relative to appropriate competitors. Winners participate in the Annual National Conference of Federal Quality and host site visits for interested agencies.

State and Local Quality Awards

In the past two decades, hundreds of corporations, nonprofits service organizations, and public agencies competed for and received awards using a standardized format based on the BNQA. Like the better-known national awards, the application and examination processes of various states provide objective feedback to public and private managers committed to service QI. Some states have given quality awards for several decades (Maryland and Virginia since 1983), whereas others created or reorganized their programs in the past few years (Colorado, Iowa, North Carolina, Pennsylvania, Utah, and Wyoming since 1999). Most states established programs between 1991 and 1994, and over half of those participating (23) have been granting awards for at least a decade. For example, Oklahoma has presented 47 awards (including 19 service organizations) since 1994. Many state awards recognize public, private, and nonprofit organizations for success in specific functions. The State of Oklahoma also won a Ford Foundation Award with its OK-FIRST program that empowers local public-safety officials to make informed decisions in weather-impacted situations through a comprehensive decision-support system with real-time weather data. Similarly, the mission of the Vermont Council for Quality is to achieve and promote performance excellence through continuous improvement and to improve the quality of life for its citizens and organizations. "It was formed as a service company that specializes in marketing organizational assessments, education, and training, and awards for excellence, all based on the Malcolm Baldrige National Quality Award criteria" (Vermont Council for Quality, 2003: 1). As in 22 other states, the council was founded as a nonprofit organization (see Table 6.1). Other state programs, such as the Florida Sterling Award and the Tennessee Quality Awards, are jointly sponsored by their governor's office and by major corporations.

Most state programs use multitiered application processes and host annual conferences to disseminate knowledge and promote applications. The multitiered approach screens out most, if not all, of those unable to document some degree of success, yet encourages others at various levels to participate. Unlike the BNQA, three-quarters of the states have multitiered awards that recognize preliminary, intermediate, and advanced levels of quality achievement. The California Awards for Performance Excellence, for instance, is a three-step application process. Winning one award does not depend on winning the previous level, and organizations can apply at any stage in the process. The first stage, called the California Challenge, designed as a self-assessment program, helps private and public sector applicants begin their journey toward performance excellence. Unlike the Baldrige and many other awards, no competitive point score or site visits take place. The second stage, the California Prospector Award, helps applicants advance their performance goals before committing to compete for the top-tier California Awards for Performance Excellence.[12] Latino businesses can apply for the *La Opinion* award for performance excellence. The Latin Business Association, along with its support entities, the Latin Business Association Institute and the Hispanic Training Council, provides the necessary support to Latino businesses for achieving world-class products and service.

State and local quality awards offer a cost-effective means to motivate organizations to manage performance and increase productivity. In addition, the winners offer a deep and wide reservoir of detailed knowledge about specific actions taken to measure and improve service quality and productivity. If catalogued and organized, these "case studies in organizational innovation" provide a rich database for benchmarking and understanding effective process improvement. Knowledge management programs can be developed to examine specific programs within certain functions, such as E-government and environmental protection (Wimmer, 2002). For example, hundreds of environmental service agencies, hospitals, and healthcare organizations, revenue departments, and school districts in the United States (including BNQA and Innovations winners in Alaska, Missouri, New York, Ohio, and Wisconsin), as well as European Quality Award winners, could be benchmarked, put into databases, and studied by other districts.

Several regional quality leaders, such as Austin, Texas; Coral Springs, Florida; Oklahoma City; Pheonix, Arizona; San Carlos and Sunnyvale, California; and Hampton, Virginia, provide benchmarks for other local governments. The Greater Austin Quality Council Award (GAQCA), a local award for organizations that display exemplary quality programs, develops partnerships between the City of Austin, the Greater Austin Chamber of Commerce, and the University of Texas at Austin. Similar to the Texas Quality Award (TQA), the Austin awards are divided into four distinct levels. The first level, the Commitment Award, identifies organizations that demonstrate a serious commitment to the implementation of a quality program. The Progress Award recognizes organizations that incorporate quality principles in daily activities and demonstrate interest in furthering their quality initiative. The Significant Merit Award rewards those who show a sound quality base and positive results stemming from the quality program. The Highest Achievement Award honors organizations that can prove outstanding examples of quality and service over a substantial period of time. The City of Sunnyvale's public-health program serves as an example of an innovative quality service designed for citizens. In 1999, the city announced plans to make Automatic External Defibrillators (AEDs) available at public buildings and to encourage employers and retailers to purchase AEDs and keep them on the premises in case of a cardiac emergency. The commitment to quality is seen in the city's statement of core values, citing long-term planning, results orientation, customer service, partnerships, prevention, continuous improvement, and community involvement as the driving forces in managing the city.

In addition to the empirical results reported in the preceding text, there is substantial other empirical evidence that quality awards play a significant role in improving organizational performance, enhancing reputations, and fostering regional economic development (Fisher, Dauerive, and Barfield, 2002; Hendricks and Singhal, 2001; NIST, 2002; Puay et al., 1998). The self-selection and multitiered processes used by many states further encourages participation and maintains a high quality standard established by outside examiners. In this respect, most state programs have been very successful. However, quality awards in the future must also acknowledge those organizations that maintain their performance after receipt of an award. Critics argue that winning an award is only a preliminary measure of success and fails to guarantee profit or customer satisfaction in the long run (Steventon, 1994). Maryland implements a program that requires organizations to constantly innovate to meet the needs of an ever-changing society. When this change is incorporated into selection criteria of all awards, then they will become much more effective in rewarding institutions that sustain long-term improvements.

Hundreds of award-winning service organizations at the state, substate, regional, and local levels provide models for others in a wide variety of functional areas, such as education, healthcare, law enforcement, parks and recreation, procurement, revenue collection, and information technology. For instance, since 1983, there have been 69 winners of the U.S. Senate Quality and Productivity Awards for Virginia, 31 (45 percent) in government services, including 12 (17 percent) school districts (Virginia Quality Awards, 2002). The State of Oregon presented 38 different awards between 1994 and 1999: 13 of those (one third) went to public and nonprofit agencies (Oregon Excellence, 2002). Since 1992, 37 organizations received Florida's prestigious Sterling Award, including the Miami-Dade County Health Department, Kendale Elementary School in Miami, Sarasota Memorial Hospital, and the cities of Coral Springs and Jacksonville (Florida Sterling Council, 2003). Of the 51 winners of the New York Empire State awards from 1992 to 2000, over half (31) were city or state governments, hospitals, school districts, or other types of service organizations (New York Empire State Awards, 2001).[13] In sum, there are now hundreds of benchmarks or models of state and local governments in a wide range of services. TQS concepts and theories are being used in a number of schools, colleges, and universities with a new generation of students learning with an environment of teamwork, shared decision-making responsibility, and accountability for results (see Case Study 6.2 and related cases in Chapter 8).

Conclusion: A 21st Century Trend or Passing Fad?

The extended use of multinational recognition programs to reward innovation confirms that most federal and state award programs successfully accomplish a majority of what they set out to achieve. All reward organizations assist applicants in improving their previous performance levels, and some expect this level to be maintained. The future success of quality awards depends on several inter-related factors, including:

- Continued evidence of a positive economic benefit from award winners
- Commitment from winners to exchange knowledge, share information, and transfer results
- Shared opportunities for applying knowledge in other types of organizations
- Expanded participation by all types of organizations

The more proof potential applicants have that quality awards can improve the internal efficiency of their organizations, increase profits, or reduce costs, the greater the number of applications. To what extent have awards encouraged other agencies to implement changes? The empirical evidence here is somewhat mixed: two thirds of the state respondents reported that as of early 2002, applications either increased or remained the same. In states where applications decreased, directors suggested that complexity of award criteria, lack of marketing, and weak regional economic conditions explained most of the decline. These negative factors were overcome in the majority of states by affiliations with corporate sponsors, partnerships with nonprofit and private organizations, strong leadership, and volunteer service. Encouragingly, despite a sluggish national economy, applications for the Baldrige awards increased in 2002.

State and local award programs reflect our federalist structure of decentralized government and are different in many ways. Some require payment of examiner's fees, whereas others award cash prizes. Some are closely affiliated with the governor's office or corporate sponsors; many are organized as nonprofits, and others have multitiered awards. However, several have common features:

1. Most state award programs depend on volunteer support and receive only limited state funding.
2. All state awards, and several private and international awards, rely on the Malcolm Baldrige National Quality Award criteria, rules, and application requirements.
3. Nearly half of the quality award organizations are independently chartered under the IRS as 501(c)3 nonprofit corporations and operate without extensive state budgetary support.
4. Three quarters (75 percent) of the states require recipients to disseminate results to other organizations.

5. Responsible officials, such as directors of quality awards programs in several states, could identify public officials (champions) who demonstrated success within certain state or local governments and are recognized statewide as quality leaders.
6. All states use common criteria and provide a standardized methodology for comparing one service function to another in diverse regions.

Customer satisfaction is becoming an obsession for many world-class service organizations, and most private companies already go beyond merely satisfying customers to exceeding their expectations. Consequently, awards, benchmarks, charter marks, and international audit standards will most likely play a more significant role by offering credibility in the eyes of citizens, customers, and employees alike. This will be especially important for corporations and governments seeking to regain public confidence and trust.

In an era in which more people depend on governments for assistance, survival, and protection, improving the efficiency and effectiveness of public services is an urgent national priority. The process that began with reinventing the government a decade ago has now evolved to a point where all public agencies are paying closer attention to their internal management processes and becoming more customer-responsive and results-driven. The critical question for future microorganizational research is: Have quality awards changed internal organizational processes and systems to provide incentives for individual employees to become more responsive to citizens and supervisors?

Rewarding customer service and performance management, part of this complex process, proves to be a useful way to share best practices, measure results, add value, and achieve quality and productivity goals. Quality awards are an underutilized resource for organizations committed to improving service quality and performance. They can serve as catalysts for change, identify areas needing improvement, support internal collaboration, motivate everyone to achieve specific goals, and provide learning tools to retain expertise. The competitive challenge and distinction that accompany pursuit of an award, charter mark, or ISO certification can be a significant source of employee motivation and pride. Perhaps most important, the data generated by various performance recognition techniques can help to develop theory to assist public managers in determining which private sector models are best suited for application in the public sector. Awards, benchmarks, citizens' charters, and audit standards will never entirely eliminate the differences between the missions of nonprofit, public, or private organizations. They can, however, provide a rich database for assisting governments in implementing change strategies, developing successful performance measures, and reaching out to all being served.

Key Terms

Intragovernmental coordination
Intergovernmental coordination
Environmental Protection Agency (EPA)
Transportation Security Administration (TSA)
U.S. Department of Homeland Security (DHS)
State quality award programs
Citizens' charters
Charter marks
Deming Prize
ISO 9000/14000
European Quality Awards
Malcolm Baldrige National Quality Award (BNQA)
Quality improvement program (QIP)
Quality improvement teams (QITs)
Policy deployment
Quality in daily work (QIDW)
Formal groups
Information central
Privatization
Ford Foundation Innovations in American Government Program
National Public Service Awards (NPSA)
Public Service Excellence Awards (PSEA)
President's Quality Award

Notes

1. In addition to surveys and telephone interviews with agency directors, several applications were reviewed and the Web sites of all agencies examined. Respondents were asked to: (1) describe application procedures, (2) list the number and types of applications received, (3) state whether the number of applications were increasing or decreasing, (4) list award criteria and give examples of successful state or local programs, and (5) describe how program successes are publicized. Surveys mailed to all 45 agencies, with 34 returned after fax and telephone follow-ups, achieved a 75-percent response rate.
2. Until recently, the phrase "public sector innovation" was regarded by many as little more than a bad joke or an oxymoron. The chaos following the 2000 U.S. presidential elections, 2002 primary elections in Florida, and the 2004 elections in Ohio resulted in part from nonstandardized voting systems and continued use of obsolete (40-year-old) technology. Failure to invest in new equipment and technologies threatens public confidence in electoral

processes. Congress has passed legislation and authorized billions of dollars to update equipment, standardize procedures, and improve training to prevent such events from happening again.

3. For a detailed and indexed guide to the use of charters, citizen participation, performance standards, charter mark awards, networks, best practices, and how to complain in the United Kingdom, see the excellent Modernizing Public Services Group Web site at www.servicefirst.gov.uk/. For lists of Deming Prize winners, see: www.deming.org/demingprize/, http://www. snqc.org/INFORMATION/QAw.htm. For European Quality Awards, see http://www.efqm.org/model_awards/eqa/intro.htm and http://www.nqi. ca/english/awards.htm; and the Baldrige Web site: www.baldrige. nist.gov.

4. This creates a "demonstration effect" where "champions" are identified as leaders of specific processes in particular agencies, within various regions. In an interview, the director of the California Quality Awards program identified specific individuals within the state who were known as leaders of the public sector quality movement.

5. The Union of Japanese Scientists and Engineers evaluates applications and makes the awards to companies and individuals who have achieved high levels of statistical quality control. Japan's leading manufacturers such as Bridgestone, Hitachi, Fuji Photo, Komatsu, Mitsubishi Electric, Nissan, Ricoh, and Toyota among many others have received Deming Prizes.

6. Of the hundreds of prizes awarded to businesses and individuals in the past 50 years, only a few have been granted to service organizations. Many Southeast Asian countries have not only received recognition, but established their own prizes modeled after the Deming award. The number of winners each year is unlimited. Any company or individual who achieves a high level of quality and is certified by examiners as meeting rigorous performance standards can be eligible to receive the award.

7. Interview with Myron Tribus, former U.S. assistant secretary of commerce, October 18, 1990. For a complete list of Malcolm Baldrige National Quality Award program recipients, contacts, and profiles, see World Wide Web at www.baldrige.nist.gov.

8. Three quarters of the states also require winners to showcase their procedures with potential applicants. The recipients of the Maryland state awards must share their information with any interested organizations and also work with the Maryland Center for Quality and Productivity. The U.S. Senate Quality and Productivity Award recipients must provide at least one person to serve as an examiner.

9. The Pearl River School District also won the New York Empire State Award in 1994. For details about 2001 education winners, see Chapter 8 and www.chugachschools.com/, www.nist.gov/public_affairs/pearlriver.htm, and www.nist.gov/public_affairs/uwstout.htm. For information on the 2002 to 2003 healthcare winners, see www.nist.gov/public_affairs/releases/ssmhealth. htm.

10. The QI story format was meant to encourage participation by the workforce, but its rigid methodology had the opposite effect. This seven-step process was inappropriately applied to too many functions. It actually

disempowered many otherwise hard-working employees who wanted to make independent decisions on behalf of customers, but were frustrated by having to apply this format to each decision.

11. Several of FPL's senior executives were actively involved in the national quality award movement and lobbied the Reagan administration for the creation of the Malcolm Baldrige award in the mid-1980s. Most felt it was not in their best interest to apply for the U.S. award due to possible accusations of conflicts of interest.

12. In 1999, the California Employment Development Department's Insurance Accounting Division won this award. The third and final stage is divided into two awards, the U.S. Senate Productivity Award and the Eureka Award for Performance Excellence. The U.S. Senate Productivity Award is reserved solely for large and small manufacturers. The Eureka Award is reserved for large and small service institutions, education, healthcare, nonprofit government, and the armed forces. The Senate Quality and Productivity Awards are reserved for the public sector, and the Eureka award recognizes both the public and private sectors. See www.calexcellence.org/cce/home/index.htm.

13. Similar numbers of nonmanufacturing private, public, and nonprofit service agencies are being recognized by other states, private nonprofit organizations, and local and regional governments. For additional examples of state and local awards programs, see www.qualitydigest.com/html/state1.html. An excellent Web site linking descriptions of all state awards is www.work-force-excellence.net/html/stateawards/default.htm.

▼

Case Study 6.1: Lessons from the Application of Total Quality Control at FPL

The positive and negative lessons learned from the FPL experience are particularly significant, as their QI efforts were initiated at a time when few services emphasized quality. Faced with an economic crisis, FPL borrowed bits and pieces from many different quality strategies, but depended heavily on Japanese statistical quality control systems (Hudiberg, 1991). Senior FPL executives visited Kansai Electric in the late 1970s and were impressed by the low-cost generating capacity of the Japanese public utility. They felt that to meet the changing demands of both the environment and customers, supply-oriented thinking had to be replaced with customer-oriented thinking.

This new strategy had to evolve from "just a new way of doing business" into a new mind-set that dominated every aspect of FPL operations. Not only did FPL import the Japanese Total Quality Control (TQC) manage-ment structure but adopted the complex and time-consuming statis-tical methodology used to subsequently demonstrate results to the Japanese who served as Deming Prize examiners. Top management guided the implementation process and gave it strong encourage-ment. Although implemented gradually in several phases, the quality philosophy was kept intact and finally spread throughout the organi-zation. Results were achieved by using a quality control system prac-ticed by a successful Japanese Power Company (Kansai Electric). The case study highlights lessons learned from the intensive and contro-versial effort to compete for a prestigious international award. Efforts to sustain the quality focus in an American, heavily-unionized, publicly-regulated workforce failed for the following reasons:

1. The goal of winning the Deming Prize consumed thousands of hours of uncompensated time and fostered resentment among the workers. Morale could not be sustained beyond the award of the prize.
2. Serious allegations were raised concerning the use of ratepay-ers' money to support the Japanese. Challenges to the Florida Public Service Commission over the costs of Japanese "coun-selors" were eventually settled by a large rebate of public funds.
3. Some senior managers underestimated their own job security as well as the complexity of changing the underlying working culture in a large service organization.
4. Creating a separate Quality Management Department did not change the underlying culture of the organization, but rather bred resentment from those not included in the separate bureaucracy.

Resistance set in, and centralization of authority became one of the major reasons that FPL's new management used to justify dismantling the program in 1989. The new chairman and CEO of FPL insisted that his decision was based on the success of the program and the fact that it had become institutionalized in the company (Broadhead, 1991). Subsequently, FPL has reduced its workforce by over 20 percent through downsizing and elimination of 3,000 jobs. Despite these short-comings, it must be remembered that FPL initiated service QIs at a time when no other large U.S. company recognized the need. Many of the improvements were institutionalized, and the company and its customers benefited in the long term. Understanding the reasons for these mistakes will help others avoid them in the future.

In the fall of 1992, during the all-out mobilization to restore power to over 250,000 customers following Hurricane Andrew, FPL crews performed almost miraculously. Within just six weeks, power was restored to all but the worst-hit areas of southwest Dade County. Contingency plans were developed during the 1980s for just such an emergency. These plans, combined with the team training in emergency response to natural disasters, combined to produce these results.

▲

▼

Case Study 6.2: Kenneth W. Monfort School of Business, University of Northern Colorado

Kenneth W. Monfort College of Business (MCB) at the University of Northern Colorado focuses on delivery of an undergraduate-only business education. The 120-credit degree program integrates business-core classes, business-emphasis classes, and business electives with a strong nonbusiness foundation in the liberal arts. MCB educates approximately 1,200 students per year with a state budget of about $4.5 million supplemented by contributions from various private foundations and a 15-year commitment from the Monfort Family Foundation ranging from $500,000 to $925,000 annually. There are 32 full-time faculty, 9 administrative staff, and 15 part-time adjunct faculty located in Greeley, Colorado.

Highlights

- From 1994 to 2004, student learning performance on the Educational Testing Service (ETS) business tests has increased 34 percent. (ETS is a national standardized educational testing and measurement organization.) Student performance at MCB consistently has been well above the national mean and in 2003 and 2004 reached the top-10-percent level, with the summer and fall 2004 results exceeding the 95th percentile, the highest scoring band available.
- On 9 of 16 student satisfaction factors measured on the 2004 Business Exit Survey by Educational Benchmarking, Inc. (EBI), MCB ranks in the top 10 percent nationally among the 171 institutions. (EBI provides comparative assessment methods, instruments, and analyses.) In 2003 and 2004, MCB scored in the top 1 percent for overall student satisfaction with the program, with performance in the top 2.5 percent for 5 consecutive years.

- In 2004, more than 90 percent of organizations employing MCB's students rated the program as good or excellent, a rating that surpasses all of MCB's major regional competitors.
- In 1984, MCB adopted a mission and vision focused only on providing high-quality undergraduate business education that has matured and flourished through three deans. This focus, combined with a strategy of high-touch (small class size), wide-tech (integrating technology throughout the curriculum), and professional depth (using highly placed executives and business-experienced PhDs as instructors), serves to differentiate the organization from its competitors. MCB is one of five under-graduate-only business schools in the nation accredited in both business and accounting by the Association to Advance Colle-giate Schools of Business (AACSB International).
- Ethical behavior is widely embedded in the classroom and over-all culture of MCB. Ethics coverage is required in every MCB course, which includes how students are to use high ethical standards as they pursue their studies. All ethical issues are addressed in the University Codification, the University Faculty Handbook, and the MCB Faculty Handbook, and are monitored by the MCB Faculty Affairs Committee and the MCB Student Affairs Committee.

Quality and Improvement Results

- For the past six years, MCB has achieved best-in-class status and has been above the 90th percentile nationally for academic rigor in their business courses, as measured by the EBI survey of exiting students. EBI results permit MCB to compare its perfor-mance with business programs at 171 schools nationwide.
- Other results show MCB in the top 10 percent nationally in areas such as "Satisfaction with Quality of Teaching in Business Courses" (top 2.5 percent in 2004 and top 10 percent since 1998); "Satisfaction with Availability of Computers" (top 5 percent in 2004 and top 10 percent for the past four years); and "Satisfac-tion with Quality of Classrooms" (top 5 percent in 2004 and top 10 percent since 1998).
- In addition, in 2004, MCB has shown strong performance against a select group of six peer institutions that includes two regional competitors. EBI provides blinded performance results for these peers. On 13 of the 16 factors reported in the EBI survey, MCB ranks first in its peer group.

■ Exiting MCB student ratings of the "Value of Investment Made in the Degree" have trended favorably from 1998 to 2004, with results in the top 2.5 percent out of 171 schools nationally in 2004 and above the top 10 percent for 5 of the last 6 years.

■ MCB has maintained a growth rate of "direct cost per credit hour" below the rate of inflation for the last three years. Despite recent cuts in state funding, MCB has increased the proportion of the state budget spent on faculty instruction. In addition, MCB's tuition levels for full-time in-state students are significantly below competitors' and 45 percent below the national average in 2003 and 2004.

■ Three key indicators of faculty satisfaction (overall evaluation of program, sharing a common vision for the school, and faculty satisfaction with computer support) demonstrated high levels of satisfaction with MCB's vision and mission. Results for Overall Evaluation of the Undergraduate Program show MCB maintaining faculty satisfaction levels in the top 10 percent of the national comparator group for at least 4 years (2000 to 2003) and in the top 2.5 percent in 2002. Despite a salary freeze and increased class loads, faculty continue to strongly support a shared vision for the college with a particular commitment to maintaining small class sizes as part of a high-touch strategy.

Processes

■ To enrich the curriculum and bring real-world business expertise to the campus, MCB's innovative Monfort Executive Professor Program invites regionally or nationally known senior executives to campus not only as guest lecturers but also to teach complete courses.

■ In addition to faculty and departmental leadership, the Dean's Leadership Council, a partnership with local, regional, and national business executives, provides input on strategies, plans, and curriculum direction, as well as student preparedness and employer requirements.

■ MCB has reduced the cycle time to launch new courses, enabling it to respond within a few months to student and employer demand for new courses to enhance the preparation and skills of graduates.

■ The college's Strategic Management Process is a multistep, systematic process aligned and integrated with its mission, vision, and values; with its shared governance structure, in which faculty, administration, students, and stakeholders participate; and with its student, stakeholder, and market knowledge processes. Key performance indicators (KPIs) and Supporting performance indicators (SPIs) are linked to MCB's strategic challenges and contribute to continuous improvement activities. The college also aligns its strategies and planning with the University's mission and values. Information from internal and external sources, including SWOT (strengths, weaknesses, opportunities, and threats) analysis and KPI/SPI results, form the basis for strategic objectives and short-term (annual) and long-term (five-year) goals.

■ MCB uses a coordinated approach to capture, review, and maintain data for management of organizational performance and knowledge management. Faculty, staff, students, and other stakeholders have real-time access to individual and aggregate data and information on SEDONA, a Web-based faculty database system, and Web sites.

■ MCB uses a comprehensive set of key process requirements for undergraduate business education. They include use of technology throughout the curriculum, small class sizes with extensive faculty–student interaction, simulation of business decisions, and hands-on learning opportunities. This contributes to MCB's strategy of high-touch, wide-tech, and professional depth.

■ All faculty and staff participate in the shared governance system that is built around councils, committees, and traditional academic departments. This structure provides the organization with its primary means to communicate throughout the organization, conduct strategic and action planning, share ideas and improvements, and manage the delivery of education programs and other processes.

Leadership and Social Responsibility

■ Students and employees are actively involved in supporting MCB's key communities as part of its organizational citizenship activities through coursework and extracurricular programs.

■ The Dean's Leadership Council (DLC), comprised of 25 Colorado professional and business leaders, helps MCB better understand and address the needs of customers, including students, alumni, students' employers, faculty, and staff.

■ The Administrative Council (ADMC), consisting of deans and department chairs, is chaired by the dean and serves as MCB's primary mission review group and functions as a communications conduit between faculty and the dean. The dean and ADMC also are active in communicating and meeting with university partners and suppliers to strengthen relationships between these partners, as well as to better understand how each functions and find ways to mutually improve service delivery. Web site: http://www.mcb.unco.edu.

Source: Baldrige National Quality Program, National Institute of Standards and Technology, U.S. Department of Commerce, Web site: www.baldrige.nist.gov.

▲

Chapter 7

Managing Performance in the Public Sector

To increase the competence, management capacity, and productivity of public employees, various competing models are used to improve the performance and responsiveness of government agencies. Since the early 1990s, many federal, state, and local agencies have applied performance management strategies based on variations of previously discussed market-driven concepts such as business process reengineering (BPR), customer relationship management (CRM), continuous quality improvement (CQI), and Total Quality Management (TQM). Reinvention, responsiveness, and restoring faith and trust in government also appeared prominently in high-level reform proposals in the United States, England, and in Europe (Gore, 1993; Hodge, 2000; Winter, 1993). Public managers now expend considerable time, effort, and resources exchanging best practices, finding best value, and rethinking government. Moreover, citizens expect public services that are as good as or better than those provided by the private sector. Whether governments can meet these expectations in today's cost conscious, results-driven, and ideologically charged political environment is often the subject of political debate.

Assessing Alternative Performance Management Strategies

Public administrators face intense political pressures to simultaneously downsize, measure performance, reduce costs, increase productivity, and provide better service to citizens. Many governments attempt to accomplish these mutually compatible public policy goals by:

1. Increasing existing organizational performance levels
2. Measuring quality and productivity
3. Improving the capacity and competence of bureaucracy to achieve results with fewer resources
4. Restoring public faith and trust in government

Citizen demands for lower taxes and political campaign rhetoric calling for leaner and meaner, i.e., more efficient and flexible, public administration ("less government that works better"), encourages many public agencies to examine how they define performance, measure productivity, and improve results. Politicians of every stripe still criticize "the bureaucracy" (ironically, the very institution they are accountable for as elected officials) as unaccountable, inefficient, and wasteful. During the 1990s, Congress passed administrative and management reforms mandating budget deficit reductions, personnel caps, and the use of results-oriented systems to implement reinvention goals.

Many government agencies now struggle to find the best strategies to implement performance-based reforms within traditional rules-driven bureaucracies. Agencies must consider strategic needs, as well as the organizational dynamics of diverse cultural, political, and social environments, to determine what aspects of private models, if any, can transfer to public agencies. Market-based models receive careful examination, especially with regard to accountability, citizenship, competition, definition of customers, and equity of services provided to citizens (Alford, 2002; Beckett, 2000; Behn, 1999; Blanchard, Hinnett, and Wong, 1998; Box, 1999a; Fredrickson, 1996; Haque, 2001; Milakovich, 2006; Wilson, 1989). As demands for lower costs and higher service quality ("less government that delivers more value") rise, relationships between suppliers and recipients of public services become increasingly complex. This requires elected officials to assume a broader role in designing and implementing systems that meet the expectations of customers, clients, and individuals. Applying profit-driven private sector management techniques to non-market-driven and regulatory organizations requires careful analysis, evaluation, and explicit criteria for selection. Many of the reforms under consideration have private sector roots, but were applied in countries with much more central government control of the economy, including Australia, Canada, New Zealand, the United Kingdom, and Chile (Armijo and Faucher, 2002; Atkinson, 1997; Durant and Legge, 2002; Forrer, 2002; Jordan, 2001; Osborne and Plastrik, 2000). Therefore, administrators must exercise care not to transfer elements from various models that might further alienate people already distrustful of government actions and motives.

Advocates of market-based reforms minimize the distinction between public and private functions and argue that government productivity improves merely with the application of competition and business "know-how" (Bush, 2001; Goldsmith, 1997; Hodge, 2000; Savas, 2000). To others, running government like a business by providing more subsidies for faith-based organizations, privatizing public functions, and outsourcing public resources, are reforms that emphasize downsizing and transfer of function rather than citizenship and political accountability. According to critics of the market model, advocates of this view disparage the public as "customers" in commercial transactions, rather than as citizens who govern themselves through active participation in democratic electoral processes (Box et al., 2001). Rather than exchanging information and designing policy with "empowered" citizens capable of democratic self-governance, those who espouse greater privatization or "contracting out" distrust "the public" and rely instead on powerful well-funded private interest groups to identify policy alternatives.

The future direction of performance management in the public sector is intrinsically linked to public trust in government's ability to resolve complex economic, political, and social problems. Public managers generally understand the concepts underlying various performance management alternatives, and some are even applying more advanced approaches, such as European ISO 9000 standards, knowledge management (KM), and Six-Sigma systems, often as a result of political pressures for expanded E-government initiatives (Barquin et al., 2001; Fountain, 2001; Gronland, 2002; Heeks, 1999; Milakovich, 2006). Still, public administrators are cross-pressured by the conflicting ideological demands of multiple interest groups, parties, and citizens. Consequently, they face difficult decisions selecting among various alternatives for improving performance.

Public agencies face difficult choices: continue to use the incremental, reinvention-based, hybrid approach of the last decade, implement "pure" private-market-based models, such as contracting out and privatization, or find a middle ground, such as joint public–private partnerships with private, volunteer, and non-government organizations (NGOs). Subtle differences between various management strategies and a lack of political consensus about which alternatives consistently work best in specific public policy arenas makes it more difficult to select a reform model. The application of "pure" QI or SPC methodologies might increase efficiency in attaining organization goals, but unique ideological and political demands on public sector decision making makes such applications difficult (Swiss, 1992). Adding urgency to the partisan debate is the grim reality that the ability of downsized and reinvented government agencies to manage performance is no longer an abstract theoretical exercise. The benchmark for successful implementation of performance management strategies for many U.S. public agencies is now their performance in protecting homeland security and fighting the war against terrorism.

Reinvention, Service Standards, and Results Orientation

The U.S. Congress supported executive branch and legislative reforms to promote entrepreneurial, market-based, and results-driven systems for distributing public resources during the reinvention era (1993 to 2001). As a result, more agencies began to decentralize decision-making authority, empower employees, and treat citizens as valued customers. Reinvention, a controversial mix of ideology, practice and theory, emphasized competitive, customer-focused, and market-based solutions to perceived inefficiencies in the delivery of government services. The principle instrument for reform, the National Performance Review (NPR), incorporated reinvention principles and exhorted federal agencies to become more efficient by downsizing, eliminating unnecessary regulation, focusing on results, and offering customer service equal to or better than "the best in business" (Carroll, 1995; Durst and Newell, 1999; Gore, 1993; Kettl, 1998; Kim and Wolff, 1994; Miller, 1994; Russell and Waste, 1998). Reinvention initiatives sought to alter organizational processes and give public administrators incentives to manage the public sector more like the private sector. Although the NPR emphasized competition, privatization, and market-driven reforms (Box, 1999a; Durst and Newell, 1999; Goldsmith, 1997), the theoretical foundations of reinvention focused on public employee empowerment, reorganization, and restructuring, rather than replacing public agencies with private providers. As a result, many public agencies realigned their organizational structures with customer-focused, performance-based, and results-oriented management systems.

There have been other high-level reform efforts targeting waste reduction and promoting managerial and technological improvements (the Ash, Hoover, Packard and Grace Commissions). Unlike its predecessors, however, the NPR managed to avoid extreme politicization and received positive evaluations for achieving most of its major goals (Kettl, 1998). Theories and methods for reform, drawn from quality management applications in Japan and the United States during the 1980s, were gradually and selectively converted to the public service sector. Reinvention stressed improvement of existing government agencies. In contrast, movement to privatize public functions originated in countries with significantly greater centralized federal control over budgets than governments in the United States (Hodge, 2000; Osborne and Plastrik, 2000).

The budget reforms, deficit agreements, and new management and performance improvement systems succeeded in reducing the size of the federal bureaucracy to its smallest level, both in total size and ratio of employees to population, since the 1950s (Milakovich and Gordon, 2004: 286). In addition, federal executive agencies must now publish and report their customer service standards, performance goals, specific measures, and results to oversight agencies, such as the Office of Management and Budget (OMB), the Congressional Budget Office (CBO), and the Government Accountability Office (GAO).[1] Federal agencies must comply with stringent laws, such as the Chief Financial Officers Act of 1990 (P.L. 101-576), the Federal Workforce Restructuring Act of 1994 (P.L. 103-226), and the Government Performance and Results Act (GPRA) of 1993 (P.L. 103-62, 107 Stat.285). The GPRA directed most federal agencies to develop performance measures to deliver better services with fewer dollars. This led to numerous demonstration projects in federal agencies, as well as in some states and local governments, and increased the potential for more effective (or selective) use of expenditures to improve (or terminate) ineffective (or politically unpopular) programs.[2] Although the Clinton Administration's capacity-building efforts received support from the U.S. Congress, many state legislatures failed to change their constituent-driven, committee-based budget procedures to make appropriations decisions, at least partially, on the achievement of customer service standards or comparative agency rankings. Nonetheless, the reinvention movement achieved important breakthroughs in changing the attitudes and motivating federal executives to implement results-oriented goals in their agencies. Most federal agencies and departments have enhanced their capacity to improve systems and processes, empower employees, improve performance, measure results, and respond to citizens as customers.

The Bush Administration shelved the reinvention initiative and mandated the use of a far more rigorous results-based management agenda for the fiscal 2003 budget cycle. Long-term goals include creating a "flatter and more responsive" bureaucracy, competitive outsourcing, expanded E-government, and integration of budget and performance indicators. President Bush's Performance Management Agenda (PMA) also emphasizes expanded competition to replace as many as 850,000 federal workers with private contractors, the creation of an Office of Electronic Government to promote E-government initiatives, partnerships with faith-based and non-profit providers, and the opening of federal contracts to "promote rather that stifle" innovation through competition (Bush, 2001).[3] It is still not clear how President Bush's vision of competitive privatization relates to more efficient delivery of public services.

Only a few federal agencies assume direct customer service responsibilities. In fact, two thirds of the federal budget consists of so-called entitlements, transfers for social insurance payments to individuals, medical services, or research grants to institutions.

The real challenge for improving performance management exists at the state and local level, where most citizens receive education, emergency management, law enforcement, healthcare, and a variety of other services directly from public officials. In many states, far less concern exists about who delivers service than about meeting current service demands and employee payrolls. Several state governments are facing 10 to 35 percent deficits in current budget projections and are being forced to increase public school class sizes, reduce social services, and release prisoners. These decisions have obvious financial implications for public budgeting, but also directly affect personnel management, labor relations, and the push for greater efficiency, effectiveness, productivity, and accountability in public management. Despite the expanded use of E-government, privatization, service standards, and results orientation, it is still too early to determine the level of commitment or the long-term impact of performance management reforms on state and local bureaucracies. Nonetheless, more governments in all countries are contracting with private providers such as Operations Management International, Inc. (see Case Study 7.1) to provide essential public services.

Restoring Faith and Trust in Public Service

Public administration is a large, multifaceted, and increasingly interconnected network of federal, state, and local service organizations, staffed by 20 million hard-working teachers, police officers, military personnel, and public officials, in all branches and at all levels of government. One in seven service industry jobs are provided directly by governments. The growth and reduction of governmental activity and public bureaucracy is one of the most significant social phenomena and the subject of considerable debate among citizens, politicians, and scholars (Behn, 1999, 2001; Svara, 1999; Wilson, 1989). Increasing public trust in the ability of governments to function effectively is an important measure of the success of such reforms.

In contrast to other advanced industrialized democracies, public institutions in the United States are both less centralized and more numerous. Public employees account for nearly 20 percent of the total U.S. workforce in over 87,000 federal, state, and local government jurisdictions (cities, counties, townships, and special purpose districts). The multiple complexities of American federalism further fragment bureaucratic authority and restrict the power of public agencies to act either accountably or undemocratically. Public administrators face immense challenges to provide essential services, such as crime prevention, public education, environmental protection, immigration control, healthcare, highway maintenance, national defense, public safety, transportation, emergency services, and assistance after natural and man-made disasters. How to identify, control, and reduce "unnecessary" bureaucracy and at the same time add value by improving the competence, management capacity, and performance of essential public services has been hotly debated during recent political campaigns. Shifts in public opinion about the performance of public agencies reflect varying levels of perceived faith and trust in government's ability to cope with basic social problems, maintain economic growth, manage programs effectively, and respond to crises. Whether or not changes in public performance management increase accountability, efficiency, and trust in government, remain open questions, subject as much to public opinion as empirical investigation.

Rebuilding Confidence and Trust

Citizens' attitudes toward the performance of both public and private bureaucracies (i.e., large organizations) are conditioned by reactions to government institutions, as well as other influential elite "actors," such as business, courts, labor, military, and the mass media. Cynicism, distrust, and skepticism about high-level public and private officials is partially explained by the "Enron effect" of scandals, official misconduct, and mismanagement of funds involving the governance of private corporations, as well as public bureaucracies. Expressions of trust or mistrust in government mirror collective feelings about the condition of the economy and incumbent national administrations. To the extent that governmental activity focuses on improving performance that the public perceives as ineffective, public confidence suffers.

Americans' confidence in public institutions declined significantly during the 1970s because of economic problems, the energy crisis, excessive levels of taxation, recession, the Iran hostage crisis, and rampant inflation. The mid-1980s brought optimism and the expectation of tax cuts, higher corporate profits, more privatization and less regulation of the economy under the leadership of President Ronald Reagan. Following the end of the Cold War, the collapse of communism, and the disintegration of the Soviet Union, relations with Russia improved, and efforts to grow the economy and curb inflation bore fruit. By the mid-1980s, public confidence and trust in government increased, but to a level well below that of the

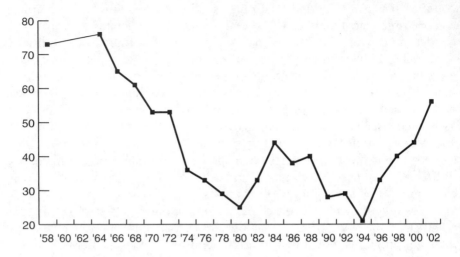

Question Text: "How much of the time do you think you can trust the government in Washington to do what is right-- just about always, most of the time or only some of the time?"

Response: Most of the time/Just about always

Figure 7.1 Trust the federal government: most of the time/just about always, 1958 to 2002. (From the NES Guide to Public Opinion and Electoral Behavior, http://www.umich.edu/~nes/nesguide/gd-index.htm#5.)

Kennedy and Johnson era in the 1960s. (see Figure 7.1.) Discussion of a "peace dividend" emerged briefly as economic conditions improved in the 1990s. Public attitudes toward government also shifted, notably in the form of rising support for government deregulation and for cuts in government spending aimed at a federal budget deficit reduction. The inevitable "downsizing" of many private sector jobs, resulting from an economic downturn since the early 2000s, significantly influenced attitudes about leaders, institutions, and policies. After declining to historic lows in the mid 1990s, public opinion on trust and confidence in government experienced an upward trend (even before 9/11), reflecting attitudes about government's ability to deal with basic social issues and increases in efficiency accompanying the reinvention movement (source: Gallup Poll and Pew Research Data).

Public impatience with governmental inefficiencies and perceived mistreatment by public administrators, together with the decade-long Vietnam War and Watergate, reduced faith and trust in government. Public opinion remained at relatively low levels during the last third of the 20th century. Fluctuations in bureaucracy's public standing coincided with increasing complexity of the nation's problems, the expansion of public services, a reduction in voter turnout, demands for entitlement programs, and (ironically) much higher levels of competence and professionalism among government workers.

Despite the expressed antigovernment attitudes, not all bureaucrats treat citizens badly, and not all government programs are ineffective. On the contrary, partially as a result of reinvention, many federal agencies receive higher customer satisfaction ratings than their private sector counterparts (Peckenpaugh, 2001), and most citizens feel satisfied with the majority of government programs (Holzer and Callahan, 1998; Goodsell, 2004; Neiman, 2000).[4] Even as politicians tried to appease public concerns about government performance by reducing the size of bureaucracies, most acknowledged the competence, honesty, integrity, and demonstrated talents of the vast majority of administrative officials. The 1990s reforms aimed at increasing the capacity and changing organizational structures to better manage performance. Assumptions about how to encourage employee motivation and recast organizational structures of large executive bureaucracies underlie these changes. Despite the impressive gains, the public sector still faces serious administrative and managerial challenges to empower, motivate, and reward employees.

Bureaucratic Empowerment and Citizen Relationship Management

Shifting to citizen-oriented, results-based, and market-driven performance management strategies entails changes in the relationships between employees, managers, and citizens. These changes can be described as citizen relationship management (CzRM). They require the empowerment of public employees, extensive development and training, and a shift from a command-and-control hierarchy to a networked organizational structure for most routine public administration activities. Public sector empowerment has been defined as the devolution of authority within preestablished limits to satisfy customer needs. Responding to citizen demands depends upon one-to-one relationships between people, not on laws, rules, structures or systems. Training must be continually updated and frontline servers drilled in organizational values, not just rules, for improving individual judgment (Berry and Parasuraman, 1991; Milakovich, 1995b; 2003). All empowered employees receive thorough training and the results of their work, at least in the initial stages, is carefully monitored. As trained workers learn how to better manage citizen relationships under a networked structure, rather than a top-down hierarchy, employees require less supervision and feel a sense of ownership; results improve and costs decrease.

Unlike the stereotypical government bureaucracy, an empowered organization grants frontline employees genuine decision-making authority, a stake in the success of the organization, tangible rewards, training opportunities, and, ultimately, process-ownership. Changes in existing organizational structures, conflicting demands and expectations among empowered employees, and results-oriented performance systems contributed in some past reform attempts to confusion and conflict among bureaucrats and citizens seeking self-governance. In exchange for full participation, workers must respond to citizen's demands in the same manner that management reacts to their own needs. This often creates problems for public managers committed to employee empowerment without a concomitant change in management systems, rewards, or organizational structure. In addition, the economic downturn has strained budgets, as well as management-labor relations, and discouraged participatory management strategies in many organizations.

In theory, empowered frontline employees earn the authority to make decisions within prescribed limits at the point of customer contact by focusing on customer service, performance, productivity, and results. This encourages more accountability to customers (citizens, users, or recipients), as well as supervisors in the organizational hierarchy. Such a transformation in thinking can be very difficult for some managers of certain types of "unreinvented" public service organizations, especially regulatory officials (e.g., law enforcement, corrections, intelligence, tax collection, and building and zoning code enforcement) committed to top-down hierarchy and often in conflict with many of their "customers." Managers in these types of agencies often believe that they are exempt from the need to empower line workers because of the evaluative judgments they exercise over the "public." Some frontline employees may indeed require closer supervision to avoid corruption, ethical lapses, liability problems, and potential conflicts of interest (Brehm and Gates, 1997; Pegnato, 1997). Guidelines for elected and appointed public officials set the standards for accountability in service quality and performance management efforts.

In exchange for increased flexibility to respond to customers at the time when help is most needed, empowering public employees imposes greater managerial discipline and results-oriented accountability on managers. Some may feel reluctant or unable (because of legal restraints) to fully empower all employees to resolve customer service issues at the point they occur; others may inadvertently exacerbate problems by not fully utilizing the capabilities of those they supervise. One reason rules-driven management is so pervasive (in both the public and private sectors) is that many managers still believe in "bureaucratic impersonality" as the basis for service among different employees and service units (Berry and

Parasuraman, 1991). Rules-driven managers insist that a standardization of services must exist among different employees and service units. Rule-driven bureaucracies tend to produce regimented Weberian-style responses that may result in bureaucratic delays, excuses for inaction, and unnecessary transfers between departments. Although bureaucratic controls are necessary for establishing accountability and equity, excessive dependency on impersonal rules contradicts the entire concept of customer service-based employee empowerment. Inflexible rules-bound bureaucracies fail to utilize the advantages that empowerment and decentralization contribute to performance management strategies that require more customized treatment and individualized decisions.

For most routine public administration actions, accountable and empowered frontline employees with specialized knowledge and expertise can learn to operate without close supervision. Problems such as bureaucratic delays can be addressed via QI methods without abandoning necessary public sector law and regulation. To achieve this, managers must carefully select those who occupy frontline positions, provide a strong organizational culture and foundation in which to work, offer strategic guidance as necessary, and supply the equipment, support, training, and technology necessary to perform jobs in an empowered organizational environment (Milakovich, 2003). Most importantly, changing the collective mindset of an organization requires delegating authority and responsibility to those who directly interact with recipients of the services.

Accountability, Ideology, and Bureaucratic Mobilization

The mission and structure of most organizations, especially those responsible for administering public policies, must undergo careful analysis when deciding whether or not to privatize critical public functions. Significant differences exist, for example, between a private sector sales transaction to purchase an airline ticket and assuming the collective responsibility for airport security at critical checkpoints to prevent terrorists from hijacking a commercial airliner. The functions of an organization, whether commercial or security, must be taken into account before implementing changes in structure or personnel. This rational approach to policymaking often conflicts with political decision-making processes.

Many citizens and their elected political representatives still feel frustrated with the amount of money collected in taxes and spent (some would say wasted) on services. They are confused about who, among the various agencies, branches, and divisions of our fragmented federal system, is accountable for managing performance, supervising operations, and achieving results. Skepticism about government spending influences attitudes toward government, especially among affluent citizens (elite opinion makers) who pay more in taxes but use minimum services from public bureaucracies. Bickering among politicians about the type of organization (public, private, or nonprofit) or level of government accountable for performing critical tasks only adds to the confusion. Bureaucratic responses to crises traditionally increase the size but not necessarily the management capacity or competence levels of government agencies (Wilson, 1989). Even during domestic and international crises, the most challenging times for all Americans, some politicians place ideological and partisan concerns above the expressed wishes of citizens.[5]

Campaign rhetoric notwithstanding, most citizens of all political persuasions strongly support efforts to improve the efficiency, effectiveness, and responsiveness of public agencies. Public officials must recommend the best policy options to elected political leaders who determine which alternatives will accomplish the task most efficiently. Controversy over who should decide how to implement the future direction of performance management in government reflects the century-old debate about the "proper" relationship between politics, policy, the public sector, and private administration.

Alternatives to Public Management

Conflicting visions of the role of the private sector in public policy decision making reflects differing definitions of public policy, administration, and management. Public policy is a complex network of government programs designed to address specific societal problems. Public administration is similarly and variously defined by leading scholars as:

> ... the use of managerial, political, and legal theories to fulfill legislative, executive, and judicial mandates for provision of regulatory and service functions ... the organization of government policies and programs ... the reconciliation of various forces in government's efforts to manage public policies and programs ... all processes, organizations, and individuals associated with carrying out laws and rules adopted by legislatures, executives, and courts ... or simply the "accomplishing" side of government (Stillman, 2005, 2–3).

As an academic discipline and also a subfield of both political science and administrative management, public administration is theoretical in concept and practical in application. The practice and study of public administration can be distinguished from public and private management by its emphasis on civic governance and political institutions, concern with equity of administering public policy, fairness in resource distribution, and the inclusion of political decision making as a related subfield of study. Unlike the private sector, public agencies are bounded by designated geographic districts and traditionally dependent on representative legislative bodies — Congress, state legislatures, county commissions, city councils, other government and special district boards and commissions — for much of their operating revenues. Public policy, expected to be competitive, responsive, and accountable to broad-based citizen preferences, articulates through interest groups, lobbies, professional associations, and political parties.

In its nearly 120-year history, the discipline and profession of public administration (and more recently, policymaking) underwent major changes in the dominant view of how the public and private sectors should or should not interact. Its most influential thinkers considered the relationship, referred to as the politics-administration dichotomy, as a conflict between *political* values such as accountability, control, and responsiveness and *administrative* values, such as efficiency, effectiveness, and performance (Taylor, 1911; Weber, 1947; Wilson, 1887). Although the theories of these "founding fathers" shaped the discipline for most of the 20th century, all had significant weaknesses: Taylor assumed that there was only "one best way" to complete a task, ignoring the limitations of U.S. federalism. Weber failed to recognize that bureaucracies could be inefficient, and Wilson naively believed that politics could be separated from administration (Behn, 1999). These flaws led others to propose theories that encouraged greater citizen choice and increased involvement by NGOs, primarily but not exclusively private firms, community service organizations, and nonprofit agencies (Greene, 2002; Savas, 2000). Governments, especially those at the local level, are increasingly rediscovering the connection between politics, productivity, and the private business market model (Blank, 2000; Goldsmith, 1997). As a result, many public agencies are applying various performance management systems derived from private sector practices and designed to run public agencies more like competitive, customer-oriented, results-driven, and market-based private businesses.

Advocates of the market model ignore another significant difference between the public and private sectors: the definition of those receiving service as either citizens or customers (or perhaps both). Public administration defines a citizen as someone who has certain rights and *responsibilities* and may be entitled (if eligible) to receive services from various governmental agencies. These services may be funded indirectly from individual income, property, and sales taxes or directly from the collection of fines, designated trust funds, service charges, or user fees. The private sector views a customer as someone who purchases a service or product from an organization that offers it at a competitive price. Businesses need customers to stay in business, whereas most citizens pay taxes whether or not they receive governmental services. Under means-tested and redistributive policy formulas, some citizens may receive more resources than they pay in taxes, whereas others pay for services that they never receive.

Conservative politicians traditionally respond to voter frustration with the perceived inefficiencies of public programs by blaming the bureaucracy and limiting general tax revenue as a source of operating expenses. This restricts the range of policy options available for reform but does not necessarily improve performance management. Responding to negative public opinion about bureaucracy, both Presidents Ronald Reagan and George H.W. Bush (1981 to 1993) contributed to the "no new taxes" attitude by supporting tax cuts and budget reductions. The cutback management movement in government, generally dating from the passage of California Proposition 13 in 1978, continues to place a major constraint on the actions of the bureaucracy. During the 2000 presidential campaign, Republican candidate George W. Bush maintained the tradition by accusing his opponent, Democrat incumbent Vice President Albert Gore, of representing "the government," whereas he (Bush) represented "the people." President Bush must now cope with the "Dubya Dilemma" that both his father and President Reagan also faced. That is, once elected, conservative chief executives must, to achieve policy goals, inspire and lead the same government they criticized. President George W. Bush's leadership challenge is even more difficult because he must mobilize many of those same much-maligned bureaucrats, as no recent president has, in the protracted "war against terrorism" (Milakovich and Gordon, 2004). Another major consequence of the "blame the bureaucracy" campaign has been a dramatic shift in the revenue base for many governments, especially at the state and local level.

Unlike profit-driven private companies, most nonprofits and other NGOs depend on government revenues and private donations for their operating revenues. Most public agencies feel no pressure to generate profits or increase market share, and rely on general revenue sources, such as taxes on personal income, property, and sales, for operating revenue. Some governments, in fact, are legally prohibited from competing with private companies for resources. To ensure fiscal accountability, public budgetary and policy decisions have heretofore focused on inputs, rather than outputs, outcomes, or results. More recently, the formation of public–private partnerships, structured to give NGOs decision-making powers over public budgets, has been used as a productivity improvement measure. Although politically attractive, this strategy raises serious questions about accountability, competition, democracy, equity, and management oversight (Beckett, 2000; Behn, 1999; Gormley and Balla, 2004; Milakovich, 2006; Osborne and Gaebler, 1992).

Motivation to initiate a performance management strategy was partly ideological (the Republican "Contract with America" in 1994, as well as public choice and privatization theories) and partly pragmatic (the Democrats' reinventing government initiative and the NPR). As a result, many state and local governments now draw greater shares of their operating revenues from proprietary services, designated trust funds, or fees collected directly from recipients for specific purposes, such as airport operations, water and sewer, or solid waste disposal. (One of the provisions of the 2001 aviation security act collects a "security fee" from all passengers to pay for new equipment and training for federal airport security officers.) In many jurisdictions, parallel public and private providers offer the same services, and service providers — as varied as airport operations, post-secondary education, mosquito abatement, utilities, and waste disposal — can only use fees for designated purposes. Regardless of the rhetoric about which models (public, private, or nonprofit) best suit the delivery of which services, federal budget caps, changing national priorities, state budget shortfalls, and local property tax restrictions fundamentally altered the sources of public revenue available to provide services. Restrictions on taxes and other general revenue sources increase the amount of money collected directly from recipients by providers of services.

The fee-based, proprietary, trust fund, and intergovernmental shares of the operating budgets of many large state and local governments now equal or exceed the amount collected from general revenue sources such as property and sales taxes. Simply put, most local governments operate closer to the people and must treat citizens as valued customers, especially when fines, license fees, service charges, and tolls are paid directly by service recipients and earmarked for the operation of specific self-supported public purposes. This is especially true for law enforcement, judicial, public safety, security, and regulatory compliance functions. The shifting revenue base of most state and local governments now favors the extended use of competitive, entrepreneurial, and market-based mechanisms for distributing public resources.

With the exception of fiscal, regulatory, and tax policy, businesses eschew greater involvement in the public arena. Decisions made by governments (even during routine times) are generally more complex, involve greater numbers of interests, and tend to be less immediate in their impacts. When compared with private sector management practices, the public sector experiences less stable leadership and fewer incentives to become results oriented and customer focused. In fact, many government functions are inherently consumptive and therefore less "profitable." (Self-interested businesspersons like to refer to themselves as the "tax-producing" sector and to government as the "tax-consuming" sector.) As monopolistic service providers, most governments isolate themselves from the pressures of private-market-based competition and have been reluctant to accept customer-focused and market-driven changes in management and performance systems. Conversely, public managers have had fewer incentives to reward empowered employees or implement results-oriented, performance-driven decision-making processes. According to popular (and largely unexamined) stereotypes, incrementalism and the status quo, rather than entrepreneurism and innovation, prevail in public agencies. Determining the optimum mix of resources for the implementation of private-market models and public–private partnerships with faith-based, volunteer, and NGOs requires more research.

Balancing Public and Private Strategies

Although many public agencies experimented with various techniques, still more failed to measure performance or respond to the needs of citizens as customers in a timely and efficient manner. Dissatisfaction with the quality of services should encourage governments to import market-driven private sector concepts, such as BPR, CRM, entrepreneurism, privatization, and TQM to improve performance, reduce costs, improve customer service quality, and enhance productivity. CRM, a widely used method in the private sector, empowers employees to respond to customers in proportion to the amount of business they contribute to the company. Its application highlights some of the problems with the direct application of private sector techniques (such as the Pareto method for prioritizing the needs of customers) by public agencies. Employees learn to discriminate among customers to provide customized service that meet individual needs.[6] If the customer's service expectations remain unfulfilled, he or she nearly always has the option in a competitive market to deal with another provider. Citizens who feel dissatisfied with public services typically have no recourse other than to purchase services (if available) from a private provider, an option that is either financially prohibitive or unavailable to all but the wealthiest citizens. Lack of competition among service providers further reduces incentives for public agencies to base performance management systems on customer satisfaction or offer customer service at lower costs.

The absence of incentives, such as competition and the profit motive, to encourage public employees to perform value-added services for citizens is a major obstacle in converting to the market-driven model (Chapter 5). Value is added when a process or series of processes that comprise a system improves by reducing variation, thereby increasing efficiency. Public agencies and nonprofit organizations almost always serve broader sets of diverse client groups and provide services that are often paid for indirectly by a third party, usually a foundation or tax-supported government agency, rather than directly by the customer. Yet, no widely accepted mechanism exists similar to CRM or the profit motive to induce either the service provider or user to demand the best value for the lowest cost. Differences in hiring procedures, mission, motivation, purpose, and structure of public and private organizations, and between the market and nonmarket model of customer service, affect what can and cannot successfully apply to improve performance.

Rather than assuming the superiority of one model over another, public managers determine the best fit between private-market-based reforms and improved performance of public agencies. The business market model emphasizes results-oriented customer service quality to increase market share and retain both external and internal customers. Businesses must provide the highest level of service to retain customers due to competition with other providers who offer the same product or service at a lower price. Successful organizations focus on creating an atmosphere of education to equip employees with the knowledge to provide value-added service (without additional costs) to greater numbers of customers within their markets. Regardless of the type of organization, training employees to think differently about customers, managers, suppliers, and themselves is critical to the application of any performance improvement effort. Individuals within an organization must develop a shared sense of common purpose by respecting the rights of customers and making their satisfaction a primary goal. Providing more responsive service by educating public employees to implement results-based systems — within Constitutional limits set by policymakers — is one promising strategy that is being implemented by several public agencies (Beam, 2001; Kettl, 1997; Milakovich, 1995b). In addition, recognizing employees as valuable internal customers and responding to their needs may help to alleviate the so-called "quiet crisis" of retiring senior executives now threatening to undercut many of the productivity gains made by U.S. federal agencies in the past several years.

Unlike private firms, public agencies must consider a wider range of noneconomic policy demands for equality, equity, and fairness in the distribution of resources. Elected representatives will always play a vital role in resolving disputes between government officials and individual constituents who feel they received unfair treatment by administrators. Many local elected officials eagerly perform this "electoral activist" role as representative and spokesperson for those who elected them (Svara, 1999). Politicians who try to "selectively" influence individual transactions between frontline administrators and citizens, however, make it more difficult for administrators to improve an organization's overall level of performance (Box, 1999b; Pegnato, 1997). Without point-of-contact accountability granted to public employees, elected officials who play the ombudsman role may become vulnerable to accusations of favoritism or worse. Satisfying constituents' interests could conflict with other public policy goals, such as program efficiency and cost effectiveness. Elected officials must be involved, as copartners with administrators, in defining how public agencies should respond to citizen expectations (Kettl, 1997). With proper models and theory to guide decisions, there is nothing inherently inconsistent about maintaining political accountability, resolving disputes among varied interests, and improving confidence in government.

Administrative processes and procedures, which uncritically favor private over public sector solutions, may discourage the development of objective outcome measures that would include all participants in reform efforts. The demonstration effect of federal reinvention on states and local governments may be limited because subnational agencies are under severe budgetary pressures, geographically isolated from Washington, and organized for top down, command-and-control governance. As mentioned earlier, federal agencies expend most of their resources (nearly $2.3 trillion) on entitlements, income or Social Security, health benefits (Medicaid or Medicare), or as grants to states and local governments. These governments, in turn, provide services directly to recipients and devote a far greater share of their budgets to employee benefits and salaries. Consequently, a far greater number of nonfederal employees risk losing their jobs from contracting out and privatization initiatives. This may explain the resistance to market-driven reinvention and performance measurement at the state and local level (de Lancer Julnes and Holzer, 2001; Sanderson, 2001). In addition, the newer collaborative and interdependent systems are built on loosely coupled horizontal, as well as vertical, networks where government becomes a broker rather than the sole provider of services (Osborne and Gaebler, 1992). Changes in attitudes required to implement this system are difficult to integrate with governmental operations in our decentralized, fragmented, and locally controlled system of federalism. Although both public and private sector advocates agree on the need to base decisions on performance and results, the research challenge for public administrators is finding ways to reinvent as well as restructure existing management systems that integrate the strongest features of both models.

Despite measurable increases in productivity, achieved primarily through spending cuts and reductions in public employment, determining the feasibility of private-market-based alternatives in specific policy areas requires more research. The data generated from evaluations of the success (or failure) of various performance management techniques will help develop theories to assist public managers in determining which private sector models (if any) are better suited for application by government. Research questions that should be addressed to assist managers in evaluating alternatives include:

- Have reinvented government agencies delivered on promises of better performance?
- How many governments at which levels have the capacity to manage performance?
- Have these reform efforts made any difference in public opinion about the productivity and effectiveness of government programs?
- Do citizens differentiate between various governmental functions in their evaluations of public service?
- What incentives can public administrators use to sustain these reforms after refocusing their mission and implementing performance management systems and techniques?
- What have we learned from states and local governments that use contracting, privatization, and public–private partnerships to deliver economic development, housing, and social services in collaborative arrangements with private developers and community based agencies?

The decision to adopt private-market-driven models, always a political one, raises difficult administrative questions. Among the other research questions necessary to address are:

- What roles should the private sector play in reinventing (or replacing) public administration?
- Are all nonprofit or private alternatives necessarily more efficient and effective service providers?
- How do administrators (public or private) manage across unclear lines of demarcation or "fuzzy boundaries" between government agencies and other entities (Kettl, 1998)?
- Does the market model eliminate democracy from public sector management (Box et al., 2001)? How will performance be measured and who will interpret the results?
- If public administrators withdraw from direct contact with citizens by outsourcing or privatization, who is accountable to whom for what results (Behn, 1999, 2001)?
- What have we learned from state and local contracting and public–private partnerships for the design and construction of public facilities that have led to innovative practices, shared efficiencies and risks, and improved delivery of services?

- If more federally supervised, privately operated "hybrids" or part-nerships are created, who is accountable for results and liable for mistakes?
- What level of confidence exists to inform future performance management efforts (Milakovich, 2006)?

Answers to these and other questions will influence public opinion and the future of bureaucratic policies at all levels of government and in the private and nonprofit sectors as well.

Restoring Faith and Trust by Improving Service Quality

The full impact of the federal government's aggressive decade-long drive to increase efficiency, measure results, and improve service quality is only now being felt (Beam, 2001; Osborne and Plastrik, 2000). Comprehensive legislation supporting downsizing, reinvention, and results-oriented man-agement prompted federal agencies to increase efficiency, establish stan-dards, develop outcome-oriented performance measures, monitor results, and publicly post key performance measures. CFOs in all federal agencies must now provide systematic performance measures and report the results to Congressional committees and to the President in detailed financial statements. Despite these reforms, the future direction of performance management in nonfederal governments remains uncertain.

No universally applicable or readily available handbook exists to guide public managers through the intricate process of selecting from among the array of choices offered in the new public management era. Many forces within and outside the public sector influence the cost, efficiency, effectiveness, quality, performance, and productivity of public services. These, in turn, influence public opinion about government performance. Before 9/11, 33-year lows in public opinion regarding faith and trust in government, anti tax movements, support for downsizing, and local incor-poration efforts reflected distrust in government. In a show of support for public institutions, these same measures spiked to 33-year highs in Octo-ber, 2001, and then returned to prior levels. (see Figure 7.2.) In addition, six out of ten Americans said they trust the federal government "to do what is right" either "just about always" or "most of the time," the highest level since 1968 (Gallup Poll, October 12, 2001). Such huge mood swings in public opinion rarely occur within the American polity, and may reflect renewed faith and trust in public sector capabilities, as well as the public's basic survival instinct when threatened by outside enemies. Partly in response to dramatically increased expectations for more efficient govern-ment to protect citizens, many more citizens now support elected officials

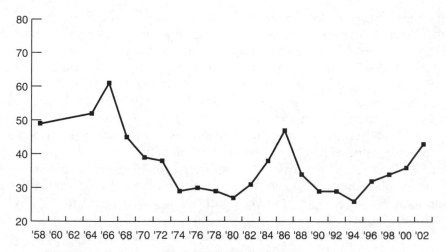

Index constructed using data from the following questions:

"How much of the time do you think you can trust the government in Washington to do what is right-- just about always, most of the time or only some of the time?"
"Would you say the government is pretty much run by a few big interests looking out for themselves or that it is run for the benefit of all the people?"
"Do you think that people in the government waste a lot of money we pay in taxes, waste some of it, or don't waste very much of it?"
"Do you think that quite a few of the people running the government are (1958-1972: a little) crooked, not very many are, or do you think hardly any of them are crooked (1958-1972: at all)?"

Figure 7.2   Trust in government: average score on index, 1958 to 2002. (From the NES Guide to Public Opinion and Electoral Behavior, http://www.umich.edu/ ~nes/nesguide/gd-index.htm#5.

and public administrators in improving government programs. In recent opinion polls, over half of all Americans want government to act more aggressively to solve the nation's problems (Gallup Poll, October 12, 2001). Public agencies can accomplish this task with their newly acquired training, tools, and support.

Public support for governmental action reached its highest level since 1968 shortly after the 9/11 attacks, but has since receded. Still, most public agencies neither fully empower government employees nor respond to the needs of citizens in a consistent, efficient, and effective manner. Many developed greater capacity and competence, but most state and local governments still lack fully functioning performance measurement systems — one of the basic requirements of more effective public management (de Lancer Julnes and Holzer, 2001; Sanderson, 2001). Performance is always difficult to measure, much less improve, and competing public and private strategies (ideologies?) do not make the task any easier. At a minimum, systems must integrate conflicting perceptions of multiple interests of administrators, citizens, lobbying groups, and politicians. Pressures for greater access to information, improved technology, international standards, fiscal pressures, voter demands, and the changing workforce further accelerate the need for performance management. The success of future initiatives, especially at the state and local level, depends on various combinations of citizen self-governance, sustained legislative oversight, and renewed motivation of senior public managers to implement new management and performance evaluation systems. Whether elected officials and senior public managers make necessary changes in management systems to accomplish the task remains to be seen. More research on value-added alternatives is needed to raise hope rather that doubt about the future of performance management.

Public management, a field of practice and study central to public administration, emphasizes internal operations of public agencies and focuses on managerial concerns related to control and direction, such as planning, organizational maintenance, information systems (IS), budgeting, personnel management, performance evaluation, and productivity improvement (Milakovich and Gordon, 2004). Advocates for more public or private management (through deregulation, contracting out, and outsourcing) typically focus on pragmatic business applications to improve system efficiency, performance, and results, rather than on systemic changes to improve delivery systems, public policy content, or political decision-making processes. Despite the accomplishments of the last decade, many ardent supporters of greater privatization view government as a large part of the problem rather than the solution for improving public management. Not surprisingly, the business community in general has been reluctant to acknowledge the profound changes in performance that occurred during the past decade of reinventing government. There are many governmental functions, however, such as aerospace technology, that public agencies are incapable of performing. Therefore, it is essential for public managers to contract services to the highest quality contractors that maintain performance standards and contribute positively to their communities. For some governmental functions, there is no alternative to the private sector as only a small number of multinational corporations are capable of meeting the quality requirements of large public agencies, such as the U.S. Department of Defense (see Case Study 7.2).

During the Clinton–Gore Administration from 1993 to 2001, critics of results-driven government accused the reinventors of going too far in changing public management practices to run operations "too much" like a business. On the other hand, many public administrators resisted such market-based reforms because their positions were threatened under a reinvented (and downsized) federal government. The election of President Bush for a second term in 2004 resulted in marginal changes in performance management strategies proposed by both the Congress and White House. Although the Bush Administration clearly signaled a preference for faith-based, private, or nongovernmental alternatives to achieve policy goals, agency administrators must decide whether to support the incremental public-oriented reforms begun in the last decade, encourage the greater use of private, market-driven options, or develop public–private partnerships. Whatever the direction of public policy, greater numbers of administrators now possess the authority, as well as the knowledge, to manage results-driven performance. In the future, both the President and the Congress must recognize a shared responsibility to initiate performance management strategies in public agencies. Administrators need theory-based research in the areas identified above to recommend effective policy changes and provide advice and expertise to elected officials.

Key Terms

Customer relationship management (CRM)
Downsizing
Government productivity
Performance management
Private-market-based models
National Performance Review (NPR)
Office of Management and Budget (OMB)
Congressional Budget Office (CBO)
Government Accountability Office (GAO)
Chief Financial Officers Act of 1990 (P.L. 101-576)
Federal Workforce Restructuring Act of 1994 (P.L. 103-226)
Government Performance and Results Act (GPRA) of 1993 (P.L. 103-62, 107 Stat. 285)
Performance Management Agenda (PMA)
Entitlements
Federalism
Enron Effect
Public administration
Bureaucratic empowerment
Citizen relationship management (CzRM)
Accountability
Decentralization
Public policy
Cutback management
Ombudsman

Notes

1. The GAO was formerly known as the General Accounting Office. The CBO, GAO, and OMB Web sites are: www.cbo.gov, www.gao.gov/gpra/index.htm and www.omb.gov. Two other comprehensive Web sites for information about recent reforms are: www.firstgov.gov and www.planetgov.com.

2. Government Performance and Results Act (GPRA) of 1993. November 15, 2000. Washington, D.C.: *National Performance Review* govinfo.library.unt.edu/npr/library/misc/s20.html. According to its sponsors, government performance under GPRA is not judged on the basis of amount of money spent or activities conducted, but rather on whether ideas and approaches produce real, tangible results for the taxpayer's dollar. For details, see www.conginst.org/resultsact and www.opm.gov/gpra/index.htm.

3. Executive Office of the President, Office of Management and Budget (2003) "Big Savings Expected from Competitive Bidding Sourcing Initiative," "Hi-Tech Community Salutes President's E-Gov Initiatives," "New Office Signals Major Step Forward for President's E-Government Initiatives," The White House, Washington, D.C. www.omb.gov.

4. Since 1984, the American Customer Satisfaction Index (ACSI) has been measuring customer satisfaction in the private sector. ACSI results now provide baseline and comparative measurement indicators for each federal agency. The University of Michigan Business School conducts customer satisfaction surveys and federal agencies are included in the comparative rankings. For full results, see Web site at www.bus.umich.edu/research/nqrc/government.html.

5. For example, during Congressional debates over aviation and homeland security, reforms in airport security were delayed for over two months after 9/11. A key point of contention was whether or not the 28,000 airline security officers would continue to work as contract employees for private security firms or become federal employees. Despite overwhelming public opinion in favor of federalizing airport security (by a margin of 70 to 30 percent), a few House of Representatives leaders held up the bill that had passed unanimously in the Senate. Several months later, the President signed a slightly modified version of the Senate bill federalizing airport security operations and placing new employees under the Transportation Security Administration (TSA). In March, 2003, the TSA became part of the new Department of Homeland Security.

6. For example, an airline sales representative handling a complaint for a passenger who flies only a few times during the year can offer a $100 voucher to satisfy the customer. The same sales rep may find the same offer would offend a businessperson who flies the airline dozens of times a year. In the latter case, a $500 voucher may be necessary to keep the dissatisfied business traveler from defecting to another airline. Most "customers" of public agencies do not receive this "value-added" differential treatment nor are they free to fly with another agency because, in most instances, there is no competitor.

▼

Case Study 7.1: Malcolm Baldrige National Quality Award Recipient, Service Category: Operations Management International, Inc.

Employee-owned Operations Management International, Inc. (OMI) runs more than 170 wastewater and drinking water treatment facilities in 29 states and eight other nations. Nearly 95 percent of OMI's customers are U.S. cities, counties, and other public entities that have outsourced the operation and maintenance of their plants. The remainder are industrial and international customers.

For all six components of customer satisfaction, scores show an eight-year improvement trend, all rising above five on a seven-point scale for which one means "very poor" and seven means "excellent."

Between 1998 and 2000, OMI's public customers realized first-year savings that averaged $325,000, their operating costs decreased more than 20 percent, and facility compliance with environmental requirements improved substantially.

OMI's total workforce of 1,400 associates is widely dispersed. Only one site employs more than 70 people; most employ fewer than 10. The company's policy is to hire workers formerly employed at facilities that OMI has been contracted to operate.

Headquartered in Greenwood Village, Colorado, OMI was formed in 1980 as part of the CH2M HILL family of employee-owned companies. It was among the first businesses to offer the service of running publicly owned wastewater and water treatment plants, concentrating on small to mid-sized facilities. Such "privatized" utility operations account for 80 percent of OMI's annual revenues, which totaled about $147 million in 2000.

Highlights

- Annual average revenue per associate improved from $92,600 in 1997 to almost $108,000 in 2000 — an increase of more than 15 percent.
- Market share in its core business segment has increased to 60 percent, up from 50 percent in 1996. Over this span, total revenue grew at an average annual rate of 15 percent, as compared with 4.5 percent for OMI's top competitor.

■ Associate turnover decreased from 25.5 percent in 1994 to 15.5 percent in 1999, better than the national average of 18.6 percent and the service industry average of 27.1 percent.

"Obsessed with Quality"

At OMI, the pursuit of quality is an admitted obsession, but there's a carefully cultured method to this self-instilled organizational approach; OMI's Obsessed with Quality process. Corresponding with the principles and criteria of the Malcolm Baldrige National Quality Award, the process spans the entire company, links all personnel levels, and creates a common foundation and focus for OMI's far-flung operations. Key elements of this integrative process include a "Quality as a Business Strategy" leadership system, a six-phase Obsessed with Quality training program for new employees, and a companywide Linkage of Process Model that facilitates systematic evaluation of more than 150 critical corporate processes.

Planning begins with the Red Team, consisting of seven top company executives and led by OMI President and Chief Executive Officer Don S. Evans, but it quickly becomes an inclusive affair. An expanded leadership team, which also includes regional executives and managers, sets organizational priorities and strategic directions, and team members communicate these to all sites. Teams at each site develop business and action plans that are consistent with the company's overall strategy, yet are specific to circumstances and customer requirements particular to their facilities.

To achieve shared focus and to coordinate efforts across sites, OMI uses a variety of approaches and tools to initiate and then drive progress toward the company's short-term and five-year improvement goals. For example, long-standing focus teams, first established in 1990, provide continuity of effort and sustain companywide commitment in five key areas: leadership, information and analysis, human resources, process management, and customer satisfaction. Like many other teams at OMI, membership cuts across the entire organization in terms of function and personnel, including top executives and hourly workers.

Other techniques to foster alignment and to ensure that important information flows to all OMI offices and facilities include newsletters, regional meetings, e-mail communications, and the company's annual Project Management Summit, a Red Team-hosted event for exchanging information among OMI-operated facilities on best practices, emerging technologies, and training needs.

OMI as a System

OMI's management views the organization as a system — an integrated whole — and it aims for synergy in its decisions and actions. Key enablers are the company's Linkage of Process Model, which defines relationships among processes, and its Family of Measures, a balanced scorecard of 20 integrated metrics. These measures of operational performance correspond to OMI's four strategic objectives — customer focus, business growth, innovation, and market leadership.

Improvement initiatives in the company's strategic plan are selected and crafted so that each initiative contributes significantly to achieving one or more strategic objectives and key customer requirements. In 2000, OMI had 26 improvement initiatives under way, each one assigned to a team led by a high-level executive. All teams write charters that state their purpose, objectives, and timeline for completion. A team charter also specifies which of OMI's more than 150 critical processes are involved, the metrics that will be used for evaluation, costs, required resources, and other information vital to the success of the initiative. Charters provide team members and company executives with the means for a quick and thorough analysis of progress toward planned goals.

Every year, the Red Team reviews the entire set of critical processes, and it ranks each process according to its perceived impact on progress toward strategic objectives. Existing processes are modified and strengthened, and new ones are conceived to advance OMI's continuous improvement efforts. The Red Team also reviews the Family of Measures to ensure that the composite set of metrics continues to provide an accurate assessment of organizational health.

Systematic attention to these and other important organizational details points the way to high-impact improvement initiatives. For example, the Red Team's review of the company's measurement scorecard suggested untapped opportunities to reduce variable operating costs at OMI-run facilities. The outcome was a recently launched plant-optimization program that aims for a 1 percent reduction in variable costs, to be achieved primarily through more systematic deployment of home-grown innovations.

"Paid to Think"

OMI works to cultivate empowerment and innovation among its employees. Associates are "paid to think," a claim that OMI backs up by providing extensive training opportunities. Skill development is a high priority, and associates are given plenty of chances to apply what they learn. All employees are authorized to improve job designs, respond directly to process problems, and address customer issues. Empowerment is reinforced by compensation, reward, and recognition systems designed to encourage workers to think and act like company owners. With labor accounting for half of total costs, the company reasons that investments to motivate associates and to increase their skills will be paid back through gains in operational performance and, ultimately, customer satisfaction.

From 1996 to 2000, OMI's expenditures on training and tuition nearly doubled. Associates are evaluated every six months, and training plans are updated as part of every evaluation. Ongoing employee focus groups, new employee surveys, and biennial internal customer satisfaction surveys help management track levels of morale and motivation. Annual regional salary surveys are used to ensure that compensation levels are competitive with the rest of the industry.

Besides empowering employees, exceeding customer expectations and enhancing the environment are the two other defining elements of OMI's culture. The company uses a variety of listening approaches — surveys, interviews, focus groups, and market research — to learn customers' current and long-term requirements. A contract renewal rate of almost 95 percent in 1999 and the industry's top rank in the average length of customer retention indicates that OMI is well-versed in the requirements of its customers.

For OMI, protecting the environment is part of its contractual obligation. However, many OMI-managed facilities are model performers. The company has won more than 100 federal and state awards for excellence in the past five years; more than half of these were earned in the last two years.

Source: Baldrige National Quality Program, National Institute of Standards and Technology, U.S. Department of Commerce; Web site: www.baldrige.nist.gov.

▲

▼

Case Study 7.2: Boeing Aerospace Support

Boeing Aerospace Support (AS) is part of the Boeing Company, the largest aerospace company in the world. Boeing AS provides products and services (including aircraft maintenance, modification, and repair, and training for aircrews and maintenance staff) to reduce life-cycle costs and increase the effectiveness of aircraft. Ninety-seven percent of Boeing AS' business comes from military customers. President David Spong leads a workforce of over 13,000 employees based at Boeing AS headquarters in St. Louis, Missouri, and nine major sites — eight in the United States and one in Australia — as well as more than 129 secondary and smaller sites. In this highly competitive industry, new orders for Boeing AS products and services have grown each year since 1999 and are significantly higher than its competitors' cumulative growth. The company's sales exceed $4 billion annually. In 1998, Boeing Airlift and Tanker Programs, which Spong led at the time, received a Baldrige award in the manufacturing category.

Highlights

- Boeing AS earnings have grown at a double-digit average cumulative rate from 1999 to 2002.
- Annual revenue has more than doubled from 1999 to 2003.
- Since 1998, Boeing AS has provided products and services within three days of a request, whereas competitors take up to forty days.
- Cash awards paid to employees for extraordinary performance have tripled from 2000 to 2002.

Growth in a Competitive Market

Traditionally, the military services have provided support to maintain military aircraft. But, in recent years, the Department of Defense has contracted with private industry to provide these services, resulting in a highly competitive market. The Boeing Company is successfully competing in this environment by leveraging its aircraft design, development, and production capabilities with the ability of Boeing AS to deliver integrated support solutions on time and at a competitive price. Key factors to the success of Boeing AS are its commitment to customer satisfaction, performance-to-plan, and on-time delivery of quality products and services. Since 1998, the "exceptional" and "very good" responses from government customers regarding Boeing AS performance have gone up 23 percent. In 2003, the exceptional responses nearly doubled those in 2002. In a survey of customers conducted by an independent third party, positive responses improved from 60 percent in 2001 to more than 75 percent in 2002. Since 1999, on-time delivery of maintenance and modification products and services, significant hardware, and other products has been between 95 and 99 percent. Quality ratings for the maintenance of

C-17 aircraft has been near 100 percent since 1998 compared to AS competitors, which trail at 70 percent in 2002 and 90 percent in 2003. A key element of AS' successful on-time delivery rate is its partnership with its suppliers to ensure high-quality services and products. As a result, the supplier on-time delivery rate has improved from about 68 percent in 1999 to about 95 percent in 2003, matching best-in-Boeing results. The quality of supplier deliverables has been above 99.5 percent for the last three years and was at 99.7 percent for 2003.

Processes are Key to Success

Carefully planned and well-managed processes combined with a culture that encourages knowledge sharing and working together have been essential to Boeing AS' ability to deliver high-quality products and services. Boeing AS has developed a seven-step approach for defining, managing, stabilizing, and improving processes. This process-based management (PBM) methodology also is used to set goals and performance metrics and requires interaction and agreement among process owners, users, suppliers, and customers. Developing a sound, long-term strategy and then turning that strategic intent into meaningful action is another of Aerospace Support's strengths and competitive advantages. AS uses an Enterprise Planning Process (EPP) comprising four process elements (Key Data Factors, Strategies, Plans, and Execution) and ten defined steps, including Lessons Learned and Process Improvements, to plan and execute key strategies. Senior leaders and business, strategic planning, and functional councils each have a role in developing and executing the EPP to ensure that all business functions and sites are integrated and aligned to the overall strategic plan. To improve performance, a five-step system helps Boeing AS select, analyze, and align data and information. The system begins by gathering requirements and expectations from stakeholders and results in a set of action plans and performance goals and metrics. A Goal Flowdown process communicates goals and directions not only throughout the organization but also to customers and suppliers. Measurement, analysis, and KM systems provide performance status and other information needed to make decisions. Finally, performance analyses and reviews are conducted regularly, resulting in recommendations or actions needed to improve performance at all levels.

Employee Involvement and Performance

Teams of employees who "own" and are responsible for the company's complex operations and processes are the core of the company's high-performance work environment. A highly structured process known as the AS People System helps to ensure that employees who constitute these teams understand priorities and expectations; have the knowledge, training, and tools they need to do the job and to assess performance against goals and objectives; and are rewarded and recognized for their accomplishments. Programs such as the Atlas Award, which recognizes outstanding team achievement with cash awards and stock options, are used to acknowledge employees who develop innovative solutions to problems. Cash awards to individuals and teams for extraordinary performance have tripled over the past three years. Employee surveys show that 66 percent of employees feel encouraged to generate new and better ways of doing things and about 65 percent are satisfied with their involvement in decision making and process improvement. Seventy percent feel their supervisor is doing a good job. In this large, widespread organization, communication is vital. Employees are encouraged to "share" information across businesses, sites, and functions. A continuous flow of information also comes from a wide range of sources including meetings, roundtable discussions, online newsletters, and functional and business councils. This culture of openness also extends to ethics. Boeing AS expects every employee to "always take the high road by practicing the highest ethical standards." Almost 70 percent of employees agree that "Management will act upon reported unethical practices," "I can report unethical practices without fear of reprisal," and "I feel free to communicate bad news to my management." This score is better than the industry average and other Boeing units. Expectations for ensuring ethical behavior are set during new employee orientation and annual refresher training. Ninety-five percent of Boeing AS staff received ethics training in 1999 and over 98 percent in 2002. A 24-hour ethics line is available to report ethical concerns or to seek advice.

Award-Winning Community Work

Boeing AS employees are involved in community activities through the company's Employee Community Fund (ECF) programs operated at all Boeing AS locations. The ECF, which is sponsored by AS's parent organization Boeing, is the world's largest employee-owned charitable organization. AS charitable contributions and community involvement activities are aimed primarily at education organizations, health and human services, culture and arts, and the environment. Although AS makes up less than 10 percent of total Boeing employees, for the last two years they have won the company's William M. Allen Award, which recognizes exceptional volunteer work by employees. Boeing AS also has received numerous awards for its efforts to protect the environment, including the Environmental Protection Agency's Clean Air Excellence Award, the gold and silver California Governor's Environmental and Economic Leadership Award, and the Kansas Water Environmental Association award.

Source: Baldrige National Quality Program, National Institute of Standards and Technology, U.S. Department of Commerce; Web site: www.baldrige.nist.gov.

▲

Chapter 8

Preserving the Future: Improving Quality in Education

Unlike almost any other country in the world, the United States has over 13,000 decentralized, fragmented, and locally controlled educational districts, mirroring the thousands of state, city, and county political systems that control their funding and resources. This structure is dominated by local community values and isolated from central government or corporate direction and control. The constitutional structure of federalism encourages such broad decentralization of power, but also makes it more difficult to define, measure, and improve quality in this vital national public service. Nearly everyone in society is either directly or indirectly a stakeholder, including taxpayers, parents, teachers, and students in private, faith-based, and public schools.

Public sector investment in education is enormous. Nearly half of all state and local personnel and budgets are devoted to elementary, secondary (K-12), and higher education, libraries, and specialized services. Citizens expect their children's public education to accurately reflect the goals of individual school districts and the values of society. Individual processes such as teacher certification, fiscal control, resource management, testing, and curriculum are among the quality processes that must be controlled and measured for improving results. Privatization is an option for many parents as many secondary schools and nearly a third of all institutions of higher education are privately operated.

American educational systems suffer from multiple problems, not the least of which is an extraordinary drop-out (or defect) rate in secondary schools, as high as 50 percent in some urban districts. Not only are the "system failures" unprepared for career and civic responsibilities, but scarce resources are wasted due to the need for rework. No industry in the world could survive such abysmal results and continue to stay in business. Nonetheless, political subsidies, state laws, and egalitarian ideology maintain an otherwise failing system. In other areas, minority students are systematically discriminated against due to extreme variations in property tax valuations that are the basis of most budgetary allocations for public education.

Analyzing education in terms of individual subprocesses is extremely important to provide better services to all students and other stakeholders as well as graduating more productive and informed citizens. Applying TQS concepts can help improve the quality of public education, focusing on new measurements and emphasizing process improvements, results, and bridging growing performance gaps between U.S. students and those of other developing and less developed nations.

Defining Quality Education

In the 1997 Academy-Award-winning motion picture *Good Will Hunting*, the central character, Will, a 20-year-old genius with little formal education, confronts a Harvard University student in a bar. The Harvard student, in true snobby, Ivy League fashion, is trying to embarrass Will's friend, who is posing as a Harvard undergrad himself. Will's friend is bombarded by a series of in-depth political questions, and Will steps in to help his friend out. Will more than holds his own as he impressively forms and defends his opinion while at the same time proving that the Harvard student is merely quoting an obscure passage from some book and trying to pass it off as his own. After asking the Harvard student if he has any independent thoughts or if he just mindlessly quotes obscure passages in hopes of feigning intellect, he leaves the dejected Harvard student with his own independent thought: "You wasted $150,000 on an education you could have got for a buck fifty in late charges at the public library."

In the context of the movie, this quote is witty and humorous. But in the context of real life, it raises serious questions about the nature of education: Are we as a society getting what we pay for when it comes to education? This question, and the many that follow from it, not only apply to higher education, as the quote in the preceding text implies, but to elementary and secondary (K-12) services as well. It is not difficult to question the value of a private institution of higher learning, especially an Ivy League education that is paid for directly out of pocket. However, it is as important to question the quality of education in our nation's public K-12 schools that are financed indirectly by taxpayers. Why is this so important?

First, public education is funded primarily by taxes from income, property, and sales, so nearly everyone who purchases goods or services, or owns or rents property, has some financial stake in ensuring quality in public education. Second, and perhaps more important, it is through K-12 education that the nation's future workers and leaders are prepared for lives as productive citizens. Primary and secondary education focuses primarily on career training, civic education, college preparation, and producing quality workers for business and government.

Producing quality individuals is a major goal, but elementary and high school education has a much broader social mission. Everyone must be concerned with the quality of processes used to fulfill this goal and to produce a competent, well-educated population capable of independence and resolving problems of society. Furthermore, schools mirror social beliefs, giving back what citizens expect from their children and themselves. Rather than merely serving as a recruiting service for industry, schools should also teach students to be critical thinkers, so that they become men and women of independent mind, distanced from the conventional wisdom of their own time and with strength and skill to change what is wrong (Postman, 1995, pp. 59–60). Concern with schools, therefore, provides society with a means to continuously reexamine values and hopes for the future. Ensuring quality in our educational system ensures quality for the future of society. Understanding this concept leads to an inevitable understanding of the importance of quality education at all levels.

Unfortunately, the question of why ensuring quality in K-12 education is important is often overlooked because the answer seems too simplistic and unworthy of any deeper consideration than a quick glance at a dictionary. As in other segments of the service economy, quality in education is viewed by many as a static notion, an adjective describing a final product. Ranking students becomes the goal and the final product of the system. As discussed in earlier chapters, there is much, much more to quality than this one-dimensional view. Successful service firms recognize the complexity and multiple facets of quality. This multidimensional nature of quality is easily seen in education. Imagine all of the different processes and components that go into delivering educational services. It is impossible to measure quality of education based solely on the final product. In fact, in the true essence of education, there is no final product.

One of the realities of the 21st-century global knowledge society is that everyone will have to relearn throughout their lives. The average person now changes jobs seven times during his or her career. With the globalization of the economy, more workers are likely to assume mobile overseas assignments requiring technical skills, a second language, or geographic knowledge not generally possessed by today's graduates. Education has become a continuous, lifelong learning process. And, although it is obvious that the foundations and motivation for lifelong learning are built into primary and secondary education, students, by definition, never become finished products. In addition, there must be a reason for seeking the additional knowledge provided in school, for being in a classroom, for listening to a teacher, for taking an examination, for doing homework, and for attending school — even though there is no immediate goal in sight. Indeed, it may take decades for many to receive a satisfactory return on investment (ROI) in time and resources devoted to learning.

Any discussion of educational quality must focus on continuous improvement, implementation, evaluation of processes, and public policies to deliver the knowledge, skills, and resources necessary to empower students to become lifelong learners. This includes current and future customers of virtual courses and degrees delivered via the Internet. The number of such programs is multiplying rapidly as more individuals and institutions recognize the need for "just-in-time learning" for new career assignments. Most college and many high school courses are now wired to the Internet and World Wide Web. Students expect courses to utilize information technology (IT), and many now conduct research and access libraries via home computers and distance learning systems.

Existing outreach programs need to be expanded to overcome funding inequities and erase the emerging digital divide that keeps some Americans underserved. Expansion could come through developing partnerships with commercial and public-interest organizations or through new technologies such as scheduled service to rural American locations using 21st-century bookmobiles featuring personal computers connected to the Internet via cellular phone links. The U.S. Postal Service has the technical and logistical capability to provide and maintain such a mobile delivery system. Kiosks and terminals in public places such as malls, libraries, schools, senior centers, government offices, and office buildings could ensure easy access to the public and the underserved population. Furthermore, training of users by government or contractors is paramount to provide for successful use once learning systems are accessed.

Educational service providers must also focus on finding a mission for schools and making sure that every stakeholder in the educational system understands and believes in the mission. The efforts of every stakeholder reflect the common goal of quality education and a sense of commitment and ownership of educational processes. This definition is multifaceted and highly complex, but its emphasis on evaluating processes, identifying a common goal and motivation, and providing ownership to each stakeholder is similar to the philosophies of quality improvement (QI) theories. Accordingly, *quality in education* is defined in terms of the principles of these theories or variations thereof (Chapter 3). Applying this new definition of quality has not been without controversy, especially when it comes to measuring educational achievement. For an example of how stakeholder-driven quality impacts primary education in one exemplary community, see Case Study 8.1.

Improving Quality Processes and Outcomes

QI is a complex activity involving people, processes, and policies. Although educational quality is a combination of all these factors, complicated by the bureaucratic and political environment in which most schools operate, it would be nearly impossible to discuss all of them at one time. Instead of identifying and discussing each component of quality in education, three specific and related areas are discussed: first, quality in teacher education and in classroom instruction, stressing the continuous development of techniques used by professionals to educate aspiring teachers and techniques used by teachers in classroom teaching and learning; next, teacher preparation and a discussion of quality in fiscal policy and resource management in elementary and secondary schools, paying special attention to improving the use of funding and resources so that they are compatible with educational goals; and last, quality in curriculum with a focus on evaluating what needs to be taught to students to improve their ability to become lifelong learners and absorb the skills and knowledge discussed previously.

Teacher Education and Classroom Instruction

Achieving high performance and quality in services means anticipating valid current and future customer needs as well as responding to them quickly and courteously with consistent, customized treatment. Although not apparent at first, TQS concepts can be applied when assessing quality in teacher education as well.

Public education has many different stakeholders in the United States and other cultures. Those paying taxes to support education certainly consider themselves to be interested customers and investors in the future of education. The most direct customers of education are the students themselves, especially as most definitions of quality (grades, test scores, rankings, etc.) center upon students. If students are indeed the primary customers of education and if quality means anticipating and responding to their needs, then those who work with students most closely must be empowered to recognize their needs and provide customized treatment. Teachers must be competent, innovative, and flexible enough to respond quickly to changing needs of students and, at the same time, knowledgeable enough to provide high-level instruction to students. The amount of training a teacher receives and the nature of that training is of the utmost importance. Employee training has become an increasingly important component of QI in many other types of businesses striving to improve service quality (Chapter 4). Thus, it is appropriate to evaluate teacher training when assessing quality in education.

In addition to the connection found in the business sector, there are significant ties between teacher training and other areas of quality assurance (QA). For example, an increase in demand for teachers in elementary and high schools across the nation has led to the hiring of people whose reasons for becoming a teacher are quite varied. Some teachers begin teaching after graduating from a certified teacher education program in college whereas others do not gain certification until after they begin teaching full-time. Many of those who did not begin as certified teachers were offered jobs based on transcript review or a history as a substitute teacher. However, a survey asking new teachers to offer their perceptions of their level of preparedness showed that certified teachers and those who had not been certified, varied considerably. Certified teachers felt significantly more prepared to teach than did those who were not certified and student performance was measurably higher in classes taught by certified teachers (Goldhaber and Anthony, 2004). Since 1987, the National Board of Teacher Certification (NBTC) has promoted national certification standards for accomplished teachers who successfully complete its rigorous certification process. In the Palatine, Illinois, school district (Case 8.1), the number of NBTC teachers increased from 2 to 48 in eight years.

Board-certified teachers are not only tested in their subject matter specialties, but are also more likely to exhibit a stronger sense of responsibility for student learning. Because it is so important for every stakeholder to feel ownership and responsibility when ensuring quality, teachers who do not feel this sense of responsibility for student learning do not provide the same level of service and more often view poor student performance as a problem for the student rather for the system. This attitude makes QI more difficult as it places blame on students rather than focusing efforts on eliminating all system-caused reasons for variation in performance (Chapter 5). Furthermore, this thinking does not allow teachers to respond to the needs of the student, because it is assumed that such needs must be met internally by student motivation and work ethic. This disparity in personal responsibility for student learning among teachers suggests that a specific understanding of the nature of education, teaching, learning, and perhaps quality theory are important in the training of new teachers and students (see Chapter 4). Teachers who do not receive specific training in these areas lack ownership of learning processes and are less likely to add value to the overall quality of education.

Over time, the concerns and goals of the nation's educational system have changed dramatically. In the past, programs were authorized to provide federal money for a variety of public policy goals. The federal government has been involved in education assistance on a limited basis since the end of World War II. The need for skilled workers after the war led to the passage of the GI Bill funding higher education for returning veterans, and fear of lagging behind the Soviet Union during the Cold War prompted funding for research in space technology. Although education has traditionally been a function of state and local governments, the federal government expanded its role in ensuring the quality of teachers in America's public schools during the 1990s. In addition, more emphasis was placed on the quality of student performance, and national standards were established to measure comparative performance between students in different states. However, policymakers failed to look at the problem from a QI standpoint.

Although results are important, it is impossible to expect higher achievement scores without improving the quality of processes. Thus, "improving the quality of teaching catapulted to the top of federal and state education policy agendas" (Koppich, 2002, p. 271). In 1994, Congress reauthorized the Eisenhower Professional Development program. The original Eisenhower program was created in the 1980s, but the new focus on teacher quality and on QI approaches toward improving education led to the reauthorization. Congress offered the following explanation:

> The federal government has a vital role in helping states and local agencies to make sustained and intensive high-quality professional development in the core academic subjects ... an integral part of the elementary and secondary education system (Koppich, 2002, p. 272).

Despite federal assistance, the extent to which programs such the GI bill, Teacher Corps, and Eisenhower program have helped actual in-class instruction is questionable. Failure to consider the broader demands for quality among multiple stakeholders limits the effectiveness of narrowly focused federal professional development programs.

Fiscal Policy and Resource Management

The effectiveness of past federal educational assistance programs is also questionable because the national government relies on narrow-purpose categorical grants to achieve broad policy objectives. Educational policymakers from Congress to local school boards have identified the importance of quality in education and understand that it can only be achieved by addressing multiple processes involved in education. This understanding is the driving force behind policy changes, but funding and guidance from the federal government still amounts to less than five percent of the total spent on education nationwide. Whatever the source of funding, states and school districts must achieve quality in fiscal policy and resource management with their own resources.

Efficient management of resources is a key to success in any sector of the economy, especially in the public sector in which funds are scarce and citizen demands are difficult to meet. One of the best ways to ensure quality resource utilization is to use cost–benefit analysis to maximize the net benefits to society, thereby providing the greatest good for the greatest number. Using statistical methods to control processes is a central notion in any attempt to improve quality. Thinking in cost–benefit terms for society when addressing resource management in education is especially appropriate when we consider that the resources allocated to school districts come directly or indirectly from taxpayers. Unless the issue of how money is spent is addressed, simply allocating more money to education will not necessarily result in increased student achievement or the reduction in pressing inequities and inefficiencies in the delivery of educational services. This is consistent with TQS principles of emphasizing processes and analyzing inefficiencies to improve quality. Many new educational initiatives involve significant expenditures, and there are increased demands from interested stakeholders for statistical evidence of positive student outcomes resulting from the outlay of public funds. Efficiency and quality in resource management in education must be seriously evaluated as new competitive providers offer alternatives to traditional geographically bounded school districts.

Citizens are increasingly aware of various service delivery options and capable of selecting among different providers. Privatization advocates assume that many citizens, if allowed to do so, would rather "shop" for the best providers of education for their children. In many public school districts, for example, academies, charter schools, and magnet programs promote local control, parental choice, student achievement, and diversity. Students with special competencies, skills, and talents no longer remain in one-size-fits-all schools, located within the borders of their residential districts. In some states, and in limited degrees from the federal government, parents who elect to send their children to private schools receive tax deductions, subsidies, or exemptions for all or part of tuition expenses. In addition, more affluent property owners, who also tend to favor lower taxes, enjoy tax deductions or exemptions for the use of property for many designated public and (some) private purposes. Furthermore, some taxpayers can deduct college expenses and tuition from their federal income tax. This benefit is generally reserved for more affluent property owners who can also reduce the proportion of real property taxes paid by hiring attorneys to challenge property tax assessments. Less affluent property owners and renters cannot choose from among competing non-government organizations (NGOs) or private institutions and depend entirely on nonprofits or public agencies for services. There is little evidence to suggest that competitive market-based reforms alone would provide additional benefits to those least able to afford the higher costs of private alternatives.

Very few states or school districts utilize cost–benefit analysis to assess resource utilization. Several studies have shown that improvement in school quality might be fostered by an increase in financial resources, but others dispute this facile notion. But until there are acceptable analyses of how those resources are being used, there is no way to know for certain if competition or additional resources lead to QI. Resource management illustrates exactly why stakeholder ownership is so important in QA as well. Such analysis would be easier to perform by including those stakeholders closest to the situation so that an accurate measure of the benefits is obtained. Quality resource management is too difficult for any one particular entity. As is the case with any quality operation, everyone must be involved and working together to make necessary improvements.

Quality of Curriculum

If schools are a mirror of societal values (as was proposed earlier) then the composition of the school curriculum is of special concern to any stakeholder. If the goals are to empower students to become more productive citizens, remedy the ills of society, and become lifelong learners, then it is imperative that students be exposed to accurate information to allow them to develop the necessary skills. Curriculum is therefore important both in composition and delivery.

How should curriculum content be decided? Some may argue that, because education is supposed to benefit society at large and because we have an idea of what we hope to gain from education, experts should draw up the best curriculum and methods for delivery. Others believe the creation of standardized, uniform lesson plans would ensure that our goals are being met and that quality education is being provided. However, those who feel this way are not approaching the issue from a quality management perspective. Teachers are an important factor, and it is important that they feel ownership in educational processes to ensure quality. Teachers are the frontline workers, having the most direct interaction with students. Teachers must be able to anticipate and respond to student needs on a continual basis.

Would teachers be able to do that if they were bound by a uniform lesson plan? Under a TQS-driven system, they would not be so limited. In fact, one study from England noted that "efforts to impose a uniform system of lesson planning in the U.K. meant that teachers did not draw on the full range of their expertise in planning lessons in diverse contexts" (Olsen, 2002, p. 131). This finding is consistent with the principles of many QI theories. Teachers would lose empowerment and the ability to react to the changing needs of each child and classes as the whole. Additionally, any effort to increase the quality of individual teachers would be wasted as professional development resources could only be used to offer standardized curricula. It follows that the best way to approach curriculum quality in K-12 education is to first provide quality teachers who understand the objectives of education and who have excellent knowledge and then empower them to meet the needs of individual students. Quality in education will only be found by ensuring quality in individual processes and linking these processes with the people involved to encourage everyone to improve.

Measuring Quality of Results in Education

Defining and improving quality in education is very complex and involves a number of processes and stakeholders. In addition to traditional measures such as graduation rates, student achievement scores, and cost per pupil, other measures include (1) improvement in reading and math scores, (2) teacher turnover rates, (3) costs of improvement per student, and (4) student satisfaction and enthusiasm for learning. QI theories applied to businesses stress that implementation must be connected to results. Constant feedback is a necessity so that quality is truly an ongoing process.

The question is how to measure results of QI in education. When recalling the less quantifiable goals of education previously mentioned (those such as shaping students to become lifelong learners who have the skills and knowledge to cure the problems of society) it is very hard to evaluate efforts to improve quality. In business, customer satisfaction is given high priority when measuring quality. In education, this is not nearly as easy. It is possible to ascertain a certain level of student enthusiasm for learning at various levels of education. Certainly students can be unhappy in their educational atmosphere. But student satisfaction is usually a combination of many other environmental and psychological factors and may not always be related to the service delivery environment.

Still, taxpayers want accountability and must be satisfied that their resources are producing measurable results. Policymakers also want results and accountability so they have some tangible success to demonstrate to constituents and critics alike. Teachers need some measure of quality, such as student evaluations, so they stay interested and committed to the profession and improve their own teaching. Accreditation associations throughout the country evaluate schools and certify teacher competencies, but they are limited in the scope of evaluation and offer few comparisons for improvement. Rather, they provide a very imprecise measure of the minimum skills required of faculty. Additionally, they often do not provide a comparable measuring stick so that schools are able to see if improvement has actually taken place. Schools need some standardized measure of quality that can be easily and often taken and compared to see if improvement has actually occurred.

Standardized testing has caused as much debate as any topic in public education at the K-12 level. The controversial No Child Left Behind Act of 2001 (PL107–110) called for schools to establish academic proficiency standards and to implement accountability measures to hold schools responsible for students' success in meeting those standards. Assessment data provides indicators to federal, state, and local policymakers who allocate public funds on the basis of students' academic progress. The Act applies national performance standards to state schools, generally without funding, to correct deficiencies. Not surprisingly, only a few districts meet such strict standards. Several states are opting out of this federal program, because they cannot raise the additional resources required if they do not meet the standards.

The goal of standardized testing is to provide a uniform measurement of student achievement while attempting to control for any spurious variables that might affect other measures, such as demographic factors and grade point averages. The theory behind standardized testing is at least partially believable as a measure of skills needed to advance to the next level with the educational system. California, Florida, and Indiana require that students pass a graduation qualifying exam known as the California's Standardized Testing and Reporting (STAR) program, Florida Comprehensive Achievement Tests (FCAT), and the Indiana Statewide Test of Educational Progress Plus (ISTEP+), respectively, to be awarded a high school diploma. The actual effectiveness of standardized tests is still subject to political interpretation.

Opponents of the controversial tests express concern about the frequency with which they have been used as well as the increasing reliance on high-stakes standardized tests and how these tests, tied to state standards, shape curriculum. Teachers often buckle under the pressure of the tests and find themselves preparing students for the test rather than truly teaching them. In many states, such as Florida, the schools themselves are graded in accordance with student achievement. This creates a similar effect as the one described earlier when a uniform lesson plan was initiated in the U.K. Strict adherence to test preparation means teachers are less likely to fully utilize their expertise and are also more likely to fail to teach students abstract concepts or life skills. Rather, focusing too heavily on standardized test preparation stresses facts over thoughts and rote memorization over reading and writing skills. By definition, standardized tests have one right answer. However, changes in educational goals stress teaching students that there is always a possibility of multiple correct answers so long as you have the verbal skills and writing ability to support your answer.

Apart from revoking the empowerment of teachers, standardized testing undermines other important facets of QA in education, opponents say. Critics argue that calls for more standardized tests come from politicians eager to prove they are serious about school reform and the need to create a high-skills, internationally competitive workforce. According to opponents of standardized testing, politicians use this route as a means to privatize schools or force the adoption of voucher plans. They claim that proponents of standardized testing pay little or no attention to more important factors that actually affect quality at the process level, unlike standardized tests that can only provide results of bad processes after the fact and without providing any real direction for improvement. Factors such as class size, teacher education, and equal and efficient distribution of resources are among those that are more closely related to quality in education. If standardized testing continues in its prominence, and issues like those previously mentioned are ignored, then results will be more than just a poor measure of quality: they could contribute to lowering overall quality in the classroom.

Furthermore, standardized tests cannot possibly reflect the complex nature of what quality means. Using test results to rank students often becomes an attempt to force schools to meet a certain standard. When that standard is not met, a game of finger-pointing instantly ensues. Politicians and administrators blame teachers for poor student performance, and students are held back or not allowed to graduate based on one test score without any consideration of that student's past performance in school. Instantly, people are blamed for shortcomings for what is perceived as their individual failures. But what is actually occurring is a failure to eliminate all causes of process variation that affect student learning. Because test results usually lead to questioning individuals and not processes, using tests only as a measure of quality cannot be considered in alignment with the principles of TQS or other QI strategies.

Some of the nation's leaders in higher education agree. The Scholastic Aptitude Test (SAT) is the most popular standardized test used by universities and colleges to predict applicants' ability to perform well academically and to ultimately select their incoming class. It has come under fierce criticism from many of its own designers. Leading the assault on the SAT has been the former president of the University of California, Dr. Richard Atkinson. An educational psychologist, Atkinson went so far as to propose that the University of California, the largest and most prestigious public university system in the country, as well as the single largest user of the SAT, no longer require the SAT for applying students. Atkinson believes that standardized tests have the capability to measure student performance but only if those exams test knowledge and skills that one would actually gain from class work. Aptitude tests, or tests designed to measure intelligence rather than the ability to learn and retain vital information, are a poor measure of the quality of a student desiring admittance into a university. Atkinson made his decision after a visit to an upscale private school, where he observed students spending substantial time working on SAT analogy questions, not developing reading and writing abilities but rather their test-taking skills. This observation underlies the earlier argument that standardized tests diminish the quality of curriculum and weaken the empowerment of teachers to help students learn more than how to take a test. The sharp criticism by Atkinson and other educators forced the makers of the SAT to reconsider the format of the exam, which has become a staple of American education.

In 2002, Education Testing Service, designers of the SAT, voted to eliminate the section of verbal analogies and add an essay-writing section to the test. These changes become effective in 2005 and suggest more emphasis on skills that can only be attained by a continual commitment by students to their overall learning process as opposed to skills that can be mastered by learning only how to take a test. The changes are a step in the right direction for critics such as Atkinson, who resigned as UC president in October 2002 to lead the fight for a revised SAT. He insists that developing new standardized tests that break from the traditional SAT will "complement K-12 reform efforts that have been launched in California and around the nation to establish clear curricular guidelines, set high academic standards, and employ standardized tests to assess student achievement" (Atkinson, 2001).

What are the alternatives to standardized testing, and are they effective measures of quality? QI theories stress that statistical analysis and control of processes are important for improving service quality. Standardized test results are a statistical way to measure academic performance. But statistics about performance on standardized tests do not accurately measure quality or processes. Several alternatives exist to measure the quality of education at individual schools. These alternatives are statistical measures of quality, whereas standardized tests are measures of statistical knowledge. Other alternatives include student portfolios that keep samples of student work, writing, and applications. Students are also asked to reflect upon the work collected in their portfolios so that they are able to think about their learning processes not just to attain high scores, but also to understand how to learn best. The student portfolio method is used in the International Baccalaureate (IB) system and is much more effective in measuring and even improving quality in education. Although more time consuming, this approach encourages teachers to regularly talk about students' work and allows more-skilled teachers to help less experienced teachers. When quality measures are being discussed on a continual basis, it is much more consistent with QI theory. Random sampling of student portfolios and evaluation by second or third parties also allows for statistical control of teaching processes that in turn makes quality more attainable.

The Pearl River school district, about 20 mi north of New York City, has deployed a measurement system that includes all stakeholders in the QI process (see Case Study 8.2). The size and diversity of the Pearl River district is representative of many public school districts in the United States. This system was among the first to win a Baldrige award for education in 2001. The Pearl River case is a positive sign of the future changes in K-12 public education in America.

Another promising alternative is known as School Quality Review Teams (SQRTs), and schools in New York, Rhode Island, and Boston have used this method in some instances to assess student performance. Parents, students, educators, and teams of trained community members are all involved in SQRT. Such inclusion of many stakeholders in reviewing quality makes this option appear to be in sync with the goals of TQS. Furthermore, these teams review more than just student academic work. SQRTs take into account the entire learning environment and the learning culture of each school, which means that the processes of education are being evaluated so that the connection between processes and results can be analyzed. However, there are obvious setbacks to this or any other alternative for standardized testing, and these setbacks are directly related to other quality issues.

First, the resources necessary to provide sufficient numbers of SQRTs are overwhelming for most cash-strapped school districts. Public schools are already under tight budget constraints, and most would be highly unlikely to receive enough funding from state or federal sources for the additional evaluators needed to evaluate performance. The only way for these teams to work on a large scale would be with a redistribution of funds or an increase in local property taxes, neither of which would be welcomed. Additionally, as is often the case with businesses that attempt to implement TQS philosophies, resistance to a new way of evaluating schools would be strong. It is always difficult to change the culture and the status quo. Another issue facing possible alternatives to standardized testing is the amount of time necessary to see results and fully implement and correct new procedures. A similar problem exists in TQS implementation in other types of services. Public sector institutions, such as schools, feel even more pressure because of the large number of stakeholders to which they are responsible and because politicians are seeking quick action and results to use for reelection campaigns. Despite serious barriers to the implementation of alternative methods of quality measurement and assurance, it is apparent that standardized tests need to be reexamined to improve quality in education

Rewarding Educational Quality Reform

Concerns for public K-12 education extend all the way to the Office of the President of the United States and have been the subject of continuous rhetoric and debate for many years. Yet, the political debate has done little to ensure long-term improvement. Politicians tend to be more concerned with quick, incremental measures than long-term solutions to difficult quality problems. Unfortunately, instituting programs that are capable of evaluation is difficult, and many come with a high level of debate and controversy. Some stakeholders involved in the debate over education reform advocate alternatives such as school vouchers, charter schools, and privatization to offer families options to improve quality. Exposing schools to market forces and allowing parents a choice of which school their children may attend, proponents say, will stimulate competition and increase the efficiency and quality of schools or force low-quality schools to improve or close. Exposing schools to business forces may or may not be the suitable response to the quality problems in education; however, exposure to quality reward systems used in business, government, and healthcare may help.

The Malcolm Baldrige award criteria are available to any school, and applying for this award, or a comparable state quality award, has the obvious benefit of providing immediate feedback and suggestions for improvement. The national award as well as the many mini-Baldrige awards at the state level recognize and promote quality and productivity in American education. These awards achieve the goal of improving and recognizing quality by objectively evaluating applicants and making recommendations for improvement to those who do not meet the high standards (Chapter 6). Opening up the BNQA to educational institutions since 1995 has allowed governments to use an existing program to help measure and improve quality in education. At the very least, the Baldrige award competition provides case studies and models for schools around the country to follow.

Applicants are reviewed in seven categories evaluated by an award committee. Each category has several subsections and action plans included, and teams are sent for on-site interviews and evaluations. The application process comprehensively evaluates the people and processes used to educate students and reflect the goals of public education. For example, the first category evaluated is leadership. Not only does this include a section on organizational leadership, but also a section on public responsibility and citizenship. Other categories include strategic planning, student, stakeholder, and market considerations, information and analysis, faculty and staff focus, process management, and organizational performance results. Together, these categories combine to provide measures of the level of quality present in the school. Furthermore, when these criteria are analyzed, they can be compared to goals and missions set forth by the school. In this way, schools retain ownership of the education they provide, and merely applying for the award or planning based on award criteria does not limit or streamline the goals of the school. Rather, schools are allowed to set their mission and goals based on the needs of the students, and applying for the award allows schools to receive independent analysis of the quality of processes in place to achieve those goals. For example, the final category, organizational performance results, states that "learning results should not only reflect what students know but also what they have learned as a result of the educational program" (NIST, 2001). Focusing on the overall learning process provides a more accurate measurement of quality.

Nearly all states have created similar awards for education, a move that encourages QI by bringing the source of the award closer to the schools and allowing more schools receive objective feedback. Also, regionalizing the awards allows for more focus on the particular challenges that might be facing a specific geographic region. For example, Florida has created the Governor's Sterling Award, which is similar to the Malcolm Baldrige award, but also has a program for self-analysis. In Georgia, the Oglethorpe Award was established in similar fashion. It provides for an education category, and it also requires that award recipients hold two Performance Excellence Showcases in the year that the award is won in hopes of providing an example to other schools. Indiana, Kentucky, and Kansas are other states that have developed affiliates of the Malcolm Baldrige award. Often, these awards are beneficial on a state level because they expose state-level policymakers to new ideas about QI. State-level policymakers tend to have more influence when it comes to educational concerns, because educational funding is assumed by the states rather than the federal government. State-level policymakers are better able to constantly keep themselves updated on educational and quality issues. State quality awards are often public–private partnerships in the spirit of the Baldrige award, which ensures that state legislators and executives are aware and knowledgeable of the award criteria.

In addition to promoting quality in education, the Malcolm Baldrige and state quality awards focus on process evaluation and satisfaction of relationships between stakeholders. They also measure results with a comprehensive method that allows schools a chance to compare how they are performing with the goals society has set for them (creating lifelong learners with the ability to be responsible, productive citizens who will be able to contribute to social problem solving). Awards such as these foster the adaptation and application of TQM philosophies in business to education. Mt. Edgecumbe High School in Alaska is one school that can attest (see Case Study 8.3).

Summary and Conclusions

The importance of quality in education is undeniable. Today's students are tomorrow's leaders and without quality education, our nation will continue to lose its competitive edge and lag even further behind the rest of the industrialized world at a time when we can least afford to fail. Society expects its education systems to achieve lofty goals, and ensuring quality is the only way to guarantee that the goals are met in a way that reflects the values and culture of society. Unfortunately, quality is difficult to define and subject to multiple interpretations in our diversified society. Quality is a function of people, processes, and policy. In education, quality must be improved in many different areas including teacher education and training, resource management, and curriculum. Unfortunately, politicians and policymakers have made it difficult to measure quality accurately because they have focused too much on standardized test results and minimum standards and have diminished quality as a result. More emphasis must be placed on how students learn and how well the processes used to teach them are working.

The BNQA and variations created by 54 states and local governments have done a great deal to offer schools a more effective means of quality evaluation based on standards used in business practices. Dozens of schools, such as Consolidated District 15, Pearl River, Mt. Edgecumbe, or the University of Wisconsin–Stout have gone even further by implementing QI strategies adjusted to fit the dynamics of local educational environments. These examples are making it difficult to argue against applications of TQS and QI methods in education. In the end, the culture of education in America must be changed if these applications are going to work on a large scale.

All stakeholders interested in preserving the future — educators, parents, students, teachers, politicians, and taxpayers — must be willing to set aside previous notions of how education should be delivered and results measured. Despite the persistent calls for continuous improvement, many fail to view education from a TQS standpoint. Doing so would force stakeholders to analyze processes involved in educational QI. If this does not occur, we will continue to raise standards for our students without providing them the means by which to reach those standards, and it will not be the students who fail. It will be our institutions.

Key Terms

Lifelong learning
Virtual courses
Just-in-time learning
Distance learning systems
Digital divide
Quality in education
Stakeholder-driven quality
Quality in teacher education
Quality in fiscal resources
Quality in curriculum
National Board of Teacher Certification
Eisenhower Professional Development Program
Categorical grants
Cost–benefit analysis
No Child Left Behind Act
STAR in California
Florida Comprehensive Achievement Tests (FCAT)
ISTEP+ in Indiana
Scholastic Aptitude Test
International Baccalaureate (IB)
School Quality Review Teams

▼

Case Study 8.1: Palatine, Illinois Community Consolidated School District 15

Community Consolidated School District 15 (D15) is a kindergarten through eighth-grade public school system serving 12,390 students in all or part of seven municipalities in Palatine, Illinois, a northwestern Chicago suburb. Its student population includes 37.5 percent minority students and 32.5 percent at the low-income level. Approximately 32 percent of D15's students come from non-English-speaking backgrounds; 72 different languages are spoken in the homes of its students. The school district has 14 kindergarten through sixth-grade schools, three junior high schools, and one alternative school. D15 operates the schools and its own transportation, maintenance, technology, and food services departments on a budget of $146.9 million, with a workforce of 1,898 faculty and staff.

World-Class Learning

For D15, "good enough" is not good enough. The district's mission is to produce world-class learners who achieve exemplary levels of understanding in academics and who can compete with any student around the globe. D15 has laid out six key goals that must be accomplished to achieve its mission: providing their students with 21st-century skills, including accessing and understanding information, communication, comprehensive reading and understanding, problem solving, and human relations skills; promoting world-class achievement; developing a connected-learning community; ensuring a caring, safe, and orderly learning environment; maintaining a high-performing staff; and implementing an aligned and integrated management system. To most effectively help all students in its diverse population achieve success, D15 has implemented a wide array of programs, including intensive reading-intervention programs in kindergarten, first grade, and second grade; the Soar to Success program to accelerate reading growth for children in grades three through six; and Read 180, which combines technology with high-interest, age-appropriate print materials for children in junior high and targeted elementary schools. Programs for English language learners include bilingual or English as a second language (ESL) classes and one-on-one or small group sessions. As a result of these programs, many students are now meeting goals and improving at an increased rate. In the 2002 to 2003 school year, results from a nationally normed test, the Iowa Test of

Basic Skills, showed that 84 percent of D15's second-grade students were reading at or above grade level.

This is an improvement of approximately 10 percentage points since 2000 to 2001, and is nearly 35 percentage points above the national average.

Highlights

■ In the 2002 to 2003 school year, 84 percent of D15's second-grade students were reading at or above grade level, nearly 35 percentage points above the national average.

■ From 2001 to 2002 to 2002 to 2003, eighth-grade students' "enthusiasm for learning," a key performance target, increased from 42 percent to 82 percent for reading, from 50 percent to 80 percent for math, and from 42 percent to 82 percent for science.

■ Turnover rate for certified staff was 11.7 percent for 2002 to 2003, compared to a national average of 20 percent.

■ At a cost per percentage point of student performance on state learning standards tests of $111.93, the district outperformed its three comparison districts, which ranged from $118.57 to $122.36.

Reaching for the Stars

D15 uses some unusual means to inspire its earthbound students to learn about science and technology, including a school bus converted into a "space shuttle"; mission control simulations; a Discovery Learning Center for earth science and geology; and involvement in actual space shuttle missions. Since 1996, junior high students with learning disabilities have participated in a week-long competition at the NASA Space Camp in Huntsville, Alabama, against nondisabled and gifted students from throughout the nation. During these seven years, the D15 students have finished first in at least one of four competition areas. In fact, the overall rate at which D15 special education students are meeting goals and exiting the special education program has shown steady improvement since 1998, reaching approximately 14 percent in 2002 to 2003 — significantly higher than both national and state comparisons of about 5 percent. For English language learners, the exit rate has increased from 8 percent in 1998 to 1999 to approximately 15 percent in 2002 to 2003, exceeding state and local comparisons. In one group of kindergarten students, 18 percent required intervention services when entering school in 2001, but this number was reduced to

1 percent by the 2003 to 2004 school year. Special education students are showing improved performance, a trend seen throughout the district. D15 students have met or exceeded state standards of learning as assessed through the Illinois Standards Achievement Test, given in grades three, five, and eight for reading and math, and in grades four and seven for science and social studies. The district equaled or outperformed its comparison district at all levels and in all subjects from 1998 to 1999 through 2001 to 2002. In addition, in 2002 to 2003, performance in third-grade math exceeded the 90-percent target and approached the state's top 3 percent benchmark. In addition, grade-five math, grade-seven science, and grade-three reading neared the 90-percent target. D15 third- and eighth-grade gifted students participating in the 2001 to 2002 World-Class Tests for math and problem solving had a higher pass percentage rate than those from the other countries participating: the United Kingdom, Australia, Hong Kong, and New Zealand.

Changing Their World

Critical to producing world-class learners is a dedicated, high-performing team of professionals, including teachers, administrators, and support staff. Highly qualified teachers, as defined in the Illinois criteria for meeting the federal "No Child Left Behind" legislation, teach 100 percent of the district's classes, and the number of its teachers who have achieved National Board Certification has increased from two from 1994 to 1995 to 48 in 2002 to 2003, the second highest number in the state. Compared to a national average of 20 percent, turnover rate in the district for certified staff is low (11.7 percent for 2002 to 2003), and attrition for first-year teachers decreased significantly, from 19.5 percent in 1996 to 1997 to 6.3 percent in 2002 to 2003, well below the 20-percent level of a comparative local school district. Among the staff, 97 percent say the environment in which they work is safe and secure. In addition, D15 motivates faculty and staff to develop and use their full potential by involving them in significant decisions about their work environment, including curriculum, instruction, and assessment issues.

Stakeholder-Driven Quality

Strategy development for D15 is led by the District Advisory Committee for Educational Excellence. This group, broadly configured from all key stakeholder segments and chaired by a community member, brings together the interests of employees, students, parents, suppliers, partners, and the community. The committee uses a nine-phase strategic planning process to translate stakeholder expectations, environmental scanning information, and organizational performance requirements into key goals and performance expectations. Through its Strategic Vision 2005, D15 converts strategies into action plans. From this guiding document containing the district's mission, core values, key goals, and student performance targets, a One-Page Plan Scorecard is developed for each department. Objectives from the scorecards are communicated to building leaders who use this information to align their own plans using a plan–do–study–act (PDSA) cycle. The strategy is further cascaded through the organization to teams and classrooms using the same PDSA process, ensuring comprehensiveness and continuity. To facilitate fact-based management, D15 has constructed a system of leading and lagging success measures aligned to its six key goals. Data is analyzed, and the results are distributed to faculty and staff to enable them to make informed decisions and develop innovations in education and support services. The district has developed innovative means of assessing performance important to key stakeholders. For example, the district's "market performance" is determined by calculating the dollar cost per percentage point of performance on state learning standards tests. This allows a value creation comparison with other districts in the state. At $111.93, D15 outperformed three comparison districts, which ranged from $118.57 to $122.36. In addition, D15 maintained a per pupil expenditure rate that is at or above the level of both comparison districts and the state average from 1995 to 2002. Over the same period, no tax referendum has been sought to increase this primary source of funding.

Source: Baldrige National Quality Program, National Institute of Standards and Technology, U.S. Department of Commerce, Web site: www.baldrige.nist.gov.

━━━━━━━━━━━━━━━━━━━━━━━━━▲━━━━━━━━━━━━━━━━━━━━━━━━━

━━━━━━━━━━━━━━━━━━━━━━━━━▼━━━━━━━━━━━━━━━━━━━━━━━━━

Case Study 8.2: Pearl River New York School District (PRSD)

Pearl River's success has not been overnight, but it has incorporated many QI strategies to reach its success, especially by including all stakeholders in the process. For example, in 1992, they initiated a process to continuously improve student performance and deliver value for the entire community, including teachers, families, taxpayers, and businesses. Each year, these same stakeholders collaborate to evaluate the school district's mission and goals to ensure that these goals are consistently being met and that the direction of these goals is consistent with an overall plan to improve quality.

In addition, PRSD has reorganized to remove structural obstacles that might distract from achievement of academic goals. The aim is to create a clear line of sight from kindergarten through high-school graduation. This line of sight includes a districtwide curriculum planner who oversees all curricula from kindergarten to high school to ensure that all teachers in the district are familiar with the goals of the district and to ensure a degree of uniform learning among students. This allows teachers in higher grades to build on the education their students received in lower grades while having familiarity with what exactly the students should have learned in previous grades, making curriculum a continuous process. The district empowered its teachers by eliminating department chairs and limiting the role of the principal to a day-to-day manager. Currently, the job of designing and delivering instructional programs belongs primarily to teachers who use PRSD's A+ Approach for Classroom Success, a variation on the PDSA method that is systematically deployed throughout all phases of the district's operations. Continuous improvement is also stressed throughout the district. The school superintendent visits each school in the district weekly to meet with principals and evaluate teachers in the classroom. Formal evaluations are held quarterly to further ensure CQI.

The new direction of the district has paid dividends. The following is a list of highlights of the district's recent success:

- Although 100 percent of all PRSD students graduate, the percentage of students graduating with a Regents diploma, a key objective, has increased from 63 percent in 1996 to 86 percent in 2001.
- Student satisfaction has increased from 70 percent in 1998 to 92 percent in 2001; parent satisfaction has increased from 62 percent in 1996 to 96 percent in 2001.
- Among PRSD's special education students, 75 percent take the SAT I exam, as compared with 3 percent statewide and 2 percent nationwide.
- PRSD's "balanced scorecard," a scannable composite of progress indicators, provides continuous, up-to-date tracking of district performance.

Additionally, students in the Pearl River district can choose to attend more than 80 private and parochial schools located within free-busing range (15 miles) of PRSD schools. However, since 1990, the proportion of eligible students choosing to attend PRSD schools rose from 71 percent to 90 percent. These numbers suggest that implementation of TQM principles can work wonders if properly applied in a uniform manner in which all stakeholders have a say and active role, even in public school districts that have previously struggled with average attainment levels.

Source: Baldrige National Quality Program, National Institute of Standards and Technology, U.S. Department of Commerce, Web site: www.baldrige.nist.gov.

▲

▼

Case Study 8.3: Mt. Edgecumbe High School

Mt. Edgecumbe High School is located in the mountains near Sitka, Alaska, far from educational rhetoric and debate, but this state school has found itself on the frontier of applying TQM to education.

The first line of the school's vision statement best illustrates the direction the school has gone with quality management: "We are innovative, constantly striving to find and create better ways of pursuing our goals." Essentially, this is the driving force behind quality management. But the school has gone further. Large sections of the school's Web site are devoted to principles of quality management. Included is an adjusted list of Deming's 14 Points as they should apply to educators (can be found at www.mehs.educ.state.ak.us/). Links to many articles and other sources on quality are also included in the school's Web site as well as links to articles written by actual students concerning QI and management in the school. Encouraging students to reflect on the quality in their education only adds to students' understanding of the educational process.

Mt. Edgecumbe is unique as it is a publicly funded school that is also a boarding school. But that has not stopped the school from becoming a model for other schools in Alaska and around the country. In fact, it is part of the school's mission to provide an example of innovation and quality to other schools. Developing a TQM philosophy has worked incredibly well. Mt. Edgecumbe has provided residents of rural Alaska with an alternative to rural schools that just are not capable of providing the high-quality education that Mt. Edgecumbe provides. Applications to the school are ever increasing, and students who attend are extremely satisfied with the experience. The school emphasizes a collective learning atmosphere and a focus more on individual student needs rather than test scores or minimum standards. Indeed, Mt. Edgecumbe is a model for other schools that are cautious about implementing quality management programs in their institutions. It also embodies all the principles of quality that have been discussed thus far by providing to the school's stakeholders inclusion in and ownership of decisions. The school empowers the teachers to work together with parents and students to ensure that teachers are able to anticipate needs and quickly meet them while being accountable and responsible to the taxpayers, who support the school financially. The school also succeeds in accomplishing many of the goals discussed for education by focusing on how students learn and by teaching based not on minimum standards or facts but rather on the idea that students must understand how to learn, how to solve problems, and how to live, work, and operate in a community setting.

Source: Abstracted from Lloyd Dobyns and Clare Crawford-Mason, *Quality or Else: The Revolution in World Business.* Boston: Houghton Mifflin, 1991, pp. 221–230.

Chapter 9

Implementing Continuous Quality Healthcare Improvement

Americans are deeply concerned about access, cost, and quality of health-care. Changes in the healthcare service delivery systems are necessary because of the following systemic problems:

- Forty-five million Americans, including thirteen million children, have no healthcare insurance.
- The cost of insurance premiums is increasing three times faster than increases in wages and salaries.
- Insurance companies charge small businesses 35 percent more than large employers.
- Only 3 of every 10 employers with fewer than 500 employees offer any choice of health plan.
- Businesses with fewer than 50 employees are not required to offer any health insurance.
- Our current system discriminates against families and small businesses as insurance companies decide whom they cover.
- Healthcare fraud and waste is costing taxpayers over 400 billion dollars a year.
- Fears of lawsuits force some doctors to practice defensive medicine by ordering inappropriate tests and procedures to protect against lawsuits.

- Consumers cannot compare doctors and hospitals as reliable quality information is not available to them.
- Twenty five cents out of every dollar on a hospital bill goes to bureaucracy and paperwork instead of patient care.

In response, many hospitals, insurance companies, and direct providers of healthcare services and supplies are adopting concepts and theories of service quality management to supplement traditional delivery systems.

Healthcare systems and services monitor services from three different perspectives: (1) the scientific-medical, (2) administrative-systems management, and (3) from the perspective of the patient, as well as other customers and suppliers. Physicians, drug companies, hospitals, nurses, and other suppliers of healthcare goods and services are now implementing continuous quality improvement (CQI) and Total Quality Management (TQM) as a vital part of comprehensive health service delivery functions, especially those related to quality assurance (QA), cost containment, and utilization management (Arndt and Bigelow, 1995; Berwick, 1989, 1996; Milakovich, 1991b; Miller et al., 1992; Motwani et al., 1996; West, 1998). For a detailed case study of how a large healthcare provider uses CQI strategies to improve patient care, see the description of BNQA winner SSM Healthcare in Case Study 9.1.

If widely adopted, a CQI strategy of "customer quality as first among equals" would also begin to achieve an important secondary goal of any healthcare system: universal access (Miller and Milakovich, 1991b). Moreover, it would improve the negative international image of U.S. medical care as too costly, elitist, and serving too few by not addressing the plight of uninsured U.S. citizens, including one out of every four children denied access because they lack health insurance. For those uninsured or unable to pay for the expensive treatment, the United States shares (with South Africa) the dubious distinction of being the only advanced industrialized nation in the world not providing healthcare for nearly 45 million persons (one seventh of its population), most of whom are women and children. The negative social consequences of limiting access to care and higher costs of delivering healthcare services favored the shift from traditional *fee-for-service* medical care to the development of *managed healthcare* systems nationwide.

Increasing Costs and Shifting Priorities for Healthcare

The creation and growth of health maintenance organizations (HMOs) since the mid-1980s encouraged healthcare professionals to think in broader, more flexible, customer-focused terms. The 1990s witnessed a shift from a physician-directed, fee-for-service system to an increasingly regulated managed care environment. Although far from the ideal reformers envisioned, proposals for more competition and cost consciousness in delivering health and medical care heralded the use of managed care (Smith, 1992; Starr, 1982, 1993). In addition to the HMOs and preferred provider organization (PPOs), government-funded healthcare buying cooperatives or "managed competitions" among private providers is viewed by many as the best way to contain costs and provide universal access. Proposed reforms stress the need to continuously monitor customers (i.e., patients) and indicators of the quality of service provided in the new managed, quasi-competitive system. Quality, cost, and access to care are critical components for ensuring the nation's well-being, as well as the health of individual citizens. The immense size of the medical–industrial complex ($1.7 trillion, or over 17 percent of the GDP) amplifies the importance of issues such as access, cost containment, insurance coverage, liability insurance, and quality of care.

One of the basic purposes of managed care, as opposed to traditional fee-for-service healthcare, is to address these systemic problems and develop delivery systems that carefully review resource utilization so all those in need of care will receive quality care. This approach increases the importance of clinical specialties such as the *QA and utilization review*, as well as administrative specialties such as cost accounting and financial performance. Designing systems that lower costs, ensure quality, and increase access at competitive prices is a continuing challenge for both managed-care and fee-for-service healthcare providers.

The primary providers of healthcare products and services have traditionally focused on the clinical–medical and financial aspects of care. Prior to the broad-scale adoption of managed care, providers of healthcare services and suppliers of medical products emphasized QA, risk management, and utilization review from strict external criteria, usually medical–clinical, or hospital accreditation standards. Healthcare policymakers, administrators, insurance companies, and allied health professionals are now developing a broader set of integrated patient-care, financial, human resources, and cost-control measures (Burnett, Quintana, and West, 2005). As members of a service industry under increasing economic, political, and social pressure, healthcare providers have fewer incentives not to horizontally integrate medical, organizational, administrative, and patient satisfaction measures into a cross-functional TQS management system. Changing national priorities, new legislation, and shifting formulas for distributing healthcare resources increase the importance of quality improvement (QI) in regard to this vital public policy issue.

Changes in nonprofit, governmental, and private health insurance policies have affected the delivery of healthcare services ever since the

Table 9.1 The Costs of Healthcare in Billions of Dollars

Year	$ Cost (Billions)	Percentage GNP	Percentage Administration
1970	74	7.3	7
1992	809	13.4	20
2000	1,516	15.2	22
2005	1,710	17.1	25
2012	3,400 (est.)	18	n/a

passage of Medicare for the elderly and Medicaid programs for the poor in 1965. Cost containment has become a major focus during the 1990s as healthcare spending grew at an average annual rate of 6.5 percent; it is predicted to increase 7.5 percent from 2003 to 2012. National health expenditures grew at an annual rate of 7.8 percent in 2000, 10.0 percent in 2001, 9.5 percent in 2002, and 7.4 percent in 2003, almost twice the rate of inflation. The slight decrease in the *rate of increase* in 2003 resulted from slower rates of growth in disposable personal income, medical price inflation, and changes in Medicare. At these growth rates, healthcare spending is projected to reach $3.4 trillion or 18 percent of the GDP in 2012 (Table 9.1). Insurance premiums per enrollee in private healthcare increased 12.2 percent by the end of 2003 and "out-of-pocket" health expenditures (paid directly by patients) are expected to grow from 14 percent in 2003 to 15 percent or higher by 2012. These changes reflect a lack of effective cost control and increasing numbers of employers who are limiting or eliminating healthcare benefits for workers and their families.

The growth rate of total healthcare spending is likely to be higher than the national rate of inflation and individual spending for the foreseeable future. Government-funded Medicare spending is increasing at 1.3 percent per year, while Medicaid spending is growing at an alarming 12.5 percent, but expected to slow to 8.5 percent by 2012. This will result in increasing numbers of poor and elderly patients having to assume a greater share of their healthcare expenses. Hospital-spending growth, driven by higher labor costs and increased hospital pricing leverage, will account for 28 percent of the increase in total healthcare spending during the decade. Prescription drugs and physician spending will each account for 17 percent of the increase. Spending on prescription drugs, the fastest-growing sector, will likely account for 14.5 percent of all health expenditures in 2012, as opposed to around 11.0 percent today.

Plainly, this mixed system of public and private revenue and divided public and private accountability creates major problems in controlling costs, setting standards, and establishing and accurately measuring critical quality characteristics for both medical and nonclinical services received by patients.

In addition, many traditionally monopolistic public agencies are being privatized; that is, their functions are being outsourced or turned over to private providers. Thus, healthcare providers are more dependant on mixed sources of public and private revenue. The reverse is also true in many private sector services that now receive revenue or the regulatory authority to operate directly from the public sector. The inflation and confusion in healthcare expenditures and management has contributed to stunning increases in non-patient-care and indirect "overhead" costs. The comparison chart (Table 9.1) shows how overhead or administrative (indirect) costs of providing care have increased and are likely to increase if current trends continue.

These trends are particularly disturbing because administrative "overhead" costs are primarily non-value-added expenses, including paperwork, data processing, and insurance forms, which do not directly benefit patients (see Chapter 5). Worse yet, the ratio of administration costs to direct costs per patient has increased in the United States during the past 35 years to one out of every four dollars (Table 9.1). If quality indicators and strict regulations were in place, the United States could reduce its total investment in healthcare by at least 10 to 15 percent without sacrificing patient-care quality. The savings generated by reducing unnecessary "overhead" costs could be redirected to the additional expenses of extending coverage to uninsured Americans. Many hospitals have assumed this responsibility voluntarily. Baptist Hospital, Inc., of Pensacola, Florida (Case Study 9.2), redistributes its "quality dividend," which totals almost 7 percent of its total revenues, to cover the costs of patients unable to pay their hospital bills. The case also lists some of the many data systems available to health administrators for monitoring clinical, financial, and operational costs.

Spiraling costs and decreasing access to healthcare services worry many citizens, especially the one in seven families without health insurance. Political mandates to measure quality, broaden access, and reduce costs were attempted, even before healthcare became a national policy issue in the early 1990s. Alternatives to individual physician visits (fee-for-service) delivery systems were created by federal and state statutes in the 1970s and receive limited subsidies from public funds. Although less comprehensive than past proposals for reform, they attempted to achieve the same goals. Thus, many of the reform proposals have been achieved, even without the formal enactment of federal legislation. Expectations for reform among stakeholders have risen. So, too, has the level of citizen awareness and concern about various alternatives.

With the passage of the controversial Medicare Prescription Drug Improvement and Modernization Act in December 2003, President George

W. Bush established privatized healthcare as one of the nation's highest priorities. The bill was designed to increase market competition and further limit government influence on healthcare decisions. Under this act, everyone eligible for federal assistance would receive a health card that guarantees healthcare coverage. Every citizen would have a choice of health plans and be able to follow their doctors into a traditional fee-for-service plan, join a PPO network of doctors and hospitals, or join an HMO. Also, insurance companies would be required to use a single claim form instead of the thousands of different forms in use today, thereby reducing overhead costs. This act would control healthcare costs by limiting how much insurance companies can raise premiums, by introducing competition to the healthcare market and by asking drug companies (but not requiring them) to hold down prescription drug choices. These goals would be accomplished by reducing paperwork and by slowing the growth of governmental programs such as Medicare. This act would also increase quality by emphasizing preventative care, giving consumers the power to judge the quality of care, reforming medical malpractice by encouraging patients and doctors to use alternative forms of dispute resolution, increasing funds for prevention research, promoting research on the effectiveness of treatments, and providing incentives for more family doctors to practice in rural and urban areas. The new system would be financed from Medicare and Medicaid savings, savings from federal employee healthcare costs, and by payroll taxes.

Despite these reforms efforts, inflation in healthcare costs continues to increase and governmental efforts to regulate the system have met with intense resistance from those who provide healthcare goods and services.

In the early 2000s, state and federal legislation encourage the creation of group medical practices, promotes free-enterprise policies, expands ownership of healthcare providers, and offers incentives for mergers of large hospital chains. U.S. medicine is being transformed from a locally controlled, fee-for-service cottage industry into a national, yet heavily regulated, competitive industry. Still, there are no quick fixes to reform the quality of healthcare services in complex, free-market economies. Why should health service providers reorient their thinking to a TQS approach?

What Is Total Quality Healthcare Improvement?

TQS is a unique combination of applied modern high technology, cognitive skills, access to facilities at reasonable costs, and patient-centered high-quality primary and specialized clinical care. All these dimensions of service are equally important. Therefore, as much effort must be devoted to designing measurement systems that assess perceived quality of care

Table 9.2 JCAHO Ten-Step Process
1. Assign responsibility.
2. Define scope of care.
3. Identify what care to monitor.
4. Identify what indicators will be used.
5. Establish threshold and minimum standards.
6. Collect and organize data.
7. Assess and evaluate care based on established standards.
8. Take appropriate action.
9. Assess actions and document results.
10. Communicate information.

provided patients as has been previously expended in designing cost accounting or narrowly focused medical care QA systems.

Tighter external review by accrediting associations (such as the American Medical Association (AMA), the Joint Commission on Accrediting Healthcare Organizations (JCAHO), Physician Review Organizations (PROs), and other means of external regulation such as Certificates of Need (CON) will have difficulty if they do not address the following: (1) control by physicians over admission to the medical profession, state licensing boards, and clinical–medical quality standards, (2) the often self-serving association — real or imagined — between cost containment efforts and "necessary" reductions in care provided restricting the scope of external review, (3) the application of stricter controls through external regulation risking massive resistance from providers of care, i.e., physicians and hospitals, and (4) no conclusive evidence that quality of patient care can be improved through tighter outside regulation.

For most healthcare managers, the trauma of learning a new language (TQS) during later professional life should be eased somewhat, as most medical facilities are already familiar, albeit not entirely comfortable, with review standards set by outside accrediting groups. Much of the information required by outside review organizations, such as the Joint Commission for Accrediting Healthcare Organizations (JCAHO) ten-step process listed in Table 9.2, can provide useful self-assessment data for a hospital. Furthermore, JCAHO has spearheaded the effort to shift the operative model from QA to QI.

As in many other services, healthcare TQS must develop from the "bottom up," but be stimulated from the "top down." Planning must be guided by a statistically based quality philosophy and supported by the massive retraining in TQS principles. Similarly, components such as cost, medical standards, and customer satisfaction must be considered together rather than separately, as has been the approach in the past. Achieving this goal not only requires disciplined top-management support, but a greater degree of cross-functional coordination than exists today among most healthcare facilities. As more administrators, suppliers, nurses, and physicians realize that tools and techniques developed in the manufacturing sector can be adapted and transferred to the healthcare service environment, more facilities are applying the systems necessary to remain competitive, increase productivity, and capture greater local and global market share. How industrial quality control differs from traditional quality control and QA is described in the following text:

- The regular use of tools to understand processes and discover flaws, such as process flow diagrams, cause–effect diagrams, control charts, data display charts such as histograms, and Pareto diagrams
- Prevention, preferable to detection
- Focus on the system, not the individual
- Centrality of the customer (internal and external)
- Endemic variation; general cause (related to the process) and special cause (not endemic to the process)
- Broader definition of quality — not just patient care (Berwick et al., 1991).

Today, most healthcare professionals realize the potential value of applying TQS theories and techniques, but some lack the time or knowledge necessary to transform these concepts into the healthcare environment. Despite volumes of research devoted to specialized areas of statistical techniques applied to manufacturing processes, there is still relatively little systematic research on customer service, on TQM and CQI concepts applied to healthcare. For this reason, as well as those discussed above, managers who continue to maintain older systems, rather than make the training investment needed to develop a TQS system, will have no accurate means to determine whether their systems are actually producing at maximum levels of both economic efficiency and quality. The economic as well as social implications of knowing how many resources are lost due to poor-quality care now exceed the excuses typically offered for failing to measure those costs. Suspecting it is costing them substantial money and staff resources, but lacking TQS systems to estimate exactly how much, most service managers (reluctantly) accept the reality of poor quality and the rework required to correct mistakes. Once measurement systems are in place, however, many are often disturbed to learn what the costs actually are. Thus, it should not be surprising to find the costs of poor quality actually increasing in the short term after a quality monitoring system is in place. Managers should be aware of this possibility and plan accordingly.

Implementing Total Quality Healthcare Improvement

Competitive markets encourage QI and cost reduction by reallocating scarce medical resources to the most efficient providers. In addition, entrepreneurship, corporate centralization, technology, and restructuring of for-profit providers increase efficiencies in delivering care. The application of expensive high-technology equipment, such as magnetic resonance imaginers (MRIs) and gamma knives (devices costing $3 million dollars that treat brain tumors without surgery), has also improved the quality of medical care for those covered by insurance. At the same time, high-tech medicine, together with other economic factors, is fueling double-digit increases in the cost of medical procedures without a corresponding increase in access to care. Access to any type of care is still limited by the maintenance of a noncompetitive, yet heavily regulated, service delivery environment.

Government reimbursement policies are aimed at "decreasing the rate of cost increase," whereas private insurers offer fixed-benefit insurance contracts as incentives for doctors and patients to become more cost conscious and efficient. Efforts to contain costs include the imposition of regulations such as Medicare's Diagnosis-Related Groups (DRGs), and Resource-Based Relative Value Scales (RBRVS), as well as fixed-cost Medicare reimbursement plans. Prompted by outside regulators, most of these policies failed to reduce costs or standardize procedures, and only marginally improved the total quality of system processes. Without the discipline of a true competitive market, there are relatively few fiscal incentives for healthcare providers to consider consumer satisfaction measures as equally important to financial and clinical–medical indicators.

Under a TQS model of healthcare, patient interpretation of quality extends beyond clinical services. Today's educated consumer looks at efficiencies in all aspects of service, including housekeeping, nursing, diagnostic and therapeutic care, as well as professional competence. Thus, patient satisfaction with hospital services is influenced by the response of the hospital personnel to patient problems, not just the technical competence of staff. Therefore, every employee must be trained to handle patient dissatisfaction at its source, before a complaint is filed.

During the managed-care expansion period in the 1990s, less attention was paid to development of customer quality measurement systems. Since the passage of Medicare and Medicaid programs, increases in the non-market (governmental) share of the nation's total medical care bill effectively discouraged healthcare providers from designing and integrating total clinical–managerial–customer quality measurement systems. Healthcare delivery systems have operated without incentives for customers (patients) to shop for the highest-quality providers at the lowest costs because medical care costs were paid indirectly by insurance companies to hospitals and doctors. What is the point of patients shopping for healthcare services when their bills are being paid by third-party providers?

Changes in marketing strategy, increased government intervention and regulation, and greater patient awareness of the costs is changing health-care delivery markets and focusing attention on integrating medical–man-agerial–customer QI systems. Ethical considerations, advanced directives, living wills, and greater patient participation in decision making have further accelerated the need for customer-driven QI (Elfenbein, Miller, and Milakovich, 1994). Healthcare professionals have been encouraged by voluntary hospital accrediting associations and government regulators to reorient their systems from the delivery of care without considerations of cost to the implementation of team-oriented, cross-functionally managed, quality-oriented, and customer-focused systems.

This reorientation requires all healthcare professionals to become far more aware of total (visible and hidden) costs of healthcare service delivery (see Chapter 5). Moreover, financial and information collection and processing systems must be integrated to increase process efficiency. Hospitals that reduce costs by increasing the efficiency of internal nonclinical processes such as admissions, laboratories, and patient services become more compet-itive. In addition, they will be favored by managed-care providers such as health maintenance organizations (HMOs), preferred provider organizations (PPOs), and the community healthcare purchasing alliances. Federal Medi-care administrators, state Medicaid programs, and private insurance compa-nies attempt to reward cost efficiencies and favor the quality providers. Simply put, those healthcare providers and suppliers that can demonstrate quality will increase market share and become more profitable.

Guaranteeing healthcare quality will always be a shared responsibility of physicians, nurses, senior hospital managers, federal and state watchdog agencies, insurance companies and (increasingly) managed care providers. Hospitals have adapted TQS and CQI systems developed in other indus-tries to meet their own special needs (Berwick et al., 1991). Pending federal legislation, continuing corporate restructuring of hospitals, insur-ance companies, and healthcare facilities encourage more consumer awareness of the costs and quality of services provided. This allows informed consumers to make rational choices of healthcare providers whose services meet their needs at costs they or their employees can afford. Many states have published data on the mortality and morbidity rates at various hospitals, giving individuals and insurers more information on which to base healthcare purchasing decisions.

Even with the increasing incentives for market competition, however, healthcare providers must still conform to external standards of medical care, at costs acceptable to patients, employers, or their insurance companies.

Third-party providers and insurance companies are encouraging primary care providers (physicians, hospitals) to think in a more "business-like" manner, contain costs and accept restricted (or capitated) reimbursements for certain predetermined procedures. This effort will not be easy and is not without controversy. Achieving these goals is made all the more difficult by the sheer numbers of hospitals (5500), diversity of structures, and complexity of healthcare delivery in the United States.

Another obstacle to developing a TQS culture in healthcare is that physicians jealously guard the prerogative of defining clinical–medical quality standards. This affects customer–supplier relationships as well as operational costs. One of the limitations is that patients are often unaware of the appropriate treatment for their particular condition, and depend on physicians for accurate diagnosis. Most doctors admit, however, that a patient's attitude about the healing process greatly influences their prognosis for recovery. To overcome the tendency to minimize patient concerns because they lack the knowledge to make complicated clinical decisions, patient relations efforts must be redesigned to include measurement characteristics for nonclinical service quality indicators. Changing doctor–hospital–patient responsibilities, coupled with the persistent demand for access to high-quality care at reasonable costs, challenges healthcare professionals to design and implement QI procedures.

When applied to healthcare services, TQS encompasses a much broader definition of QA than that traditionally focusing narrowly on professional, i.e., medical, definitions of the quality of services provided, usually through retrospective review. Surviving in the new competitive–regulated managed care environment requires providers to offer services on the basis of total quality, rather than either lower cost or strict clinically defined QA. Everyone must learn and apply TQS principles in continuously meeting or exceeding customer expectations, consistently doing the correct things right the first time.

Implementing continuous quality in healthcare requires active management participation and includes all traditional measures of cost and QA, cross-functional teamwork, and statistical evidence of compliance with medical standards. In addition, it requires surveys monitoring customer satisfaction and dissatisfaction, and measures of the quality of goods and services provided by suppliers. The differences between traditional QA (retrospective quality assessment) and QI are presented in Table 9.3.

Changing Attitudes, Globalization, and Managed Healthcare Competition

International economic competition, a reputation for shoddy domestic services, poor educational performance, and the need to increase productivity

Table 9.3   Comparing QA with CQI

QA	CQI
Vertical orientation	Horizontal orientation
Retrospective blame assignment	Concurrent evaluation
Inspection and "policing"	Team interplay
Suppresses stimulation	Promotes stimulation
Top-down communication	Communication up-down
Promotes autonomy	Promotes accountability
External standards	Internal standards

to decrease costs combined to motivate U.S. service providers to apply total quality healthcare concepts. American industry has already made remarkable progress toward achieving both higher quality and greater productivity, while remaining price competitive in world markets. Still, our economic competitors and trading partners (Canada, China, Germany, Great Britain, and Japan) are far more efficient at increasing access to healthcare services and controlling costs. As a percentage of GNP, these countries spend half to one third less, provide universal access to care, and demonstrate better quality results than U.S. doctors and hospitals. As a result, these nations can devote a greater share of their national resources to other vital areas such as education, medical research, research and development, social security, job creation, and crime protection.

Prior to the first Bush Administration, employers assumed the primary responsibility for providing healthcare insurance because the majority of those at risk were employed at least part-time. Many employees are now in danger of becoming indigent because all their financial resources are being decimated as a result of reduced coverage, natural disasters, or catastrophic illness or disease. The vital connection between global competitiveness, employment, and a healthy workforce is clearly seen with the increase in healthcare expenditures (which have risen faster than inflation) and the trend in outsourcing jobs. Together, these developments have negatively impacted industry's ability to compete in global markets. Corporate healthcare benefits have soared to a point where they now consume over half the net profit of American firms. Senior managers in private companies have a strong profit motive for controlling healthcare costs. Until recently, no similar motivation to change management practices existed in the public or service sector in general, or in the competitive–regulated healthcare service delivery sector in particular. Large employers such as General Motors and Chrysler-Daimler Corporation have taken the lead in promoting more cost-conscious managed healthcare delivery systems.

To control costs and increase access, many employers favor a managed competition system dominated by large, heavily regulated HMO-type healthcare purchasing cooperatives. The State of Florida passed a similar law (The Florida Healthcare and Insurance Reform Act of 1993) to ensure its 15 million residents access to high-quality, affordable healthcare. Florida was the first state to adopt the managed-competition model of healthcare delivery and extend medical coverage to state employees and its 2.5 million uninsured residents. Those covered by universal insurance may be offered a basic package of services meeting minimum standards of care. If statistical evidence is provided that such care meets or exceeds customer care expectations, then the substantial cost savings resulting from switching to the lower-cost, comparable quality approach can be applied to increasing access for all those who need treatment, without loss of acceptable levels of quality care (Miller and Milakovich, 1991a).

Historically, healthcare service providers depended on third-party payers and direct consumer spending for most of their operational funds. Third parties are private insurance companies or government funding agencies, which together pay 86 percent of the nation's healthcare bill. The public share has increased dramatically in the four decades since federal subsidies were first enacted. In 1960, for example, prior to Medicare and Medicaid, these two sources accounted for 81 percent of total revenues, with public funds contributing less than 20 percent. By 2003, the healthcare system received its largest single share (52 percent) of direct support from federal, state, and local governments. Another one third came from other third-party providers, corporations, and private insurance companies, whereas the remaining 14 percent was paid for directly by patients.

Attempts to regulate, reallocate, reduce, or even ration public expenditures for healthcare have been resisted by healthcare professionals. Many have responded defensively with real or threatened restrictions of access to services. Still others think of quality as a fixed commodity, rather than a variable customer-defined service responsive to such factors as system improvement, customer quality characteristics, or reduction in non-value-added (administrative) costs. Despite these self-serving objections, many healthcare experts emphasize that cost containment policies need not result in lower quality care, if appropriate systems are in place to measure and control quality results (Ullmann, 1985; Burnett, Quintana, and West, 2004). Within the medical profession, there is less agreement about the role that customer (patient) satisfaction should play in the QA process. Several user-oriented studies have shown that patients could perceive "good" hospitals as treatment centers or as "homes away from home," thereby accelerating the treatment and healing process. Increasing numbers of healthcare practitioners recognize that achieving and producing health and satisfaction is the ultimate measure of the quality of care. Comparing patient perceptions with actual clinical outcomes reveals that patients do possess accurate knowledge of the quality of care they are receiving.

In sum, for the necessary transition in thinking about managing health-care quality to occur, the technical language and concepts of TQS must be translated into a common set of relevant healthcare examples. Guided by quality theory and principles, these cases should illustrate the application of statistical quality tools and assist healthcare managers in their knowledge of how to improve their facilities. The essential elements of this new way of thinking are: (1) all actions must be guided by principles of CQI, (2) there must be active involvement of the providers of care, in teams and problem-oriented workgroups, (3) decisions are based on facts, data, outcome measurements and statistical information, and (4) leaders must be personally involved and committed to serving customers, broadly defined as anyone impacted by the actions of the organization (Milakovich, 1991b). For a recent example of such as system in practice, see Case Study 9.3 of the Robert Wood Johnson Hospital in New Jersey.

With these processes in mind, we turn now to a more complete description of how TQS principles are being applied to measure results in healthcare and patient services.

Strategies for Measuring Patient Satisfaction

For most types of service industries, information about consumer attitudes regarding quality is critical for their economic survival. In a healthcare organization, not only the patient, but also the patient's family must be recognized as one of the consumers in the extended customer network in healthcare, inclusive of all "customers'" healthcare processes (Figure 9.1).

The key to providing quality service is to balance all the customer's expectations with their perceptions of quality in all related healthcare services, such as nursing care, employee attitudes, technology, hospital administration, appearance of physical facility, convenience and access, food service, and even presence of the governing board. In the past, administrators focused on attracting and retaining qualified physicians, who in turn brought in patients. Today, however, hospitals and healthcare institutions must develop a broader range of measures reflecting patient as well as employee perceptions of care. St. Luke's Hospital of Kansas City (Case Study 9.4) uses 12 customer-contact requirements to respond to patient complaints within 24 hr or less. To ensure that everyone understands the hospital's focus, all employees take part in the performance management process.

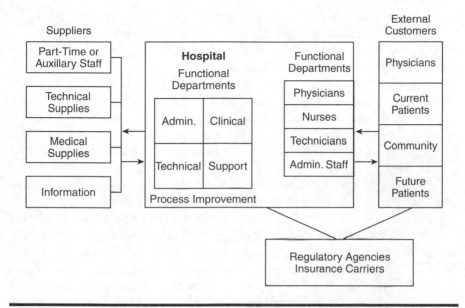

Figure 9.1   The extended customer network in healthcare.

One area that holds great promise for incorporating total quality into healthcare is patient satisfaction measurements. This refers to the recipients' reaction to critical aspects of their service experience. Plagued by rising costs, increasing regulations, and growing consumer interest in reducing costs, healthcare professionals can achieve gains by concentrating on patient-centered service QI. This happens because it simply costs less to provide higher quality care than continuing to offer poorer quality. Process improvement centers on the elimination of wasteful, inappropriate, or unnecessary services, while providing better clinical outcomes, fewer avoidable complications, and greater patient satisfaction. All types of service organizations can learn from patient–customer perspectives on service. Patient evaluation can lead to more structured processes for gathering patient satisfaction measures and more accurate "voice of the customer" information.

No QA system will ever be perfect. Gaps may occur in systems designed to monitor quality due to the incongruence between what matters to customers and what matters to those providing service. Once expectations are identified, gaps may still exist because of the difference in service quality definitions and the ability of the organization to meet these standards. One method of overcoming these gaps in service quality is to use the patient's knowledge to improve the healthcare process (Zeithaml, Parasuraman, and Berry, 1990:31). Quality patient satisfaction also plays a vital role in establishing institutional loyalty, usage patterns, and word-of-mouth communications.

Healthcare service providers have tended to react to patient complaints, rather than anticipate patient needs. Patient complaints, both oral and written, are typically handled by a single individual, usually a nurse or public relations officer, designated as the patient relations coordinator. The coordinator is responsible for resolving complaints by negotiating with attending physicians, risk managers, QA professionals, and administrators. The goal of a patient satisfaction system is to encompass all aspects of patient relations activities into a comprehensive, effective, and efficient proactive system that is consumer oriented and addresses the quality of patient services.

This strategy assists healthcare professionals in becoming less defensive and more aware of patient needs and how their behavior impacts the quality of healthcare services. Furthermore, listening to the customers allows for evaluation of "gaps" resulting from differences between patient and staff perceptions of service encounters. It promotes CQI rather than merely reacting to complaints. Designing a quality patient satisfaction system involves five primary activities: (1) benchmarking best practices of one's own institution or other hospitals or related service industries, (2) obtaining customer feedback, (3) considering complaints as opportunities for improvement, (4) empowering a QI lead team or council, and (5) institutionalizing follow-up service evaluations and surveys. The preceding activities are further considered in the following text:

- *Benchmarking:* Designing a patient satisfaction monitoring system could begin with a review of the facility or business organizations outside of healthcare (see Chapter 2). Obvious related service industries are hotels and food service. Firms known for their commitment to QI such as Hyatt Hotels, Ritz-Carlton, and Marriott Corporation are being benchmarked for systems to (1) measure customer satisfaction from check-in to check-out, (2) train employees to become more aware of the customer's needs, (3) encourage customers to complete surveys, (4) developing top-management commitment to quality assessment and improvement, and (5) continually adjusting processes to obtain desired outcomes.
- *Data sources:* The second component is monitoring patients' feedback on the care received while hospitalized. Consumer assertiveness has challenged healthcare professionals to devise new ways to incorporate patient input into TQS management systems. Techniques designated to solicit patient feedback are available and have helped expand professionals' definitions of quality. Some of these data-gathering techniques are:
  - Telephone interviews
  - One-on-one interviews

- Complaint inquiries
- Patient and other customer surveys and questionnaires
- Focus groups made up of past, current, or future patients
- Referral information services
- Patient questionnaires are generally divided into sections that pertain to the patient's experience during hospitalization, from admission to discharge. After collecting and examining patient questionnaires, the knowledge gained can be used to focus on improvement opportunities. This form of scenario writing (see Chapter 4) aids management in eliminating the root causes of problems in specific departments or hospital services. Another advantage of using systematically collected patient input data is that by encouraging responses other than "yes or no," respondents can express their true feelings and attitudes toward their hospitalization. This methodology removes the likelihood of obtaining skewed data and, when analyzed, will increase the validity of patient satisfaction data.

■ *Redesigning Patient Relations:* A third component of a successful quality patient satisfaction model is the establishment of an appropriate organizational center that encourages interdepartmental communication and serves to address patient complaints about healthcare services. Each complaint should be viewed as a QI opportunity. The information could be received formally from written complaints, as well as orally from appropriate reporting personnel or directly from the patient. Patient relations problems can be reported directly to the QA director, whose mission is to integrate departments in achieving QI goals.

■ *QA committee:* The inherent goal of any TQS healthcare improvement effort is to positively impact the quality of health services provided to patients. For the process to succeed, extensive input must be gained from all individuals directly or indirectly involved in patient satisfaction. The fourth component of the proposed model is the establishment of a QA team, an interdisciplinary council to address patient-care issues. The purpose of this group is to use an interdisciplinary framework to monitor all patient complaints obtained from various data sources and to ensure corrective actions are implemented in a reasonable timeframe. The chairperson could be the hospital chief executive officer (CEO), and the committee could comprise the medical directors, QA director, volunteer coordinator, patient relations director, and a representative from the nursing and medical staff. In addition, because of their impact upon patient satisfaction, food services and environmental service departments could be part of follow-up team if these areas are identified as needing improvement. Other ancillary departments are included on an "as-needed" basis. Lead team members serve as resource persons in identifying and prioritizing patient complaint issues, developing corrective actions, and monitoring the effectiveness of process improvements. All of the components are important, but a well-functioning QA team may be the most important.

■ *Follow-up and evaluation:* As with so many other services, patient complaints are rarely even considered until the patient communicates dissatisfaction to a service provider, which may not occur until after discharge. Once the patient's hospitalization comes to an end, follow-up and evaluation of the quality of health services delivered is often neglected. In many cases, it is too late to effectively respond. Mechanisms must be put in place to anticipate patient grievances by continuously monitoring attitudes and perceptions to improve quality processes. The fifth and final component of the model is the follow-up and evaluation. Automobile dealerships have been benchmarked in this area for many years. Following the purchase of an automobile and after each service encounter, service representatives personally contact customers to solicit feedback on the satisfaction of the service. Many hospitals now do the same. For the service quality leaders, customers have now come to expect personalized follow-up evaluation. The customer is usually pleasantly surprised and willing to share thoughts, attitudes, evaluations, and even make improvement recommendations. This information is analyzed and integrated into the QI system. Implementing a callback system or similar method of responding to patients in a timely fashion is critical to the patient's perception of service quality.

As mentioned earlier, the average business does not hear from 95 percent of its dissatisfied customers. However, the lack of complaints does not signify the absence of dissatisfaction. It has been noted that for every complaint, there are as many as six others with serious problems and thirty less serious complaints that have not been expressed. In a hospital setting, this ratio may be magnified because patients have been conditioned to believe that passive and compliant behavior is safer and less damaging to their care.

Quality patient and other customer satisfaction is oriented toward providing timely information that can be used in an external marketing campaign. As competition increases, market segmentation in healthcare is also increasing. By offering fitness classes, postoperative rehabilitation programs, and other nonclinical services, medical facilities hope to capture distinctive markets by restructuring their delivery systems to offer alternative services. As healthcare providers attempt to develop these alternative quality systems, emphasis has been on the selection, location, and availability of services. Through the use of patient satisfaction programs, providers may discover that rather than the issues currently advertised, they would have greater success in positioning themselves in the market by addressing issues of the patient–physician interaction, staff competence, and actual medical care. In the search for the market niche, knowledge concerning consumers and their perception of the facility are vital.

The rationale behind using patient satisfaction monitoring is that patient perceptions can aid healthcare organizations in a variety of ways, such as monitoring quality of care, reducing the cost of care, and providing useful marketing surveys to encourage the use of services by others. Whatever the results, these solid facts provide an excellent basis for preparing an advertising campaign. With accurate information about service quality, a hospital can differentiate itself from others in the marketplace without relying solely on reputation or specialization.

There are a number of forces increasing pressures for QI in healthcare. In addition to the previously mentioned competitive service environment, these include the high liability insurance premiums for hospitals and physicians, tougher state regulations, and JCAHO requirements. In addition, the area of quality assessment is a growing part of the healthcare evaluation process. The ultimate purpose of quality monitoring is to exercise surveillance so that departure from standards can be detected early and corrected, before it negatively impacts patient care.

Structured approaches to improved patient satisfaction focus on the institutional aspects of care, such as hospital policies, staff qualifications, physical facilities, and the organizational framework in which the caregiver and the patient interact. Structural evaluation focuses on the system, whereas process evaluation focuses on the implementation of care provided by a facility. Actions taken by health professionals are measured by "outcome" evaluation, which stresses the end result of care or the change in the patient's health status as a result of treatment. By implementing a patient satisfaction program, a healthcare facility can monitor the quality of structural, process, and outcome measures from a clinical, managerial, and patient's point of view.

Defining standards for quality of care requires a definition of the characteristics of care as well as criteria that constitute good care. The management of illness can be divided into two sections: the technical and the interpersonal. It is important to remember that the quality of interpersonal encounters may affect the quality of the technical care provided as well as eliminate expensive "below-the-surface" hidden costs of poor quality.

Patients often play an important role in defining what constitutes quality care by determining which values are associated with different outcomes. Determining patients' perceptions also provides information about the performance of healthcare professionals. Without using inspection as a tool, a well-designed comments form acts as a monitoring device for the availability and performance of personnel. This adds a measure of accountability for employees, physicians, and managers in terms of meeting or exceeding the customer's technical and emotional needs. It also reduces the probability of malpractice cases and reduces the need for risk management policies.

Patient satisfaction is promoted when healthcare service encounters are tailored to individual needs and wants. This requires that patients understand treatment options and their expectations be both heard and acted upon. The process of shaping expectations should begin before the patient's arrival and should continue after discharge. Patient participation in making treatment and other healthcare-related decisions restores a patient's sense of control and encourages the healing process.

Healthcare QI is a complex and dynamic activity involving thousands of organizations and millions of individuals. An attempt is made below to summarize some of the more successful QI techniques and how they could be adapted to hospital or healthcare environments, emphasizing proved methods that managers can use to implement change within their own organizations.

Implementing Organizationwide Healthcare Quality

Experience in manufacturing as well as in other service organizations confirms that the best-designed QI systems are only as good as the people who implement them. This is especially true when measuring behavioral as well as technical aspects of quality healthcare. There are no significant differences in the need to measure quality in both areas, except that measurement can be more difficult when no tangible product results from a process. Measurement characteristics in service organizations are more difficult to define and monitor accurately, primarily due to the dependence on *human sensors* rather than scientific instruments for data collection and interpretation (see Chapter 5). Human sensors must be more sophisticated and sensitive, capable of overcoming natural tendencies to make judgments according to their biases. Careful training is the key to overcoming these tendencies.

For successful implementation to take place, all departments in a health service organization must be involved, but one person should initially accept the responsibility to serve as quality coordinator. Ideally, this person should be at or near the top-management level within the organization, preferably the CEO or president. As a practical matter, considering the various routine QA data collection efforts required of most facilities, a senior vice president or comparable appointee will typically initiate and coordinate the process review. As long as the person assigned the task has authority commensurate with the responsibilities, and the effort has the full support of the senior-level staff, organizationwide actions can begin.

If one does not already exist, the first order of business is creating or updating of an organization's *mission statement.* The second step in the implementation process is the *formation and training* of teams representing each unit in the organization. These teams will meet initially to discuss the goals and objectives of the quality review, to establish targets for improved process efficiency, and to develop measurement characteristics appropriate for each "quality function" within the work unit. Several quality measurement characteristics may already be available within the existing information collection process; others may have to be created by departmental teams. In a department such as patient accounts payable, for example, measurement characteristics could be the number of rebills, number of billing delays, number of patient inquiries about mischarges, and other indices. Each departmental team member is responsible for developing a set of items that are directly related to the quality of the team member's section of the work unit. Brainstorming and focus-group sessions can be used to narrow and refine the team-generated lists of quality measures.

Team leaders are appointed or elected by team members themselves and given additional training in QI theory and techniques. They must be carefully chosen and thoroughly trained to communicate the purposes and goals of the activity to their respective work units. Team leaders must understand the concept and principles of CQI, explain the necessity of developing appropriate measurement characteristics, and facilitate the identification and collection of data from each department. All members of the department, workgroup, or subunit must be included in the process. Team leaders must explain the TQHI concepts at the departmental level, conduct brainstorming sessions with all members to develop complete lists of quality characteristics, and represent the department or subunit in cross-functional planning with other units. Further, top management must support departmental quality projects and encourage small group quality efforts until quality planning becomes a routine part of the quality measurement collection process.

In all likelihood, most line workers, especially nurses, are already overburdened with paperwork, data to collect, forms, and other procedures to be monitored. Most white-collar service employees will not be unfamiliar with CQI techniques and they are likely to be dubious of the need for yet another form to fill out. Thus, the purpose of the TQS process improvement exercise such as the cause–effect diagram (see Chapter 5) as a bottom-up exercise in total organizational QI must be clearly and succinctly communicated to everyone to gain cooperation and sustain momentum.

Collecting data on the costs of poor quality is not an inherently difficult task, yet it is rarely done in the hospital or healthcare setting because clinical care and financial reporting requirements dominate the data collection efforts. Many hospitals and other healthcare facilities fail to collect data to determine whether "valid" customer requirements are being met. If customer satisfaction data is collected, it is rarely integrated with clinical and financial systems. With sufficient resources to support the effort, the outlines of a TQS system can be put together in just a few months of team effort. The first data collection effort may get only 70 to 80 percent of the total data required, but analysis of this data would provide sufficient "shock value" that most facilities will not need the remaining 20 to 30 percent of the data for some time. As more data is collected, the quality review process can be calibrated, and teams expanded as necessary to collect additional information.

Members of each department's team and the team leader should discuss their lists of quality characteristics with other departments. Departmental facilitators summarize and condense the lists and provide a summary of key indicators. Department liaisons or team leaders would then meet with other departmental representatives during cross-functional focus-group exercises to discuss strategies for identifying the costs associated with each quality indicator. Here, representatives from staff areas such as nursing, patient relations, finance, and accounting could also be consulted as part of a cross-functional team-building exercise to attach costs to each of the measurement characteristics proposed by departmental teams.

All departmental team leaders then discuss their quality indicators with the QI coordinator, who in turn devises a monthly reporting system using feedback from each of the departmental reporting team sessions. Team members would then meet and discuss progress on a continuous basis and review the statistics being generated by each department. Adjustments to the process (or "fine-tuning") are made as necessary, based on this statistical data. In this way, all members of the organization begin to develop fact-based approaches to the solution of departmental QI problems. Above all, the system problems that cause flaws, rather than the people who work in a flawed system, must be addressed (Berwick et al., 1991).

Healthcare managers must develop multiple measurement systems capable of monitoring the full range of clinical services, products from suppliers, and patient satisfaction with services. Within most medium-to-large facilities, it is possible to automate a good portion of the data collection and reporting effort to reduce the paperwork burden on employees. The development of fact-based information collection and processing systems capable of accurately assessing various measurement characteristics is as important as the change in thinking required of all employees. To some in any organization, the preceding data collection and reporting steps may appear to be overly detailed and time consuming. As detailed earlier, the use of organizational change strategies, training, systems thinking, and statistical methods also provides everyone with a better understanding of the differences between common and special causes of variation within the system.

Conclusions and Action Steps

TQS implementation and patient satisfaction plans vary from more conceptual, philosophical approaches to a more detailed and hands-on approach. Following an organizationwide commitment to TQS, decisions on the depth, breadth, and scope of the effort are made by senior management. Although specific plans vary depending on the size, mission, and function of a particular facility, there are several general steps that can be taken to strategically improve healthcare quality:

1. Study the literature, read and disseminate appropriate *case studies* of QI efforts in other settings, especially BNQA and state award winners such as those highlighted in this chapter. CQI has only been applied to healthcare since the late 1990s. Influential academic and practitioner journals are recognizing the importance of the subject and publishing increasing numbers of studies to assist professionals in all types of facilities to develop case applications appropriate to their particular institutions.

2. *Personal commitment and involvement* on the part of top management to QI efforts is essential to initiate and sustain the process of top-down–bottom-up implementation. Lacking top-down encouragement, efforts initiated from the bottom are more difficult to sustain.

3. *Recognize poor quality cost practices* as a necessary transition step. Integrate cost measures with patient-care, financial, and clinical–medical data. Here, top management must support small group QI efforts as part of routine information collection processes.

4. *Ensure patient privacy* as well as the *professional autonomy* of physicians, psychologists, nurses, and other state-licensed professions, while at the same time involving all professions in QI plans.

5. *Develop bottom-up work-unit-based measures* consistent with professional discretion and patient requirements, designed to meet extended definitions of customer expectations.
6. Encourage *cross-functional coordination* both vertically and horizontally between line and staff functions within the facility, using training and small-group problem identification techniques.
7. Implement *quality function deployment* to merge customer requirements with organizational process controls and QA standards to minimize costly resistance during the critical start-up phase and sustain continuous improvement process (Omachanu, 1991).

In addition to the preceding guidelines, healthcare administrators must communicate precisely why and how a strategy of service QI differs from other management systems. Moreover, they must stress the importance of extended definitions of customer satisfaction, assume the lead in training all employees, and develop multiple measures and key characteristics of quality (Milakovich, 1991b).

Key Terms

Information processing system
Health Maintenance Organizations (HMOs)
Fee-for-service healthcare
Managed healthcare
Quality assurance and utilization review
Medicare
Medicaid
Out-of-pocket expenses
Medicare Prescription Drug Improvement and Modernization Act
Preferred Provider Organizations (PPOs)
Preventative care
Diagnosis-Related Groups (DRGs)
Resource-Based Relative Value Scales (RBRVS)
Community Health Purchasing Alliances (CHPAs)
American Medical Association (AMA)
Joint Commission on Accrediting Healthcare Organizations (JCAHO)
Physician Review Organizations (PROs)
Certificates of Need (CON)
Extended definition of processes
Customer-contact requirements
Scenario writing

------------------------------▼------------------------------

Case Study 9.1: SSM Healthcare

Founded more than 130 years ago and sponsored today by the Franciscan Sisters of Mary, SSM Healthcare (SSMHC) is a private, not-for-profit healthcare system based in St. Louis, Missouri, that provides primary, secondary, and tertiary healthcare services. The system owns, manages, and is affiliated with 21 acute care hospitals and three nursing homes in four states: Illinois, Missouri, Oklahoma, and Wisconsin. With operating revenues of approximately $1.7 billion, SSMHC provides a wide range of medical services including emergency care, surgery, oncology, mental health, obstetrics, cardiology, orthopedic, pediatric, and rehabilitative care. Nearly 5,000 physician partners and 23,000 employees work together to provide healthcare services through inpatient, outpatient, emergency departments, and ambulatory surgery settings. To support its core hospital business, SSMHC offers additional services that include physician practices, residential and skilled nursing, home care and hospice, and information services.

SMHC has made technology a key part of its delivery of medical services. An innovative, automated information processing system allows physicians to access clinical, patient, and other data through personal computers, personal digital assistants, pagers, and fax machines. Physicians connected to the information system have increased steadily from 3,200 in 1999 to 7,288 in 2002.

SSMHC's mission is: "Through our exceptional healthcare services, we reveal the healing presence of God." Its core values are compassion, respect, excellence, stewardship, and community. SSMHC's "Healthy Communities" initiative launched in 1995 and its charity care policy help the organization address its mission and vision. SSMHC requires each of its entities to engage in one or more community projects such as free dental clinics and campaigns to reduce teen drinking and smoking. Since 1999, SSMHC has exceeded its charity care goal of contributing a minimum of 25 percent of its operating margin (before deductions) from the prior year. Currently, in excess of 33 percent of SSMHC's previous year's operating margin (before deductions) is used to provide care to people who cannot pay.

Highlights

- In 1999, SSMHC started a clinical collaborative program with 4 teams to improve patient outcomes. By 2002, 85 teams had been involved in 6 clinical collaboratives. Physicians connected to an

automated information system have increased steadily from 3,200 in 1999 to 7,288 in 2002.
- For 4 consecutive years, SSMHC has maintained an investment AA credit rating — a rating attained by less than one percent of U.S. hospitals.
- SSMHC's share of the St. Louis market increased over each of the past 3 years to 18 percent, while 3 of its 5 competitors lost market share.

Values Are the Cornerstone of SSMHC

SSMHC is a mission- and values-driven organization where every executive leader is responsible for ensuring that SSMHC's mission and values are communicated and deployed. System management, networking, and entity leadership are responsible for establishing, communicating, and deploying strategic goals throughout the organization.

Organizational short- and long-term strategic direction and performance expectations are established through a strategic, financial, and human resource planning process (SFPP). Extending over a 12-month cycle, the SFPP combines direction setting, strategic development, human resources, and financial reporting and involves all of the organization's networks, entities, departments, and employees. Through the SFPP, process improvement goals are established that consider the needs of key stakeholders — patients and their families, employees, physicians, major suppliers, and payers.

A performance management process (PMP) is used to assess organizational performance as it relates to achieving SFPP short- and long-term goals and in meeting changing healthcare service needs. The PMP defines the roles and responsibilities of executive leadership groups in managing performance of SSMHC and its entities, outlines a consistent set of performance-reporting tools, and establishes standardized definitions and indicators to ensure consistency in measurement and performance evaluation.

Communication is critical to the process. Through a systemwide tool called "Passport," employees develop goals that support short- and long-term entity goals, overall organizational goals, and performance expectations. The Passport contains the SSMHC mission and values; the characteristics of exceptional healthcare services; spaces for entity, departmental, and personal goals and measures; and a place for the employee and manager to sign and date. The passport creates a "line of sight" from personal goals to the organization's goals.

Fostering Continuous Improvement throughout SSMHC

SSMHC's commitment to CQI has put it at the forefront of the health-care industry and has fostered an environment that empowers and encourages all employees to be innovative and to seek the knowledge they need to anticipate and manage change.

SSMHC gathers critical information about its customers, competitors, employees, market share, and clinical outcomes. A variety of listening and learning tools, such as surveys, interviews, complaint systems, feedback, and patient follow-up calls, are used on an ongoing basis to rapidly identify and correct potential problems and improve service delivery. Environmental scans are conducted to gather market research, analyze market share by product line, review population trends, and conduct an inventory of competitors. SSMHC uses all of this information to establish customer and market share goals and performance measures at the network and entity levels. SSMHC's use of DI Diver software reflects the organization's focus on using data to make decisions. The software segments patient satisfaction and clinical data for analysis to improve procedures and decision making. It also compares performance across facilities.

Improving Clinical Outcomes

Persistently and creatively finding ways to improve patient care is part of SSMHC's commitment to CQI. Physicians work together with other caregivers, administrators, and staff using an innovative model called "Clinical Collaboratives" to make rapid improvements in patient care. In 2002, 85 teams, up from 4 in 1999, were involved in the clinical collaborative process.

The results from SSMHC's clinical collaboratives for patients with congestive heart failure and ischemic heart disease demonstrate levels that approach or exceed national benchmarks. For example, more than 80 percent of SSMHC's patients who have congestive heart failure and atrial fibrillation receive coumadin treatment compared to the benchmark of 64 percent. Also, SSMHC has attained national benchmark levels of patients receiving lipid-lowering agents to decrease the morbidity and mortality in patients who have suffered heart attacks.

Employees Drive Success

SSMHC puts its patients and their families first and understands that engaged physicians and employees are keys to its success. Because of the critical role physicians play, SSMHC develops partnerships through a physician-partnering process and other means to focus on physician relations, recruitment, and retention.

In the highly competitive healthcare market, a premium is placed on attracting, recruiting, and retaining a highly qualified workforce. SSMHC is able to achieve this, in part, through its tailored benefits package that offers flexibility and responds, in particular, to women, who comprise 82 percent of its workforce. SSMHC offers flexible work hours; work-at-home options; long-term care insurance; insurance coverage for legally domiciled adults; retreats, and wellness programs. Tuition assistance and student loan repayment programs are highly regarded as significant benefits differentiating SSMHC from its competitors. SSMHC has reaped the benefits of being a flexible employer; the turnover rate for all employees has been reduced from 21 percent in 1999 to 13 percent as of August 2002.

SSMHC maintains a continuous focus on increasing the number of minorities in professional and managerial positions. Minorities in professional and managerial positions increased from almost 8 percent in 1997 to 9.2 percent in 2001, a result that is considerably better than the healthcare industry benchmark of 2 percent.

Source: Baldrige National Quality Program, National Institute of Standards and Technology; U.S. Department of Commerce, Web site: www.baldrige.nist.gov.

▲

▼

Case Study 9.2: Baptist Hospital Inc.

The First Baptist Church of Pensacola, Florida, established Baptist Hospital in 1951 as a community-owned healthcare facility founded on Christian values. Today known as Baptist Healthcare (BHC), that single hospital has evolved into the largest, most comprehensive healthcare system in the Florida Panhandle. Baptist Hospital, Inc. (BHI), a subsidiary of BHC, has two hospitals, Baptist Hospital of Pensacola, a 492-bed tertiary care and referral hospital, and Gulf Breeze Hospital, a 60-bed medical and surgical hospital, and an ambulatory care complex, Baptist Medical Park, which delivers a wide array of outpatient and diagnostic services.

A New Direction

In the mid-1990s, low satisfaction marks, not only from patients and their families but also from staff and doctors, were becoming a trend at Baptist Hospital, Inc. BHI leaders decided that just improving was not enough. With the lofty vision of becoming the best health system in America, BHI leaders decided to rebuild the organization by engaging its staff and listening to its patients. One of their first actions was to create a flat, fluid, and open leadership system based on communication. Under this new system, staff are not just encouraged, they are expected to contact anyone in the organization, including President John Heer, at any time to discuss work issues and improvement opportunities. Senior leaders also serve as role models and are personally engaged in creating a "no-secrets" environment through activities such as the Daily Line-up, in which all leaders and employees gather at each shift to review information in the *Baptist Daily*, and in quarterly around-the-clock employee forums.

Leaving nothing to chance, BHI has created a multifaceted, systematic approach to building customer relationships that begins with BHI's Standards of Performance in areas such as attitude, appearance, safety, and even elevator etiquette. Potential job applicants are required to read and agree to abide by these standards before completing an application. "Scripting" helps to ensure that all patients and other customers receive the same high level of personal interaction. For example, any employee who sees a visitor who appears lost will ask, "May I take you to where you are going?" Upon leaving a patient's room, employees always ask, "Is there anything else that I may do for you? I have the time."

Highlights

- Overall satisfaction for inpatients, outpatients, ambulatory surgery patients, and home healthcare services has been near the 99th percentile for the past several years.
- Positive morale for hospital staff has risen from 47 percent in 1996 to 84 percent in 2001 (the most recent survey), compared to 70 percent for staff at its closest competitor hospital.
- Senior leaders serve as role models and are held accountable for organizational performance through a "No Excuses" policy.
- BHI provides 6.7 percent of its total revenue to indigent patients, compared to 5.2 and 4 percent for its competitors

Pillars of Excellence

Five "Pillars of Operational Excellence" line the hallways of BHI and literally and figuratively form the foundation for BHI's culture of excellence and its mission to "provide superior service based on Christian values to improve the quality of life for people and communities served." The pillars are people, service, quality, finance, and growth. All of BHI's activities are driven by and centered around the five pillars. Using external and internal inputs, BHI's senior leaders and Strategic Measurement Team develop the goals for each pillar. These goals cascade into leader goals, 90-day action plans, senior management priorities, and budgets. BHI uses 90-day action plans for short-term goals. A five-year plan helps balance the time needed for capital commitments and state approvals, and also anticipates advances in medical technology and practices.

Programs such as "Bright Ideas" encourage employees to contribute innovative suggestions for improving operational processes and customer service or reducing costs. Since 1998, the number of improvement ideas has increased from 1,400 to 6,800 in 2003, and the number of ideas implemented during this time has increased from 370 to 5,000. In 2002, BHI exceeded both its goal of two implemented "Bright Ideas" per employee and its cost-saving target of $2.1 million. BHI uses a variety of tools and processes to gather results, information, and data that can lead to improvements. For example Clinical Accountability Report of Excellence (CARE) captures clinical quality data results and trends in more than 50 departments throughout the hospital. One indicator measures patients' adverse reactions to medication, including medication errors. In fiscal year 2000, 2.5 medication error events occurred per 10,000 doses dispensed, whereas only 1.5 events occurred per 10,000 doses dispensed in fiscal year 2002; the VHA benchmark for this measure is 18. (VHA is a private, for-profit cooperative serving not-for-profit healthcare organizations nationwide.) BHI also makes extensive use of information technology (IT) to gather and pass on information. The Hospital Information System helps BHI collect and integrate data for tracking overall organizational performance, as well as financial, clinical, and operational data and information, and identifies opportunities for CQI. The HIS systems are accessed through mobile terminals, kiosks, and the Medical Information Data Access System (MIDAS) for physicians. In 2001 and 2003, *Hospitals and Health Networks* magazine gave BHI its "Most Wired" award for effective use of technology.

Excellence Leads to Results

BHI's new approach to doing business is resulting in significant improvements. Since 1998, the Press Ganey survey has shown BHI to be near the 99th percentile for overall satisfaction for both inpatients and outpatients in the areas of ambulatory surgery, home healthcare, and emergency room service. (Press Ganey Associates is a leading independent vendor of satisfaction measurement and improvement services for the healthcare industry.) Also, staff in the hospital facilities and LifeFlight, BHI's helicopter air ambulance service, have earned at or near a 99 percent satisfaction rating for the past several years for their sensitivity, attitude, concern, and overall cheerfulness. In a highly competitive market, BHI has become an employer of choice by offering employees a combination of empowerment and extensive training and development programs. In 2003 BHI was named a "Top 50" learning organization by *Training* magazine. In both 2002 and 2003, Baptist Healthcare was ranked in the top 15 in *Fortune*'s 100 Best Companies to Work For in America. Since 1997, the employee turnover rate has declined from 31 percent to 13.9 percent in 2003. These rates are more favorable than the northwest Florida and national averages, and are at the best-in-class level. Although turnover is on the decline, morale at BHI is on the rise, from 47 percent of staff reporting positive morale in 1996 to 84 percent in 2001.

Healthy Community

For more than 50 years, BHI has had a strong commitment to improving the quality of life for the communities it serves. BHI provides a number of free health programs for the area's poor and uninsured. Heart risk screenings have increased from 1,100 in fiscal year 2000 to more than 2,400 in fiscal year 2003. BHI's new Women's Heart Advantage program was established to improve awareness of heart disease among women, provide education on healthy lifestyles, and give them easy access to cardiac testing and treatment. BHI's goal is to provide 2,500 screenings to women in 2003. BHI provides 6.7 percent of its total revenue to indigent patients compared to 5.2 percent for its closest competitor. In fiscal year 2002, 2,700 prescriptions valued at more than $550,000 were provided to hospital patients too poor to pay, and another $250,000 worth of prescriptions were provided to over 1,100 low-income outpatients through its various programs for the uninsured. From October 2001 through September 2002, BHI's outpatient clinic had 26,000 visits from 16,000 indigent patients.

Source: Baldrige National Quality Program, National Institute of Standards and Technology; U.S. Department of Commerce, Web site: www.baldrige.nist.gov.

▲

------------------------------▼------------------------------

Case Study 9.3: Robert Wood Johnson University Hospital Hamilton — Baldrige National Quality Award, Healthcare

A private, not-for-profit acute care community hospital, Robert Wood Johnson University Hospital Hamilton (RWJ Hamilton) provides healthcare services to more than 350,000 residents in its service area through its network of caregivers. Primary services include medical, surgical, obstetric, cardiology, orthopedic, and intensive care for both adults and critically ill infants and children. Outpatient services provided at the hospital include diagnostic and therapeutic care, ambulatory surgery, medical and radiation oncology, and emergency services, including emergent angioplasty. Community services include health education, health screenings, and disease prevention programs.

- Web site: http://www.rwjhamilton.org/
- Revenue: $160 million (annually)
- Workforce: 1,734 employees, and an additional medical staff of more than 650
- Location: RWJ Hamilton is based in Hamilton, New Jersey

In September 2004, RWJ Hamilton opened its Center for Health and Wellness, located 4 miles from the hospital. The Center for Health and Wellness focuses on community wellness, education, and physical therapy.

Highlights

With more than 70 percent of inpatient admissions initiated through RWJ Hamilton's emergency department, it is the community's "front door" to the hospital. In 1998, RWJ Hamilton implemented the "15/30" program, which guarantees that patients coming into the emergency department will see a nurse within 15 minutes and a physician within 30 minutes. This program, combined with improvement in physician satisfaction, has improved patient satisfaction with the emergency department from 85 percent in 2001 to 90 percent in 2004, exceeding the national benchmark. In addition, emergency department volume has grown 100 percent from 1999 to 2003. With steadily rising volume over the last four years, RWJ Hamilton's emergency department is a market leader in the area. Over the past five years, RWJ Hamilton has been New Jersey's fastest-growing hospital and has steadily improved its market share, whereas its closest competitor's share has remained the same or declined. For example, RWJ Hamilton's market share in cardiology has grown from approximately 20 percent in 1999 to nearly 30 percent in 2003; in surgery, its market share has increased from approximately 17 percent in 1999 to 30 percent in 2003; and market share in oncology has increased from approximately 13 percent in 1999 to above 30 percent in 2003.

RWJ Hamilton's Patient-Focused Model includes fully deployed goals and expected outcomes based on input from a multidisciplinary care team. Care plans are evaluated daily and patients are included in the assessment and planning process through inclusion of their language preferences, cultural needs, lifestyle, quality-of-life issues, and organ donation wishes. All employees are expected to provide customers with "Excellence through Service" and agree to uphold RWJ Hamilton's 5-Star Service Standards in eight areas including commitment to customers, commitment to co-workers, courtesy and etiquette, communication, privacy, and safety awareness.

Employees are recruited, selected, and evaluated using these standards. RWJ Hamilton's senior leaders and staff are committed to improving community health through a number of activities, including financial contributions, charity care, education programs, health fairs, and screening services. On average, free health screening is provided to more than 900 community residents per month. Donations to community organizations have increased to approximately $140,000 in 2003, up from approximately $80,000 in 1999. Charity Care Dollars have increased from approximately $5 million in 1999 to approximately $23 million in 2003. Community contributions by RWJ Hamilton staff members included serving meals at a local soup kitchen once a month, serving on 88 community boards, and raising nearly $100,000 for several local programs in 2003.

Quality and Improvement Results

Inpatient satisfaction with nursing and with nursing courtesy has improved from 70 percent in 1999 to more than 90 percent in 2004 and meets or exceeds the Press Ganey Top 10 percent level. (Press Ganey Associates provides nationally normed healthcare satisfaction measurements.) The results are further reinforced by the Gallup Community survey results, ranking RWJ Hamilton as having the best nurses among local competitors in 2000 and 2002. Medications such as aspirin and beta blockers, which help to reduce the heart's workload and lower blood pressure, commonly are used by hospitals to treat patients who have suffered a heart attack or congestive heart failure. From 2002 to 2004, patients receiving this treatment at RWJ Hamilton have performed better than those at the top 10 percent of hospitals evaluated by the Joint Commission on Accreditation of Healthcare Organizations. Results for patient mortality rates at RWJ Hamilton show a steadily downward trend from 1999 to 2003, meeting the Agency for Healthcare Research and Quality (AHRQ) Best Level in 2003. For example, mortality rates for patients with congestive heart failure decreased from nearly 8 percent in 1999 to 2.5 percent in 2003. According to the QuadraMed Clinical Performance System, the expected rate in 2003 was 6.2 percent. (QuadraMed is a national organization providing comparative statistics for clinical operations.) RWJ Hamilton's results for hospital-acquired infections, such as ventilator-associated pneumonia and urinary tract infections, all demonstrate favorable downward trends since 2000. For example, ventilator-associated pneumonia rates have decreased from approximately 10 per 1,000 device days in 2000 to two per 1,000 device days in 2004. This exceeds the top 10 percent of organizations as reported by the National Nosocomial Infection Surveillance, a comparative database for hospital-acquired infections. Between 2001 and the first quarter of 2004, RWJ Hamilton's many safeguards to prevent patients from receiving the wrong medication were successful in about 93 percent of cases, far exceeding the national median of approximately 64 percent. As a result of RWJ Hamilton's continuous investment in its technology, equipment, and facilities, occupancy rates have increased from 70 percent in 1999 to 85 percent in 2003 while the best competitor's rates ranged from approximately 57 percent in 1999 to nearly 60 percent in 2003. In the 2002 Gallup Community Survey of customer loyalty, RWJ Hamilton ranked first among all local competitors in all nine "positive" attributes, including most improved; most personal care to patients; advanced, state-of-the-art technology and equipment; best doctors; and best nurses. Seventy-three percent of the customers said they were likely to use RWJ Hamilton again. Over the past four to five years, employee satisfaction has risen in a number of key areas. Satisfaction with benefits rose from nearly 30 percent in 1999 to slightly above 90 percent in 2003; satisfaction with leadership increased from nearly 90 percent in 1999 to almost 100 percent in 2003; satisfaction with participation in decisions grew from slightly above 40 percent in 1999 to 90 percent in 2003; and satisfaction with employee recognition has improved from 70 percent in 1999 to 97 percent in 2003. Retention rates for registered nurses as well as other employees show positive trends: registered nurse retention has improved from 94 percent in 2001 to 99 percent in 2003 and retention of other employees has gone from 80 percent in 2001 to 98 percent in 2003. Training hours for full-time employees has increased from approximately 38 hours in 2002 to approximately 58 hours in 2003.

Processes

To determine patient and customer preferences, RWJ Hamilton analyzes industry, customer satisfaction, and physician referral trends, examines market research, demographics, and information on competitors, and evaluates community surveys. Information is captured in a database called Voice of the Customer. Relying on its Excellence Through Service Leadership System, its Five Pillars of Excellence (service, finance, quality, people, and growth), and its strategic planning process and associated measurement systems has helped RWJ Hamilton successfully develop and deploy objectives and detailed action plans throughout the organization. To improve key processes, meet patient and other customer needs, and achieve its overall vision, RWJ Hamilton uses its Organizational Performance Measurement System to track daily performance and operations. Key performance indicators are reviewed weekly by senior leaders, monthly by manager, and quarterly by all employees. RWJ Hamilton shares best practices and other organizational knowledge through a variety of methods, including the Learning Center Web site and a program called "Walk in My Shoes," in which employees spend time working in and learning the processes of an area or department other than their own.

Leadership/Social Responsibility

RWJ Hamilton has a "zero tolerance" policy for unethical behavior. The principles of ethics are built into the 5-Star Service Standards to ensure integrity in every encounter. All employees are encouraged and empowered to report any potential breach of ethical standards anonymously through the Compliance Hotline or to the corporate compliance officer. Clinical ethical concerns are addressed by a multidisciplinary group of physicians, employees, and administration. Ongoing communication by senior leaders about organizational performance helps to reinforce accountability, identify opportunities for improvement, and underscore a focus on results. Each executive management team member, including the CEO, attends daily briefings in designated department areas to share current information with the staff and to answer questions.

Source: Baldrige National Quality Program, National Institute of Standards and Technology; U.S. Department of Commerce, Web site: www.baldrige.nist.gov.

▲

▼

Case Study 9.4:
Saint Luke's Hospital of Kansas City

Saint Luke's Hospital (SLH) is the largest hospital in the Kansas City, Missouri, metropolitan area. Affiliated with the Diocese of West Missouri of the Protestant Episcopal Church, it is a not-for-profit comprehensive teaching and referral healthcare organization that provides 24-hour coverage in every healthcare discipline. SLH is driven by its vision, "The Best Place to Get Care, The Best Place to Give Care," and its core values of quality and excellence, customer focus, resource management, and teamwork. Saint Luke's employs 3,186 staff and 500 physicians and is committed to providing leadership, volunteers, and funding to many community health organizations, including the federal Women, Infants, and Children Program, the Metropolitan Organization to Counter Sexual Abuse, and The Cancer Institute. The level of financial commitment to community healthcare education has steadily increased from $9.6 million in 1999 to $12.7 million in 2002.

Specialized care capabilities for very ill people are Saint Luke's hallmark. These include the Mid America Heart Institute, which treats complex cardiovascular diseases; the Mid America Brain and Stroke Institute, which includes a nationally recognized program dedicated to preventing and treating stroke; a highly rated trauma center and neonatal intensive care nursery; and the only comprehensive maternal and fetal diagnostic and treatment center in the Kansas City area. From 1999 to 2002, SLH's financial performance has steadily improved, showing that pursuing and implementing innovative treatments is compatible with sound business practices. In total margin and operating margin, SLH currently ranks among the top five percent of the nation's hospitals. In total revenues, SLH outperforms the Council of Teaching Hospitals top quartile.

Listening, Learning, and Improving

Saint Luke's Hospital accomplishes its mission of "providing excellent health services to all patients in a caring environment" by listening to its customers and designing new and improved ways to deliver healthcare. SLH uses a continuous-loop model, known as the Performance Improvement Model, to plan, design, measure, assess, and improve the way it delivers healthcare services. Used in all hospital departments, employees are introduced to the model during orientation, and process owners and PI team members receive extensive training on its use. Saint Luke's "Listening and Learning" process helps to determine patients' requirements. The process includes formal methods, such as surveys, focus groups, and follow-up calls, and informal ones, including daily conversations that SLH employees have with patients, families, and others. A customer satisfaction research program continuously gathers customer and market requirements and helps measure customer satisfaction. One outcome of this input is a better understanding of how patients want to be treated and a set of 12 customer-contact requirements known as the "Commitment to the Four Core Values." The 12 requirements include "Address patients/guests by last name unless otherwise told" and "Address all complaints within 24 hours or less." All employees carry these requirements on a Very Important Principles Card and they are prominently posted throughout the hospital.

Highlights

- In 2002, Consumer's Checkbook ranked SLH 35th in the nation out of 4,500 hospitals evaluated.
- Since 1997, studies of regional healthcare providers by the National Research Corporation have shown that patients believe SLH has the best quality healthcare and the best doctors and nurses of the 21 facilities in the market area.
- SLH has 12 customer-contact requirements, including "Address patients/guests by last name unless otherwise told" and "Address all complaints within 24 hours or less."
- SLH outperforms the Council of Teaching Hospitals top quartile in financial performance and ranks in the top five percent of hospitals nationwide in total margin.

Care Pathways

To ensure the best possible clinical outcomes and high patient satisfaction, multidisciplinary care teams, comprising physicians, residents, students, clinical nurses, patient-care technicians, and information associates, work with patients and their families to design individualized "care pathways." Patients get their own version in a format that allows both the patient and the family to understand and follow the day-to-day delivery of healthcare. Teams also have developed 134 clinical pathways for high-volume, high-cost diagnoses that standardize care and reduce variation in treatment. Sixty percent of SLH patients receive care that is based on a clinical pathway. The constant cycle of listening, learning, and improving is paying off in patient satisfaction.

In 2002, Consumer's Checkbook, a consumer education organization, ranked SLH 35th in the nation out of 4,500 hospitals evaluated. The hospital received an overall score of 7669 compared to a national average of 5418. Consumer's Checkbook rating for SLH physicians was 86 percent compared to a national average of 33 percent. An independent study by the National Research Corporation shows that patients believe SLH delivers the best quality healthcare and has the best doctors and the best nurses of the 21 facilities in the market area. This top position has been sustained since 1997. Additionally, the study found that patients believe that SLH delivered the best cardiac, neurology, and orthopedic care, and ranks it among the top four hospitals in obstetrical care.

A Focus on Excellence and Employees

Saint Luke's "Leadership for Performance Excellence Model" captures all of the elements that drive its focus on performance improvement and excellence, including the strategic planning and performance management process, process improvement model, and a commitment to excellence assessment model based on the seven BNQA performance excellence categories. Saint Luke's vision, mission, core values, and strategy sit at the top of the model and influence all of the organization's plans and processes. A robust strategic planning approach consists of three phases and seven steps that integrate direction setting, strategy development and deployment, financial planning, and plan management. At a series of retreats, the leadership team develops strategy and a 90-day action planning process to deploy the strategy to all departments. The balanced scorecard process produces a measurement system that aligns all departments with the strategy and ensures the proper focus in key performance areas throughout the organization. A highly empowered, high-performing workforce is key to Saint Luke's success. To ensure that everyone is in tune with the hospital's focus, all employees take part in the Performance Management Process. The process helps employees develop action plans and goals that are aligned with the organization's strategy and core values and identify personal commitments that contribute to SLH's values. The process also defines primary customers and competencies needed for each position and sets expectations for each employee.

A Process Improvement Model provides employees with the information they need to effectively design, manage, and improve hospital processes. Factors that determine employee well-being, satisfaction, and motivation are uncovered through formal surveys, open forums with senior leaders, targeted focus groups, senior leader "walk rounds," "staying" and "exit" interviews, and the Peer Review Grievance Process. An intense focus on ensuring that its workforce reflects the diversity of the community, including diversity training for all employees and "Lunch-and-Learn" sessions about diversity-related topics, has led to an increase in minority managers and professional staff, from 3 percent in 1998 to almost 10 percent in 2002. Employees also are staying longer, another indicator of growing employee satisfaction. For the past five years, results for employee retention have exceeded the Saratoga Institute's median and are approaching 90 percent.

Source: Baldrige National Quality Program, National Institute of Standards and Technology; U.S. Department of Commerce, Web site: www.baldrige.nist.gov.

▲

Chapter 10

Leadership for Service Quality Improvement

Never tell people how to do things. Tell them what you want to achieve, and they will surprise you with their ingenuity.

— Gen. George S. Patton, 1944

This concluding chapter begins with a brief summary of the key points discussed in earlier chapters. After this review, we identify barriers to achieving quality in services, and discuss action strategies to overcome these obstacles. Leadership challenges for those committed to achieving customer service quality are presented, within the broader context of developing high-performance organization in global service delivery environments. The reader is once again reminded that total quality service (TQS) is not a destination, but rather a continuous journey, and that those seeking "quick fixes" or easy solutions for service quality problems will be disappointed.

Meeting both high *internal* performance standards and *external* customer service quality requirements means anticipating valid future customer needs and responding to them quickly and courteously with consistent, personal, and customized treatment. This requires responsiveness to customers needs for flexibility, genuine employee empowerment, and the capacity to exceed, rather than merely meet, customer expectations. Anticipating valid demands for better service further empowers everyone involved in service delivery processes and encourages employee ownership and confidence in responding to customers' needs. Recall how St. Luke's Hospital integrates its performance measurement systems by encouraging employee participation (Chapter 9). Quality outcomes depend heavily on one-on-one contact between those providing and those receiving service. In most organizational cultures, employee satisfaction with the way they are treated significantly improves customer satisfaction with the services they receive. Without employee dedication, participation, and support, the best-designed and most generously funded quality and productivity improvement efforts are doomed to failure.

Leadership is key to employee empowerment. Leaders are not necessarily defined by rank, but include all those who own, or seek to own, or enable others to continuously add value by improving processes within their organizations (Chapter 5). Leaders know how to continually improve systems and services to anticipate customer needs. They also appreciate the complexity of strategies and tactics needed to transform existing service cultures into those focused on customer-driven quality. In the competitive profit-driven private sector, achieving customer-driven product and service quality absolutely determines a firm's future economic survival. Delivering TQS is no less important in the non-market-driven, regulated, "noncompetitive" public and nonprofit sectors. In fact, it may be more important as lack of a quality focus perpetuates waste and breeds further antagonism between the "paying customers" (citizens and taxpayers) and those providing services (government employees and bureaucrats). Recall how public opinion polls show that trust and confidence in public institutions increases as performance management initiatives increase (Chapter 7). Leaders are applying TQS principles to merge knowledge and quality management thinking and guide all types of organizations: private businesses, nonprofit agencies, schools, hospitals, and governments.

In our diverse global free-market economy, quality improvement (QI) principles have spread rapidly, albeit unevenly, in services since the 1990s. Despite some early failures, false starts and frustrations, many organizations find that application of quality theories and techniques improves efficiency, reduces waste, decreases costs, and improves customer satisfaction. Increased customer loyalty is accompanied by productivity gains and an enhanced global competitive position. In those highly publicized instances in which quality failed to deliver as expected (i.e., FPL, McDonnell-Douglas, and Wallace Corporation), the causes could be traced to changing markets, new management, or lack of leadership consistency and commitment. Instances of successful service quality implementation at Caterpillar Financial Services, Community Consolidated School District 15, FedEx, St. Luke's Hospital, BI, and Pearl River School District, among many others, far exceed failures.

Implementing TQS for High Performance

Specific strategies must be custom-fitted to each service culture, and successful implementation of TQS requires action in the following areas:

1. Integrating management functions, promoting teamwork, and flattening hierarchies
2. Defining customer service quality requirements
3. Strengthening customer–supplier relationships
4. Empowering employees to respond to customers
5. Understanding and eliminating the causes of system variation
6. Continuously improving processes
7. Reducing the costs of poor-quality practices

Several prominent "world-class" quality theorists enhance our knowledge of quality leadership and process improvement. It is important to understand the influential quality pioneers and their theories, but empowered process owners are best able to select and apply the appropriate elements to improve their work environments.

Understanding quality leadership from the perspective of customers requires a general knowledge of the theoretical basis for the various approaches to QI and how those theories can be applied to change attitudes and organizations (Chapter 2 and Chapter 3). W. Edwards Deming observed that "experience teaches nothing without theory." The opposite is also equally true: knowledge of theory without empirical applications and validation is useless. To consistently and effectively apply theory to achieve organizational goals requires an understanding of the interrelationships between basic quality concepts and how they affect the substructure of particular service organizations. An example of understanding this relationship is the connection between systems thinking and continuous quality improvement (CQI) (presented in Figure 2.8).

Although the major theories of the world-class quality masters have been highlighted in the preceding pages, the emphasis throughout the book has been on generic rather than brand-name, quality concepts. Among those elements common to all efforts are the following: establishing better coordination between functions within organizations, promoting teamwork, focusing on customer-driven definitions of quality, maintaining closer customer–supplier relations, continuously improving everything, thinking systematically, and eliminating non-value-added costs, process variation, and poor-quality cost practices. Consistently achieving these goals allows more resources to be devoted to individualizing treatment for the unique circumstances and needs of every customer.

Regardless of the size of the organization or the nature of the service being provided, leading TQS efforts is a team-based, interdisciplinary, theory-driven activity. In many respects, Xerox Corporation, the State of Connecticut, Ford Motor Company, Levi Strauss, and USAA insurance and financial services are similar. Yet, in other respects they differ. Although a process orientation allows for comparisons within and between critical functions of different types of organizations, all processes differ slightly. Deming also observed that "inefficiency in a service organization, just as in manufacturing, raises prices to the consumer and lowers his standard of living. The principles and methods are the same for service as for manufacturing. The actual application differs, of course, from one product to another, just as all manufacturing concerns differ from one to another" (Deming, 1982, p. 183). Moreover, service organizations generally do not produce a standard product at a uniform cost as do manufacturers. Rather, they provide customized treatment for each recipient, emphasizing their differing needs. For this reason, training in the "high-touch" human relations elements of TQS is as important as training in technology, statistics, and measurement (Chapter 4 and Chapter 5).

The four key components of a TQS model are leadership, teamwork, customer orientation, and systems thinking (Figure 4.1). They must be carefully balanced to meet the special needs of particular customers for a specific service. Successful leadership for achieving quality and productivity goals is theory based, results oriented, focused on action, and transformational. Widespread, decentralized, and nonhierarchical participation in self-managed work teams is another goal. Achieving such a cooperative workforce requires a far different leadership style from that which is practiced in most organizations. Executives who have reached senior positions under the old system may have trouble empowering those "beneath" them in competitive nonhierarchical networked organizations.

Transforming the behavior of individuals within service organizations is an essential leadership component of TQS, which views human, technical, and management subsystems as team based, customer oriented, and interrelated with the organizational mission. Service processes can be constantly improved by creating opportunities for participation, stressing knowledge management (KM) as well as results, and using appropriate statistical methods and tools shared by the entire workforce. Ten principles of human resource quality management guided the discussion of how to achieve the transformation to a TQS culture:

1. Inspire top-management commitment and leadership.
2. Anticipate customer needs.
3. Educate all employees for self-improvement.
4. Continuously improve processes and systems.
5. Create a work environment free from fear.
6. Develop a stimulating work environment.

7. Teach and practice teamwork.
8. Stress communication, not inspection.
9. Think statistically.
10. Encourage personal commitment to change.

Human resource training principles are particularly useful in organizations in which skills need to be updated frequently, and continuous just-in-time learning is valued. This strategy reflects a process in which knowledge is created through the transformation of experience. Those organizations that master the art and science of knowledge transfer between component subsystems quicker and more effectively than the competition increase their chances of global survival. They also build the confidence levels of all participants and create a cadre of able and willing leaders upon whom quality results depend.

For those eager to learn how to change faster than the competition to survive changing business environments, the full array of QI options can be very confusing. Various approaches with acronyms such as BPR, CQI, CRM, JIT, QA, QC, SPC, STSM, TQM, and TQC have been introduced to the business and government vocabularies throughout America. When applied to services, they are widely viewed as a means of achieving the illusive goals of economic efficiency and increased productivity. Too often, however, the precise meaning of these terms varies with the depth of one's own understanding or, more commonly, that of one's consultant. Talking about the potential rewards for quality improvement is less difficult (and far more common) than actually implementing QI systems. Advocates of the various approaches can point to success stories, usually in another industry. Extreme care should be taken not to assume that successes in one sector can be automatically transferred to another.

As we have seen, rigid organizational structures and hierarchies are inconsistent with TQS. At the same time, TQS does not abandon accountability, command and control, and results, the traditional justifications for bureaucratic hierarchy. Rather, TQS principles are designed to provide flexibility instead of uniform responses, allow action to respond to customers at the point of contact, empower employees to act in the customer's best interest, and monitor process results. Effective leadership for process improvement requires both a systemwide perspective and a greater team responsibility for demonstrating results. Training and empowerment permit individuals, as members of self-directed work teams of committed workers, to address and eliminate problems at their source and respond to the expressed needs of customers, without depending on time-consuming and rigid command-and-control structures. The worst excuse a service worker can give a loyal customer is: "I am sorry. I'll have to check with my supervisor on that!"

The power of QI principles depends less on the use of consultants' jargon, confusing acronyms, or complicated tools than on the capacity to learn and teach individual responsibility. Enhanced responsiveness to all customers, true empowerment of employees, members or associates through teamwork, participation, and systematic analysis of task-related problems are essential for learning concepts and applying skills to improve customer service processes. This is a global phenomenon as customers everywhere seek competence, empathy, and responsiveness from service employees.

Operational processes within organizations are complex, so implementing TQS not only requires system changes, but also an understanding of the appropriate tools and techniques used to encourage systems thinking among process improvement teams. Problem identification techniques, such as brainstorming, nominal group technique, and cause–effect diagrams, can help reduce the causes of variation within existing processes. When blended together, they can yield valid service quality measurement characteristics that then become operational measures for monitoring the needs of customers. Statistical quality control (SQC) tools (group decision making, Pareto analysis, cause–effect diagrams, check sheets, control charts, and run charts) can eliminate non-value-added steps and monitor performance. Understanding the definition and application of quality measurement characteristics is at the heart of process analysis and system improvement.

The ultimate goal of process improvement is to eliminate non-value-added steps in response to customer requirements. It is equally important to integrate TQS principles and traditional approaches to cost containment and productivity improvement. Numbers-driven productivity measurements are an established management method. Most managers who lack quality training will be unfamiliar with certain aspects of the "softer" TQS approach. Fear of change or not wanting to get caught with extensive knowledge of last year's fad can be a barrier to implementation, as well. Some theorists have argued that productivity cannot be raised beyond a certain level using traditional tools without applying the hard-numbers statistical process control (SPC) approach. There are many examples of the effective use of SPC to raise productivity, increase outputs, and either reduce inputs or utilize "excess" inputs to expand operations or diversify. Components of SPC are logical extensions of traditional productivity tools; combining those tools with TQS principles inevitably leads to a higher productivity ceiling. In private service industries, where competitors are destroying past paradigms and making quantum leaps in productivity, a blend or mixture of the soft and hard approaches may be necessary.

TQS serves as a bridge between traditional productivity methods and two familiar perspectives: the marketing-based customer service approach

(Zeithaml, Parasuraman, and Berry, 1990), and the more statistically based companywide quality control (CWQC) system, the mainstream management philosophy in Japanese private and public sectors (Ishikawa and Lu, 1985). Although TQS can be employed as a transitional tool, when combined with SPC, it provides an effective means for organizational transformation, cost containment, and productivity improvement. In today's interconnected global markets, local cultures, diverse languages, and regional economic needs must also be considered when applying quality improvement systems.

TQS improves competitiveness in world markets and in domestic services, as well. Multinational firms deploying QI principles have obtained competitive advantages and cost reductions by enlisting employees, suppliers, and customers in the continuous improvement of processes. The same techniques can be applied, albeit carefully, in regulated services, such as governments, schools, and public utilities. Actions to promote quality leadership include benchmarking the Malcolm Baldrige National Quality Awards (BNQA), the Presidential Quality awards, and numerous state and private sector awards. In Europe, the International Standards Organization (ISO) and the European Quality Awards have performed a similar role (Chapter 6). These models parallel ongoing governmental efforts to deregulate, privatize, and devolve functions to levels closest to the customers.

Interest in applying TQS techniques to a wide range of public services is spreading to all levels of government, the primary suppliers of essential education, healthcare, law enforcement, and retirement services for tens of millions who cannot afford to purchase them from private providers. TQS provides a promising model for launching a nonpartisan quality revolution for the American public, nonprofit, and private sectors. There is an increasing need to improve customer service quality in all functions and at all levels of American public services (Chapter 7). Despite the need, few governments have implemented the changes in attitudes and organizational cultures necessary to empower employees, eliminate poor-quality costs, or respond effectively to citizen complaints about service quality. Past failures of governmental productivity efforts increase the willingness of elected and appointed public officials to experiment and innovate. Still, there is as yet no reward equivalent to the bottom line (e.g., increased profit and market share) in the public service sector. Successful TQS strategies result in higher productivity per worker, greater job satisfaction, reduced waste, and lower operating costs. Citizens, taxpayers, and voters, the true "customers" of public service agencies, benefit from greater returns for their investment in more efficient and effective governance.

No advanced industrial nation can survive without a strong public education system. Our federalist structure of divided national, state, and local government makes it more difficult to define, measure, and improve quality in this vital national service. Indicators of educational productivity and quality in the United States have been declining for several decades (Chapter 8). Without comprehensive reform based on quality improvement principles, more jobs will be outsourced and the economy will suffer. Today's students are tomorrow's leaders and without quality education, we will continue to lose our competitive edge and lag even further behind the rest of the industrialized world at a time when we can least afford to fail. Ensuring educational quality is the only way to guarantee that national goals are met in a way that reflects the values and culture of society. Unfortunately, quality is difficult to define and subject to multiple interpretations in our diversified society. Quality is a function of people, processes, and policy. In education, quality must be reflected in many different areas including teacher education and training, resource management (RS), and curriculum.

Despite the prospect of change, immense challenges confront those intent on applying TQS in a health service delivery environment. Chronic waste of resources accompanies our increasingly mixed system of public and private health delivery. Nearly half the general population (the elderly, poor, disabled, and those whose incomes fall below the poverty line) are eligible to receive government-subsidized healthcare. With the "graying of America," corporate downsizing, and continued loss of jobs to outsourcing, this number is becoming much higher. If universal health insurance is enacted through a system of "managed competition," the efficiency of delivering services will become even more important. Hospital, medical, and healthcare services have traditionally emphasized retrospective quality assurance (QA) and externally imposed regulatory standards from a strict clinical perspective (Chapter 9). Historically, health professionals lacked incentives to integrate services into a TQS system to improve medical, organizational, administrative, and patient evaluation processes. Today, the complexity of measuring clinical outcomes combined with the new competitive, cost-conscious, regulated service environment requires an integrated view of quality. TQS is more than QA or QC; continuous improvement requires strategic management actions based on a clear understanding of extended customer requirements and a precise mission statement. Combined with regulation and cost competition, TQS is becoming a primary policy implementation strategy for healthcare institutions seeking to lower costs, raise productivity, and enhance profit in the ultracompetitive healthcare market of the 2000s. This is especially important to control costs and provide universal access to healthcare for all Americans.

The most common barrier to achieving quality in services is failure to train employees to respond effectively to customers. Not unlike manufacturing, service organizations must adopt modern training methods or risk being unable to compete in global marketplaces. The potential impact of combining global standardization with ISO 9000, European quality standards, Baldrige award criteria, statistical process control, and TQS is significant and impressive, especially in a hyper-competitive environment of declining markets and shrinking resources. Using these techniques increases an organization's proportion of visible (useful) output and decreases its invisible (wasted) output (see "Iceberg" Figure 5.2). Training must be focused on learning quality strategies to distinguish between value-added and non-value-added components of processes. Everyone must understand concepts such as variation (common and special), value addedness, team-based evaluation, the difference between QA, QC, and quality improvement, and how these concepts and techniques are integrated to better serve customers.

Barriers to Achieving TQS

The regulated monopolistic character of many service industries, especially — but not only — those offered by the public sector, tends to discourage new ideas, competition, and innovation. Poor training, obsolete knowledge, concerns about rank and status within existing hierarchies, employment insecurity, and other attitudinal barriers have inhibited customer service quality improvement. These structural and behavioral barriers are rapidly breaking down as once-protected public and private service "monopolies" face the same competitive challenges confronted by American manufacturing industries in the last two decades. Leaders of the service quality revolution possess the knowledge of past attempts to change manufacturing and are more likely to avoid the obvious pitfalls.

There are various reasons for the failure of U.S. industries to respond to the global challenge of service quality improvement. Although their origins are complex and all the reasons have not been fully explored, the primary barriers are suggested in the following text:

1. *Over dependence on top-down management:* Despite calls for greater employee participation and empowerment, the Weberian model or "chain-of-command" hierarchy still predominates. This is the primary management method taught by most business school courses and practiced in most American organizations. Based on ancient religious and military doctrine, and advanced to theory status in the mid-1800s, the Theory X model was applied at the beginning of the Industrial Revolution to discipline and control an illiterate workforce. It is antithetical to the knowledge revolution of the 21st century. Not surprisingly, it actively discourages participation

in customer service improvement, problem solving, or goal setting. It disempowers rather than empowers workers. One costly symptom of its perpetuation is divisive American labor–management relations. American industry has paid a heavy price for continued distrust between workers and owners. Dependence on top-down management is slowly declining with evidence of successful union–management cooperation, "gain sharing" in the United States, joint ventures with other countries, and harmonious management–worker participation in Northern Europe and Japan. Over a decade ago, futurist Alvin Toffler recognized the importance of reducing hierarchies in all types of organizations, but especially among global "knowledge workers," who work primarily in service organizations (Toffler, 1990).

2. *Management by objectives:* First proposed by Peter Drucker in the mid-1950s, MBO was applied to the U.S. Department of Defense for the explicit purpose of gaining control of the defense industry workforce in the 1960s. Study after study shows that MBO has failed in both goal attainment and internal process improvement. Yet, as if tradition somehow requires it, MBO continues to dominate public and private graduate management education, as well as government and private industry administrative practice. Management by control must be reexamined and replaced by total quality leadership, horizontal rather than vertical management, and empowered employees trained to respond to, not hide from, customers. Leaders must provide a secure environment, support, resources, and education to train and empower workers and help the organization reach its goals (Greebler-Schepper, 1993).

3. *Annual review and the (de)merit system:* Prior to the reemergence of the service quality movement in the United States, there were few incentives to change individual performance appraisal systems. The merit system currently used to set pay and bonuses encourages destructive ("I win, you lose") competition, destroys morale, creates fear, and inhibits cooperation. Employees are not rewarded on responsiveness to customers or quality of services provided, because performance appraisal and merit selection processes (if examined at all) emphasize results and pleasing superiors, not system improvements. Some are rewarded and others punished without examining the underlying causes for system variation (Deming, 1986). Without statistical verification, it is assumed that greater productivity *per se* leads to higher quality. Peter Scholtes says flatly that individual performance appraisal is antithetical to quality improvement (Scholtes, 1993). James Bowman argues that if you have to do it, tie performance appraisal to quality evaluation

(Bowman, 1994). Whatever strategy is adopted to improve service quality, a thorough restructuring of human resources processes must be undertaken, emphasizing incentives for employees to work together to uncover and eliminate non-value-added costs and the systemic causes of customer-defined problems.

4. *Overspecialization in job descriptions:* All knowledge-based services are to some extent provided within bureaucratic structures that are hierarchical, specialized, fragmented, and compartmentalized to allow a professional staff or "experts" to exercise control over employees and maintain authority over customers. This is especially true of construction, healthcare, education, government and other "credentialed" services. So long as personnel and hiring rules specify specialized skills in job descriptions, further fragmentation is likely, making it more difficult to promote teamwork and break down barriers to cooperation. Lacking integration with other functions within organizations, overspecialization continues as a barrier used by technical "experts" in dealing with nonspecialized recipients of services. TQS principles can be used effectively to overcome overspecialization, which distances service providers from those being served.

5. *Ineffective productivity measurement techniques:* The widespread misuse of productivity measurement techniques in most public (and many private) organizations is a further barrier to TQS. The prevailing myth that productivity declines as quality increases also inhibits change. Leaders of businesses, public organizations, and universities fear the use of quality and productivity management techniques could render bonuses, merit procedures, step increases, and other productivity tools obsolete. Reluctance to train employees in quality concepts may reflect insecurities among well-intended senior managers who are themselves not prepared for the changes. Many leaders continue to practice the traditional methods and techniques that took them to leadership positions in their organizations. Implementation of quality is a delicate process, and its long-term success depends upon changing leadership principles, long after a particular leader has departed. The inability of senior managers to empower employees is one of the key leadership challenges of implementing TQS (Drath, 1993; deLancer Julnes and Holzer, 2001; Sanderson, 2001). Far more leaders should be committed to transforming the current system to improve it.

6. *Resistance to change:* TQS must be approached with an open mind. Fear of acquiring new knowledge that conflicts with that previously learned remains one of the primary obstacles to permanent service quality improvement. Although implementing new

approaches disturbs many senior managers who are either incapable or unwilling to change their management practices, it is often welcomed by those who embrace change. Upon first exposure to Deming's teachings, many managers dismiss his 14 points as naive, utopian, too complex, socialist, or with less flattering (and unprintable) adjectives. Most soon realize, however, that much of what they have previously learned about management is outmoded and dysfunctional. At the very least, exposure to Deming's principles causes many to question the conventional wisdom about how best to achieve quality and productivity improvement (Milakovich, 1990a).

These barriers limit the acceptance of TQS theories and techniques in the service sector. To overcome them, manufacturing support and service firms have taken bold steps, including decentralization of operations and abolition of the merit system, to remove implementation barriers with stunning success. Successful experiences in other sectors of the economy provide the broad policy guidelines for achieving the transformation of the service sector.

Action Strategies for Service Quality Improvement

First, flatten hierarchies that discourage teamwork and create barriers between departments.

If each department and every individual within each department acts to optimize itself, himself, or herself, then the effectiveness of the organization as a whole is reduced. Teamwork can be achieved by implementing cross-functional management (CFM), flowcharting of processes, identification of internal and external customers' needs, and, as necessary, the use of statistical tools to monitor customer satisfaction. Eliminating barriers between departments, establishing trust and cooperation rather than fear-based competition, and providing training for teamwork are all necessary to accomplish the transformation. The most challenging element in the promotion of teamwork is to create equality and mutual respect among team members. Empowered teams are then able to eliminate the causes of variation within systems and processes. Members whose tasks are interdependent develop mutual respect for each other and, in training for teamwork, develop a shared common vision transmitted throughout the organization. Even in highly unionized organizations, it is still possible to break down barriers if TQS implementation is mutually agreed to and written into contracts. Ironically, with or without union cooperation, experience has shown middle management is more likely to resist quality implementation.

Second, formulate a mission statement that reflects the shared values and operationally defines the vision of the organization.

Once the mission statement has been written, it must be published as official company policy so that each and evey employee understands his or her role in accomplishing the mission. Teams can then be trained to implement their part of the mission. Senior TQS managers, who act more like coaches or facilitators than inspectors or judges, must guide the preparation of a mission statement articulating the vision. The identification of internal customers and the flowcharting of processes not only increases internal efficiency and defines tasks more clearly, but also empowers employees to cope with their environment not as "the system," but as a series of interconnected processes and subsystems over which they exert control.

Third, empower employees, do not threaten them.

Similar to many other healthcare service organizations, a hospital decided to implement quality. In the opening training session on CQI theories and techniques, the consultant hired to conduct quality training said, "In five years, most of you will not have a job!" This caught the audience's attention but in precisely the wrong way to prepare anyone for the journey. On another occasion, the chief executive officer of an organization said, "This [quality] is our goal. We may never reach it, but we are going to come as close to it as we can. We will use whatever means necessary to achieve this, and anyone who gets in had better join in or ship out." This is more important today as more employees of service organizations are aware of the negative effects of outsourcing to developing economies.

During the early phases of the ill-fated Florida Power & Light QIP described in Chapter 6, the chairman and chief executive officer produced a videotape that was required viewing by the entire workforce. The purpose of the video was to encourage a then-skeptical workforce to implement quality the way that had apparently succeeded in the Japanese utility used as a model for FPL quality efforts. The message was clear and professionally presented, but the ending portended the rocky road ahead. Near the end of the video, the speaker said, "The train is rolling, either get on board, or get out of the way!" With this introduction and unforgiving attitude, it was not surprising that the workforce later rebelled over the amount of extra work required to please senior management and the Japanese examiners to win the Deming Prize.

These fear-based statements reflect a dilemma shared by managers in many competitive industries: how do they "empower" when they have achieved rank and status by not sharing power or authority with others? In theory, most managers value empowerment of subordinates, but have a difficult time putting the concept into practice (Drath, 1993). Making coercive statements in a service organization reflects a fundamental problem with implementing action strategies in a diverse workforce. Leadership style must be consistent with the mission of the organization. If empowerment and participation are valued, then threats and intimidation are inconsistent with the mission.

Fourth, pay more attention to your customers and suppliers.

If not doing so already, develop systems to survey and collect feedback from all customers. Do not wait for complaints, because by then it is usually too late. Even public agencies that serve large numbers of persons who cannot or will not purchase services from private providers are setting customer service standards, empowering employees to act in the recipients' interest, and monitoring results. Obviously, the complexity of public services requires a phased-in approach to customer-driven TQS. In some service areas, the transition to TQS will be easier than others. Increasingly, user fees are being charged for the delivery of basic services; a citizen who pays for a service directly has every right to demand that the service be performed to his or her satisfaction. Service satisfaction measures are being widely applied in the emerging entrepreneurial public service sector.

Fifth, begin slowly and do not create unrealistic expectations.

Evidence presented here shows numerous successful (and some less so) efforts to apply quality principles in services. Important lessons can also be learned from failed attempts. It is important to be aware of the basic tenets of quality, referred to here as TQS. In addition, the manner in which quality concepts and productivity principles are introduced is equally important. Emphasis should be placed on internal rather than external rewards for quality improvement. Not every company providing a quality service at a reasonable cost needs to apply for an award, nor should all quality firms invest the time or resources. However, the BNQA provides a useful self-assessment checklist to determine if your organization is maintaining quality standards (Appendix E). Those willing to participate in the TQS effort should be forgiven for early mistakes in judgment. The learning and organizational change process requires patience and understanding. Results will come, but slowly, as working cultures change.

Sixth, anticipate, and continually adapt, to change.

Political and social environments are continuously changing as world markets expand, definitions of product and service quality merge, and as TQS strategies are successfully applied to more and more different types of services. Even those services protected by domestic regulations and tariffs are no longer immune from global competition. Failure to recognize market changes is a common reason for businesses to lose market share and disappear. Learning is encouraged as organizations, similar to individuals, adapt to changes in business environments. The "light at the end of the tunnel" for future service quality leaders is not a certificate or a diploma or an award: it is the achievement of a cultural change that allows everyone to continuously improve processes.

Lastly, adopt a leadership style consistent with changing organizational cultures.

Responding to change is as important to the ultimate success of quality efforts as listening to the customers and responding to their needs. But it is only one element, along with customer orientation, learning how to change, true empowerment, and systems thinking. Leaders must strive to understand the discipline and balance their quality and productivity improvement strategies with the needs and expectations of those who must actually deliver the service. It is unwise to get too far ahead of those upon whom you depend to accomplish organizational goals. Without support from those who must actually control processes, make the decisions, and deal with customers, even the most enthusiastically supported and generously funded strategies will fail.

Leadership Challenges

Never underestimate the difficulty of convincing an organization made up of diverse interests that quality is always the answer to every problem. Unless required by your mission, never threaten or intimidate people into producing more. In an educated workforce delivering customer-contact airline, banking, educational, or healthcare services, these tactics will be resisted; both quality and productivity will plummet. Initiating permanent QI requires sound theory, consistency, hard work, discipline, and confronting realities about the basic structures of the organization that might have to be changed. Above all, a personal commitment to the success of the change is required.

During the early stages of any QI effort, some obvious areas of conflict are likely to arise. These include:

- Getting used to a networked, rather than a hierarchical command-and-control managerial approach to decision making
- Developing collective team-based performance measures

- Applying continuous quality improvement, rather than QC standards
- Learning to work within the more flexible yet closely monitored performance structures

All of these changes will require training within the context of a comprehensive strategic QI plan.

In the past, changes such as MBO, planning–programming–budgeting systems (PPBS), or zero-based budgeting (ZBB) were initiated as short-term responses to the latest financial crises or in reaction to customer complaints. If these are the primary motives, then changes are destined to fail. To succeed, fundamental and lasting organizational changes must be accompanied by resources and training necessary to achieve quality improvement results.

Leadership for quality improvement means motivating others to do what is best for the organization for their own reasons (creating a win-win situation). Managers should learn how to think and act like coaches, teachers, or facilitators, rather than administrators, inspectors, or bureaucrats. New roles include teacher, benchmarker, motivator, mentor, and entrepreneur. Realistically, not all managers or employees are capable of the personal commitment required to learn and practice these new skills. Those who cannot commit should at least learn how to coexist in a win-win environment and not resist the change effort (Milakovich, 1993).

Change can be frustrating. It is often hard enough to change one's own behavior, much less that of an organization made up of diverse individuals, not all of whom welcome change. How does a committed quality leader handle resistance? Not in the traditional control-dominated, John Wayne macho, "take no prisoners" or "shoot the messenger" style. Resistance from employees, like complaints from customers, is a critical barrier that cannot be ignored. Causes must be understood and action taken by empowered teams to eliminate the reasons for the dissatisfaction. Understanding why some may not assist in the TQS effort will help to overcome resistance. The reasons include:

- They are afraid to speak out.
- They are unaccustomed to being asked to participate.
- They are afraid of appearing stupid in front of others, especially those with whom they work.
- They do not believe it will do any good, so why bother.
- They distrust calls for cooperation when competition has prevailed in the past.
- The new roles are uncomfortable at first.

- Those involved in the change process are uncertain if the change will last.
- They do not know how to "look good" in the new roles.

Overcoming these and other valid employee concerns depends on committed leadership from senior officials. Leaders in quality-oriented service cultures generally adopt a transformational leadership style, as opposed to a traditional or situational approach. The new roles for leaders to play in guiding the internal transformation are:

- Acting as coaches for CQI teams, defining ultimate objectives, training teams, and facilitating successful performance
- Offering constructive advice on the formulation of policy to support a TQS culture
- Creating an environment free from traditional barriers and promoting open communications

Among the most important leadership challenges to succeed in these new roles are developing a vision of the service responsive to customers and implementing this strategy with the full cooperation of employees. This must be accomplished without resorting to threats of downsizing, layoffs, outsourcing or sham productivity efforts that produce the same results. Important transitional steps for achieving these results are delegating responsibility to the lowest levels (empowerment) and using pilot projects on a small scale to demonstrate results.

Finally, incentives and reward systems must change to recognize, not punish, those willing to assume responsibility for managing nontraditional applications such as benchmarking, gain sharing, and performance measurement on a broad scale in the service sector. To continuously improve service quality, new leadership styles combined with better measures of customer satisfaction are needed. Application of techniques described in this book provides a framework for rethinking current management practices. As implementation breakthroughs occur in greater numbers of services, TQS will be seen as offering an alternative road map for the transformation. Why is it important to transform basic structure?

It is very difficult to prepare a workforce for impending changes without threatening them with dismissal if they demand to be included, or raise questions about the pace of change. There is a backlash resulting from the frustrations experienced by those who must ultimately implement quality improvements. Total Quality Management (TQM) was criticized as a cult; others refer to their attendance at Deming seminars as a religious experience. In different ways, both criticisms are correct.

In his seminars, Deming frequently talked about recruiting "joyful bosses" and restoring "joy in work." In his sincere effort to restore everyone's reason for working, he may been offering an operational definition of the illusive "self-actualized" personality that Abraham Maslow defined five decades ago as the optimum strategy to motivate workers and managers (Maslow, 1954). For many in today's workplace, this is a very compelling message. Beyond a certain point, most people do not work solely for money. In a fully operational TQS environment, other forms of reward such as peer recognition and greater responsibility become important. This was nicely summed up by a sales executive at a seminar who described the difference as working to achieve the mission of the organization versus just working to receive a paycheck.

Leadership is the art of persuading others to internalize opportunities for adopting cooperative win-win solutions, rather than creating competitive zero-sum internal conflict. In many ways, quality leaders behave more like elected political representatives than either managers or appointed permanent bureaucrats. In an American workforce increasingly made up of diverse interests and individuals, leaders must practice a form of leadership analogous to a political campaign, where broad-scale participation and assumption of individual responsibility are encouraged. Political leadership skills in dealing with varied interests and resolving conflicts peacefully among different groups are valued. As opportunities for participation increase, everyone is happier because the size of the pie being sliced is bigger.

In practice, the real power of quality theories lies not in their theoretical promise, but in their proven success to positively change attitudes and opinions. A word of caution: If not properly introduced, QI could make things worse. Moreover, they require changes in work environments that could threaten existing hierarchical relationships. In the initial stages, TQS organizations must be forgiving of mistakes, especially when all causes of system variation have not been discovered and eliminated. Individuals must not be blamed for mistakes caused by the system. Quite often, in non-TQS organizations, part or all of the blame for a mistake falls upon an undertrained, low pay-grade, overworked employee. There are some simple things that any organization can do to prevent these special causes of variation and assist every employee to maximize his or her self-improvement efforts.

When top management encourages every individual to improve, the total sum of human resources available to serve customers increases, at little additional cost to the organization. Elimination of barriers and the establishment of cooperative (win-win) work environments rather than fear-based competitive workplaces provide the basis for the trust and teamwork necessary to accomplish the transformation.

Examples of successful quality applications to improve products, services, processes, and systems abound. Thousands of American firms have made the commitment to customer satisfaction and are reaping the benefits of increased profit, lower costs, higher productivity, and greater market share. Virtually all American consumers are aware that at Ford Motor Company, "Quality is Job One and a Job Continues." At leading firms such as Citigroup, Marriott Corporation, and Southwest Airlines, employee dedication to customer needs is expected from the beginning. At Motorola, Six-Sigma quality (less than 2 ppb defective) became an attainable goal as well as an operational management philosophy. At Florida Power and Light Company, the first large American public service utility to institute total quality control (TQC), "breakthroughs" in service quality were incorporated into company policy. At FedEx, dedication to customer satisfaction, reliability, on-time delivery, and continuous monitoring of performance produced measurable results.

Despite these and many other successes highlighted in previous pages, the quality revolution is still unfinished in services, especially in small businesses, nonprofit organizations, regulated monopolies, and public agencies. Implementing the principles outlined in the preceding text achieves demonstrable cost savings, increases the numbers of satisfied customers, reduces lost work time from fewer on-the-job injuries, and offers the prospect of better service reliability. When changes are made, everyone benefits as customers and suppliers of higher-quality goods and services for consumers in domestic and global markets.

Appendix A

The Eternally Successful Organization Grid

	Comatose	Intensive Care	Progressive Care	Healing	Wellness
Quality	Nobody does anything right around here	We finally have a list of customer complaints	We are beginning a quality improvement process	Customer complaints are practically gone	People do things right the first time routinely
	Price of nonconformance = 33 percent	Price of nonconformance = 28 percent	Price of nonconformance = 20 percent	Price of nonconformance = 13 percent	Price of nonconformance = 3 percent
Growth	Nothing ever changes	We bought a turkey	The new product isn't too bad	The new group is growing well	Growth is profitable and steady
	Return after tax = nil	Return after tax = nil	Return after tax = 3 percent	Return after tax = 7 percent	Return after tax = 12 percent
Customers	Nobody ever orders twice	Customers don't know what they want	We are working with customers	We are making many defect-free deliveries	Customers' needs are anticipated
	Customer complaints on orders = 63 percent	Customer complaints on orders = 54 percent	Customer complaints on orders = 26 percent	Customer complaints on orders = 9 percent	Customer complaints on orders = 0 percent

	Nothing ever changes	Nobody ever tells anyone anything	We need to know what is happening	There is no reason for anyone to be surprised	Change is planned and managed
Change	*Changes controlled by Systems Integrity = 0 percent*	*Changes controlled by Systems Integrity = 2 percent*	*Changes controlled by Systems Integrity = 55 percent*	*Changes controlled by Systems Integrity = 85 percent*	*Changes controlled by Systems Integrity = 100 percent*
Employees	This place is a little better than not working	Human Resources has been told to help employees	Error Cause Removal programs have been started	Career path evaluations are implemented now	People are proud to work here
	Employee turnover = 65 percent	*Employee turnover = 45 percent*	*Employee turnover = 40 percent*	*Employee turnover = 7 percent*	*Employee turnover = 2 percent*

Source: Philip B. Crosby, *Quality Is Free: The Art of Making Quality Certain*, New York: McGraw-Hill, 1969, p. 31.

Appendix B

Deming's 14 Points

1. Create constancy of purpose toward improvement of product and service with a plan to become competitive and to stay in business. Decide to whom top management is responsible.
2. Adopt the new philosophy. We are in a new economic age. We can no longer live with commonly accepted levels or delays, mistakes, defective materials, and defective workmanship.
3. Cease dependence on mass inspection. Require, instead, statistical evidence that quality is built in to prevent defects rather than detect defects.
4. End the practice of awarding business on the basis of price tag. Instead, depend on meaningful measures of quality, along with price. Eliminate suppliers that cannot provide statistical evidence of quality.
5. Find problems. It is management's job to work continually on the system (design, incoming materials, composition of material, maintenance, improvement of machines, training, supervision, retraining, etc.).
6. Institute modern methods of training on the job.
7. The responsibility of foremen must be changed from sheer numbers to quality ... [which] will automatically improve productivity. Management must prepare to take immediate action on reports from foremen concerning barriers such as inherited defects, machines not maintained, poor tools, and fuzzy operational definitions.
8. Drive out fear so that everyone may work effectively for the company.

9. Break down barriers between departments. People in research, design, sales, and production must work as a team to foresee problems of production that may be encountered with various materials and specifications.
10. Eliminate numerical goals, posters, and slogans for the workforce, asking for new levels of productivity without providing methods.[1]
11. Eliminate work standards that prescribe numerical quotas.
12. Remove barriers that stand between the hourly worker and his right to pride of workmanship.
13. Institute a vigorous program of education and retraining.
14. Create a structure in top management that will push every day on the preceding 13 points.[2]

Notes

1. According to Deming, individual goals are necessary, but "numerical goals set for other people, without a road map to reach a goal, have [negative] effects opposite to the [positive] effects sought" (Deming, 1986, p. 69).
2. Deming has stated that if a critical mass equal to the square root of the number of people within the organization accepts his 14 Points, then the organization will successfully transform. However, he may have underestimated the resistance to change in many American service firms.

Appendix C

Crosby's 14 Steps

1. *Management Commitment* — Management must commit to all parts of quality management.
2. *Quality Improvement Team* — Crosby's QITs are cross-functional management teams that consist of department heads during the first cycle and either department heads or high-level designates thereafter.
3. *Quality Measurement* — Choose the quality output measures and begin to measure them (i.e., percentage of late reports, time lost due to equipment failure, etc.).
4. *Cost of Quality Evaluation* — The cost of poor quality is the shortfall in bottom-line profits because everything is not done right the first time; it includes but is not limited to insurance protection against litigation, inspection costs, lost sales or the equivalent, and costs of providing guarantees, warranties, and allowances.
5. *Quality Awareness* — This includes but is not limited to employee training in quality; disseminating brochures, memoranda, etc., about quality; and making public within the organization the quality output measures and the cost of poor quality.
6. *Corrective Action* — Required to change organizational systems to eliminate poor-quality practices.
7. *Ad Hoc Committee for the Zero Defects Program* — This is an interdepartmental committee whose job is to implement DIRFT (Do It Right the First Time) and supervise the transition to Zero Defects Day, the one day when the organization has absolutely no defects.

8. *Employee Education* — To define the training needed by all employees to actively carry out their roles in the quality improvement process.

9. *Zero Defects Planning and Zero Defects Day* — See Step 7 for details. In addition, the CEO should give a face-to-face speech to employees on this day. The speech should be about the importance of zero defects and conformance to requirements.

10. *Goal Setting* — After Zero Defects Day, every employee in the organization meets with his or her superordinate to negotiate 30-day, 60-day, and 90-day quantifiable goals. The superordinate tries to coordinate these goals to encourage teamwork.

11. *Error Cause Removal* — A one-page form is disseminated throughout the organization on which every employee is asked to list in specific terms his or her greatest problems. Cross-functional groups will be established to process these forms within set time limits (24, 48, or 72 hours).

12. *Recognition* — Present workers with nonfinancial rewards for outstanding achievement in quality improvement in front of their peers.

13. *Quality Councils* — The QIT chairpersons and the quality professionals meet regularly as a quality council to discuss how to continuously improve the quality program.

14. *Do It Over Again* — Reaffirm management's commitment (Step 1) and begin the cycle again.

Appendix D

2004 Criteria for Performance Excellence — Item Listing

2004 Categories and Items		Point Values
1	**Leadership**	**120**
	1.1 Organizational Leadership	70
	1.2 Social Responsibility	50
2	**Strategic Planning**	**85**
	2.1 Strategy Development	40
	2.2 Strategy Deployment	45
3	**Customer and Market Focus**	**85**
	3.1 Customer and Market Knowledge	40
	3.2 Customer Relationships and Satisfaction	45

2004 Categories and Items   Point Values

4   Measurement, Analysis, and Knowledge
**   Management**   **90**

    4.1   Measurement and Analysis of Organizational
        Performance   45
    4.2   Information and Knowledge Management   45

5   Human Resource Focus   **85**

    5.1   Work Systems   35
    5.2   Employee Learning and Motivation   25
    5.3   Employee Well-Being and Satisfaction   25

6   Process Management   **85**

    6.1   Value Creation Processes   50
    6.2   Support Processes   35

7   Business Results   **450**

    7.1   Customer-Focused Results   75
    7.2   Product and Service Results   75
    7.3   Financial and Market Results   75
    7.4   Human Resource Results   75
    7.5   Organizational Effectiveness Results   75
    7.6   Governance and Social Responsibility Results 75

Total Points   **1000**

Source: Baldrige National Quality Program; National Institute of Standards and Technology; U.S. Department of Commerce; Web site: www.baldrige.nist.gov.

Appendix E

Are We Making Progress?

Your opinion is important to us. There are 40 statements in the following text. For each statement, check the box that best matches how you feel (strongly disagree, disagree, neither agree nor disagree, agree, and strongly agree). How you feel will help us decide where we most need to improve. We will not be looking at individual responses but will use the information from our whole group to make decisions. It should take you about 10 to 15 minutes to complete this questionnaire.

Senior leaders, please fill in the following information:

_____
Name of organization or unit being discussed

Category 1: Leadership

	Strongly Disagree	Disagree	Neither Agree nor Disagree	Agree	Strongly Agree
1a I know my organization's mission (what it is trying to accomplish).	☐	☐	☐	☐	☐
1b My senior (top) leaders use our organization's values to guide us.	☐	☐	☐	☐	☐
1c My senior leaders create a work environment that helps me do my job.	☐	☐	☐	☐	☐
1d My organization's leaders share information about the organization.	☐	☐	☐	☐	☐
1e My senior leaders encourage learning that will help me advance in my career.	☐ ☐	☐ ☐	☐ ☐	☐ ☐	☐ ☐
1f My organization lets me know what it thinks is most important.					
1g My organization asks what I think.	☐	☐	☐	☐	☐

Category 2: Strategic Planning

	Strongly Disagree	Disagree	Neither Agree nor Disagree	Agree	Strongly Agree
2a As it plans for the future, my organization asks for my ideas.	☐	☐	☐	☐	☐
2b I know the parts of my organization's plans that will affect me and my work.	☐	☐	☐	☐	☐
2c I know how to tell if we are making progress on my workgroup's part in the plan.	☐	☐	☐	☐	☐

Category 3: Customer And Market Focus

Note: Your customers are the people who use the products of your work.

	Strongly Disagree	Disagree	Neither Agree nor Disagree	Agree	Strongly Agree
3a I know who my most important customers are.	☐	☐	☐	☐	☐
3b I keep in touch with my customers.	☐	☐	☐	☐	☐
3c My customers tell me what they need and want.	☐	☐	☐	☐	☐
3d I ask if my customers are satisfied or dissatisfied with my work.	☐	☐	☐	☐	☐
3e I am allowed to make decisions to solve problems for my customers.	☐	☐	☐	☐	☐

Category 4: Measurement, Analysis, and Knowledge Management

	Strongly Disagree	Disagree	Neither Agree nor Disagree	Agree	Strongly Agree
4a I know how to measure the quality of my work.	☐	☐	☐	☐	☐
4b I know how to analyze (review) the quality of my work to see if changes are needed.	☐	☐	☐	☐	☐
4c I use these analyses for making decisions about my work.	☐	☐	☐	☐	☐
4d I know how the measures I use in my work fit into the organization's overall measures of improvement.	☐	☐	☐	☐	☐
4e I get all the important information I need to do my work.	☐	☐	☐	☐	☐
4f I get the information I need to know about how my organization is doing.	☐	☐	☐	☐	☐

Category 5: Human Resource Focus

	Strongly Disagree	Disagree	Neither Agree nor Disagree	Agree	Strongly Agree
5a I can make changes that will improve my work.	☐	☐	☐	☐	☐
5b The people I work with cooperate and work as a team.	☐	☐	☐	☐	☐
5c My boss encourages me to develop my job skills so I can advance in my career.	☐	☐	☐	☐	☐
5d I am recognized for my work.	☐	☐	☐	☐	☐
5e I have a safe workplace.	☐	☐	☐	☐	☐
5f My boss and my organization care about me.	☐	☐	☐	☐	☐

Category 6: Process Management

	Strongly Disagree	Disagree	Neither Agree nor Disagree	Agree	Strongly Agree
6a I can get everything I need to do my job.	☐	☐	☐	☐	☐
6b I collect information (data) about the quality of my work.	☐	☐	☐	☐	☐
6c We have good processes for doing our work.	☐	☐	☐	☐	☐
6d I have control over my work processes.	☐	☐	☐	☐	☐

Category 7: Business Results	Strongly Disagree	Disagree	Neither Agree nor Disagree	Agree	Strongly Agree
7a My customers are satisfied with my work.	☐	☐	☐	☐	☐
7b My work products meet all requirements.	☐	☐	☐	☐	☐
7c I know how well my organization is doing financially.	☐	☐	☐	☐	☐
7d My organization uses my time and talents well.	☐	☐	☐	☐	☐
7e My organization removes things that get in the way of progress.	☐	☐	☐	☐	☐
7f My organization obeys laws and regulations.	☐	☐	☐	☐	☐
7g My organization has high standards and ethics.	☐	☐	☐	☐	☐
7h My organization helps me help my community.	☐	☐	☐	☐	☐
7i I am satisfied with my job.	☐	☐	☐	☐	☐

Would you like to give more information about any of your responses?
Please include the number of the statement (for example, 2a or 7d) you are discussing.

_____

_____

_____

_____

Source: Baldrige National Quality Program; National Institute of Standards and Technology; U.S. Department of Commerce; Web site: www.baldrige.nist.gov.

Appendix F

State Quality Award Programs

- Alabama Quality Award (2003) <www.alabamaexcellencc.com/>
- Arizona State Quallty Award (2003) <www.arizona-excellence.com>
- Arkansas Quality Award (2003) <www.arkansas-quality.org>
- California Council for Excellence (2003) <www.calexcellence.org>
- Colorado Performance Excellence (2002) <www.coloradoexcellence.org>
- Connecticut Quality Improvement Award (2003) <www.ctqualityaward.org/>
- The Council for Excellence in Government (2003) <www.excelgov.org>
- Delaware Quality Award (2003) <http://www.accoladealliance.org/DQA02.htm>
- Deming Prize (The Deming Prize Guide) (2003) <http://www.deming.org/demingprize/>
- European Organization for Quality — SME Awards (2003) <www.eoq.org>
- Florida Sterling Council (2003) <www.floridasterling.com>
- Georgia Oglethrope Award (2003) <www.georgiaoglethrope.org>
- Government Performance and Results Act (GPRA) of 1993. November 15, 2000. Washington, D.C.: *National Performance Review* <govinfo.library.unt.edu/npr /library/misc/s20.html>

- The Hawaii State Award of Excellence (2003) <www.asqhawaii.org>
- Idaho Quality Award (2003) <www.idahoquality.org>
- Illinois: The Lincoln Foundation for Performance Excellence (2003) <www.lincolnaward.org>
- BKD Indiana Quality Improvement Award (2003) <www.indianabusiness.com/quality/>
- Innovations in American Government — Ford Foundation (2003) <www.excelgov.org/displaycontent.asp?keyword=aiHomePage>
- Iowa Quality Center (2003) <www.iowaqc.org>
- Kansas Award for Excellence Foundation (2003) <www.kae.myassociation.com/home.jsp>
- Kentucky Quality Council (2003) <www.kqc.org>
- The Louisiana Quality Foundation (2003) <http://www.loyno.edu/~lqf/>
- Malcolm Baldrige National Quality Award (2003) <www.baldrige.nist.gov >
- Margaret Chase Smith Maine State Quality Award (2003) <www.maine-quality.org>
- MAX: MassExcellence (2003) <www.massexcellence.com>
- Michigan Quality Council (2003) <www.michiganquality.org>
- Minnesota State Quality Awards (2003) <www.workforce-excellence.net/html/stateawards/state-mn.htm>
- Mississippi Quality Award (2003) <http://www.sbcjc.cc.ms.us/progs.html>
- Missouri Quality Award (2003) <www.mqa.org>
- National Public Service Awards (2003)<www.aspanet.org/awards/npsaguidelines.html>.
- Nebraska: Edgerton Quality Awards (2003) <assist.neded.org/edgerton/>
- New Hampshire: Granite State Quality Council (2003) <www.gsqc.com>
- NIST Update (2002), "Study Shows $25 Billion in U.S. Economic Benefits from Baldrige." <www.nist.gov/public_affairs/update/upd011029.htm>
- New York: Empire State Advantage (2003) <www.empirestateadvantage.org/>
- Ohio Award for Excellence (2003) <www.oae.org>
- Oklahoma Quality Award Foundation (2003) <www.oklahomaquality.com>
- Oregon Excellence Award (2001) <www.oregonexcellence.org>
- Pearl River School District. Malcolm Baldrige National Quality Award 2001 Award Recipient. December 5, 2001 <www.nist.gov/public_affairs/peralriver.htm>

- President's Quality Award Program (2003) <www.opm.gov/quality>
- Public Employees Roundtable Awards, Public Service Excellence Awards (2002) <www.theroundtable.org/prevawds.html>
- Quality New Jersey (2003) <www.qnj.org>
- Quality New Mexico (2003) <www.qualitynewmexico.org/>
- Quality Texas (2003) <www.texas-quality.org>
- Rhode Island: Race for Performance Excellence (2003) <www.rirace.org/home.asp>
- South Carolina's Quality Forum (2003) <www.scquality.com>
- Tennessee Center for Performance Excellence (2003) <www.tqa.org>
- Utah Quality Award (2003) <www.utahqualityaward.org>
- University of Maryland Center for Quality and Productivity. December 4, 2001 <http://www.umcqp.umd.edu/Index.htm>
- Vermont Council for Quality (2002) <www.vermontquality.org>
- The United States Senate Productivity and Quality Award for Virginia (2002) <www.gmupolicy.net/quality>
- Washington State Quality Award (2003) <www.wsqa.net>
- Wisconsin Forward Award (2003) <www.forwardaward.org>

Appendix G

Bibliography

Agor, W.H. (1997), The measurement, use, and development of intellectual capital to increase public sector productivity, *Public Personnel Management*, Vol. 26, No. 2, pp. 175–187.

Albrecht, K. and Zemke, R. (1985), *Service America!: Doing Business in the New Economy*, Homewood, IL: Dow Jones-Irwin.

Albrecht, K. (1992), *The Only Thing That Matters*, New York: Harper Business.

Alford, J. (2002), Defining the client in the public sector: a social-exchange perspective, *Public Administration Review*, Vol. 62, No. 3, pp. 337–346.

American Quality Foundation and Ernst and Young (1992), *The International Quality Study Best Practices Report: An Analysis of Management Practices that Impact Performance*, Cleveland, OH: Ernst and Young.

Ammons, D. (2000), Benchmarking as a performance management tool: experience among municipalities in North Carolina, *Journal of Public Budgeting, Accounting, and Financial Management*, Vol. 12, No. 1, pp. 106–124.

Ammons, D., Coe, C., and Lombardo, M. (2001), Performance-comparison projects in local government: participants' perspectives, *Public Administration Review*, Vol. 61, No. 1, pp. 100–110.

Arcaro, J.S. (1995), *The Baldrige Award for Education: How to Measure and Document Quality Improvement*, Delray Beach, FL: St. Lucie Press.

Armijo, L.E. and Faucher, P. (2002), We have a consensus: explaining political support for market reforms in Latin America, *Latin American Politics and Society*, Vol. 44, No. 2, pp. 1–40.

Arndt, A. and Bigelow, B. (1995), The implementation of total quality management in hospitals: how good is the fit?, *Health Care Management Review*, Vol. 20, No. 4, pp. 7–14.

Atkinson, P.E. (1997), New Zealand's radical reforms, *OECD Observer*, No. 205, p. 43.

Atkinson, R. (2001), Standardized Tests and Access to American Universities, The 2001 Robert H. Atwell Distinguished Lecture delivered at the 83rd Annual Meeting of the American Council on Education.

Auger, D.A. (1999), Privatization, contracting, and the states: lessons from state government experience, *Public Performance and Management Review*, Vol. 22, No. 4, pp. 435–454.

Barnard, C. (1938), *The Functions of the Executive*, Cambridge, MA: Harvard University Press.

Barquin, R.C, Bennet, A., and Remez, S. (2001), *Knowledge Management: The Catalyst for Electronic Government*, Leesberg, Virginia: Management Concepts.

Beam, G. (2001), *Quality Public Management: What it Is and How it Can Be Improved and Advanced*, Chicago: Burnham Publishers.

Beckett, J. (2000), The "Government should be run like a business" mantra, *American Review of Public Administration*, Vol. 30, No. 2, pp. 185–204.

Behn, R. (1999), The new public management paradigm and the search for democratic accountability, *International Public Management Review*, Vol. 1, No. 2, pp. 131–165.

Behn, R. (2001), *Rethinking Democratic Accountability*, Washington, D.C.: The Brookings Institution Press.

Bennis, W. and Nanus, B. (1986), *Leaders: Strategies for Taking Charge*, New York: Harper and Row.

Berry, T. (1991), *Managing the Total Quality Transformation*, New York: McGraw-Hill.

Berry, L. and Parasuraman, A. (1991), *Marketing Services: Competing Through Quality*, New York: The Free Press.

Berry, L. and Parasuraman, A. (1992), Prescription for a service quality revolution, *Organizational Dynamics*, Vol. 21, No. 4, pp. 5–15.

Berry, L. and Parasuraman, A. (1997), Listening to the customer — the concept of a service-quality information system, *Sloan Management Review*, Vol. 38, No. 3, pp. 65–76.

Berwick, D.M. (1989), Continuous Improvement as an Ideal in Health Care, *New England Journal of Medicine*, Vol. 320, pp. 53–56.

Berwick, D.M. (1996), A Primer on Leading the Improvement of Systems, *British Medical Journal*, Vol. 312, pp. 619–622.

Berwick, D.M., Godfrey, A.B., and Roessner, J. (1991), *Curing Health Care*, San Francisco: Jossey-Bass.

Blakeslee, J.A. (1999), Implementing the Six Sigma Solution, *Quality Progress*, Vol. 32, No. 7, pp. 77–85.

Blanchard, L.A., Hinnant, C., and Wong, W. (1998), Market-based reforms in government, *Administration and Society*, Vol. 30, No. 5, pp. 483–513.

Blank, R. (2000), Can public policy makers rely on private markets? The effective provision of social services, *Economic Journal*, Vol. 110, No. 462, C34–50.

Block, P. (1991), *The Empowered Manager*, San Francisco, CA: Jossey-Bass.

Boseman, B. (1987), *All Organizations Are Public*, San Francisco, CA: Jossey-Bass.

Bothe, D.R. (2003), Improve Service and Administration, *Quality Progress*, Vol. 36, No. 9, pp. 53–57.

Boyne, G. and Walker, R. (2002), Total quality management and performance: an evaluation of the evidence and lessons for research on public organizations, *Public Performance and Management Review*, Vol. 26, No. 2, pp. 111–131.

Bowman, J. (1989), Quality Circles: Promises, Problems, and Prospects in Florida, *Public Personnel Management*, Vol. 18, No. 4, pp. 375–403.

Bowman, J. (1994), At last, an alternative to performance appraisal: total quality management, *Public Administration Review*, Vol. 54, No. 2, pp. 129–137.

Box, R.C. (1999a), Running government like a business: implications for public administration theory and practice, *The American Review of Public Administration*, Vol. 29, No. 1, pp. 19–43.

Box, R.C. (1999b), Lessons learned from electricity restructuring: running government like a business: implications for public administration theory and practice, *The American Review of Public Administration*, Vol. 29, No. 1, pp.19–43.

Box. R.C., Marshall, G., Reed, B.J., and Reed, C. (2001), New Public Management and Substantive Democracy, *Public Administration Review*, Vol. 61, No. 5, pp. 608–619.

Brehm J. and Gates, S. (1997), *Working, Shirking and Sabotage: Bureaucratic Response to a Democratic Public*, Ann Arbor, MI: University of Michigan Press.

Broadhead, J.S. (1991), The Post Deming Diet, *Training*, Vol. 28, No. 1, pp. 41–43.

Brown, S.A. (1992), *Total Quality Service: How Organizations Use It to Create a Competitive Advantage*, Englewood Cliffs, NJ: Prentice-Hall.

Brown, M.G., Hitchcock, D., and Willard M. (1994), *Why TQM Fails and What to Do About It*, New York: McGraw-Hill.

Brown, M.G. (2004), *Baldrige Award Winning Quality* (13th ed.), Milwaukee, WI: ASQ Press.

Brown, R. and Murti, G. (2003), Student partners in instruction: third level student participation in advanced business courses, *Journal of Education for Business*, Vol. 79, No. 2, pp. 85–90.

Burnett, R, Quintana, O., and West, J. (2004), Hospitals: Defining a Framework to Manage the Environment and Improve the Bottom Line, unpublished paper.

Bush, G.W. (2001), Improving Government Performance, President's Management Agenda, accessed at www.whitehouse.gov/omb/budget.

Camp, R. (1989), *Benchmarking: The Search for Industry Best Practices that Lead to Superior Performance*, Milwaukee, WI: ASQC Press.

Carr, D. and Littman, I. (1990), *Excellence in Government: Total Quality Management in the 1990s*, Arlington, VA: Coopers and Lybrand.

Carlzon, J. (1987), *Moments of Truth*, New York: Ballinger.

Carroll, J.D. (1995), The rhetoric of reform and political reality in the national performance review, *Public Administration Review*, Vol. 55, No. 3, pp. 302–312.

Chu, P-Y. and Wang, H-S. (2001), Benefits, critical process factors, and optimum strategies of successful ISO 9000 implementation in the public sector, *Public Performance and Management Review*, Vol. 25, No. 1, pp. 105–121.

Chuan, T.K. (2000), A detailed trends analysis of national quality awards worldwide, *Total Quality Management*, Vol. 11, No. 8, pp. 1065–1080.

Clemmer, J. (1992), *Firing on All Cylinders*, Homewood, IL: Business One Irwin.

Coe, C. (1999), Local government benchmarking: lessons from two major multi-government efforts, Public Administration Review, Vol. 59, No. 2, pp. 110–115.

Cohen, S.A., Herman G., Robin W., and Josefowitz N. (1992), *Effective Behavior in Organizations*, Homewood, IL: Irwin.

Cole, R. (1993), *The Life and Death of the American Quality Movement*, San Francisco: Jossey-Bass.

Cole, R. (2002), From continuous improvement to continuous innovation, *Total Quality Management*, Vol. 13, No. 8, pp. 1051–1057.

Coplin, W. and Dwyer, C. (2000), *Does Your Government Measure Up?: Better Tools for Local Officials and Citizens*, Syracuse, NY: Syracuse University Community Benchmarks Program.

Crosby, P.B. (1979), *Quality is Free: The Art of Making Quality Certain*, New York: McGraw-Hill.

Crosby, P.B. (1984), *Quality Without Tears,* New York: New American Library.

Davison, J. and Grieves, J. (1996), Why Should Local Government Show An Interest in Service Quality?, *The TQM Magazine*, Volume 8, No. 5, pp. 32–38.

Debia, N.S. (2001), Global perspectives on quality, *Total Quality Management*, Vol. 12, No. 6, pp. 657–668.

DeFeo, J.A. and Janssen, A. (2001), The Economic Driver for the Twenty-First Century: Quality, *The TQM Magazine*, Vol. 13, No. 2, p. 92.

deLancer Julnes, P. and Holzer, M. (2001), Promoting the Utilization of Performance Measures in Public Organizations: An Empirical Study of Factors Affecting Adoption and Implementation, *Public Administration Review*, Vol. 61, No. 6, pp. 693–708.

Deming, W.E. (1950), *Some Theory of Sampling*, New York: John Wiley & Sons.

Deming, W.E. (1982), *Quality, Productivity, and Competitive Position*, Cambridge, MA: MIT Center for Advanced Engineering Study.

Deming, W.E. (1986), *Out of the Crisis*, Cambridge, MA: MIT Center for Advanced Engineering Study.

Deming, W.E. (1993), *The New Economics of Industry, Government, and Education*, Cambridge, MA: MIT Center for Advanced Engineering Study.

Dervitsiotis, K. (2004), The design of performance measurement systems for management learning, *Total Quality Management and Business Excellence*, Vol. 15, No. 4, pp. 457–472.

DiIulio, J., Garvey, G., and Kettl, D.F. (1993), *Improving Government Performance: An Owner's Manual*, Washington, D.C.: The Brookings Institution.

Donaldson, L. (1999), *Performance-Driven Organizational Change*, Thousand Oaks, CA: Sage.

Douglas, T.J. and Judge, W.Q. (2001), Total quality management implementation and competitive advantage: the role of structural control and exploration, *Academy of Management Executive*, Vol. 44, No. 1, pp. 158–177

Drath, W.H. (1993), *Why Managers Have Trouble Empowering: A Theoretical Perspective Based on Concepts of Adult Development*, Greensboro, NC: Center for Creative Leadership.

Durant, R.F. and Legge, J.S., Jr. (2002), Politics, public opinion, and privatization in France: assessing the calculus of consent for market reforms, *Public Administration Review*, Vol. 62, No. 3, pp. 307–323.

Durst, S.L. and Newell, C. (1999), Better, faster, stronger: government reinvention in the 1990s, *The American Review of Public Administration*, Vol. 29, No. 1, pp. 61–76.

Dzikowski, D. (1997), Looking to outsource, *Fairfield County Business Journal*, Vol. 36, No. 4, pp. 22–24,

Eggers, W.D. and O'Leary, J. (1995), *Revolution at the Roots*, New York: Free Press.

Elfenbein, P., Miller, J., and Milakovich, M. (1994), Medical resource allocation: rationing and ethical considerations, *Physician Executive*, Vol. 20, No. 2, pp. 3–8.

Evans, J.R. and Lindsay, W.L. (2005), *The Management and Control of Quality (6th ed.)*, Mason, OH: Thomson Southwestern.

Feigenbaum, A.V. (1991), *Total Quality Control*, 3rd ed., rev. New York: McGraw-Hill.

Fisher, C., Dauterive, J., and Barfield J. (2002), Economic impacts of quality awards: does offering an award bring returns to the state?, *Total Quality Management*, Vol. 12, No. 7,8, pp. 981–987.

Flynn, B. and Saladin, B. (2001), Further evidence on the validity of the theoretical models underlying the Baldrige criteria, *Journal of Operations Management*, Vol. 19, No. 6, pp. 617–653.

Fontenot, G., Behara, R., and Gresham, A. (1994), Six sigma in customer satisfaction, *Quality Progress*, Vol. 27, No. 12, pp. 73–76.

Forrer, J. (2002), Private finance initiative: a better public-private partnership?, *Public Manager*, Vol. 31, No. 2, pp. 43–48.

Fountain, J. (2001), *Building the Virtual State*, Washington, D.C.: Brookings Institution.

Fredrickson, G. (1996), *The Spirit of Public Administration*, San Francisco, CA.: Jossey-Bass Publishers.

Furlong. G.P. and Johnson, L. (2003), Community of practice and metacapabilities, *Knowledge Management Research and Practice*, Houndmills, Vol. 1, No. 2, pp. 102–137.

Galloway, R.A. (1992), Quality improvement and heightened self-esteem: the Brighton police story, *Journal of Organizational Excellence*, Autumn, pp. 453–461.

Gartman, J.B., and Fargher, J. (1988), Implementing Gainsharing in a Total Quality Management Environment, Proceedings of the International Industrial Engineering Conference.

Garvin, D.A. (1984), What does "product quality" really mean, *Sloan Management Review*, Vol. 26, No. 1, pp. 25–43.

Garvin, D.A. (1987), Competing on the eight dimensions of quality, *Harvard Business Review*, Vol. 65, No. 6, pp. 101–109.

Gass, G.L. (1992), Measuring TQIM Efforts: Management By Fact, Total Quality Insurance Conference, Orlando, Florida, June 4–5.

Gibbons, S. and Gogue, J-M. (2001), Starting alone, *Journal of Quality and Participation*, Vol. 24, No. 4, pp. 28–32.

Gilbert, R. (1992), *The TQS Factor and You*, Boca Raton, FL: Business Performance Publications.

Ginnodo, W.L. (1989), How to build commitment, *Journal of Organizational Excellence*, Vol. 8, No. 3, pp. 249–260.

Giovannetti, E., Kagami, M., and Tsuji, M. (2003), *The Internet Revolution: A Global Perspective*, Cambridge: Cambridge University Press.

Gitlow, H. and Gitlow, S. (1987), *The Deming Guide to Quality and Competitive Position*, Englewood Cliffs, NJ: Prentice-Hall.

Gitlow, H. S. (1990), Planning for Quality, Productivity, and Competitive Position. Homewood, IL: Dow Jones-Irwin.

Gitlow, H. (1991), Lecture on Deming's Management Method, University of Miami Institute for Quality in Service and Manufacturing's Quality Forum, March 1991.

Gitlow, H. and Levine, R. (2005), *Six Sigma for Green Belts and Champions*, Upper Saddle River, NJ: Prentice-Hall.

Gitlow, H.S., Gitlow, S., Oppenheim, A., and Oppenheim, R. (1989), *Tools and Methods for the Improvement of Quality*, Homewood, IL: Irwin.

Gitlow, H., Oppenheim, A., Oppenheim, R., and Levine, D. (2005), *Quality Management* (3rd ed.), New York: McGraw-Hill.

Goldhaber, D. and Anthony, E. (2004), *Can Teacher Quality Be Effectively Assessed?*, Seattle: Center for Reinventing Education, accessed at www.crpe.org/workingpapers/pdf/NBPTSquality report.pdf.

Goldsmith, S. (1997), Can business really do business with government?, *Harvard Business Review*, Vol. 75, Issue 3, p. 110–121.

Goodsell, C.T. (2004), *The Case for Bureaucracy: A Public Administration Polemic*, Washington, D.C.: CQ Press.

Gore, A. Jr. (1993), *From Red Tape to Results: Creating a Government that Works Better and Costs Less*, Report of the National Performance Review, New York: Times Books, Random House.

Gormley, W. and Balla, S. (2004), *Bureaucracy and Democracy: Accountability and Performance*, Washington, D.C.: CQ Press.

Government Performance and Results Act (GPRA) of 1993 (P.L. 103-62, 107 Stat.285). November 15, 2000. Washington, D.C.: National Performance Review, accessed at: www.npr.gov/library/misc/s20.html.

Greebler-Schepper, C. (1993), The psychology of continuous improvement: understanding human behavior; The first the most critical step, *Personal correspondence*, October 1993.

Green, R. and Brill, R. (2002), State Quality Awards Directory, *Quality Digest*, pp. 40–45, accessed at http://www.qualitydigest.com/mar02/html/ redir.html and http://www.qualitydigest.com/pdfs/statedir.pdf

Greene, J. (2002), *Cities and Privatization: Prospects for the New Century*, Upper Saddle River, NJ: Prentice-Hall.

Griffin, A. and Hauser, H.R. (1993), The voice of the customer, *Marketing Science*, Vol. 12, No. 1, pp. 1–27.

Gronland, A. (2002), *Electronic Government: Design, Applications and Management*, Hershey, PA: Idea Group Publishing.

Groocock, J.M. (1986), *The Chain of Quality: Market Dominance Through Product Superiority*, New York: John Wiley & Sons.

Hackman, J. and Wageman, R. (1995), Total quality management: empirical, conceptual and practical issues, *Administrative Science Quarterly*, Vol. 40, No. 2, pp. 309–342.

Haines, S.G. and McCoy, K. (1995), *Sustaining High Performance: The Strategic Transformation to a Customer-Focused Learning Organization*, Delray Beach, Florida: CRC Press.

Hammer, M. and Champy, J. (1993), *Reengineering the Corporation*, New York: Harper Business.

Haque, M.S. (2001), Public service: The diminishing publicness of public service under the current mode of governance, *Public Administration Review*, Vol. 61, No. 1, pp. 65–82.

Harrington, H.J. (1987), *Poor Quality Costs*, Milwaukee: Marcel Dekker-ASQC Press.

Harvard University, John F. Kennedy School of Government (2002), Innovations in American Government awards, accessed at: www.innovations.harvard.edu/home.html.

Hauser, J. R. and Clausing, D. (1988), The house of quality, *Harvard Business Review*, Vol. 66, No. 3, pp. 63–73.

Heeks, R. (1999), *Reinventing Government in the Information Age*, London: Routledge.

Heinrich, C., Lynn, A., and Hill, G. (2000), *Governance and Performance: New Perspectives*, Washington, D.C.: Georgetown University Press.

Hellein, R. and Bowman, J. (2002), The process of quality management implementation, *Public Performance and Management Review*, Vol. 26, No. 1, pp. 75–93.

Hendricks, K.B. and Singhal, V.R. (2001), The long-run stock prices performance of firms with effective TQM programs as proxied by quality award winners, *Management Science*, Vol. 47, No. 3, pp. 359–368.

Herzberg, F. (1966), *Work and the Nature of Man*, Cleveland: World Publishing.

Hill, C.W.L. (2003), *International Business: Competing in the Global Marketplace*, 4th ed., New York: McGraw-Hill/Irwin.

Ho, A.T. (2002), Reinventing local governments and the e-government initiative, *Public Administration Review*, Vol. 62, No. 4, pp. 434–441.

Hodge, G. (2000), *Privatization: An International Review of Performance*, Boulder, CO: Westview Press.

Hogan, R. and Fernandez, J. (2002), Syndromes of Mismanagement, *Journal of Quality and Participation*, Vol. 25, No. 3, pp. 28–32.

Holzer, M. and Callahan, K. (1998), *Government At Work: Best Practices and Model Programs*, Thousand Oaks, CA: Sage Publications.

Hudiberg, J. (1991), Winning With Quality: The FPL Story. New York, White Plains.

Hufbauer, G. and Wong, Y. (2003), Security and the economy in the North American context: the road ahead for NAFTA, *Canada-United States Law Journal*, Vol. 29, pp. 53–70.

Hunt, V.D. (1992), *Quality in America: How to Implement a Competitive Quality Program*, Homewood, IL: Business One Irwin.

Hyde, A.C. (1991), Reserving quality measure from TQM, *The Bureaucrat*, Vol. 19, No. 1, pp. 16–20.

Imai, M. (1986), *KAIZEN: The Key to Japan's Competitive Success*, New York: Random House.

Ingraham, P., Thompson, J.R., Sanders, R.P. (Eds.) (1998), *Transforming Government: Lessons from the Reinvention Laboratories*, San Francisco: Jossey-Bass.

Ishikawa, K. (1985), *What is Total Quality Control? The Japanese Way*, Translated by David J. Lu. Englewood Cliffs, NJ: Prentice-Hall.

Johnson, C.N. (2002), College and university programs in quality, *Quality Progress*, Vol. 35, No. 10, pp. 33–43.

Johnson, H.T. and Kaplan, R. (1987), *Relevance Lost*, Cambridge, MA: Harvard Business School Press.

Johnson, H.T. (1991), *Relevance Found: The Rise and Fall of Managerial Accounting*, Boston, MA: Harvard Business School Press.

Joiner, B.L. and Scholtes, P. (1986), The quality manager's new job, *Quality Progress*, Vol. 19, No. 10, pp. 52–56.

Jordan, A. (2001), Special education in Ontario, Canada: a case study of market-based reforms, *Cambridge Journal of Education*, Vol. 31, No. 3, pp. 349–371.

Juran, J.M. (1964), *Managerial Breakthrough: A New Concept of the Manager's Job*, New York: McGraw-Hill.

Juran, J.M. and Gryna, F.M. Jr. (1980), *Quality Planning and Analysis: From Product Development through Use*, 2nd ed., New York: McGraw-Hill.

Juran, J.M. (1988), *Juran on Leadership for Quality*, New York: McGraw-Hill.

Juran, J.M. and Gryna, F.M. Jr. (1999), *Juran's Quality Control Handbook*, 4th ed., New York: McGraw-Hill.

Kanigel, R. (1977), *One BestWay: Frederick Winslow Taylor and the Enigma of Efficiency*, New York: Viking Press.

Kano, N. and Gitlow, H. (1989), Lectures on Total Quality Control and the Deming Management Method, University of Miami Quality Program, Coral Gables, Florida (unpublished lecture notes).

Kano, N. (1993), A perspective on quality activities of American firms, *California Management Review*, Vol. 35, No. 3, pp. 12–31.

Katzenbach, J.R. and Smith, D. (1992), *The Wisdom of Teams*, Cambridge, MA: Harvard Business School Press.

Keehley, P., Medlin, S., MacBride, S., and Longmore, L. (1997), *Benchmarking for Best Practices in the Public Sector: Achieving Performance Breakthroughs in Federal, State and Local Agencies*, San Francisco, CA: Jossey-Bass.

Kelman, S. (1994), *Procurement and Public Management: The Fear of Discretion and the Quality of Government Performance*, Washington, D.C.: AEI Press.

Kember, D. (2002), *Action Learning and Action Research: Improving the Quality of Teaching and Learning*, Sterling, VA: Stylus.

Kettl, D. (1997), The global revolution in public management: driving themes, missing links, *Journal of Policy Analysis and Management*, Vol. 16, No. 3, pp. 446–462.

Kettl, D. (1998), *Reinventing Government: A Fifth-Year Report Card*, Washington, D.C: The Brookings Institution.

Kettl, D. (2000a), *Has Government Been "Reinvented"?* Washington, D.C.: House Committee on Rules; Senate Committee on Governmental Affairs, Joint Hearing, May 4, 2000.

Kettl, D. (2000b), Relentless Reinvention, *Government Executive*, Vol. 32, No. 1, pp. 12–23.

Kettl, D. (2002), *The Global Public Management Revolution: A Report on the Transformation of Governance*, Washington, D.C.: The Brookings Institution.

Kettl, D. (2003), *Team Bush: Leadership Lessons from the Bush White House*, New York: McGraw-Hill Trade.

Kim, P. and Wolff, L. (1994), Improving government performance: public management reform and the national performance review, *Public Performance and Management Review*, Vol. 18, No. 1, pp. 73–87.

King, B. (1987), *Better Designs in Half the Time: Implementing QFD in America*, Methuen, MA: GOAL/QPC.

Koch, J. and Fisher, J. (1998), Higher education and total quality management, *Total Quality Management*, Vol. 9, No. 8, pp. 659–669.

Koch, J. (2003), TQM: Why is its Impact in Higher Education so Small?, *The TQM Magazine*, Vol. 15, No. 5, pp. 325–332.

Koehler, J.W. and Pankowski, J.M. (1996) *Quality Government: Designing, Developing, and Implementing TQM*, Delray Beach, FL: St. Lucie Press.

Kolb, D., Rubin, I.M., and McIntyre, J.M. (1984), *Organizational Psychology*, Englewood Cliffs, NJ: Prentice-Hall, 1984.

Koppich, J.E. (2002), Federal Role in Teacher Professional Development, *Brookings Papers on Educational Policy*, Washington, D.C.: Brookings Institution.

Kravchuk, R.S. and Leighton, R. (1993), Implementing total quality management in the United States, *Public Productivity and Management Review*, Vol. 17, No. 1, pp. 71–82.

Laszlo, G.P. (1996), Quality Awards — Recognition or Model?, *The TQM Magazine*, Vol. 8, No. 5, pp. 14–18.

Latzko, W.J. (1986), *Quality and Productivity for Bankers and Financial Managers*, New York: Marcel Dekker/ASQC Press.

Leadership for America: Rebuilding the Public Service (1990). The Report of the National Commission on the Public Service and the Task Force Reports to the National Commission on the Public Service, Lexington, MA: Lexington Books. (See also, Volcker, P.)

Lewis, R. and Smith, D. (1994) Total Quality in Higher Education. Delray Beach, FL: St. Lucie Press.

Liebowitz, J. (2003), Aggressively pursuing knowledge management over 2 years: a case study at a U.S. Government organization, *Knowledge Management Research and Practice*, Houndmills, Vol. 1, No. 2, pp. 69–75.

Lillrank, P. and Kano, N. (1989), *Continuous Improvement: Quality Control Circles in Japanese Industry*.

Liswood, L. (1990), *Serving Them Right: Innovative and Powerful Customer Retention Strategies*, New York: Harper and Row.

Lowery, D. (1999), ISO 9000: a certification-based methodology for reinventing the federal government, *Public Performance and Management Review*, Vol. 22, No. 2, pp. 232–250.

Lumney, K. (2000), Eight Agencies Honored for Peak Performance, *Government Executive*, accessed at www.govexec.com/dailyfed/0700/070500m1.htm.

Maslow, A. (1954), *Motivation and Personality*, New York: Harper and Row.

Masternak, R.L. (1993), Gainsharing boosts quality and productivity at a BF Goodrich plant, *Journal of Organizational Excellence*, Vol. 12, No. 2, pp. 225–239.

McGregor, D. (1960), *The Human Side of Enterprise*, New York: McGraw Hill.

Milakovich, M.E. (1990a), Total quality management for public sector productivity improvement, *Public Performance and Management Review*, Vol. XIV, No. 1, pp. 19–32.

Milakovich, M.E. (1990b), Enhancing the quality and productivity of state and local government, *National Civil Review*, Vol. 79, No. 3, pp. 266–277.

Milakovich. M.E. and Dan, S. (1990c), Achieving quality at Florida Power and Light: the pursuit of the Deming prize, *Quality Digest*, Vol. 10, No. 11, pp. 38–50.

Milakovich, M.E. (1991a), Total quality management in the public sector, *Journal of Organizational Excellence*, Vol. 10, No. 2, pp. 195–215.

Milakovich, M.E. (1991b), Creating a total quality health care environment, *Health Care Management Review*, Vol. 16, No. 2, pp. 9–21.

Milakovich, M.E. (1992), Total quality management for public service productivity improvement, in *Public Productivity Handbook*, Marc Holzer (Ed.), Milwaukee, WI: Marcel Dekker, pp. 577–602.

Milakovich, M.E. (1993), Leadership for public service quality management, *The Public Manager*, Fall, 1993, Vol. 22, No. 3, pp. 49–52.

Milakovich, M.E. (1995a), How quality oriented have state governments really become?, *Journal of Organizational Excellence*, Vol. 14, No. 1, pp. 38–50.

Milakovich, M.E. (1995b), *Improving Service Quality: Achieving High Performance in the Public and Private Sectors*, Boca Raton: St.Lucie Press.

Milakovich, M. (1998), The status of results-driven customer service quality in government, *Journal of Organizational Excellence*, Vol. 17, No. 2, pp. 47–54.

Milakovich, M. (2002), From Democracy to E-mocracy: Using the Internet to Increase Citizen Participation in Government, in Maria Wimmer (Ed.), *Knowledge Management in e-Government*, Vienna: Trauner Druck, pp. 138–154.

Milakovich, M. (2003), Balancing customer service, empowerment, and performance with citizenship, responsiveness and political accountability, *International Public Management Review*, Vol. 4, No. 1, pp. 61–82.

Milakovich, M. (2004), Rewarding Quality and Innovation: Awards, Charters, and International Standards as Catalysts for Change, in Maria Wimmer (Ed.), *Knowledge Management in Electronic Government*, Berlin: Springer, pp. 64–75.

Milakovich, M.E. (2006) "Comparing Bush–Cheney and the Clinton–Gore Performance Management Strategies: Are They More Alike than Different" *Public Administration,* in press.

Milakovich M.E. and Gordon, G.J. (2004), *Public Administration in America*, Belmont, CA: Thomson Wadsworth.

Miller, H.T. (1994), A Hummelian view of the Gore Report: toward a post-progressive public administration?, *Public Performance and Management Review*, Vol. 18, No. 1, pp. 59–71.

Miller, J. and Milakovich, M. (1991a), Total quality management and the utilization review process, *Physician Executive*, Vol. 7, No. 6, pp. 8–11.

Miller, J. and Milakovich, M. (1991b), Improving access to health care through total quality management, *Quality Assurance and Utilization Review*, Vol. 6, No. 4, pp. 138–141.

Miller, J., Rose, M., Milakovich, M., and Rosasco, E.J. (1992), Application of TQM principles to the utilization management process: a case report, *Physician Executive*, Vol. 7, No. 6. pp. 10–16.

Moon, M.J. (2002), The evolution of E-government among municipalities: rhetoric or reality?, *Public Administration Review*, Vol. 62, No. 4, pp. 424–433.

Moskowitz, M. (2003), *The 100 Best Companies to Work for in America*, New York: Doubleday.

Motwani, J., Sower, V., and Brashier, L.W. (1996), Implementing TQM in the health care sector, *Health Care Management Review*, Vol. 21, No. 1, pp. 73–82.

Murgatroyd, S. and Morgan, C. (1993), *Total Quality Management and the School*, Buckingham, England and Philadelphia: Open University Press.

Nakhai, B. and Neves, J.S. (1994), The Deming, Baldrige, and European quality awards, *Quality Progress*, Vol. 27, No. 1, pp. 36–37.

National Commission on the State and Local Public Service (1993), *Hard Truths/Tough Choices: An Agenda for State and Local Reform*, Albany, NY: Nelson Rockefeller Institute of Government. (See also, Winter, W.)

Neiman, M. (2000), *Defending Government: Why Big Government Works*, Upper Saddle River, NJ: Prentice-Hall.

New York State Police, *The Governor's Excelsior Award*, 1992 Public Sector Award Winner, Interview with Col. John Wallace, New York State Police, June 21, 1993.

NIST (National Institute for Standards and Technology), *Malcolm Baldrige National Quality Award*, 2001 Award Recipient, Education Category, Pearl River School District, http://www.nist.gov/public_affairs/peralriver.htm, accessed June 2003.

Oliver, W. (1990), The quality revolution, *Vital Speeches of the Day*, Vol. 56, No. 20, p. 625.

Olsen, J. (2002), Systemic Change/Teacher Tradition: Legends of Reform Continue, *Journal of Curriculum Studies*, Vol. 34, No. 2, pp. 129–137.

Omachanu, V. (1991), *Total Quality Productivity Management in Health Care Organizations*, Norcross, GA: Institute of Industrial Engineers.

Omachanu, V. (2004), *Principles of Total Quality Management*, Boca Raton, FL: CRC Press.

Osborne, D. and Gaebler, T. (1992) Reinventing Government. Reading, MA: Addison-Wesley.

Osborne, D. and Plastrik, P. (2000), *The Reinventor's Fieldbook*, San Francisco, CA: Jossey-Bass.

Ouchi, W. (1981), *Theory Z: How American Business Can Meet the Japanese Challenge*, Reading, MA: Addison-Wesley.

Ouchi, W. (1984), *The M-Form Society*, Reading, MA: Addison-Wesley.

Parasuraman, A., Berry, L., and Zeithaml, V. (1988), SERVQUAL: a multi-item scale for measuring customer perceptions of service quality, *Journal of Retailing*, Vol. 64, No. 1 Spring, pp. 12–40.

Parasuraman, A., Zeithaml, V., and Berry, L. (1994), Alternative scales for measuring service quality: a comparative assessment based on psychometric and diagnostic criteria, *Journal of Marketing*, Vol. 74, No. 3, Fall, pp. 201–230.

Peckenpaugh, J. (2001), Feds Top Private Firms in Customer Satisfaction, *Government Executive Magazine*, December 17, 2001, accessed at www.govexec.com/news/index.cfm?mode=report&articleid=21868.

Pegnato, J. (1997), Is a citizen a customer?, *Public Performance and Management Review*, Vol. 20, No. 4, pp. 397–404.

Peters, T. and Waterman, R.H. (1988), *In Search of Excellence: Lessons from America's Best Run Companies* (Revised edition), New York: Warner Books.

Peters, T. (1987), *Thriving on Chaos: Handbook for a Managerial Revolution*, New York: Knopf.

Preuss, G. (2003), High performance work systems and organizational outcomes: the mediating role of information quality, *Industrial and Labor Relations Review*, Vol. 56, No. 4, pp. 590–605.

Postman, N. (1995), *The End of Education*, Vintage Books: New York.

Puay, S.H., Tan, K.C., Xie, M., and Goh, T.N. (1998), A Comparative Study of Nine National Quality Awards, *The TQM Magazine*, Vol. 10, No. 1, pp. 30–39.

Romero-Simpson, J.E. (1990), A Quality-Improvement Oriented Organizational Behavior Course, paper presented at the OBTC Meeting, University of Richmond, Virginia, June 13, 1990.

Rosander, A.C. (1989), *The Quest for Quality in Services*, Milwaukee, WI: ASQC Quality Press.

Rosen, B. (1998), *Holding Bureaucracies Accountable*, Westport, CT: Greenwood Publishing.

Russell, G. and Waste, R. (1998), The limits of reinventing government, *American Review of Public Administration*, Vol. 28, No. 4, pp. 325–346.

Ryan, K.D. and Oestreich, D. (1991), *Driving Fear Out of the Workplace*, San Francisco, CA: Jossey-Bass.

Salamon, L. (1981), Rethinking public management: third-party government and the changing forms of government action, *Public Policy*, Vol. 29, No. 3, pp. 255–275.

Sanderson, I. (2001), Performance Management, Evaluation and Learning in "Modern" Local Government, *Public Administration*, Vol. 79, No. 2, pp. 297–313.

Sarbaugh-Thompson, M. (1998), Change from below: integrating bottom-up entrepreneurship into a program development framework, *American Review of Public Administration*, Vol. 28, No. 1, pp. 3–25.

Savas, E.S. (2000), *Privatization and Public Policy Partnerships*, Chatham, NJ: Chatham House.

Schaeffer, P.V. and Loveridge, S. (2002), Toward an understanding of types of public-private cooperation, *Public Performance and Management Review*, Vol. 26, No. 2, pp. 169–189.

Scherkenbach, W.W. (1988), *The Deming Route to Quality and Productivity*, Washington, D.C.: CEEP Press.

Scherkenbach, W.W. (1991), *Deming's Road to Continual Improvement*, Knoxville, TN: SPC Press.

Schiavo, L.L. (2000), "Quality Standards in the Public Sector: Differences Between Italy and the UK in the Citizens' Charter Initiative," *Public Administration*, Vol. 78, No. 3, pp. 679–698.

Schmidt, W.H. and Finnigan, J. (1992), *The Race without a Finish Line: America's Quest for Total Quality*, San Francisco, CA: Jossey-Bass.

Schneider, B. and White, S. (2004), *Service Quality: Research Perspectives*, Thousand Oaks, CA: Sage Publications.

Scholtes, P. and Hacquebord, H. (1987), *A Practical Approach to Quality*, Madison, WI: Joiner Associates.

Scholtes, P. and Hacquebord, H. (1988), Beginning the quality transformation, part I, *Quality Progress* Vol. 21, No. 7, pp. 28–33.

Scholtes, P. (1988), *The Team Handbook: How to Use Teams to Improve Quality*, Madison, WI: Joiner Associates.

Scholtes, P. (1993), Total quality or performance appraisal: choose one, *Journal of Organizational Excellence*, Vol. 12, No. 3, pp. 349–365.

Sedell, K. (1991), The Relationship between Quality and Productivity, unpublished research paper, Political Science Department, University of Miami.

Senge, P. (1990), *The Fifth Discipline*, New York: Doubleday.

Senge, P.M. et al. (1994), *The Fifth Discipline Fieldbook*, New York: Doubleday.

Senge, P.M. (1996), *Leading Learning Organizations, Training and Development*, Vol. 50, No. 12, pp. 36–7.

Sensenbrenner, J. (1992), Quality comes to city hall, *Harvard Business Review*, Vol. 69, No. 2, pp. 64–75.

Seymour, (1992), *On Q: Causing Quality in Higher Education*, New York: Macmillan Publishing Company.

Shewhart, W.A. (1931), *Economic Control of Quality of Manufactured Product*, New York: Van Nostrand Reinhold.

Shewhart, W.A. (1939), *Statistical Method from the Viewpoint of Quality Control*, Ed., W. Edwards Deming, Lancaster, PA: Lancaster Press.

Shingo, S. (1986), *Zero Quality Control: Source Inspection and the Poka-Yoke System*, Translated by Andrew Dillon, Cambridge, MA: Productivity Press.

Shingo, S. (1989), *A Study of the Toyota Production System*, Translated by Andrew Dillon, Cambridge, MA: Productivity Press.

Shonk, J.H. (1992), *Team-Based Organizations*, Homewood, IL: Business One Irwin.

Sink, D., Developing world-class quality and productivity management efforts, in Sumanth, D.J., Edosomwan, J.A., Sink S., and Werther W. Jr. (1991), *Productivity and Quality Management Frontiers III*, Norcross, GA: Industrial Engineering and Management Press, Institute of Industrial Engineers, pp. 210–216.

Sinn, V. (2002), Education and the Future of Quality, *Quality Progress*, Vol. 35, No. 3, pp. 69–74.

Smith, D.G. (1992), *Paying for Medicare: the Politics of Reform*, New York: Aldine De Gruyter.

Spechler, J. (1991), *When America Does it Right: Case Studies in Service Quality*, Norcross, GA: Industrial Engineering and Management Press.

Starr, P. (1982), *The Social Transformation of Medicine*, New York: Basic Books.

Starr, P. (1993), *The Logic of Health-Care Reform*, Knoxville, TN: The Grand Rounds Press, Whittle Books.

Steventon, D. (1994), Quality Awards — A Means to an End or an End in Themselves?, *The TQM Magazine*, Vol. 6, No. 5, pp. 7–8.

Stiglitz, J. (2002), *Globalization and Its Discontents*, New York: W.W. Norton.

Stillman, R. (2005), *Public Administration: Concepts and Cases* (8th ed.), Boston: Houghton-Mifflin.

Sumanth, D. (1984), *Productivity Engineering and Management*, New York: McGraw-Hill.

Sureshchandar, G.S., Rajendran, C., and Anantharaman, R.N. (2001), A holistic model for total quality service, *International Journal of Service Industry Management*, Vol. 12, No. 4, pp. 378–412.

Svara, J. (1999), The shifting boundary between elected officials and city managers in large council-manager cities, *Public Administration Review*, Vol. 59, No. 1, pp. 44–53.

Swiss, J.E. (1992), Adapting Total Quality Management (TQM) to Government, *Public Administration Review*, Vol. 52, No. 4, pp. 356–362.

Szilagyi, A.D. Jr. and Wallace, M.J. Jr. (1990), *Organizational Behavior and Performance*, Scott, Foresman, Glenview, IL.

Taguchi, G. (1986), *Introduction to Quality Engineering: Designing Quality into Products and Processes*, White Plains, NY: Quality Resources and the Asian Productivity Organization.

Taguchi, G. and Clausing, D. (1990), Robust quality, *Harvard Business Review*, January–February, pp. 65–75.

Taylor, F.W. (1911), *Principles of Scientific Management*, New York: Norton Free Press.

Thompson, J.D. (1967), *Organizations in Action*, New York: McGraw-Hill.

Thompson, A.A. and Strickland, A.J. (2002), *Strategic Management: Concepts and Cases*, Burr Ridge, IL: McGraw-Hill.

Tisch, J. (2004), *The Power of We,* New York: John Wiley and Sons.

Toffler, A. (1990), *Power Shift: Knowledge, Wealth, and Violence at the Edge of the 21st Century*, New York: Bantam.

Townsend, P. and Gebhardt, J.E. (1990), *Commit to Quality*, New York: John Wiley & Sons.

Tribus, M. (1990), Interview at Deming Seminar, Costa Mesa, CA, February.

Tummala, V.M., Rao, and Tang, C.L. (1994), Strategic quality management, Malcolm Baldrige and European quality awards and ISO 9000 certification: core concepts and comparative analysis, *International Journal of Quality and Reliability Management*, Vol. 13, No. 4, pp. 8–38.

Ullmann, S.G. (1985), The impact of quality on cost in the provision of long-term care, *Inquiry*, Vol. 33, No. 4, pp. 292–306.

U.S. General Accounting Office (1991), *Management Practices: U.S. Companies Improve Performance Through Quality Efforts*, GAO/NSIAD-91-190.

U.S. General Accounting Office (1992), *Quality Management: Survey of Federal Organizations*, Washington, D.C., Document GAO/Ggd-93-9BR.

U.S. Secret Service and Department of Education (2002), "Threat Assessment in Schools: A Guide to Managing Threatening Situations and to Creating Safe School Climates," Washington, D.C.
<www. secretservice.gov/ntac/ssi_guide.pdf>

Van Thiel, S. and Leeuw, F.L. (2002), The performance paradox in the public sector, *Public Performance and Management Review*, Vol. 25, No. 3, pp. 267–281.

Vassekuil, B., Fein, R., Reddy, M., Barum, R., and Modzeleski, W. (2002), *The Final Report and Findings of the Safe School Initiative: Implications for the Prevention of School Attacks in the United States*, United States Secret Services and Department of Education, Washington, D.C.

Volcker, P. (1990), *Chair, Leadership for America: Rebuilding the Public Service*, The Report of the National Commission on the Public Service and the Task Force Reports to the National Commission on the Public Service, Lexington, MA: Lexington Books.

Walton, M. (1986), *The Deming Management Method*, New York: Dodd, Mead.

Walton, M. (1990), *Deming Management at Work*, New York: G.P. Putnam's Sons.

Wang, X. (2001), Assessing Public Participation in U.S. Cities, *Public Performance and Management Review*, Vol. 24, No. 4, pp. 322–336.

Weber, M.V. (1947), *The Theory of Social and Economic Organization*, New York: Free Press.

West, J.P, Berman, E., and Milakovich, M.E. (1994), Total quality management in local government, chapter in *1994 Municipal Yearbook*, Washington. D.C.: International City/County Management Association.

West, T.D. (1998), Comparing change readiness, quality improvement, and cost management among Veterans Administration, for-profit, and nonprofit hospitals, *Journal of Health Care Finance*, Vol. 25, No. 1, pp. 46–58.

West, D.M. (2001), *Assessing E-Government: The Internet, Democracy, and Service Delivery by State and Federal Governments*, 2000, accessed at: www.inside-politics.org/egovtreport00.html.

Wheeler, D.J. and Chambers, D. (1992), *Understanding Statistical Process Control*, 2nd ed., Knoxville, TN: SPC Press.

Whitney, J. (1989), Columbia University Insurance Study, Interview at Deming seminar, Costa Mesa, CA, July, 1989.

Wilson, J.Q. (1989), *Bureaucracy: What Government Agencies Do and Why They Do It*, New York: Basic Books.

Wilson, W. (1887), The Study of Administration, *Political Science Quarterly*, Vol. 2, pp. 197–222.

Wimmer, M. (Ed.). (2002), *Knowledge Management in e-Government*, Vienna, Austria: Trauner Druck.

Wimmer, M. (Ed.) (2004), *Knowledge Management in Electronic Government*, Berlin: Springer.

Winn, B.A. and Cameron, K.S. (1998), Organizational quality: an examination of the Malcolm Baldrige national quality framework, *Research in Higher Education*, Vol. 39, No. 5, pp. 491–512.

Winter, W. (1993), Chair, National Commission on the State and Local Public Service, *Hard Truths/Tough Choices: An Agenda for State and Local Reform*, Albany, NY: Nelson Rockefeller Institute of Government, State University of New York, Albany.

Wisniewski, M. and Donnelly, M. (1996), Measuring Service Quantity in the Public Sector: The Potential for SERVQUAL, *Total Quality Management*, Vol. 7, No. 4, pp. 357–365.

Woodall, J. (1988), Policy Deployment: How FPL Focuses for Improvement, University of Miami Quality Program, October, 1988. (unpublished)

Zbaracki, M. (1998), The rhetoric and reality of total quality management, *Administrative Science Quarterly*, Vol. 43, No. 3, pp. 602–636.

Zeithaml, V., Parasuraman, A., and Berry, L. (1990), *Delivering Quality Service: Balancing Customer Perceptions and Expectations*, New York: The Free Press.

Zemke, R. and Schaaf, D. (1989), *The Service Edge*, New York: New American Library, 1989.

Appendix H

Glossary and Acronyms

Glossary

Acceptable quality level (AQL) — (1) an operational definition of quality, (2) adjusting specifications so that tolerances are not tighter than what is required (i.e., using high-grade material when a low-grade will produce the same performance; using bearings that last 20 years on a component with a planned obsolescence of 10 years), (3) the "acceptable" fraction of defects.

Accountability — a political principle according to which agencies or organizations, such as those in government, are subject to some form of external control, causing them to give a general accounting of, and for, their actions; an essential concept in democratic public administration.

Advanced tools — design of experiments, Taguchi experiments, regression analyses, sampling plans, and multivariate analyses used for statistical process control.

American Medical Association (AMA) — political interest group primarily composed of professionals within the medical field; as an emerging secondary service, the AMA also works to ensure quality within the medical profession.

Andon cord — a rope suspended above the Toyota production line that allows any worker to stop the entire process if he/she observes a defect; see also, *empowerment.*

Appraisal costs — the cost of ensuring that standardized activities are performed as designed; part of direct quality costs.

Assignable quality costs — see *controllable quality costs.*

Attribute check sheet — check sheet that tabulates attribute data.

Attribute data — data that falls into a category.

Baldrige National Quality Program — presents Malcolm Baldrige National Quality Award (BNQA) established by the U.S. Congress to certify that winners meet a specified level of quality assurance. Purpose is to reward organizations excelling in the development of quality within their respective fields. Up to two awards are handed out yearly in each of five categories.

Bar chart — see *histogram*.

Basic tools — brainstorming, flowcharting (classical and deployment), cause–effect diagrams (positive and negative Ishikawa diagrams), check sheets, Pareto charts and diagrams, histograms, run charts, control charts, scatter diagrams, and stratification.

Benchmarking — a quality and productivity improvement methodology that examines those organizations best able to perform a certain process or set of processes (for example, employee relations) and then transplanting the methods into another organization. See also, *quality position*.

Brainstorming — a method designed to extract unconstrained ideas from a working group or team of people involved in total quality improvement and to free individuals from traditional or restrictive mindsets that inhibit them from discovering new approaches and new conceptualizations regarding present and future processes.

Breakthrough — when the level of quality attained for one cycle sets a new record and this rise in quality is attributable to human intervention in the process. See also, *Joseph M. Juran*.

Bureaucratic empowerment — concept of empowerment applied to government agencies; see also, *empowerment*.

Business process reengineering (BPR) — fast-track and radical form of quality management proposed by Harvard business professors Hammer and Champy.

California's Standardized Testing and Reporting (STAR) — standardized statewide achievement tests.

Categorical grants — federal grants that may be spent only for narrowly defined purposes; recipients often must match a portion of the federal funds.

Cause-and-effect (C–E) diagram — a graphic tool to collect and organize ideas about possible root causes of a problem. Categories of causes including the "Seven M's" (Manpower, Machines, Materials, Methods, etc.) appear as bones branching off the spine of a fish. The head of the fish is the problem of effect. Also known as a *fishbone chart* or *Ishikawa Diagram*.

Certificate of need (CON) — required by any person, partnership, or corporation proposing to construct, develop, or establish a new healthcare facility, service, or home healthcare agency.

Chain reaction of quality improvement — shows how improved quality reduces waste and rework, and increases efficiency with better use of people, time, materials, and equipment. See discussion of Deming Method, Chapter 3.

Charter marks — public recognition based on specified criteria for excellence; marks are displayed in windows and can be used in promotional advertising.

Check sheet — a table indicating the frequency with which an event or category of events has occurred.

Chief executive officer (CEO) — the senior manager within the organization, ultimately responsible for the day-to-day operation of the organization.

Chief Financial Officers Act of 1990 — federal legislation creating financial officers within federal executive agencies. Purpose is to strengthen management capacity.

Citizen charters — written standards of service, similar to guarantees, which entitle customers to receive certain levels of service; more common in Europe.

Citizen relationship management (CzRM) — concepts of customer services and customer relationship management (CRM) applied to relationship between citizens and government.

Code of Hammurabi — one of history's oldest codes of law (ca. 2150 BC) dating back to Babylonian times showed that society was willing to impose severe penalties to deter those who practiced unsafe production and service techniques.

Commitment to the customer — fundamental principle of all quality improvement systems supporting customer-driven definitions of quality characteristics measured to meet or exceed customer standards.

Common causes of variation — process variations that occur within upper and lower specification limits when a process is in statistical control.

Communication — process of bringing together divided labor; emphasis on common or compatible objectives, harmonious working relationships, and the like; linked to issues involving centralization–decentralization, information technology, and leadership.

Companywide quality control (CWQC) — (also known as total quality control) uses statistical process control, statistical quality control, and total care concept for both quality assurance and quality control. Ishikawa and Taguchi are known for CWQC.

Competitive position — domestic and international market share relative to others in the same "line of business" (applies to public, private, and nonprofit sectors).

Congressional Budget Office (CBO) — created by the Congressional Budget and Impoundment Control Act of 1974. CBO's mission is to provide the Congress with the objective, timely, nonpartisan analyses needed for economic and budget decisions and with the information and estimates required for the Congressional budget process.

Continuous quality improvement (CQI) — *Kaizen* (Japanese) applied to every aspect of an organization; also called total quality improvement.

Control chart — a run chart that also depicts the arithmetic mean of the values and the upper and lower control limits (known also as Shewhart control chart).

Controllable quality costs — costs that management has direct control over to ensure that only accepted services are delivered and to ensure that standardized activities are performed as designed.

Cost–benefit analysis —analysis technique designed to measure relative gains and losses resulting from alternative policy or program options; emphasizes identification of the most desirable cost–benefit ratio, in quantitative or other terms.

Costs of poor quality — analysis of the sum of the price of conformance and nonconformance.

Critical mass — the number of people inside an organization who must believe in the quality approach for a quality transformation to occur; Deming estimates that this critical mass is equal to the square root of the number of employees.

Crosby, Philip B. — one of the most prominent quality gurus, Crosby's name is perhaps best known in relation to the concepts of Do It Right First Time and Zero Defects. He considers traditional quality control to be acceptable quality limits and waivers of substandard products to represent failure rather than assurance of success.

Cross-functional (horizontally integrated) management (CFM) — solving problems that cut across staff areas by forming teams such that each team has a facilitator and a representative of each of the responsible work units; refers also to two-way transmission and discussion of information and suggestions across staff areas.

Cross-functional teams — implement cross-functional management and deal with problems that cut across organizational barriers, such as accounts payable; for examples, see Florida Power and Light Quality Improvement Program, Chapter 6.

Cumulative distribution function (CDF) — see *Pareto diagram*.

Customer — the receiver of a product or service, internal or external to an organization.

Customer-contact requirements — standards for point-of-contact accountability between employees and customers.

Customer relationship management (CRM) — methodology for assessing customer satisfaction.

Customer satisfaction — various means of determining if customers receive satisfactory service quality.

Customer-driven quality — identifying internal and external customers, implementing the extended process, and setting as a goal meeting valid extended customer requirements while engaging in continuous quality improvement.

Customer–supplier relationship — the concept of the customer or user as the final judge of quality standards, including internal customers (employees in departments, divisions, and bureaus) and external customers (buyers, vendors, and regulators) of products and services.

Cutback management — or "downsizing." Current fiscal pressures on public organizations have spawned the need for downsizing in many places, forcing leaders to use a variety of new tactics. At the same time, they must strive to maintain organization morale and performance levels, while holding the negative effects of organizational decline to a minimum.

Decentralization — an organizational pattern of system that distributes power broadly within an organization.

Deming Prize — prize created by the Japanese Union of Scientists and Engineers in 1950 to commemorate Dr. Deming's contribution to the quality field and promote the continued development of quality control. The Deming Prize, especially the Deming Application Prize given to companies, has exerted an immeasurable influence directly or indirectly on the development of quality control and management.

Deming, Edwards W. — renowned quality expert who was a consultant for 40 years, with a practice worldwide. His clients included railways, telephone companies, motor freight carriers, manufacturing companies, consumer research, census methods, hospitals, legal firms, government agencies, research organizations, and universities. He is best known for his work in Japan, which commenced in 1950 and created a revolution in quality and economic production. See also, *Deming Prize.*

Demonstration effect — once someone respectable in a certain field has done something with great success, then publicizing that fact leads to others attempting to mimic that person's success.

Department of Homeland Security (DHS) — was created by legislation in 2002 and officially established on March 1, 2003, with the merger of 22 existing divisions of various federal agencies. Its mission is to coordinate intelligence from various services and protect Americans against further acts of political violence.

Departmental facilitator — see *facilitator*.

Deployment flowchart — a chart showing who is responsible for doing what while depicting all of the different permutations of a process; developed by Dr. Myron Tribus.

Diagnosis-Related Groups (DRGs) — groups of diseases and medical procedure categories based on related diagnoses and similar hospital requirements.

Digital divide — refers to the increasing disparities between the technological "haves" and "have-nots"; those who can afford home computers and fast Internet connections and those who cannot.

Direct quality costs — controllable quality costs plus resultant costs.

Distance learning systems — long-distance learning systems assisted by personal computers and the Internet. See also, *virtual courses*.

Downsize — to drastically reduce the number of workers a company or government employs to reduce costs. See also, *outsourcing*.

Dual Factor Theory — originated by Frederick Herzberg. For example, hygienic factors cause worker dissatisfaction, and motivating factors cause worker satisfaction.

Education and self-improvement — goal of quality improvement training programs.

Eisenhower Professional Development Program — Federally funded teacher development program.

Electronic data interchange (EDI) — methodologies for enhancing global communications networks enabling transfer of information between remote geographic locations.

Empowerment — an approach to management that stresses extended customer satisfaction, examines relationships among existing management processes, seeks to improve internal agency communications, and responds to valid customer demands; in exchange for the authority to make decisions at the point of customer contact, all empowered employees must be thoroughly trained, and the results must be carefully monitored.

Enron Effect — general descriptive term referring to corporate corruption, mismanagement, and scandals.

Entitlements — programs of government financial assistance (mainly to individuals) created under legislation that defines eligibility standards but places no limit on total budget authority; the level of outlays is determined solely by the number of eligible persons who apply for authorized benefits under existing law

Environment, free from fear — principle number 8 of Deming's 14 points; goal of quality improvement training and process improvement to permit workers to make judgments without fear of failure or unnecessary supervision.

Environmental Protection Agency (EPA) — federal regulatory agency that ensures that all manufacturing companies are in line with federal environmental standards; also initiates prosecutions of companies not in compliance with federal regulations.

European Quality Awards — quality awards for members of the European Union; comparable with BNQA in the United States.

European Union (EU) — political and economic union between 25 member states in Europe that creates a stronger, more competitive, and unified Europe.

Experiential learning — lessons gained by experience or from experience.

Extended customer requirements — valid customer requirements of customers identified by the extended definition of process. See also, Figure 2.2.

Extended definition of process — the critical concept that an entire chain of production from raw materials to finished product being purchased by the end user, regardless of the number of intermediaries, are a set of interlinked systems that should be directed to reducing overall costs and increasing customer satisfaction through coordination between intermediaries; commitment to quality improvement by companies, customers, organizations, and suppliers that spreads quality standards in a continuing series of processes.

External customers — receivers of a product or service produced by a work unit external to the external customer's organization.

Extrinsic motivation — attempts to motivate workers or employees by bonuses, pay-for-performance, or other nonintrinsic rewards.

Facilitator or departmental facilitator — someone who is beyond the control of team members, who is trained in organizational behavior and group dynamics (and sometimes also industrial psychology), and who chairs team meetings.

Federal Workforce Restructuring Act of 1994 — legislation that authorized non-DoD agencies to offer buyouts of as much as $25,000 to voluntarily leave the workforce. This was done to avoid reductions-in-force and to give federal agencies the same downsizing tools commonly used by private companies.

Federalism — a constitutional division of governmental power between a central or national government and regional governmental units (such as states), with each having some independent authority over its citizens.

Feedback — related to systems theory, the process whereby data (analytic, descriptive, or enumerative) and information are used as the basis for reaction to a process, system, or worker that in turn affects the process on which data is being collected.

Fee-for-service healthcare — traditional manner by which doctors charge patients directly for medical services.

Feigenbaum, Armand V. — one of the leaders of the quality realm, considered the founder of the total quality control approach; see also, *hidden plant*.

Fishbone chart — a Cause–Effect or an Ishikawa diagram.

Flattening the hierarchy — a service quality movement created to encourage employee empowerment and reduce the arbitrational friction found within a top-down chain of command in a company.

Florida Comprehensive Achievement Tests (FCAT) — standardized achievement tests for all public school students in Florida.

Florida Power and Light Company (FPL) — an electric utility that services approximately half of Florida; part of FPL Group, Inc.

Flowchart — a chart, with standardized shapes to denote different types of internal work processes, which depicts all of the possible work steps and their interrelationships, the output to the customer, and the input from suppliers.

Ford Foundation Innovations in American Government Program — competitive award program for states and local governments, awards include money.

Ford, Henry — industrialist, capitalist, and founder of Ford Motor Company.

Formal groups — within an organization whose memberships are officially delineated (i.e., department heads, marketing, personnel office, etc.).

Funnel experiment — Deming's classic experiment that shows the negative effects of tampering with "out of control" management systems.

Gain-sharing — a system whereby an employee or group of employees receive either a bonus or commission determined by a sliding scale based upon the amount of money said employee or employees either save or generate for the organization by a cost-cutting or productivity-improving suggestion.

Global competition — the increased competition among nations impacting the daily operations of public, nonprofit, and private organizations in a variety of ways — definitions of service quality are merging, business environments are changing; information, capital, products, and services flow across international borders at increasing speeds; and unfortunately, jobs disappear, as well.

Global service markets — worldwide access to and competition for services.

Government Accountability Office (GAO) — the investigative arm of Congress that helps oversee federal programs and operations to ensure accountability to the American people through a variety of activities including financial audits, program reviews, investigations, legal support, and policy and program analyses.

Government Performance and Results Act (GPRA) of 1993 (P.L. 103-62, 107 Stat. 285) — federal legislation requiring performance-based and results-driven budgeting processes for executive agencies.

Government productivity — the measurable relationship between the results produced and the resources required for production or delivery of a public service; a quantitative measure of the efficiency of the organization.

Gross domestic product (GDP) — refers to the sum of goods and services produced by the economy, including personal consumption, private investments, and government spending.

Health maintenance organizations (HMOs) — managed healthcare organizations.

Hidden plant — the proportion of plant capacity that exists to rework unsatisfactory parts.

Hierarchical structure — when an organization is organized so that there is a top-down successive order of levels; every manager has 1 to 15 people immediately subordinate to him or her, not including personal staff (secretaries, etc.); an employee only reports to those on a level equal to or greater than her or his superordinate(s) through said superordinates.

High-performance service organizations — world-class quality organizations delivering measurable high-quality goods and services to customers.

Histogram — depicts the number of times every given value of a given quality characteristic has occurred, known also as a bar chart.

Horizontal service networks — flexible, cross-functional, horizontally oriented goods and services delivery management systems designed for global 21st-century management. See also, *Theory Z.*

Human relations — an approach to organizational behavior which emphasizes the behavior of individual workers. See also, *Theory Y.*

Human resources — refers to personnel or human assets within an organization.

Human sensors — like highly sensitive instruments, trained workers detect problems and prevent them from worsening; perform the vital "early warning" function. Trained to detect quality characteristics that are precise, valid, and reliable — easily understood by those who must perform critical tasks within limits of bias, error, and precision. See also, *sensing device*.

Human subsystem(s) — personnel united by some form of regular interaction and interdependence.

Humanware subsystem(s) — personnel; see also *human subsystem(s)*.

Important few — see *vital few*, in reference to Pareto diagram.

Indiana Statewide Test of Educational Progress Plus (ISTEP+) — standardized statewide achievement tests.

Indirect quality costs — losses that are not reflected in a standard accounting ledger, including loss of repeat business and the effects of negative ripple effects.

Informal groups — influential cliques that form within organizations that are not reflected in chains of command or official organization procedural materials.

Information — data that is timely, reliable, accurate, and of direct usefulness.

Information central (IC) — monitors progress of quality improvement teams; part of the quality improvement program approach to quality.

Information processing system — processes for collection, analysis, and storage of information such as customer-contact requirements essential for data-based statistical quality improvement; see especially Chapter 9 on healthcare information systems.

Inherited defects — defective inputs from other shifts in the same work unit or from suppliers.

Institutional memories — the cumulative knowledge possessed by experienced workers in an organization.

Intergovernmental coordination — all the activities and interactions occurring between or among governmental units of all types and levels within the American federal system.

Internal customers — receivers of a product or service produced by another work unit within the organization.

International Baccalaureate (IB) — based in Geneva, Switzerland, a rigorous academic program for students who perform successfully on the six external examinations. Students may earn college credit and advanced standing at institutions of higher learning throughout the world.

Intragovernmental coordination — refers to coordination and communication efforts within states and between states and local governments.

Intrinsic motivation — motivating workers or employees by the value of the job or work itself.

Ishikawa diagram — a catalog of everything that needs to go right for a process to work, organized by ever more specific categories, beginning with machines, materials, methods, environment, and personnel. Also known as *fishbone diagram*.

Ishikawa, Kaoru — Japanese quality guru credited with developing quality control circles and total quality control.

ISO 9000/14000 — widely used European International Standards Organization quality auditing and accreditation system.

ISTEP in Indiana — standardized achievement tests for all public school students in Indiana.

Japanese Union of Scientists and Engineers (JUSE) — the most prestigious academic organization in Japan; in the quality science and quality management science fields, they are just as exemplary. The Emperor of Japan is the titular head. JUSE is devoted to promoting communication and cooperation between scientists and engineers and between academia, research laboratories, and industry. They award the Deming Prize.

Joint Commission on Accrediting Healthcare Organizations (JCAHO) — private-hospital-accrediting association.

Juran, Joseph M. — major contribution has been in the field of quality management. Dr. Juran has been called the "father of quality." Perhaps most important, he is recognized as the person who added the human dimension to quality, broadening it from its statistical origins.

Juran Trilogy — basis of Juran quality method: planning, control, and breakthrough form a cycle, interlocked with a second cycle: the old standard, breakthrough, and the new standard (Chapter 3, Figure 3.2). The Juran Trilogy is repeated in a never-ending cycle of continuous improvement. Proper quality planning yields processes that reduce poor-quality costs by meeting quality control goals. This, in turn, leads to a new zone of quality control.

Just-in-time (JIT) production — working with suppliers to keep inventories and backlogs low using frequent deliveries; applies to both products and services. See also, *Kanban*.

Just-in-time learning — analogous to JIT production applied to higher and continuing education.

***Kaizen* (Japanese)** — the philosophy that every characteristic of a product, service, or task can and should be continually improved, and that it is the responsibility of everyone involved, including the end user, to do so.

***Kanban* (Japanese)** — see *just-in-time (JIT) production* in the preceding text.

Knowledge management (KM) — application of new technologies to achieve communication breakthroughs and systems improvements in a wide range of areas including electronic transfer of information, education, biomedical engineering, space exploration, and energy. See also, *knowledge revolution.*

Knowledge revolution — a social phenomenon of the past 50 years, particularly in Western industrial nations, creating new technologies and vast new areas of research and education; examples include biogenetic engineering, information systems, the Internet, space exploration, mass communications, nuclear technology, and energy research.

Less developed countries (LDCs) — countries within the early stages of economic development that characteristically have low living standards, as well as low levels of productivity and economic and social cohesion.

Lifelong learning — requirement for updating career skills, see also, *distance learning* and *virtual courses.*

Malcolm Baldrige National Quality Award — see Baldrige National Quality Program.

Managed healthcare — see *health maintenance organizations (HMOs).*

Management by exception — every problem is treated as though it were already identified as a special cause of variation.

Management by fact — using data collected about a task as a basis for action or reaction.

Management by objectives (MBO) — (1) using Theory X with both personal staff (secretaries, aides, etc.) and immediate subordinates within a hierarchical structure; (2) using Theory X with immediate subordinates and Theory Y with personal staff (secretaries, aides, etc.) within a hierarchal structure.

Management systems — with built-in procedures to formalize the gathering of data, decision-making processes, and decision-making rules for routine, tactical, and strategic management decisions.

Marketing operations — either the people who do the work or the work itself of determining what the needs of the customer are and will be in the future.

Matrix organization — nonhierarchical integrated management systems.

Medicaid — federal healthcare program operated by the states to assist the poor.

Medicare — a program under the U.S. Social Security Administration that reimburses hospitals and physicians for medical care provided to qualifying people over 65 years old.

Medicare Prescription Drug Improvement and Modernization Act of 2003 — provides seniors and those with disabilities with prescription drug benefits, more choices, and improved benefits.

Merit increases — a raise in salary given because the employee has received a fixed number of performance appraisals for which the overall score is "above average" or "outstanding."

Monitor — in statistical quality control and statistical process control, a person or device that determines whether or not a stable process exists.

Motivating factors — are related to higher-level needs in Maslow's hierarchy of needs than are hygienic factors; also part of Herzberg's dual factor theory.

Motor device — that which takes action to adjust a process if necessary; part of the Juran school of thought of quality.

Multidimensional quality — defined in terms of the quality characteristics of performance, features, reliability, conformance, durability, serviceability, aesthetics, and perceived quality; developed by David Garvin.

Multinational corporations (MNCs) — corporations whose physical plants and offices span the geography of several nations with no binding ties to a single state.

National Board of Teacher Certification — established in 1987, concentrates on education reform in the classroom, in which teaching and learning take place. National Board certification demonstrates a teacher's practice as measured against high and rigorous standards. For details, see www.nea.org.nationalboard.

National Performance Review (NPR) — Clinton administration government reform effort (1993 to 1997); also known as the National Partnership for Reinventing Government (1998 to 2001).

National Public Service Awards (NPSA) — recognize individuals who exhibit the highest standards of excellence over a sustained period of time as career managers at all levels of the public service and nonprofit organizations.

Necessary many — the many causes that actually represent a minority of the problems facing a manager, refers to Pareto analysis.

Negative Ishikawa diagram — see *reverse Ishikawa diagram.*

Network model — horizontally-oriented, flexible management system designed for just-in-time production. See also, *horizontal service networks.*

No Child Left Behind Act of 2001 — the Bush administration's controversial educational reform program designed to improve student achievement and change the culture of America's schools. For details, see http://www.ed.gov/nclb/landing.jhtml.

Non-market-driven services — see *regulated service monopolies.*

North American Free Trade Agreement (NAFTA) — North American Free Trade Agreement involving the United States, Canada, and Mexico; provides for increased economic and strategic cooperation.

Office of Management and Budget (OMB) — part of the Executive Office of the President; OMB receives budget requests from executive agencies, prepares the President's budget (which is submitted to

Congress for approval), prepares economic projections, and supervises executive branch spending.

Ombudsman — of Scandinavian origin, referee or arbitrator of disputes between individuals and corporations or governments.

Operational definition — has three components: specification, test, and criterion; an example would be that a room is stuffy if the oxygen content falls below 20 percent (specification), and a specific model of a specific sensor gave a reading (test) below 19.5 (criterion), which allows for the uncertainty in the measurement.

Out-of-pocket expenses — costs of healthcare services paid directly by patients.

Outsourcing — the process in which a company reallocates jobs to a much more favorable environment (i.e., lower wages, less taxes, less regulation, etc) for employment, usually seen as pattern of movement from developed countries to developing ones.

Overcontrol — too much intervention in a system or process that results in greater variation than if no intervention at all had been applied to the system or process.

Pareto analysis — using Pareto charts and Pareto diagrams to prioritize actions or problems.

Pareto chart — a type of bar chart ranking by frequency (number of times) or severity (usually in dollars or time) of problems resulting from a given cause and its percentage of total frequency or severity of problems facing a manager or work team.

Pareto diagram — a graphic representation of a Pareto chart.

Pareto optimization — a ranking of causes by direct and indirect costs of problems resulting from each cause and the costs' percentages of total costs on the list; which is followed by estimated costs of correcting the vital few; which is followed by a ranking of causes by the ratio of costs to not fixing these costs to fixing these problems.

Pareto principle — mathematical concept that confirms that 80 to 85 percent of all problems are caused by 15 to 20 percent of the customers.

Participatory management (Theory Z) — a system is in place whereby suggestions from employees are formally reviewed for possible implementation.

Patient satisfaction — operational measures of patient satisfaction with healthcare services.

PDCA cycle — see *Shewhart cycle*.

PDSA cycle — see *Shewhart* or *PDCA cycle*.

Performance appraisals — when a superordinate fills out a standardized form rating a subordinate's performance along a list of categories. The rating system uses terms such as poor, fair, below average, average, above average, good, and outstanding. A number is associated with each rating (i.e., average = 3) and an overall score is generated (i.e., a sum of ratings = 56, divided by 20 categories, means an overall score of 2.8). Usually, the average score on performance appraisals is well above the score associated with average.

Performance management — measurement of results and use of results to guide decision making.

Performance Management Agenda (PMA) — Bush administration proposals for improved performance of federal agencies.

Personal Application Assignments (PAAs) — written goal statements from individual team members designed to reflect learning from a specific exercise, knowledge of the readings, application to real situations, and self-knowledge. They also help participants express problems in such a way that the problems can be addressed by other team members.

Physician Review Organizations (PROs) — provides case reviews for hospitals, management care organizations, major insurance companies, and private physician practices to ensure informed, confidential, and objective reviews.

Plan–do–check–act cycle — see *Shewhart cycle.*

Planning Programming Budgeting System (PPBS) — a budgeting process including annual program memoranda (short-term budgeting and planning), multiyear program and finance plan (long-term budgeting and planning), and special studies (analytic basis for program memoranda).

Pluralism — a political concept emphasizing the importance of group organization, and diversity of groups and their activities, as a means of protecting societal interests; assumes group competition will benefit the public interest.

***Poka-Yoke* (Japanese)** — concept credited to Shigeo Shingo (1986) of "fool-proofing" industrial systems that allows manufacturers to fail-safe their processes from human error.

Policy deployment — identifying and eliminating the vital few; part of FPL quality improvement program.

Poor-quality costs — the cost of not having quality.

Preferred Provider Organizations (PPOs) — group of healthcare professionals or hospitals that contract with an employer or insurance company to provide medical care to specified groups of employees.

President's Quality Award — recognize federal agencies that demonstrate performance excellence and document world-class results.

Preventative care — healthcare emphasizing prevention of disease as well as treatment.

Price of conformance — what it would cost to meet the customer's requirements.

Price of nonconformance — all expenses paid for doing things wrong, not meeting the customer's requirements.

Private-market-based models — see *privatization*.

Privatization — a practice in which governments either join with, or yield responsibility outright to, private sector enterprises, for provision of services previously managed and financed by public entities; a pattern especially evident in local government service provision, though with growing appeal at other levels of government; converting a public sector function into a private sector function.

Process orientation — focusing one's attention upon improving the process or processes.

Process variation — see *common* and *special variation*.

Productivity — the ratio of the direct and indirect costs of inputs to the value of outputs.

Productivity ceiling — theoretical limit of the application of productivity improvement tools.

Public administration — (1) all processes, organizations, and individuals acting in official positions associated with carrying out laws and other rules adopted or issued by legislatures, executives, and courts (many activities are also concerned with formulation of these rules); (2) a field of academic study and professional training leading to public service careers at all levels of government.

Public management — the subfield of management applied to the public sector.

Public policy — (1) the organizing framework of purposes and rationales for government programs that deal with specified societal problems; (2) the complex of programs enacted and implemented by government.

Public Service Excellence Awards (PSEA) — supports governments to educate American citizens about the contributions made by public employees to the quality of their lives; to encourage *esprit de corps* among government employees; and to promote public service careers.

Purchasing agents — employees within the organization who spend the organization's money to obtain goods and services from those outside the organization, usually based upon the requests of others within the organization.

Quality approach — using Total Quality Management, total quality improvement, quality assurance, statistical quality control, and statistical quality assurance.

Quality assurance (QA) — minimizing defects in a product or service received by an end user by preventing defects before it is produced.

Quality assurance/quality control — see *quality control*.

Quality characteristic — attributes of a process or service deemed important enough to warrant some control; that which is being measured as part of an operational definition of quality.

Quality consensus — the tendency of high-performance quality organizations to do business with other quality companies and organizations; companies and organizations not using the quality approach must either adopt the quality approach or lose business.

Quality control — (1) minimizing defects in a product or service received by an end user by detecting defects using sampling after it is produced; (2) in both versions of total quality control, minimizing defects by any means (including both quality control definition 1 and quality assurance).

Quality control circles — a work unit minus the manager together with a facilitator who meet to identify problems, potential problems, and solutions; used to create employee empowerment.

Quality element — see *quality characteristic*; part of total quality service.

Quality function deployment (QFD) — a methodology developed by John R. Hauser and Don Clausing that balances "the voice of the process" against "the voice of the customer" and can be applied multidimensionally regardless of the number of "voices" with which the processes and the customers speak; in the two-dimensional case, the resultant chart is known as "the house of quality."

Quality improvement (QI) principles — generic term referring to various approaches to and models of quality improvement such as Total Quality Management, continuous quality improvement and total quality control.

Quality improvement program (QIP) — FPL group, Inc., and Qualtech's "school" of thought about quality.

Quality improvement teams (QIT) — workgroups whose purposes are to develop the skills, abilities, and attributes of the team members as well as to improve the quality of the services of the organization as a whole.

Quality in daily work (QIDW) — applying quality improvement program techniques when using an individual worker as the unit of analysis.

Quality measurement characteristics — quality characteristics that have been operationally defined and for which a nominal has been established; compare with *valid customer requirements*.

Quality objective — the ideal expressed in the organization's or project's mission statement.

Quality of conformance — the degree to which goods and services are consistent with the intent of design. Factors that influence conformance include: the capability of equipment, the training and skills of employees, process monitoring to assess conformance, worker motivation, and management commitment.

Quality of design — reflects the designer's intention to include specific features (such as size, weight, or color) in a finished product. Design choices demanded by customers typically originate from marketing representatives who listen to and gather information from external customers. Because production resources are always limited, the end product or service usually reflects some compromise between the "voice of the customer" and the "voice of the process."

Quality of performance — encompasses the reliability of the original product and service as well as the competence, integrity, and promptness of staff and support services.

Quality position — how an organization ranks vis-à-vis its competitors or, in the case of public sector, vis-à-vis similar organizations elsewhere, in implementing quality within the organization and using quality as a competitive tool. See also, *benchmarking*.

Quality science — the science of implementing and maintaining quality assurance and quality control.

Quantitative systems — the academic subfield that deals with mathematics as applied to management.

Red bead experiment — Deming's classic experiment showing how nothing an individual worker can do in an out-of-control system affects outcomes.

Regulated service monopolies — services provided directly by or regulated by governments; they are monopolies because there is no competition for an industrial sector or geographic service area. See also, *non-market-driven services*.

Relearning — learning to do the job again because the job has changed.

Resource-based relative value scales (RBRVS) — method to statistically benchmark medical practices and individual physicians.

Resultant poor-quality costs — internal and external costs of errors.

Results and customer feedback — information received from customers about the quality of service provided. See also, *customer-driven quality* and *voice of the customer*.

Results orientation — focusing attention upon descriptive statistics about results of a process instead of analytic data about the process or results.

Return on investment (ROI) — business accounting principle referring to the time needed to recover capital investment.

Reverse Ishikawa diagram — a catalog of everything that can possibly go wrong, organized by ever-expanding categories, leading eventually to machines, materials, methods, environment, and personnel; invented by Dr. Myron Tribus.

Rework — (1) correcting defects or mistakes made in a product or service; (2) scrapping and redoing a finished product or work done on a project because it has a defect in it.

Ripple effect — word-of-mouth good or bad advertising by customers to other potential customers.

Role playing — using mathematical models by themselves or in conjunction with individuals who serve as actors to determine the effects of an action and reaction pair.

Run — a sequence of one or more consecutive observations; see *run chart.*

Run chart or check sheet — a chart with a column for each observation using the height of a marking to depict the magnitude of the value of each observation, also used to isolate unusual or out-of-control factors.

Scatter diagram — uses height to indicate the value of a quality characteristic for a given observation and uses the number of graphic marks at that height to indicate the frequency with which that value was obtained; different units can be depicted using different areas of the same chart.

Scenario — or future scenario, the result of scenario writing.

Scenario writing — taking a well-defined set of assumptions and developing an imaginative conception of what a future process, product, or service would be like if these assumptions were true.

Scholastic Aptitude Test (SAT) — standardized test used by colleges for admissions.

Scientific management — basis of efficiency in industrial processes; the idea that there is one best and most efficient way to do any task; compare with scientific quality management. See also, *Taylor, Frederick W.*

Self-actualization — Abraham Maslow's highest stage of individual job satisfaction.

Sensing device — something or someone that detects what is occurring or has occurred pertaining to some quality characteristic; part of the Juran school of thought on quality.

Service quality revolution — refers to the global market for services made available though information technology, the Internet, and the World Wide Web.

SERVQUAL — widely used methodology for measuring gaps between customer perceptions and expectations of service quality.

Seven advanced quality control tools — see *advanced tools.*

Seven indispensable tools for quality control — see *basic tools.*

Seven management quality control tools — see *intermediate tools.*

Shewhart cycle — a never-ending cycle of plan, do, check, act, plan, do, check, act, etc. Plan the activity, Do a trial run, Check the results, and Act upon the results to improve performance.

Shewhart, Walter — first introduced statistical process control charts to monitor quality in mass production manufacturing, See also, *Shewhart cycle.*

Sigma — 1 sigma = 1 standard deviation, 1.3 sigma = 1.3 standard deviations, 2 sigma = 2 standard deviations, etc.

Six-Sigma quality — Motorola and other firms' quality goal, 99.7 percent perfect. Having such a high level of quality assurance or quality control that the ratio of the number of products or tasks either produced or which reach the customer (depending upon the operational definition of "quality") that contain defects to the total number of products or tasks either produced or that reach the customer (depending upon the operational definition of "quality") is equal to 1 minus twice the Z-score associated with 6 standard deviations.

Software subsystems — policies, procedures, their interdependence, and their interactions.

Special variation — also known as "random" causes, vary outside upper and lower control limits of a process; occur more frequently when system is out of control.

Stakeholder-driven quality — broader definition of customer-driven quality to include all stakeholders.

Stakeholders — all of the people affected by a process or organization; for a business, the stakeholders include stockholders, employees, suppliers, and customers.

Standard deviation — the geometric mean divided by the square root of the number of values.

STAR — standardized tests in California.

State award programs — listed alphabetically in Appendix F.

Statistical analysis — the objective of statistical analysis is to make decisions about a process under conditions of uncertainty and imperfect information.

Statistical control chart — see *Shewhart control chart*.

Statistical control methods — basic, intermediate, and advanced tools.

Statistical frame — a list of all sampling units in a given population.

Statistical process control (SPC) — developed at the Western Electric Bell Labs factory in Chicago during the 1930s, SPC techniques were expanded by Shewhart and his colleagues as an efficient method for controlling the quality of mass-produced goods. SPC uses statistically valid methods for the collection of statistics and provides statistically valid feedback to those statistics, using measured responses to do both quality assurance and quality control. They were expanded, perfected, and successfully applied to the mass production of weapons and war materials during World War II.

Statistical quality control (SQC) — using scientific quality management to perform quality control instead of quality assurance.

Statistical quality control chart — a Shewhart control chart used for the purposes of statistical quality control.

Statistical thinking — scientific quality management plus management by fact.

Statistics — the academic discipline concerning the systematic classification, collection, interpretation, and tabulation of numeric data as a basis for the formation and testing of hypotheses.

Stockholders — individuals and institutions who own shares of publicly traded companies.

System variation — common and special variation in a system.

Systemic cause of problems — a reason why a problem occurred that was identified by using a process orientation, when the problem can be corrected by modifying the system.

Systemic interrelationships — systems theories applied to organization relationships; methods of understanding how processes fit together to form systems.

Systems approach — one of eight models of policy analysis; the idea that rules are promulgated and events occur as a result of the interaction of systems.

Systems theory — the theoretical basis of the systems approach.

Taylor, Frederick W. — one of the most influential contributors to the field of management science; the theorist credited with the creation of the field and organizational theory.

Teamwork — the encouragement for the distribution of responsibility between several people rather than one, acting upon a basis of consensus and cooperation.

Theory X — assumptions about individual motivation and leadership; command-and-control structure; information flows up; orders flow down; people are inherently lazy and require direction.

Theory Y — people want to do a good job, so they should be allowed some limited autonomy within a limited area ("kept on a leash"); orders are discussed between a subordinate and superordinate before they are finalized, but the final decision is the superordinate's.

Theory Z — Japanese management system that stresses deliberative, "bottom-up" collective accountability and decision making, long-term planning, and closer relationships among managers and workers.

Third-party cooperative partnerships — describes mutual-support relationships between faith-based, nonprofit, private firms, and government agencies. Under IRS section 501(c) 3, donations to nonprofit agencies are tax deductible, members serve without pay, and rules are stricter than those applying to private sector corporate boards.

Time-motion studies — a study that attempts to maximize efficiency by analysis and modification of what individual workers physically do to perform their tasks.

"Top-down" management — see *Theory X.*

Total care concept — dividing employees into "permanent" employees and those "on probation"; "permanent" employees receive in-house travel agency services, assistance in locating child and elderly care facilities, assistance in placing children in schools, locating housing, etc.; dual-career couple recruiting and employee assistance programs are used.

Total Quality Control (TQC) — (1) the Japanese model of quality control that uses FIIS, statistical process control, statistical quality control, and total care concept for both quality assurance and quality control. Ishikawa and Taguchi are known for TQC. This definition of TQC is also known as *companywide quality control*. (2) a model of total quality improvement first espoused by Armand V. Feigenbaum.

Total Quality Management (TQM) — (1) attempts to prevent defects instead of catching them after they have been made, (2) involves participative management, (3) is oriented towards both identifying and satisfying both internal and external customers, (4) drives out fear, and (5) establishes pride of workmanship.

Total Quality Service (TQS) — a process of continuous improvement involving all stakeholders in meeting customer expectations by doing the correct things right the first time. Key components of a TQS model are leadership, teamwork, customer-orientation, and systems thinking (Chapter 4, Figure 4.1). They must be carefully balanced to meet the special needs of particular customers for a specific service. Successful leadership for achieving quality and productivity goals is theory based, results-oriented, focused on action, and transformational.

Transportation Security Administration (TSA) — a federal agency established with the passage and subsequent signing of the Aviation and Transportation Security Act of 2001. The TSA was founded as a subdivision of the Department of Transportation; it was reorganized as a division of the Department of Homeland Security in 2003 and has significant responsibility for maintaining security at U.S. seaports and airports

Trivial many — see *necessary many*.

Union of Japanese Scientists and Engineers — see *Japanese Union of Scientists and Engineers*.

User-based quality definitions — quality from the perspective of the academic discipline of marketing systems; a reflection of customers' preferences; developed by David Garvin.

Valid customer requirements — operational definitions of what will fulfill the nonspurious needs or desires of the customer.

Validated measure — an operational measure that has been determined to be statistically valid.

Value-added processes — the results of successful actions to reduce variation within processes and add value without additional cost to customers.

Value-based quality definitions — quality from the perspective of the academic discipline of production management; conformance to design specifications at a reasonable cost; developed by Garvin.

Values — ideas that group members share about desirable goals and purposes.

Variability — see *variation*.

Variable check sheet — check sheet or data record in which a frequency distribution expresses the arithmetic measurements of a process.

Variation — along any and every quality characteristic, no two tasks or products are exactly the same; variation is the way the characteristic varies.

Vendor — those outside an organization from whom an organization purchases goods or services.

Vertical hierarchies — traditional corporate or governmental command-and-control systems that tend to isolate managers, centralize authority, and distance those accountable from their customers. See also, *Theory X*.

Virtual courses — see also, *distance learning*.

Vital few — the few causes that cause the majority of the problems facing a team or manager.

"Voice of the customer" — (1) valid and spurious customer requirements and customer desires; (2) feedback from customers to a vendor about a product or service.

"Voice of the process" —restraints placed by the resources available and practical considerations as to what can be done; developed by William W. Scherkenbach.

Weber, Max — Max Weber is best known as one of the leading scholars and founders of modern sociology, but Weber also accomplished much economic work in the early 20th century. Weber's main contribution to economics and the social sciences was his work on methodology.

Work unit — the basic building block of all quality improvement theories; groups of workers organized in teams having direct contact with customers. See also, *quality improvement teams* and *teamwork*.

Acronyms

AMA — American Medical Association
AQL — Acceptable quality level
BPR — Business process reengineering
BNQA — Baldrige National Quality Award
CBO — Congressional Budget Office
CDF — Cumulative frequency distribution
CEO — Chief executive officer
CFM — Cross-functional management
CON — Certificate of need
CQI — Continuous quality improvement
CRM — Customer relationship management
CzRM — Citizen relationship management
CWQC — Companywide quality control
DHS — Department of Homeland Security*
DRG — Diagnosis-related group
EAP — Employee assistance plan
EDI — Electronic data interchange
EOP — Executive Office of the President (U.S.)*
EU — European Union
FADE — Focus–analyze–develop–execute
FCAT — Florida Comprehensive Achievement Tests
FPL — Florida Power and Light
GAO — Government Accountability Office (U.S.)*
GATT — General Agreement of Trade and Tariffs
GDP — Gross domestic product
GPRA — Government Performance and Results Act
HMO — Health Maintenance Organization
IC — Information Central
IPA — Independent provider affiliate
IPPMC — Integrated project planning and management cycle
ISO — International Standards Organization
JCAHO — Joint Commission on Accrediting Healthcare Organizations
JIT — Just-in-time delivery
JUSE — Japanese Union of Scientists and Engineers
KM — Knowledge Management
MBO — Management by objectives
MNC — Multi-national corporation
MSC — Management by self-control
NAFTA — North American Free Trade Agreement

---

* Denotes U.S. government agency, branch, or commission.

NGT — Nominal group technique
NPR — National Performance Review (Clinton)*
OMB — Office of Management and Budget (U.S.)*
OPM — Office of Personnel Management (U.S.)*
PACE — Planning–activation–control–evaluation
PD — Policy deployment
PDSA — Plan–do–study–act
PIP — Productivity improvement program
PMA — President's Management Agenda (Bush)*
PPBS — Planning–programming–budgeting system
PPO — Preferred Provider Organization
PRO — Physician review organization
QA — Quality assurance
QCC — Quality control circles
QI — Quality improvement
QIDW — Quality in daily work
QIP — Quality improvement program
QIT — Quality improvement team
QM — Quality management
SAT — Scholastic Achievement Tests
SERVQUAL — Methodology for measuring service quality
SPC — Statistical process control
SQC — Statistical quality control
TCC — Total care concept
TPM — Total productivity model
TQC — Total quality control
TQM — Total quality management
TQS — Total quality service
TSA — Transportation Security Agency*

Index

A

absenteeism, 118, 147, 148*fig*, 155
acceptable quality level (AQL), 94
accomplishments, 29, 121, 192, 228, 237
   and Maslow's hierarchy of needs, 118
   in learning how to learn, 121
accreditation, 22, 179
   audit-based, 179, 181
   in education, 249
   in healthcare, 267, 298
accountability, 76, 178, 209, 213, 216,
      217–220, 276*fig*, 299, 309
   clinical, 294
   fiscal, 220
   for results, 35, 195, 249
   for schools, 249
   for solutions, 49
   point-of-contact, 224–225
   privatization and, 22
   problems with, 268
   taxpayers, 249
   to customers, 142, 216, 284
   political, 209, 218, 219, 224
aesthetics, 42
after-sales service, 92, 149
Agor, W., 174
Albrecht, K., 17, 22, 37, 38
Alford, J., 208
American Customer Satisfaction Index
      (ACSI), 24*n*, 170, 230*n*
American Express Co., 16
American Heart Association, 15

American Medical Association (AMA), 271
American On-line (AOL), 16
American Quality Foundation, 21
American Telephone and Telegraph (AT&T),
      34
   case study of Universal Card Services, 56,
      69–72
Ammons, D., 43, 44
andon cord, 53, 84
annual review, 314
Austin, Texas, 194
anxiety, 120
appraisal costs, 152
AQL, see acceptable quality level
Arcaro, J.S., 61
Armijo, L.E., 209
Arndt, A., 266
Atkinson, P.E., 209
Atkinson, R., 251
AT&T, see American Telephone and
      Telegraph
attitude, 60, 91, 117–119, 153, 293–295, 322
   about patients, 275
   about healthcare competition, 275–278
   about patient satisfaction, 278–282
   empowerment and, 51
   Crosby methods and, 95
   Deming methods and, 83, 123
   FPL and, 317
   human resource management and, 109,
      115, 117–119
   Juran Trilogy and, 86
   leadership and, 311

management and, 37
Maslow and, 119
mistrust and, 123
 of citizens, 213
 of *Kaizen,* 93, 118
 of team members, 186
 of TQS, 146, 322
reinvention and, 211
toward government, 213–220, 224
toward globalization, 2–3, 80, 275–278
toward student performance, 244
Auger, D.A., 12
automobile manufacturing, 5*fig,* 80
awards, 188–195
Axland, S., 24

B

Baldrige National Quality Award (BNQA), 8,
 34, 96, 179, 193
 as a model for state awards, 196
 banking and, 110
 criteria for performance excellence, 333
 comparisons with other awards, 179–183
 competition for, 182
 creation of, 182
 education and, 8, 257–262
 examination categories, 333–334
 healthcare and, 8, 289–303
 hotel service and, 114, 135–138
 increases in applications for, 196
 list of winners website, 34, 182
 self-assessment and, 335–339
Baptist Healthcare, xi
Baptist Hospital of Pensacola, Florida, 269
 case study of, 292–295
bar chart, 86
Barquin, R.C., 209
basic tools, 146
Beam, G., 14, 223, 226
Beckett, J., 208
Behn, R., 208, 212, 225
Bemowski, K., 24
benchmarking, 43–44, 51, 64
 in healthcare, 280
benefits, 47, 107, 292, 323
 employee, 93, 103, 155–157, 224
 fringe, 119
 health, 155, 224, 268, 277
 of participation, 11
 of reducing non-value added costs, 141
 of secure work environments, 118

 of teamwork, 122
 to society, 246–247
Bennis, W., 114
Berman, E., 43, 48
Berry, L., 12, 39, 43, 58*fig,* 215, 216, 279, 311
Berry, T., x, 37, 185
Berwick, D.M., 266, 272, 274, 286
Bethleham Steel, 18
BI, BNQA case study of, 101–104
Blakeslee, J.A., 146
Blanchard, L.A., 208
Block, P., 39
BNQA, see also Baldrige National Quality
 Award
Boeing Aerospace Corp., xi
 case study of, 234–238
Bothe, D.R., 63*n*
Boyne, G., 7
Bowling Green (Kentucky) University, 18
Bowman, J., 21, 43, 90, 124, 314, 315
Box, R.C., 208, 209, 210, 223, 225
BPR, see business process reengineering
brainstorming, 90, 108, 151, 285, 310
Brehm, J., 142, 216
breakthroughs, 37, 54, 59*fig,* 84, 86, 96, 122,
 186, 211, 322, 323
Broadhead, J.S., 201
Brown, M.G., 7, 181
Brown, R., 18
Brown, S.A., 22
Burnett, R., 267, 277
Bush, G.W., 21, 188, 209, 211, 220, 228, 229,
 270
business process reengineering (BPR), 6,
 207, 222, 309
business results, 26, 64
 BNQA and, 334
Business-to-Business (B2B) relationships, 10

C

cable TV, 13, 34, 36
California Awards for Performance
 Excellence, 192–193, 199*n*
California Standardized Testing and
 Reporting (STAR) program, 249
Camp, R., 43, 63*n*
Carlzon, J., 113
Carr, D., 11
Carroll, 210
Caterpillar Financial Services Corp.,
 case study of, 169–172

causes of problems, 315
  analysis of, 286, 310
  systemic, 54, 84
cause-and-effect diagram, 146, 272, 286
certificates of need, 271
CFM, see cross functional management
chain reaction of quality improvement,
    80–81
Chambers, D., 63*n*
Champy, J., 39
change, adapting to, 318–319
charters, 177–178
  indexed guide to website, 198*n*
charter marks, 178–179
check list, 318
check sheet, 146
Chief Financial Officers Act, 211
China, 2–3, 18, 23*n*, 276
Chuan, T.K., 177, 188
Citigroup, xi, 46, 56, 107, 146, 323
  case study of universal card services,
    69–72
citizen
  complaints, 110, 312
  defining needs of, 176
  demands, 208, 216, 246
  expectations, 11, 224
  participation, 10–11, 179, 199*n*
  responsibilities, 219
Citizen Relationship Management (CzRM),
    215–217
Clarke American Checks, 34
Clarke, J.P., 99*n*
Clausing, D., 63*n*, 93
Clemmer, J., 37
Code of Hammurabi, 74
Coe, C., 43, 44
Cole, R., 7, 54
Columbia University, 19
commitment, xiii, 17, 21, 35, 61, 74, 301–302,
    308, 319–323
  community, 131
  for empowerment, 27, 48
  management, 41, 114, 127, 280, 308
  personal, 112, 115, 126–127, 288, 309,
    319–320
  public sector and, 194, 196, 212
  to CQI, 59, 78, 95, 114, 142, 168, 194,
    280, 291, 297
  to the customer, 111, 163, 180, 235, 323
  to TQS, 44–45, 115

quality education and, 242, 251, 300
  quality theory and, 94
common variation, 93, 100*n*, 144–146
communication, 4, 9, 48, 111, 124–125, 156,
    188, 190*fig*, 237, 257, 276*fig*, 290,
    293, 297, 299, 309
  channels, 123
  cross-functional, 47, 55, 173, 187, 281
  Deming Prize and, 180
  empowerment and, 48, 51
  global, 9
  internal, 51, 57
  interpersonal, 117, 165
  labor-management, xii
  leadership and, 127
  training, xiii,
company-wide quality control (CWQC), 37,
    78, 93, 116, 131*n*, 311,
  origins and evolution of, 78
competition, 12–13, 21, 188, 165, 313, 320
  BNQA and, 182–183
  CQI and, 59
  global, xiii, 2, 4, 6, 11, 16, 20, 36, 83,
    309, 319
  in education, 20, 24*n*, 61, 247, 253–254
  in government, 210–211, 222–223
  in healthcare, 267, 270, 274, 275–278
  market-based, xiii, 16, 208–209, 220, 222,
  managed, 15, 312
  outsourcing and, 188
  performance appraisal and, 124, 314
  service quality and, xiv, 141, 156. 169
competitiveness, 311, see also specific topics
  international, xiii, 3, 8, 12, 59, 100*n*, 159,
    276
  governmental, 183, 185, 210–211
  Malcolm Baldrige National Quality
    Award, 183
  Toyota and, 92
  United States and, xiv, 8
complaints, 28, 30, 49, 56, 188, 318, 326*fig*
  citizen, 110, 311
  customer, 13, 16–17, 28, 68, 113, 133,
    148*fig*, 153, 155, 178, 320
  employee, 57, 122
  patient, 278, 280–282, 301
conformance, 42, 85
  design, 41
  price of, 150–151
  quality of, 40
  to requirements, 94–95, 184, 332

to standards, 40*fig,* 150
Confucious (Chinese Philosopher), 33
Congressional Budget Office (CBO), 211,
    230*n*
consensus building, 108*fig*
consistency, 57, 115, 155–156, 167, 291, 306,
    320
constancy of purpose, 81
continuous quality improvement (CQI), xi,
    6, 35, 58–59, 129, 207, 307, 320
    in healthcare, 266
    human resource management and, 129
    origins and evolution of, 58–59
    changing definitions of, 39–43
Contract with America, 221
control center, 87
control chart, 87
controllable quality costs, 151
coordination and cooperation,
    intragovernmental, 173
    intergovernmental, 173
Coplin, W., 44
Corning Glass Works, 101*n*
corrections, 13, 216
corrective action, 331
cost-benefit analysis, 92–93, 156, 246–247
cost containment, 154, 159, 266–268, 271,
    278, 310–311
costs of poor quality,147–154
    analysis, 272
    direct, 152
    eliminating, 159
    indirect, 153
    in healthcare, 82, 286
    hidden, 63*n,* 150, 283
    reducing, 59–60, 127, 147–149, 307
    visible, 60, 149
CQI, see continuous quality improvement
credibility, 42, 114, 197
Crosby, P., 37, 38*fig,* 60, 62*n,* 94–96, 121n,
    326–327
    absolutes, 94–95
    Eternally Successful Organizational Grid
        (Appendix A), 326–327
    Fourteen Steps, 331–332
cross-functional, 20, 44
    communication, 173
    coordination, 272
    integration, 42
    management (CFM), 20, 31, 38, 47, 56,
        111,

see also, horizontal management
    and FEDEX, 31, 46
    planning, in healthcare organization,
    teams, 46, 71, 111, 164, 186, 275
        in healthcare, 267
    total quality service and, 37, 44
Custom Research, Inc.,
    case study of, 166–169
customer, see also external customer;
        internal customer
    commitment to, 111, 163, 180, 235, 323
    expectations, x, 7–8, 22, 39, 42, 53, 110,
        122, 153, 166, 234, 275, 305
    healthcare, see patient
    needs, internal and external, 21–23
    retention, 113, 137, 153, 234
customer-defined quality, 35, 55, 141
customer feedback, xiii, 45, 50, 166, 280
customer focus, 71, 104, 233, 300
    quality improvement and, x
BNQA and, 333
customer orientation, 60, 108*fig,* 129, 308,
    319
customer quality characteristics, 50, 278, 301
customer contact requirements, 48, 73, 142,
    278
Customer Relationship Management (CRM),
    44, 207
customer responsiveness training, 113
customer retention, 113, 137, 234
customer satisfaction, 9, 16, 21–23, 24*n,*
        26–32, 39, 45, 51, 56–58, 64–65,
        69–72, 109–10, 155–156, 178,
        181*fig,* 197, 230*n,* 248, 271, 275,
        282, 286, 288, 316, 321, 323
    BI and, 101–03
    Boeing and, 235
    Caterpillar Financial Services and, 172
    Citigroup Card Service and, 69–2
    Custom Research, Inc. and, 166
    Dana Commercial Credit and, 162–165
    FEDEX and, 30–31
    FPL QIP and, 185
    Los Alamos National Bank and, 133
    Operations Management International
        and, 231–4
    Ritz-Carlton and, 136
        public sector and, 215, 222
        six sigma and, 146
customer service, xi, 11–12, 22, 34, 37, 39,
        52, 55, 93, 97,109, 142, 151–54,

160*n*, 210–212, 222–223, 272, 294,
307, 310, 312, 318
customer service approach, 310
customer–supplier processes, 49–51
customer–supplier relationships, xi, 8, 45,
48–51, 129, 275, 307
in healthcare, 275
customized treatment, 217, 243–244, 305,
308
cutback management, 220, see downsizing
CWQC, see Company-Wide Quality Control

D

Dana Commercial Credit Corp., 34, 140
case study of, 162–165
Dan, S., 187
data systems, 280–281
Davis, Gov. Gray, 35
recall petition and, 35
Davison, J., 177
deadly diseases (Deming's), 81–83
Debia, N.S., 177, 188
Debra robata, 90
decentralization, 14, 217
decision-making processes, 44–45, 217, 222,
228
under conditions of uncertainty, 140
DeFeo, J.A., 16
deLancer Julnes, P., 176, 223, 227, 315
delayering, 47
Dell Computer, xi, 2, 5, 16, 34
complaints about outsourcing, 28
tech support, 28
Delphi method, 108*fig*
Delta Airlines, 16
Deming, W.E., 37, 39, 50, 62*n*, 77, 79–84,
81, 100*n*, 123, 161*n*, 199*n*, 201,
308, 314, 330*n*
Fourteen Points, see also 14 Points, 37,
329–330
Deming Prize, 179–180, 201, 317
FPL and the, 184–188
list of winners website, 199*n*
Department of Defense (DoD), U.S., 228,
314
Department of Education, U.S., 44
deployment flowchart, 50
deregulation, 214, 228
Dervitsiotis, K., 7
design, quality of, 40–41
detecting devices, 124–125, see also, sensor

diagnosis, 84, 86, 143, 275
diagnosis-related groups (DRGs), 273
diagnostic arm, 88
DiIulio, J., 57
direct quality costs, 151
DIRFT, 331
Disney Corp., 107
division of labor, 75
DoD, see Department of Defense
Donaldson, L., 176
Douglas, T.J., 7
Dow Chemical Corp., 4
downsizing, xiv, 17, 209–210, 220, see also
cutback management
Drath, W.H., 315
drive out fear, 157, 329
Drucker P., 38, 314
Dual Factor Theory, 119, 157, see also
Maslow
durability, 42
Durant, R.F., 209
Durst, S.L, 210

E

EAP, see Employee Assistance Plan
e-commerce, x, 8, 10, 15, 16
e-government, 44, 188, 194, 212
initiatives, 10, 209, 211, 230*n*
technology and, 10, 179
education, 239–264
as service and product, 6
business, 19
classroom instruction and, 243–245
curriculum quality and, 247–248
decentralized structure of, 239
defining quality in, 6, 240–243
drop-out rates in, 240
federalism and, 239–240
fiscal policy and resource management,
246–247
for self-improvement, 111, 115–116
improving processes, 243–248
learning customer-driven TQS and, 17–22
measuring results in, 248–253
national performance standards and,
249–253
public sector and, x,
quality improvement in, 243
rewarding quality reform in, 183,
253–255
school quality review teams and, 252

teacher education and, 243–245

EDI, see electronic data interchange

effectiveness, 159, 190, 192, 197, 212, 218–219, 226, 246, 249, 270, 282, 316

efficiency, xiv, 4–5, 16, 159, 187, 190*fig*, 196, 209, 212, 214, 218–219, 226, 312, 317
    chain reaction of quality and, 81
    defined, 154
    in education, 253
    in healthcare, 252, 274, 285
    of government services, 13, 192, 197, 222
    scientific management and, 75

Eggers, W.D., 12

ego satisfaction, 118

Eisenhower Professional Development Program, 245

Elfenbein, P., 274

Electronic Data Interchange (EDI), xii, 9, 22

employee
    assistance plan (EAP), 93
    benefits, 93, 103, 155–157, 224, see benefits
    empowerment, 27, 45, 51, 139, 210, 216–217, 305–306
    involvement, 158, 167, 236
    motivation, 81, 197, 251
    participation, 21, 50, 78, 100*n*, 111, 306, 313
    responsibility, 22
    retention, 52, 101, 104, 156, 172, 292, 298, 303
    turnover, 65, 136, 148*fig*, 295, 327*fig*

empowerment, 22, 27, 51–53, 57, 61, 76, 129, 215–217, 305–306
    bureaucracy and, 215
    citizen relationship management and, 215–217
    of employees, 39, 45, 51–53, 132–134, 310, 317
    of teachers, 248–251
    Theory X and, 142, 313
    Theory Y and, 52

enthusiasm, 121, 142, 248, 258

entropy, 41

Enron Corp., 4, 181, 213, 228

"Enron effect", 213

environment, 50*fig*, 122
    healthcare, 267, 272–273, 275, 283, 291–293, 312

improving workplace, 39, 51, 81, 90, 118, 236, 260, 308, 314

learning, 114–117, 120–121, 252, 257

political, 176, 207, 243

QIDW and, 112

Environmental Protection Agency (EPA), 10, 174

error cause removal, 327, 332

Eternally Successful Organization Grid (Appendix A), 326–327

European Union (EU), 14–15
    and trade liberalization, 15

European Quality Awards, 181, 194

Evans, J.R., x, 54

Exemplary State and Local (EXCL) Awards, 189–191

expectations, x, 7–8, 22, 39, 42, 53, 110, 122, 153, 166, 234, 275, 305

experiential learning, 116

extended process model, 49, 113
    in healthcare, 279

external customer, needs of, 21–22, 51, 113, 305

F

facilitator, 90, 111, 186

FADE, see
        Focus–Analyze–Develop–Execute, 55

Fargher, J., 63*n*

fear, 57, 121, 308
    of change, 310
    freedom from, 118–122
    managing and, 118–120
    public sector and, 157
    work environment and, 52, 322

features, 40, 41–42, 77, 157, 224
    of quality control circles, 91
    of *Kanban* systems, 93
    of state quality awards, 196

Federal Express (FEDEX), xi, 107
    case study of, 29–32
    1:10:100 Rule, 30
    service quality indicators, 31

federal government, quality management in, 11, 157

federal procurement standards, 14, 44, 160*n*

Federal Workforce Restructuring Act, 211

FEDEX, see also Federal Express

Federalism, 196, 213, 219, 224, 239

feedback, 50*fig*, 88–89, 120–122, 144*fig*

BNQA and, 253–254
corrective actions and, xiii
cycle, 110n
developing a TQS culture and, 45
diagnostic arm and, 88
education and, 248
employee, 128–129
external, 57, 60
FEDEX and, 29
monitoring results and, 50, 56, 166–168
patient, 280–282, 291
sensing device and, 87
service standards and, 178
statistical control and, 140
voice of the client and, 68
feedback loop, 87, 124–125, 144*fig*
fee-for-service healthcare, 266
Feigenbaum, A.V., 62n, 88–89
financial services, 15, 66–69, 96, 105, 107,
        131–134, 162–165, 169–172, 308
BNQA and, 183
Caterpillar Financial and, 146, 169
Citigroup and, 69
Dana Commercial Credit and, 163
Los Alamos National Bank and, 131
Merrill Lynch and, 66
similarities with other services, 308
USAA and, 96, 105
Fisher, C., 194
fitness for use, 85
flattening hierarchies, 316
flexibility, 60, 79, 132, 164, 132–133, 166,
        216, 292, 305, 309
Florida Comprehensive Achievement Tests
        (FCAT), 249
Florida Health Care and Insurance Reform
        Act, 277
Florida Power & Light Company (FPL),
        184–188, 200–202, 306, 318
case study of, 200–202
Deming Prize and, 184–188
flow chart, 49, 146
Flynn, B., 188
focus group, 285–286
Focus–Analyze–Develop–Execute Cycle, 55
follow-up services, 35
Fontenot, G., 146
Forbes, L., xvii
Ford, H., 17, 75
Ford Foundation *Innovations in American
        Government Awards*, 189–191

Ford Motor Company, 4, 18, 34
Forrer, J, 209
Forrester Research, 13
Fountain, J., 177, 209
Fourteen Points, see Deming, W.E.
FPL, see Florida Power & Light Company
Franciscan Sisters of Mercy, SSM Healthcare,
        289–292
Fredrickson, G., 208
fulfillment, 91, 118, 122
Furlong, G.P., x
functional teams, 186
funnel experiment, 83, 124

G

Gaebler, T., 14, 220, 224
Gain sharing, 51, 63n, 156, 158, 314, 321
Galloway, R.A., 43
GAO, see Government Accountability Office
gap analysis, 57–58
Gartman, J.B., 63n
Garvin, D.A., 41–42, 112
Gass, G.L., 97
GDP, see also Gross Domestic Product
General Accounting Office (GAO), see also
        Government Accountability
        Office, 39
General Electric (GE), 146
General Motors, 4, 18, 276
Germany, 2
Gibbons, S., xii
Gilbert, R., x, 22, 39
Gilbreth, F., 38*fig*
Gilbreth, L., 38*fig*
Ginnodo, W.L., 158
Giovannetti, E., 9
Gitlow, H., x, 62n, 120, 123, 146
globalization,
        competition and, xiii
            ISO 9000 and, 51, 180–181
        environment and, ix
        knowledge management and, 179
        service markets and, ix
Globe Metallurgical, 99n
GNP, see Gross National Product
goal setting, 314, 332
Goldhaber, D., 244
Goldsmith, S., 12, 188, 209, 210
Goodsell, C., 215
goodwill, 155, 159
Gordon, G., 75, 77, 211, 220, 228

Gore, A., 14, 207, 210, 220
government, 15, 46, 74, 176–177, 196,
    207–238,
  BNQA and, 182
  comparisons with other countries, 209
  customer satisfaction and, 24n, 44, 161n,
    230n
  education and, 241–242, 245–246,
  electronic, 10, 44, 179, 188, 194, 209,
    211–212, 230n
  empowerment and, 216, 227
  downsizing, 17, 210, 220
  inefficiencies, 13
  improving performance in, 183, 211, 215,
    227, 306
  gain sharing and, 156
  group conflicts and, 12, 217–218
  healthcare and, 267–268, 273–274
  innovation in, 13–14, 189
  market-driven, 209, 225, 228
  productivity and, 219
  public administration and, 218
  quality awards in, 190–191fig, 195, 200n,
    341–343
  reinvention, 14, 189, 197, 207, 210, 221
  regulation, xiii, 6, 13
  results-driven, 44, 57, 228
  services, 5, 22, 34, 192,
  third-party, 12, 15, 223
  total quality public service and, 173
  to business exchanges (G2B), 10
  to citizen transactions (G2C), 10
  trust in, 16, 214, 227, 208, 212–215,
    214fig, 224, 226–229, 227fig
Government Accountability Office (GAO),
  211, 230n
Government Performance and Results Act
  (GPRA), 24n, 181, 211, 230n
GPRA, see Government Performance and
  Results Act
Greebler-Schepper, C., 314
Green, R., 188
Griffin, A., 63n
Gronland, S., 177, 209
Groocock, J.M., 81
Gross Domestic Product (GDP), x, 2
Gross National Product (GNP), 82, 268, 276
groups,
  formal, 117
  informal, 117
Guyna, F., 100n

guilds, 74

H

Hackman, J., 7
Hammer, M., 39
Haque, M., 176, 208
hardware, 109
Harrington, H.J., 151
Harvard University, 189
Hauser, H.R., 63n
Hauser, J.R., 63n
healthcare, 265–303
  BNQA and, 183, 199n
  continuous quality improvement in,
    56fig, 266, 270–275
  costs of, 266–270, 268fig, 277
  deadly diseases and, 82
  fraud and abuse, 265
  hidden and visible costs of, 148, 274
  implementing organization-wide quality,
    284–287
  managed competition, 15, 275–278
  public administration and, 213
  shifting national priorities for, 266–270
  strategies for measuring patient
    satisfaction, 278–284
  systemic programs in, 265–266
  total quality, 266, 285
  universal, 100n, 266–267, 276–277, 312
health insurance, excessive costs, 268
health maintenance organization (HMO),
  266–267
Heeks, R., 177,209
Heinrich, C., 177
Hellein, R., 21, 43
Hendricks, K.B., 194
Herzberg, F., 119, 157
Hewlett-Packard Corp., 2, 16, 18
hidden plant, 89
hierarchical management, 76, see also,
  Theory X
  command and control, 76
  structures, 47
  vertical, 9
hierarchy, flattening the, 45
hierarchy of needs, 118
high performance, xii, 46, 188, 305
  service organizations, xii
higher education, 17–20, 24n, 35, 42, 61,
    239–241, 245
Hill, C.W.L.,14

histogram, 86, 146, 27
HMO, see Health maintenance organization
Ho, A.T., 177
Hodge, G., 12, 207,211
Hoffer, E., 107
Hogan, R., xii
Holzer, M., 189, 215
Homeland Security (DHS), Department of, 174
horizontal management, 10
  service networks, 10
Hudiberg, J., 200
Hufbauer, G., 14
human relations, 18, 37, 76, 257, 308
human resources, 29, 107–138, 147, 164, 180–181, 327*fig*
  characteristics of, 110
  facilitators and, 186
  improvement guidelines for, 111–112
  management of, 110
  organizational behavior and, 77
  productivity and, 116
  teamwork and, 350
  total quality service training and, 53, 110–111, 127–129
human sensors, 140, 284
humanware, 109–110
Hunt, D., x
Hyatt Hotels, 107

I

IBM, 2, 4
Imai, M., 92, 125
incentives, xi, 8, 24*n*, 34, 59, 101–104, 133, 149, 222, 225, 274–275
  gain sharing and, 156, 158
  removing dissatisfiers and, 157
  rewards as, 173, 180, 189, 197, 222, 315, 321
  tax, 165
independence, 118, 241
India, 3, 10, 18, 28, 176, 180
Indiana Statewide Test of Education Progress Plus (ISTEP+), 249
indirect quality costs, 151–154
industrial cycle, 89
Industrial Revolution, 1, 4, 74–76
information, ix, 9, 91, 124, 141, 144, 228,
  analysis and, 181*fig*, 234–238, 254
  BNQA and, 181
  central, 29, 186,

exchange, 12–13, 173, 196, 209
healthcare and, 271, 279*fig*, 281–287, 294
Internet and, 8
knowledge and, 177, 334
lines, 124–125
technology and (IT), 9, 13, 32, 71, 133–138, 166, 242, 171, 178, 195, 242, 294
sensor and, 87
Ingraham, P.W., 14
innovation, 13, 92, 132, 174, 187–192, 195, 198*n*, 222, 313
input, xiii, 6, 11, 154, 161*n*, 281,
inspection, 40*fig*, 75–78, 95, 111, 123–124, 148*fig*, 152, 276*fig*, 309, 329, 331
insurance, 16, 22, 149, 212, 274–275,
  healthcare, 82*n*, 147, 265–270, 279*fig*, 312
  hierarchies, 47
  liability, 21, 74, 283
  malpractice, 148
  USAA, 96–97, 105, 308
interchangeability of parts, 75
Intel Corp., 2, 5, 34
internal customer, 50, 78, 234
  definition of quality, 40, 50
  needs of, 21–23
Internal Revenue Service (IRS), 10,
  Section 501[c]3 organizations, 12, 189, 196
International Baccalaureate (IB) system, 252
International Standards Organization, see also ISO 9000
Internet, 4, 8–11, 10, 105, 111, 131, 134, 242,
interviews, 198*n*, 234, 254, 280, 303
IRS, see Internal Revenue Service
Ishikawa, K., 37, 49, 62*n*, 89–94
ISO 9000, 51, 179–181, 209, 313

J

Japan, 2, 3*fig*, 60,
  approach to total quality control, 60–61,
  impact on U.S. manufacturing, 20–21, 98
  origins and evolution of total quality control, 78, 89
  quality control circles in, 91–94
Japanese Union of Scientists and Engineers, 37, 38*fig*, 199*n*
JCAHO, see Joint Commission on Accrediting Healthcare Organizations
JIT, see *kanban* or just-in-time

job descriptions, 115, 315
job security, 47, 74, 81, 119, 201
Johnson, C.N., 19, 24*n*
Johnson and Johnson Corp., 34*n*
Joint Commission on Accrediting Healthcare
       Organizations (JCAHO), 271
Jordan, A., 209
Juran, J.M., 1, 16, 37, 62*n*, 84–88, 100*n*, 150,
       161*n*
Juran Trilogy, 85
JUSE, see Union of Japanese Scientists and
       Engineers,
just-in-time (JIT) or *kanban*, 92, 181*fig*, 242

K

kaizen, 86, 111, 116–118, see also
       continuous quality improvement
kanban, 92, 181*fig*, 242
Kanigel, R., 23*n*
Kano, N., 52, 93, 109
Kansai Electric Company, 201
Katzenbach, J.R., 46
Keehley, P., 43, 44
Kelman, S., 14
Kember, D., 61
Kettl, D., 11, 57, 177, 210, 223, 224,225
King, B., 63*n*
Kim, P., 210
Knight-Ridder, 107
knowledge management (KM), x, xiii, 9,10,
       173–175, 178, 194, 205, 209, 236,
       308, 334
   BNQA and, 334, 337
   defined, 371
   developmental assistance and, 9
   globalization and, 179
   linking databases, 174, 194
knowledge revolution, 4–9, 75, 313
Koch, J., 7, 19
Kodak, 146
Koehler, J.W., 188
Kolb, D., 116, 128
Koppich, J., 245
Korea, 3*fig*, 18
Kravchuk, R.S., 43

L

labor-management committees, 115, 156
law enforcement, x, xi, 13, 43, 44, 60, 142,
       153,195, 212, 216, 221, 311

lawyers, 82
leadership, 64, 81, 83, 108*fig*, 181*fig*,
       305–325, 333
   BNQA and, 205–207, 232–237, 254, 333
   challenges, 220, 305, 315, 319–323
   commitment by, 61, 114
   communication and, 127–128
   defined, 322
   empowerment and, 306
   focus,117
   for change, 83, 86, 87, 125, 127
   for achieving high-performance quality
       improvement, x, 306
   for service quality improvement, 305–323
   multi-national corporations and, 5
   performance excellence and, 302–303
   roles redefined, 10
   social responsibility and, 205–206, 299
   theories, 78
   training, 127–130, 133
   TQS and, 108*fig*, 142, 308
lead teams, 186
Leighton, R., 43, 48
less developed countries (LDCs), 9
Levering, R., 24*n*
liability costs, 82, 147, 150
Liebowitz, J., x
lifelong employment, 100*n*
Lillrank, P., 93
Liswood, L., 113
Littman, I., 11
L.L. Bean, 107
local governments, 46, 173, 212, 312
Loew's Hotels, 108
Los Alamos National Bank, 110
   case study of, 131–134
lower control limit, 87
Lumney, K., 189

M

MacGregor, D., 9, 52, 77
Malcolm Baldrige National Quality Award,
       see Baldrige National Quality
       Award (BNQA)
managed healthcare, 266, 273–276
   changing attitudes toward, 266
managed competition, 15, 277, 312
management, see also specific systems
   control systems, 21
   by exception, 108
   by fact, FPL QIP and, 29, 67, 185

by objectives (MBO), 37, 88, 108, 314
by self-control (MSC), 88
   human resource, 109
participatory, 76, 92, 157, 158, 216
performance, 142, 178, 181*fig*, 182, 189,
   197, 207–229, 278, 290, 302, 306
productivity, 4
systems, xi, 3, 5, 7, 9, 14, 17, 37, 39, 55,
   58*fig*, 139, 175
manifest destiny, 1
manufacturing, ix, 4, 9, 18, 38*fig*, 96, 109
   BNQA and, 182–183
   China and, 23*n*
   comparisons between services and, 5,
      149, 188, 308
   competition and, 35
   entrophy and, 41
   healthcare, 272
   Japan and, 41, 49, 93, 98
   market share and, 80
   origins and evolution of quality control
      in, 38*fig*, 36–39
   U.S. economy and, 2–3, 20, 313
manufacturing-based quality, ix
marketing, 39
market-based models, 208
market share, 4, 5, 6, 63, 66, 69, 74, 223,
   291, 297
   losses in, 5, 80, 153, 319
   improving, 6, 11, 21, 35, 48–49, 80, 107,
      220, 223, 274
Marriott Corporation, xi, 108
Maryland Center for Quality and
   Productivity, 199*n*
Maslow, A., 118, 322
mass inspection, 123
mass production, 2–5
Masternak, R.L., 63*n*
matrix organization, 76
MBO, see Management by objectives
MBQA, see Malcolm Baldrige National
   Quality Award
McDonald's Corp., 2
measurement, 9, 39, 52, 124–126, 136,
   139–154, 144*fig*, 159, see also
   statistical analysis
   characteristics, 86, 101, 109, 140, 154,
      285, 310
   educational, 249, 252–254
   healthcare, 27–275, 285–287, 291, 295,
      299

key indicators, 57
performance, 192, 224, 227, 299, 306,
   315, 321
Medicaid, 82, 224, 268, 270, 274, 275, 277
medical costs, see Healthcare
Medicare, 82, 224, 268–270, 273, 274, 275
Medicare Prescription Drug Improvement
   and Modernization Act of 2003,
   269–270
merit system, 314, 316
Merrill Lynch Credit Corp. (MLCC), 50
   case study of, 66–69
   empowerment and, 68
   voice of the client and, 68
Metlife, 107
Microsoft Corp., 2, 5, 18, 34
Milakovich, M.E., xiii, 7, 11, 12, 16, 34, 44,
   111, 142, 157, 176, 183, 188, 211,
   216, 217, 220, 223, 228, 266, 288,
   316, 320
Miller, H.T., 210
Miller, J., 266, 277
Milliken & Company, 101*n*
mission, xi, 34, 39, 40*fig*, 48, 53, 81, 119,
   BNQA, 183
   educational, 242, 254, 257–263
   FPL, 184
   Monfort College of Business, 203–206
   PSEA, 192
   public sector and, 177, 192, 217, 225, 241
   pyramid concept and, 136
mission statement, 158, 164, 170, 312, 317
   healthcare, 281, 285, 287, 289, 290, 300,
      302
Monfort College of Business, University of
   Northern Colorado, 19
   BNQA and, 203–206
   case study of, 202–205
monitoring results, xi, 45, 57, 140, 139–172,
   318
Moon, M. J., 177
morale, 60, 83, 126, 136, 148*fig*, 155–156,
   159, 201, 234, 295, 315
moments of truth, 113
Morgan, C., 61
Moskowitz, M., 24*n*
Motwani, J., 266
motivation, xii, 8, 9, 41, 42, 81, 82, 185, 198,
   215, 223, 228, 242
   intrinsic, 122
   external, 119

motor device, 87
Motorola Corp., 34, 100*n*
    six sigma and, 146
MSC, see management by self-control
Mt. Edgecumbe High School, Alaska, 255
    case study of, 262–263
multi-national corporations (MNCs), 2, 3, 4,
        8
multivoting, 108*fig*
Murgatroyd, S., 61

N

NAFTA, see North American Free Trade
        Agreement
Nakhai, B., 188
Nanus, B., 114
National Institute for Standards and
        Technology (NIST), 195
National Performance Review (NPR), 210
National Public Service (NPSA) Awards,
        189–191
National Quality Improvement Act, 182
necessary many, 86
Neiman, M., 215
network model, 10, 319
    barriers to, 34
New Mexico State Quality Award, 110
New York Life, 107
New York State Police, 43
NIST, see National Institute for Standards
        and Technology
No Child Left Behind Act, 249
Nokia Corp., 5
nominal group technique, 108*fig*, 310
nonmarket driven services, xi, 34, 45
    challenges for, 12
    defined, 34
    frustration levels with, 35
non-conformance, price of, 150
non-government organizations (NGOs), 9,
        12, 209, 219, 220, 222, 247
    partnerships with, 12
non-market sector, continued neglect of, 16
non-profit organizations, 15
    challenges for, 34
non-value-added costs, 9, 48, 59, 140, 142,
        148, 151, 308, 315
    elimination of, 48, 59, 140, 157,
North American Free Trade Agreement
        (NAFTA), 14–15

NPR, see National Performance Review,

O

Oestreich, D., 118
Office of Electronic Government, 211
Office of Management and Budget (OMB),
        211, 230*n*
Office of Personnel Management (OPM),
        24*n*, 191*fig*, 231*n*
Ohmae, K., 101*n*
Ohne fehler, 90
oil consumption,
    and China, 3
    global, 3
Oliver, W., 12
Omachonu, V.K., x, 54, 288
OMB, see Office of Management and Budget
Ombudsman, 224
on-time delivery, 8, 29,235, 236, 323
open system, 117, 128
operational definitions of customer
        requirements, 141, 329
operational measures of customer
        characteristics, 141, 142, 155, 310
Operations Management International
        (OMI), 34
    case study of, 231–234
OPM, see Offic of Personnel Management
Oppenheim, A., 100*n*
Oppenheim, R., 100*n*
Oracle Corp., 18
Oregon State University, 19
organizational behavior, 37, 77, 109–111,
        117–118
organizational humanism, 119
organizational socialization, 127–128
organizational theory, 52
organizational values, 40*fig*, 174, 215
Osborne, D., 14, 209, 224, 226
Ouchi, W., 39, 77
output, 5, 6, 35, 56,90, 116, 142, 155, 161*n*,
        313
    statistical process control and, 144–145
outsourcing, xiv, 8, 17, 28, 36, 188, see also,
        downsizing
    Dell, case study of, 28
    implications of, 13
    in healthcare, 269
Overcontrol, dangers of, 83, 120, 123
Overspecialization, 315

P

PAA, see personal application assignment
PACE, see planning, activation, control, evaluation
Palatine, Illinois, school district, 244
case study of, 257–260
Pal's Sudden Service
benchmarking and, 63
case study of, 63–66
Parasuraman, A., 13, 39, 43, 57, 58*fig*, 215, 217, 279, 311
Pareto method, 87, 222
analysis, 86, 146, 151, 310
diagram, 272
principle, 85
participation, see also human resource management
participatory management, 76, 92, 157, 158, 216
partnerships, 188
cooperative, 12
patient privacy, 287
patient satisfaction, strategies for measuring, 278–284
Patton, Gen. George S., 305
Paul Revere, 107
PCMI, see President's Council on Management Improvement
PD, see Policy Deployment
PDSA, see plan–do–study–act
Pearl River, New York, School District, 183, 199*n*, 252, 342
case study of, 260–262
Peckenpaugh, J., 215
Pegnato, J., 142, 216, 223
perceived quality, 42, 270
performance, quality of, 41
and the need to improve, 175–177
performance appraisal, 123–124
performance management, 142, 178, 181*fig*, 182,189, 197, 207–229, 278, 290, 302, 306
assessing alternatives for, 208
public trust and, 209
Performance Management Agenda (PMA), 211
performance measurement, 88, 176, 177, 192, 224, 227, 299, 306, 321
personal application assignment (PAA), 121, 124

personal commitment, 112, 115, 285, 309, 320, 321
Peters, T., 24*n*, 39
physical surroundings, 109, see also environment
Physician Review Organizations (PRO), 271
pinches, 124
PIP, see Productivity Improvement Program
plan–do–study–act (PDSA), 53, 54, 56*fig*, 59, 79, 93, 187, 260, 261
FPL QIP and, 185
planning, x, 22, 26, 31, 65–67, 105, 110, 114, 126, 137, 187, 189, 232, 271, 297
annual, 169
business, 67, 132
cross-functional, 285
cycles, 53, 54, 85, 101
enterprise, 236
financial, 290
Juran method and, 85–86
long-term, 194
PPBS and, 108, 320
public administration and, 228
quality, 69,150, 161, 285
strategic, 26, 52, 64, 102, 117, 136–137, 181, 189, 205, 236, 254, 260, 290, 299–302, 333–336
planning–activation–control–evaluation (PACE), 53–54
planning–programming–budgeting–system (PPBS), 108, 320
pluralism, 12
Poka-Yoke, 93
policy deployment (PD), at FPL, 184
poor quality, cost of, see Cost of poor quality
Postal Service, U.S., 242
Postman, N., 241
PPBS, see planning–programming–budgeting –system
PPO, see preferred provider organization
Preferred provider oganization (PPO), 267
Preuss, G., xii
Presidential Award for Quality, 189–191
prevention, 48, 86, 94, 141, 151–152, 154, 272
price of conformance, 150
price of non-conformance, 150
pride, 60, 119, 131, 197
in accomplishment, 121
of workmanship, 129, 158, 330
primary care providers, 275

privatization of public services, 188, 209,
213, 224–225, 228, 239,246, 253
Bush Administration and, 212, 228
Contract with America and, 221
partnerships and, 209
market-driven concepts and, 222
reinvention and, 210
process, 139–172, 40, 54, 64–71, 122, 141,
185–187, 285–288
adding value to, 9, 92, 140, 222,
appraisal, 133
defined, 143
control techniques, 41, 74, 78, 117, 142,
148, 180, 250,
experiential learning and, 116
extended, 49*fig*,
focus, 55
human resource management and, 125
improvement, 21, 34, 37, 40*fig*, 45, 48–49,
53, 57, 102–103, 113, 116, 121, 126,
141, 170, 236, 237, 240, 279,
302–303, 307, 309–310
continuous, x, 85, 86, 117, 123, 140, 148,
159, 163, 260–261
in healthcare, 150, 271–272, 275, 277,
279, 282–288
teams, public sector and, 197
inspection and, 77
learning, 118, 120, 124–126, 242, 251,
254, 301
management, 102, 334, 338
measurement, 25–27, 30–31, 45, 156, 233,
284, 299, 309
orientation, 108, 111, 125, 128
ownership, 39, 51, 142, 167, 216, 236, 307
partnering, 292
problem solving, 54
quality control and, 75
quality control circles and, 90
reengineering, 6, 52, 207
six sigma, 146, 170
statistical control of, xi, 20, 36, 83, 87,
93, 125, 141, 145–147, 313
transformation, 144
variation, 59, 78, 83, 142–145, 250, 307
voice of the, 50–51, 155
1:10:100 Rule and, 30
procurement, 9, 10, 14, 44, 78, 92, 160*n*,
187, 195
productivity, 7–11, 50*n*, 116, 139–171,
154–158, 312

BNQA and, 182
changing definitions of, 99*n*, 156–159,
161*n*,
concepts of, evolution, 37, 40*fig*, 74–77,
Deming and, 79–82,
improvement in, x, 4, 8, 16, 18–19, 45,
61, 92, 104, 110, 154–158, 171, 194,
228
ineffective measurement techniques and,
16, 147, 223, 315, 321,
management of, 3, 18, 306, 315
market share and, 6, 22
public sector, 190–191*fig*, 207–209, 219, 223,
253, 311
quality management and, 47, 57, 59, 84,
157, 159
strategies for, 12, 113, 156
work environment and, 142,
U.S. Senate Awards and, 195, 199*n*, 200*n*
productivity ceiling, 155, 310
professional autonomy, 287–288
Puay, S.H., 177, 182, 195
public administration, 178, 190*fig*, 208, 212,
215, 217–219, 228
public policy, 208, 209, 218–219, 224,
228–229, 245, 267
public safety, see also law enforcement
public sector, 17, 207–238, see also
government
high performance in, xii
innovation, 13, 179, 198*n*
lack responsive in, 11
market-based alternatives to, 224
privatization and, 188, 210, 218
total quality public service, 50
vulnerability of, 13
public services, 11, 46, 283, 297, 207–208,
212–213, 215, 226, 311–312, 318
Public Service Excellence Awards (PSEA),
189–191
purchasing, see also procurement

Q

QA, see Quality assurance
QCC, see Quality control cycle
QDW, see Quality in Daily Work
QI, see quality improvement
QIP, see Quality Improvement Program
QIT, see Quality Improvement Team
quality, see also specific topics
as customer determines, 42

assurance (QA), 6, 18, 77, 150, 153, 180, 244, 266, 312
awards, 177–183, 190–195
BNQA and, 8, 34, 96, 179, 182, 193
changing definitions of,41, 43, 279,
characteristics, 42, 50, 141, 144, 151, 269, 276, 285, 310
consensus, xiii
defined, 41–43, 62, 112
Deming Prize for, 38, 97, 179–180, 184–188,
evolution of, 77–78
healthcare, 266–267, 276
government and public sector, 15, 46, 74, 176–177, 182, 196, 207–238
human resources, 107–129
leadership for, 305–323
multidimensional view of, 42
of conformance, 40–41
of design, 40
of performance, 41
of student performance, 245
origins and evolution of, 58–59
story technique, 90
vision, xiii, 21, 53, 117, 170, 187, 212, 316–317, 321
quality awards, 187–195
quality characteristic, 42, 87
as operational definitions, 141
defined, 141
SMART, 141
quality control, 2, 22, 38*fig*,73–78
concepts of, 39–43
definition of, 39–43
evolution of concepts, 73–78
origins and evolution of, 73–78
quality consensus, xiii
quality control circle (QCC), 90–92, 111
quality function deployment (QFD), 38*fig*,51,
quality improvement (QI), xi, 6, 36, 58–59, 85*fig*, 129, 207, 307, 320,
see also specific topics
as a journey, 21
in healthcare, 276
guidelines for, 111–130
human resources and, 109–111, see also human resource management
leadership for, 305–324
masters of, 78–94
rewarding, 173–197

strategies for, 6–8, 12, 222–226
selection of strongest features and strategies, 12, 96–97
story, 185, 199*n*
teams, 84, 101
theoretical understanding of, 36
Quality Improvement Program (QIP), FPL, 184–185
Quality Improvement Teams (QIT), FPL, 185
Quality in Daily Work (QIDW), 184
quality management, x, 9, 17–19, 34, 42, 60, 88, 122, 146, 180, 210, 266, 308
quality of conformance, 40–41
quality of design, 40
quality of performance, 41

R

random variation, see special variation
rate of process improvement, 141
recognition, 16, 111, 118, 154, 189, see also specific topics
employee, 174, 298
public sector and, 179, 189, 197
of quality, 16, 114, 180,
systems,158, 164
red bead experiment, 83–84, 126
Red Cross, 15
reengineering, 6, 207, 222, 309
referral information services, 281
regulation, government, 10, 14, 111, 176, 210, 217, 271,
of service monopolies, 6
of non-market services, xi
reinventing government, 14, 189, 197, 207, 210, 221
reliability, 5, 8, 36, 41–42, 50, 140, 323
resistance, 7, 14, 34, 61, 79, 82, 86–87, 108, 224, 253, 270–271, 288, 315, 320, 330*n*
resource-based relative value scales, 273
respect for people, 78
FPL QIP and, 185
responsiveness, 21–22, 42, 46, 76,110, 113, 207, 218–219, 305, 310, 315
resultant costs, 151–152
restructuring, 7, 16, 78, 156, 158, 210, 273–274, 283, 315
retention, 52, 101, 104, 156, 172, 292, 298, 303
retirement services, 311
retraining,17, 45, 78, 156, 271, 329–330

return on investment (ROI), 5, 11, 242
revenue collection, 43, 195
rewards, 44, 59, 103–104, 119, 125–126, 127,
    151, 156, 158, 173, 189, 194, 216,
    309, 318
Ricoh, 199*n*
Ritz-Carlton Hotel Company, xi, 108,114
    case study of, 135–138
Robert Wood Johnson Hospital, New Jersey,
    278
    case study of, 296–299
Rochester Institute of Technology, 19
ROI, see also Return on Investment
Romero-Simpson, J.E., 110, 112, 121, 122
root cause, 31
Rosander, A.C., 39
run chart, 146
Russell, G., 210
Ryan, K.D., 118

S

Salamon, L., 12
Samford University, Birmingham, Alabama,
    19
Sanderson, I., 176, 177, 224, 227, 315
Saratov system, 90
Saturn Automotive, 99*n*
Savas, E., 12
Scandinavian Airlines, 38*fig*
scatter diagram, 146
scenario writing, 281
Schaaf, D., 39
Schaeffer, P.V.,12
Scherkenbach, W.W., 50
Schiavo, L., 178
Schmidt, W.H., x
Schneider, B., 22
Scholastic Aptitude Test (SAT), 251
Schwarzenegger, Gov. Arnold, 35
    recall petition and, 35
Scholtes, P., 47, 112, 122, 123, 314
scientific management, 1, 76
scorecards, 141, 164, 260
Sedell, K., 88, 156, 157
self-actualization, 118
self-directed work teams, 71, 309
self-improvement,111–112, 308
    human resource management and,
    115–116
self-managed work teams, 38, 53, 79, 141,
    308

Senate Productivity Award, U.S., 199*n*, 200*n*
Senge, P., x, 53, 143, 174,
sensing device, 87
sensor, 87
Seymour, D., 19
service industries, ix, x, 4, 6, 77, 114, 280,
    310, 313
    contrast with manufacturing, 5, 36, 39
    U.S. work force and, 3,
service networks, horizontal, 10
service quality, x, 21, 35, 96, 108–109, 143,
    149, 216, 222–223, 305, 307
    action strategies for improvement of,
    316–319
    awards and, 197
    BNQA and, 179
    charter marks and, 178
    competition and, 11, 12, 306
    concern with, 34, 39, 151
    definitions of, 42–43
    e-commerce and, 9, 22,
    employee training and, 53, 110–111,
        127–129, 244, 315
    FEDEX and, 20, 30–32
    global movement for, 8, 9, 12, 17
    healthcare, 279, 282–283
    leadership for, 319–323
    monitoring, 50, 82, 139, 149, 310
    outsourcing and, 100*n*
    President's Quality Awards and, 190*fig*
    raising standards for, xi, xii, 23, 39,
    revolution, 14, 23, 38*fig*, 140–141, 314
serviceability, 42
SERVQUAL methodology, xii, 57–58
Seymour, D., 19
Shewhart, W., 36–37, 143, 145
Shewart cycle, see plan–do–study–act,
Shingo, S., 92–94, 97
Singo Prize, 97
Sisters of Mary (SSM) Healthcare, 266
    case study of, 289–292
six sigma, 146, 209
Scholtes, P., 47,112, 122–123, 314
Shonk, J.H., 47
short-term thinking, 81
Sink, D.S., 154
Sinn, V., 18
SMART, see quality characteristics
STMicroelectronics Corp., 34
Smith, A., 75
Smith, D., 46, 48

Smith, D.G., 267
socialization, 127, 129
Social Security Administration (SSA), 10,
    160*n,*
software, 109–110
Solectron, 34
SPC, see Statistical Process Control
span of control, 76
Spechler, J., 14
special variation, 145
SQC, see statistical quality control
SSA, see Social Security Administration
St. Luke's Hospital, Kansas City, Mo., 278
    case study of, 300–303
stability, 3,4, 155, 159
stakeholders, 11, 252–255, 269
standards, xiii, 58, 96–97, 118, 174–177,
    177–183, 210–212, 216, 249,
    277–283, 305
    audit, 197
    for customer service, 7, 10, 22, 34, 39,
        114, 211, 154–155, 318
    government, 12, 22, 24*n*, 34, 209, 226
    external, 40*fig*, 274, 276*fig*
    high performance, 21, 26, 44, 72, 87, 111,
        192, 199*n*, 229, 245
    healthcare, 267–268, 271, 275, 277, 279,
        297,
    history of, 74–75
    internal management and , xiii, 44,
        276*fig*, 305,
    professional, 41,150,
    quality, 48, 52, 74, 98, 139, 288
    regulatory, 312
    Ritz-Carlton gold, 136–138
    security, 134
    survey methodology, 141
standard operating procedures (SOP), 109
state and local government quality awards,
    192–195
    website listing programs, 200*n*
state governments, 195, 212
    quality award programs, 189–197
    award program websites, 342–343
statistical analysis, , see also measurement
statistical control, 37, 87, 93, 144–145, 252
    charts, 83
statistical process control (SPC), xi, 20, 36,
    83, 141, 145–146, 310, 313
    origins and evolution of, 36–37
statistical quality control (SQC), 199*n*, 200

quality control circles and, 151, 156
statistical tools, 87, 112, 126, 128, 140, 316,
    see also specific tools,
Steventon, D., 195
Stillman, R., 218
Stirling (Florida) Award, 193
strategic planning, 26, 52, 64, 102, 117,
    136–137, 181, 189, 205, 236, 254,
    260, 290, 299–302, 333–336
stress, in the work environment, 118, 120,
    147, 155
stockholders, 48, 110
Sumanth, D., 154
Sunnyvale, California, 194
supplier relationships, xi, 8, 45, 48–51, 129,
    275, 307, see also
        customer–supplier relationships
Sureshchandar, G.S., 22, 142
surveys, 198*n*
Svara, J., 212
Swiss, J., 210
systems, x, xiii, 3, 4, 5, 7, 9, 14, 17, 37, 39,
    55, 58*fig*, 139, 175
    approach, 78, 79
    causes of problems, 54, 84
    governmental, 4
    improvement, management commitment
        and, 111
    integrity, 327–328
    monitoring and, xiii
    processes, 109–110
    open, 117, 128
    service, 2
    thinking, 53–54, 108, 112, 125
Szilagyi, A.D., 117

T

Taiwan, 18
Taguchi, G., 92–93
task forces, 115, 156
task team, 186
taxpayer, 14
    discontent, 20
Taylor, F.W., 23*n*, 75, 88,
TCC, see Total care concept
teams, 37, 47, 84, 102, 122, 129, 139, 141,
    285, 308, 317
    cross-functional, 46, 71, 111, 164,
    empowered, 59, 116, 316, 320
    in healthcare organization, 285, 291, 301
    FPL and, 185, 186

leader, in healthcare organization, 285
school quality review, 252
self-managed, 79, 308, 309
teamwork, 20, 45–48, 53, 108*fig*, 117, 123,
        128, 131, 189, 307, 308, 316
    CQI and, 278, 321
    cross functional management and, 316
teacher education, 243–245
    certification and, 244
    quality assurance and, 244
    quality and, 245
technology, 8
    obsolescence of, 14
telecommunications, 6, 7, 9, 11, 13, 18, 22
Texas A & M University, 19
Texas Instruments, 34
theory X management systems, 9, 47, 76,
        157, 313
theory Y management systems, 52, 76
theory Z management systems, 76–77
third-party providers, 11
    cooperative partnerships, 12
Thompson, A.A., 189
Thompson, J. D., 52, 117
Thompson, J.R, 14
Tisch, J., 108
3M Corp., 34
Toffler, A., 314
top–down–bottom–up implementation, 287
top–down management, 313–314
total care concept (TCC), 93
total productivity model, 154
total quality control (TQC), 6, 38*fig*, 78,
        89,94, 180, 323
    Deming Prize and, see Deming Prize
    Florida Power and Light (FPL) and,
        200–202
    origins and evolution of, 37
total quality management (TQM), ix, xii, 6,
        96, 157, 266
    criticisms of, 321
    government services and, 207
    Japanese management and, 36
total quality service (TQS), xi, xii, 33–63, 73,
        see also specific topics
    as an integrative concept, xi
    barriers to achieving, 312–316
    benchmarking and, 43–44
    changing values and, 40*fig*
    continuous quality improvement (CQI)
        and, 58–59

components of the model, 108fig, 308
cross-functional management and, 45–48
culture and, 48
customer-driven, 21, 141
customer satisfaction and, 108
customer–supplier relationships and,
        48–51
definition of, 21, 44–60
delayering hierarchy and, 45, 47
demanding, 11–17
empowerment and, 51–53
evolution of, 38*fig*
extended process and, 49*fig*
flexibility and, 309
guidelines for training, 111–127
human resource management and,
        109–111
implementing to achieve high
        performance, 46
in government, 46
in healthcare, 46, 275
interactive model for, 108*fig*
leadership for achieving high-
        performance quality
        improvement, 108, 305–323
learning customer-driven, 17
model, 108*fig*
monitoring results, 56–58
organizational feedback and, 50*fig*
origins and evolution of, 36–39
principles of, 47
quality and control, changing
        perspectives on, 39–43
quality improvement strategies, 6–8, 12,
        222–226
redefining, 20–22
reducing costs and, 59–60
systemic relationships and, 53–56, 108
teamwork and, 45–48, 60, 108
Toyota Motors, 53, 84, 92–93, 153–154
TQC, see total quality control
TQM, see total quality management
TQS, see total quality service
trade associations, 74
training, xi, xii, 8, 14–15, 17, 27, 30, 47,
        65–67, 73, 81, 86, 90, 94, 98, 151,
        168, 188, 223, 234, 241, 244–245,
        284–285, 312–313, 317–321, see
        also human resource management
BNQA and, 182

critical elements in, 37, 98, 140, 159, 223, 308
customer responsiveness, 46, 77, 149
empowerment and, 41, 48, 51–53, 79, 174, 217, 221
human resources, 108–130
Japanese and, 91
in public sector, 176, 215
teacher, 61
transcendent quality, 41
transformation process, 144, Figure 5.1
Transportation Security Administration (TSA), U.S.174, 230n
Treasury Department, U.S. see also Internal Revenue Service
Tribus, M., 49, 199n
Tummala, V.M., 177
trust, 214
    restoring faith and, 212–215, 226–229
    public opinion and, 213–214, 226–227
turnover, 148fig, 155, 248, 326–327fig

U

Ullmann, S.G., 277
Union of Japanese Scientists and Engineers (JUSE), 37–38
United Services Automobile Association (USAA), xi, 96–97, 105, 107
United States, xi, 1–2,
    competition and, 3, 19, 80
    need for improved service quality, 20, 182
    recognizing quality in, 75, 177 see also Baldrige National Quality Award
United Way, 15
universal healthcare, 100n
Universities of
    Arizona, 19
    California, 251
    Miami, 19
    Michigan, 19, 230
    Minnesota, 19
    Northern Colorado, 202–206
    Pennsylvania, 19
    Tennessee, 19
    Texas A & M, 19
    Wisconsin–Madison, 19
    Wisconsin–Stout, 183, 256
upper control limit (UCL), 87
USAA, see United Services Automobile Association

user-based quality, 41
utilization management, in healthcare, 266

V

value-added processes, 140, 228
value-based quality, 41
values, 111
    administrative, 219
    political, 219
Van Thiel, S., 177
variation, 59, 78, 83, 142–145, 250, 307
    in healthcare, 307
Vassekuil, B., 44
veterans Hospitals, 82
vision, 21, 53, 117, 170, 187, 212, 316–317, 321
vital few, 86, 102
voice of the process, 40, 50fig, 51, 155
voice of the customer, 50, 68, 279

W

Wallace, M.J., 117
Wal-Mart Corp., 2, 5
warusa-kagen, 124–125
Weber, M., 75–76
West, D.M., 177
West, J.P., 43
West, T.D., 266
Wheeler, D.J., 63n
Whitney, E., 75
Whitney, J., 47
Winn, B.A., 182
Wilson, J.Q., 208, 212, 218
Wimmer, M., x, 174, 177, 193
Wisniewski, M., 57
Woodall, J., 186
work environment, see environment
work unit, xiii
worker–organization bonding, 127
worker participation, 37, 77–78, 314
work force, see human resource management
World Wide Web, 9, 11, 199n, 242 see also Internet
    service quality revolution and, 379

X

Xerox Business Services,
    case study, 25–28

Xerox Business Products and Systems, xi, 34

Z

Zbaracki, M., 7

Zeithaml, V.A., 39, 43, 57, 279, 311
Zemke, R., 39
zero-based budgeting, 320
zero defects, 94–96, 331–332
Zografos, K., 99n